Java™ Application Frameworks

Darren Govoni

Wiley Computer Publishing

John Wiley & Sons, Inc.
NEW YORK · CHICHESTER · WEINHEIM · BRISBANE · SINGAPORE · TORONTO

Publisher: Robert Ipsen

Editor: Theresa Hudson

Assistant Editor: Kathryn A. Malm

Electronic Products, Associate Editor: Mike Sosa

Managing Editor: Micheline Frederick

Text Design & Composition: North Market Street Graphics

Designations used by companies to distinguish their products are often claimed as trademarks. In all instances where John Wiley & Sons, Inc., is aware of a claim, the product names appear in initial capital or ALL CAPITAL LETTERS. Readers, however, should contact the appropriate companies for more complete information regarding trademarks and registration.

This book is printed on acid-free paper. ∞

Published by John Wiley & Sons, Inc.

Published simultaneously in Canada.

This publication is designed to provide accurate and authoritative information in regard to the subject matter covered. It is sold with the understanding that the publisher is not engaged in professional services. If professional advice or other expert assistance is required, the services of a competent professional person should be sought.

Library of Congress Cataloging-in-Publication Data:

Govoni, Darren, 1970–
    Java application frameworks / Darren Govoni.
        p.   cm.
    Includes bibliographical references.
    ISBN 0-471-32930-4 (pbk.)
    1. Java (Computer program language)   2. Application software—Development.   I. Title.
    QA76.73.J38G69   1999
    005.2'762—dc21

99-24509
CIP

Printed in the United States of America.

10 9 8 7 6 5 4 3 2 1

Contents

Acknowledgments

Special thanks to the following individuals for their insight, support, and various contributions to this effort: Michael Alexander, Dave Bock, Madeline Li, Chris Bailey, Russ Bailey, Kevin Trent Smith, and Dennis "Govassic Park" Govoni.

About the Author

Darren Govoni is an engineer and researcher specializing in distributed architectures and complex adaptive systems with Java. Over the past 10 years, he has focused his research efforts in areas such as distributed computing, mobile agents, expert systems, and adaptable fractal architectures. Currently, he is exploring new technologies that permit the dynamic evolution of software systems and applications. He also researches architectures based on framework components, and organized the 1998 Object-Oriented Systems Languages and Applications (OOPSLA) midyear workshop on Java Frameworks. When he's not absorbed by technology, he enjoys basketball and golf, and frequently embarks on expeditions to far away places.

About the Artists

Chris Bailey

Chris Bailey is a graphic artist specializing in Web design. He has worked extensively in both digital and traditional media, and is currently squandering his gift on several cartooning projects in his copious free time. Chris designed the diagrams in this book using Adobe Illustrator, and with the help of many fine caffeinated beverage products.

Russ Bailey

Russ Bailey is a member of a visual design team at FGM, Inc. in the Washington, DC, area. Previously, he spent three years teaching printmaking, painting, and multimedia at Uludag University in Bursa, Turkey. He has been a political cartoonist, a book and magazine illustrator, and a struggling artist at various times and to varying degrees during the past three and a half decades.

Kevin Trent Smith

Kevin Trent Smith is a senior systems engineer at BTG, Inc., where he manages small projects and specializes in Java solutions for collaboration and network security. For the last two years, he has focused much of his research on distributed object technology. He has degrees in Computer Science from the College of William and Mary and George Mason University. Kevin lives in Fairfax, Virginia, with his wife, Gwen, and their pets, Fox and Malory.

Introduction

With the advent of the Java platform and programming language, the way we think about and develop software systems has received a firm thrust in the direction of objects with the promise of reusability. One of the reasons developing software with Java is so appealing is the enormous number of classes, libraries, APIs, and frameworks that are part of the standard platform, in addition to those available commercially. This alone can translate into enormous savings for developers and companies alike.

Overview of the Book and Technology

In today's software development arena, time and cost are forever interwoven, and many software projects have overrun on both accounts. Consequently, corporations are realizing the importance of leveraging reuse and are embracing the market supply of usable objects and components to build future systems. It has proven uneconomical to build entire systems from scratch when many of the needed components have already been built and made commercially available. Such components include specialized middleware, widget libraries, database interface packages, visualization objects, report generators, objects, and frameworks of various types. Over the years, many of the common elements appearing in applications of all levels (up to the enterprise level) have been distilled into separate reusable components and frameworks as commercial vendors began to answer the demand for such items. That demand is on the rise.

Definition of a Framework

An *application framework* represents a collection of specialized classes designed to solve a particular (application-level) class of problem, such as graphing, user interface, or object persistence. Over the past 20 years, extensive studies have been conducted on reusable methods of software development. Notably, work by Ralph Johnson (of Gang of Four recognition) has demonstrated a clear evolution toward the idea of aggregated reusable entities such as patterned architectures and frameworks. Frameworks are implemented to be reused; they represent an architectural approach to a given problem domain. Because a framework encapsulates an architectural solution to a particular problem, developers are freed from understanding the complexities and scaling the hurdles needed to implement that solution; instead, they have only to utilize the interfaces provided by the framework.

How Frameworks Are Used

Application frameworks are designed from the ground up to be reusable components that can be applied in many application contexts. For this reason, they are characteristically flexible and often extensible. A framework is often considered a form of application template. They typically provide a semi-complete application architecture for some particular purpose. Application developers are required to complete the framework architecture by integrating their application-specific code or objects into the framework. These so called *plug points* are where developers can tailor the exact functionality of the framework to a specific application context. It is through this facility that frameworks find widespread appeal as class-category solutions (e.g., data access, visualization, GUI, etc.). The plug points of a given framework represent the variability between applications, and allow the framework proper to be adapted to many application situations as they relate to the problem addressed by the framework.

Types of Reuse

Frameworks that offer a strict comprehensive interface to expose its functionality provide a form of reusability known as *black box* reuse, meaning simply, that no specialized knowledge of the inner mechanics of the framework is necessary to utilize its functionality within an application. In contrast, *white box* implementations require some knowledge about the *object* and *collaboration models* provided within the framework.

Frameworks versus Class Libraries

Frameworks have different characteristics from simple class libraries. Specifically, frameworks tend to embed a process from which application code is subsequently executed. That is, the framework will often control the flow of execution to application client objects, rather than the inverse, which is typically how we utilize simple class libraries. A framework will ideally provide a complex set of behaviors whose purpose is to address a specific problem domain, such that a developer utilizing the framework can embed his or her code to complete the overall application or system architecture. The framework provides an architecture for a particular purpose and that architecture is reused across subsequent applications whose purposes may themselves vary. This is, indeed, the most compelling use (or reuse) of the framework concept. The separation between class libraries and frameworks is one most clearly represented as a continuum, and although the extremes may be well defined and separated, a gray area exists where it becomes difficult to quantify the "framework-ness" of a given specialized class library. Indeed, variations of frameworks address areas ranging from specialized domains such as banking, commerce, and the like to low-level capabilities such as distributed objects and networking protocols.

Patterns in Frameworks

Frameworks are usually composed of a collection of similarly related classes grouped into a *pattern* or series of patterns. The sum of such patterns constitute the *architecture* implemented by the framework. A pattern or *design pattern* is an abstracted collaboration of objects that have a specific objective. This concept and these patterns are well documented in the book *Design Patterns: Elemento of Reusable Object-Oriented Software* (Erich Gamma; Richard Helm; Ralph Johnson; John Vlissides; Addison-Wesley, 1995.). Somewhere in between objects and frameworks lie the notion of patterns. Whereas patterns represent reusable micro-architectures and may consist of only a few object types or roles, the reusable properties of objects are seen to aggregate into collaborations as patterns, which subsequently may aggregate into larger bodies such as frameworks.

At some point, it became clear that many programming problems encountered in object-oriented development could be extracted, defined, and solved for future use. Subsequently, programmers identified this new "pattern language" with which they could communicate and recognize reoccurring problems in object-oriented software development. This has proven to be an immensely important and valuable discovery, and has saved many a programmer time and effort addressing common problems. In that same vain, the goal of framework development and usage attempts to fill a larger, more specific domain of reusability with which systems and software architects can use to build larger complex systems.

Build versus Buy

Exploring the use of prefabricated frameworks within large software systems is proving to be an invaluable practice. Furthermore, corporations are realizing that creating solid reusable foundations upon which future products and systems can build is important to application and system longevity. From this methodology, two distinct classes of software developers have emerged: Those who operate at the higher, architectural level, defining systems in terms of course-grained components and frameworks, and those who specialize in particular application-level domains and instantiate applications within larger architectural systems. This is a simple differentiation that may be characterized as architecture versus application.

How This Book Is Organized

The structure of this book is designed to lay a natural progression from concept to practice to implementation, migrating from fine-grained topics and discussion (such as objects) to course-grained topics (such as system architectures). In addition, the discussion migrates from *within* frameworks to *outside* frameworks in an effort to scope the entire domain of practice from designing frameworks to using them within larger architectures and contexts.

 Chapter 1, "Framework Concepts" Lays foundation for the reader to grasp and understand the definition of a framework and the many focus areas surrounding them. It presents concepts relating to the design, implementation, and usage of frameworks at different levels within an organization; specifically, from the perspective of individual developers, teams of developers, and at the corporate level where strategic views of enterprise development can be based upon reusable framework foundations.

 Chapter 2, "Java Framework Design" Covers design practices that can be applied to general framework implementation. It discusses the concept and importance of *abstraction* and the role it plays in separating interface and implementation within a framework. Three models are posed for separating concerns in a framework design: namely, the object, organizational (or composition), and collaboration models. The differences between *inheritance* and *composition* from an *object model* perspective are addressed. The reader will also learn about the Java 2 Collections Framework, how it is constructed, and how it can be used. This framework demonstrates a solid implementation of the concepts discussed in this and the previous chapter and therefore serves as a good instructional aid.

 Chapter 3, "Using Design Patterns" Introduces and discusses design patterns and their importance and use within frameworks. The chapter breaks down pertinent patterns presented in the aforementioned *Design Patterns: Elements of Reusable Object-Oriented Software,* and offers further analysis for framework inclusion. Each pattern is accompanied by a Java example and some discussion about the usefulness and applicability of the pattern in general and within frameworks.

Chapter 4, "JavaBean Components" Introduces JavaBean components, what they are, and how they're used. The idea of JavaBeans within frameworks is compelling, as they share a common theme centered on reusability. JavaBean objects (or components) are based on standard naming conventions and patterned models. Using them as a basis for framework components and adopting the JavaBean event-listener model for certain client-framework interactions is an interesting concept for consideration.

Chapter 5, "Analysis of Java Frameworks" Links the previous two chapters on patterns and JavaBeans by exploring two interesting and useful Java frameworks: JFC/Swing and InfoBus. Both of these frameworks make extensive use of design patterns and JavaBean components and naming conventions. The reader will find it both valuable and interesting to make use of the topics discussed in prior chapters while gaining the knowledge of how to use these powerful devices for application/framework development.

Chapter 6, "Composite Foundation Architecture" Presents an architectural view of complex applications through layering (and buffering) frameworks. Simple visualization techniques and mental models useful at system architecture time are defined. Java packages are covered in detail, and readers will learn how segmenting a system through clever packaging schemes can facilitate external knowledge about how a complex system is organized and/or layered. Complexity and reusability management are addressed by creating abstracted foundations upon which successive layers of implementation and specialization of frameworks and applications can be achieved.

Chapter 7, "Java Application Architectures" Focuses on various architectural concerns important in application development beyond the internal nature or design of frameworks. Architectural patterns useful for designing applications in Java are presented. These include database integration, user interface architectures, and distributed objects using RMI. The concept of a *business object* is discussed, followed by descriptions of good practices for separating logic and implementation in such objects. Readers will find the wider scope of this chapter useful in understanding the bigger picture of application and systems development, enabling them to identify other areas where frameworks will prove to be useful devices.

Chapter 8, "Enterprise Frameworks" Presents two important enterprise frameworks for creating distributed applications with Java. Although many strategies are cropping up that enable distributed applications, Enterprise JavaBeans and CORBA represent two dominant technologies in this arena. Having discussed the concept of distributed applications and objects in Chapter 7, this chapter gives the reader two invaluable frameworks for creating enterprise class applications. It also discusses the notion of distributed frameworks.

Who Should Read This Book

This book assumes a working familiarity with Java and a solid understanding of general object-oriented programming (OOP). It is intended for individuals who want to understand and learn techniques for developing and using Java-based applications frameworks. It is useful for novice and intermediate software developers and architects, as well as those exploring ways to optimize reusability and architect large distributed systems using Java and frameworks. The goal of this book is to address concerns that range from the small to the large, and in doing so to bring together a comprehensive picture of application development using frameworks. Because the discussions often represent but a fraction of the combined knowledge in a particular area, additional sources are provided as gateways to more in-depth information on those subjects. Expert developers may want to skip or skim Chapter 5 on Java framework analysis, and possibly Chapter 8 on enterprise frameworks, save the last section on distributed frameworks. Experts on JavaBeans will be able to skim Chapter 4, perhaps perusing the sections on JavaBeans and integration with frameworks.

What's on the Web Site

The companion Web site, located at **www.wiley.com/compbooks/govoni**, contains the code examples from the chapters. You also will find links to pertinent studies, research, and information from individuals, corporations, and universities, on the following topics:

- Object-Oriented Programming
- Frameworks
- Design Patterns
- Java 2
- Java Collections Framework
- JFC/Swing
- InfoBus
- JavaBeans
- Enterprise JavaBeans
- Software Architecture

Summary

As object-oriented programming continues to accelerate in popularity, the goal of enterprisewide reusability will allow for the reduction of time and monetary costs on projects of all sizes. The commercial market recognizes the value of reusable components, as is obvious in the growing number of toolkits, APIs, and frameworks available for developers to design and build systems.

Frameworks represent a course-grained approach to reuse, as they encapsulate solutions to a generally complex problem. Sparing the effort to address complex, recurring problems in systems development will surely save countless hours of work. Companies of the future will capitalize on this trend by building large, scalable foundations of reusable solutions.

Framework Concepts

Object-oriented design and programming is dominating today's software development world with its flexible and extensible models and components. Systems built using object-oriented languages and technologies (e.g., Java) are proving to be easier to develop and longer lived than previous systems. The longevity of systems built using object-oriented languages and techniques can be attributed to their potential to adapt and change over time.

This capability is critical for a system's future success with users and developers. Concepts such as pluggable components and frameworks are becoming more important in mainstream software development because they provide systems with this capability. In addition, technologies like networks and distributed systems are increasingly relying on development and computing models that offer new levels of flexibility and adaptability over time. As software systems grow in terms of project size and scope, adopting design approaches that facilitate these two characteristics is becoming prevalent.

Software companies are also realizing that buying or reusing code and components is key to long-term success. Solving a class of problems for a given application or set of applications and making that solution template available for future efforts is what makes application frameworks useful.

The Framework Paradigm

The concept of reusing code or parts of code isn't new. Code reuse is important for many reasons other than simple economics. Programmers often find themselves "reinventing the wheel," thus decreasing their efficiency as well as the efficiency of their projects. A good programmer finds ways to optimize his or her time, whether it's maintaining his or her own library of developed objects or components, or simply by cutting and pasting lines of code from other projects. This process of reuse is ever present at many levels in software development. Specifically, developers are realizing that for large systems, reuse is extremely important.

Large systems are, by definition, complex and costly. Once a large system is developed, changes that involve redesigning and modifying it are even more complex and costly. In my experience, systems that are designed to achieve a particular goal seldom undergo architectural or design reevaluation once that goal has been reached. This could be in part because, economically, it would be too costly to repair something that appears to operate properly. However, goals change, and sometimes pieces of a system become nonfunctional or obsolete, and are therefore subject to redesign or replacement in order to keep the system viable and to avoid creating a new one from scratch.

No one wants to reinvent the wheel if a good one already exists. The automobile industry is a great example of reuse in motion. Often, many cars developed by the same manufacturer include the same parts, such as an alternator, wheel bearings, or a gas filter. If this were not the case, cars would be too expensive to make and certainly too expensive to buy. The software industry has been struggling with models of reuse that can perform equally well. The concept of a specialized framework that performs a well-defined objective that developers can tap into is one way to achieve reuse.

Framework Definitions

A *framework* is an abstracted collection of classes, interfaces, and patterns dedicated to solving a class of problems through a flexible and extensible architecture. Frameworks encapsulate critical design architectures specific to their purpose. In doing this, classes of frameworks can be utilized by developers to save time otherwise wasted reinventing common application problems.

Frameworks have been defined in many ways:

> "A framework is a collection of classes that provide a set of services for a particular domain; a framework thus exports a number of individual classes and mechanisms which clients can use or adapt."
>
> —GRADY BOOCH, *Object-Oriented Analysis and Design*

"A framework is a set of prefabricated software building blocks that programmers can use, extend, or customize for specific computing solutions."

—TALIGENT, *Building Object-Oriented Frameworks*

"A framework is more than a class hierarchy. It is a class hierarchy plus a model of interaction among the objects instantiated from the framework."

—TED LEWIS, *Object-Oriented Application Frameworks*

These definitions indicate that a framework can include more than simply a collection of classes, and may also present a defined process or method of interaction between its objects. Combining objects and interactions provides a truly useful environment in which categories of problems can be addressed in far less time than it would take to reanalyze the problem and invent new solutions.

A framework may also present an abstracted application architecture that allows developers to plug in the pieces that define application-specific functionality. Because most of the architectural decisions are already made within the framework, the developer does not need to be overly concerned with the details of how the framework solves problems. Instead, the framework can be perceived as a *black box* entity in which implementation details within the framework are more or less concealed.

It would seem from this discussion that the design and adoption of frameworks is geared more toward developers. Most of the time, developers will realize a savings in time when they adopt a previously constructed framework to solve a problem. Naturally, adopting a framework involves a learning curve. But if a new approach is perceived to take longer to learn or use, chances are the developer will simply find another solution, possibly inventing it him- or herself. Therefore, if a framework is to be useful to a developer, it needs to be easy to understand and capable of being utilized quickly. However, there are exceptions to this. Sometimes, it serves the best interest of the project or company to migrate to framework implementations across their projects. In this case, the migration period can involve more steps than simply directly addressing application-level problems. Nevertheless, it is generally perceived that adopting framework-based solutions has, at the very least, a longer-term benefit on a larger scale as well.

Collaboration of Objects

In addition to a rich set of usable interfaces, abstract classes, and possibly patterns, frameworks provide semantics for how these entities interact. These semantics usually includes internal algorithms for controlling message passing between objects in the hierarchy. For example, the Java AWT event model defines an interface called MouseListener. Objects wishing to receive messages pertaining to mouse events implement this interface (shown here) and register themselves with the object that generates the event.

```
public class MyMouseListener implements MouseListener {

    public void mouseClicked(MouseEvent event)
    {
        ...
    }

    public void mousePressed(MouseEvent event)
    {
        ...
    }

    ...
}

    MyMouseListener mouseListener = new MyMouseListener();
    JButton myButton = new JButton("Button");

    // This method invocation establishes an interaction between
    // the object "myButton" and the object mouseListener.
    myButton.addMouseListener(mouseListener);
```

The interaction between the event model and the supplied listener is governed by the process of the Java AWT event model. That is, a listener is plugged into an existing framework process that controls the flow of execution to the listener.

NOTE This is an example of the adapter design pattern, discussed in Chapter 3, "Using Design Patterns."

One of the unique characteristics that distinguish frameworks from simple class hierarchies is that the model of interaction defined by a framework controls the flow of invocation to your client objects, as opposed to client objects initiating flow control entirely themselves.

In procedural languages like C and Pascal, invocations to functions are made with input parameters. When the function returns, its side effects are the resulting changes on the data structures it received. This model is considered function-centric for this reason. Figure 1.1 shows how a data pointer called entity is passed into various functions that perform some action involving the received data. However, in object modeling, objects are defined in terms of their attributes and the operations on those attributes or operations on associated objects. In other words, the flow of control is not centralized; objects react to one another in well-defined and specific ways. Figure 1.2 shows the data object entity that now contains the processes previously held internally in functions. These methods are triggered from other objects through the appropriate message; for example, store(), process(), or load(). Because the data is

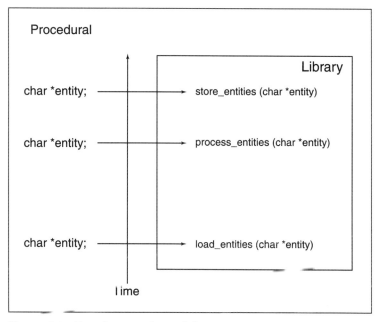

Figure 1.1   Function-centric model.

encapsulated in the object entity (in this example), there is no need to pass it through method invocations.

An object-oriented framework defines the roles of *client* objects that extend or implement interfaces provided by the framework. A client object is any object interacting with the services of the framework as supplied by the application designer. The logical flow or reactions between objects is a natural part of the framework and addresses the goal for which the framework was created. Because of this, developers do not need to be overly concerned with the

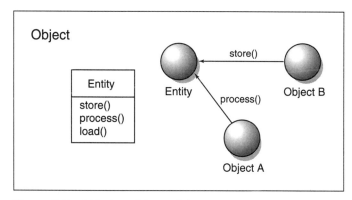

Figure 1.2   Object-centric model.

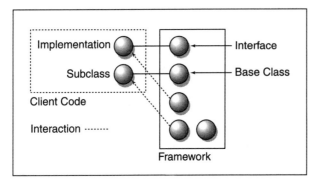

Figure 1.3 Relationship between client-code implementation classes and framework base classes.

internal mechanics of a framework that has solved a particular class of problems. The developer only needs to provide the level of utilization demanded by his or her application needs. This may involve extending the frameworks core classes and implementing abstract behaviors or implementing interface methods in an application-specific manner. When those methods are invoked is often controlled from within the framework itself. Figure 1.3 shows the relationship between a framework's definitions and a client application that utilizes those definitions. In this scenario, the client implements one of the framework interfaces and extends one of its foundation classes. The process control within the framework interacts with the client objects created in a particular application.

Class Libraries and Frameworks

A *class library* is a collection of classes designed for a variety of purposes. For example, java.io and java.net are simple packages containing classes that perform more or less similar capabilities. To a degree, these classes can interoperate with each other, but the fundamental method of use is for the application developer to utilize the class library directly and provide the ways in which individual classes collaborate. A framework, on the other hand, provides a model of collaboration and often executes application code directly from within the framework model. The framework presents an architecture as a pattern or series of patterns [Gamma et. al, 1995] through which an application designer can plug in implementations at specified locations.

In reality, however, measuring the differences between some class libraries and frameworks is often difficult and subject to interpretation. Most frameworks are at least a collection of classes; therefore, a class library is often part of the framework. The line between what is strictly a class library and what is strictly a framework can be gray and undefined. Part of this problem, in my opinion, centers around the lack of size and scope in the definitions of frameworks. For example, you wouldn't think of two classes collaborating as a framework; but legitimately, they could very well be. Frameworks tend to be larger because they often solve complex problems, and reusing solutions to complex problems is more attractive to third-party individuals. One way of looking at the two is as a spectrum, with class libraries on one end and frameworks on the other.

Framework Granularity

The granularity of the problem addressed by a framework can vary. For example, a framework could provide for object persistence of some kind. Object persistence could be transferable across applications. A variety of useful applications could be built by reusing the object persistence framework. This could be perceived as a lower level of granularity. In other words, the problem domain of the framework is broad and general. On the other hand, you could construct a framework that deals with a more specific type of problem. Consider a framework that provides classes and processes for creating inventory control programs. Such a framework would provide the necessary elements and definitions upon which actual applications could be implemented. A variety of needs could be met from an inventory control program. The framework could be reused to service the range of needs for inventory control applications. Because this type of framework specializes in the inventory control domain, it may be referred to as a *domain-specific* or a *domain type framework*. The object persistence framework performs a utilitarian function, namely storing and retrieving objects, and may be referred to as a *utility framework*.

NOTE Be careful not to confuse the generic meaning of the word *domain* in this context, which means the origin of the problem as it exists in a real-world context. Anything can be thought of as having a problem domain, but this usage does not imply the real-world context in which solutions are to be inserted.

Framework Characteristics

As discretely defined entities, frameworks should represent certain traits or characteristics that support their definition. The following subsections list some of the more important characteristics that apply to frameworks in general.

Frameworks Should Be Reusable

Frameworks are built to be used and reused. Before a framework can be reusable, however, it must first be usable. The particular domain of problem a framework addresses should be well defined by the framework documentation. This is extremely important because the framework is intended to be reused by many other developers. Defining the scope of the framework allows the developer to understand how it can be applied toward his or her objective. Saving time by eliminating frameworks that don't apply is just as important as choosing the right one. To promote reusability, it is necessary to select an appropriate problem set for which the framework provides solutions and to document it well.

There are actually two fronts where reusability comes into play with frameworks. The framework itself can be reused across applications to address similar problem domains. Also, by delegating problem sets within your application, specific implementations can be removed and replaced by other implementations, thereby reusing the rest of your application. Sometimes, changing a component within an application results in redesign to accommodate the new functionality. Previous objects within the system are not reusable as-is, and must undergo some revision to adopt new pieces into the application. Because frameworks provide the necessary abstractions to facilitate the easy removal and replacement of key implementations, other components of the existing application will undergo little or no redesign. This, essentially, allows the developer to continue to use, or reuse if you will, existing components.

Figure 1.4 illustrates this principle with a framework view of an application. The application is constructed of three primary frameworks, one to handle the graphical user interface (GUI), one to handle business or domain objects, and one to handle object persistence. Because of the way the frameworks interact, any changes to the persistence mechanism is hidden or abstracted from the GUI framework, making it reusable in the new context of a different framework implementation for object persistence. Likewise, the framework implementation can be reused elsewhere. Complex systems can benefit from buffering frameworks, or foundation layering, because it isolates specific technologies used as implementations of layers within the system. The propagation of effects is minimized or localized, and therefore the effects of redesign can be essentially muted.

There are a few basic flavors of reuse worth mentioning. In the context of a framework, the focus is on how the framework exposes itself to the outside world—that is, at which points within the framework do developers focus their attention, and exactly how much of the internal structure of the framework should they know about?

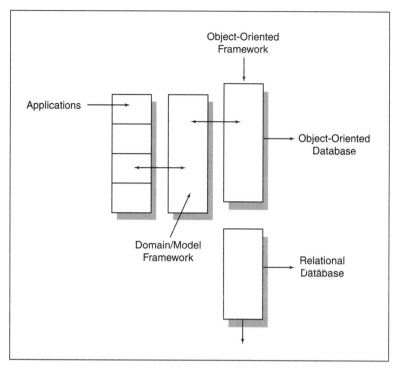

Figure 1.4   Replacing one framework implementation with another.

Black Box

The term *black box* is an elementary perspective on the encapsulation facility of basic objects. The insides of an object cannot be seen directly and thus are "black." In addition, only certain inputs need be known about the black box, and the outputs will result from its internal processing. *Black box reuse* [Szyperski, 1998] applied to frameworks means essentially the same thing. These types of frameworks expose strict interfaces and do not allow the framework internals to be explored or modified. In the Java world, this would equate to having only the class or JAR files for a framework while the documentation outlines only the necessary interface elements pertinent to the application developer. The rest is intentionally concealed.

White Box

White box reuse is the opposite of black box in that, although it reveals fragments of its components through interfaces, full utilization and understanding comes through examining the actual implementations provided by the framework. In this sense, white box reuse can be considered as having the source code for a framework and enabling the exploration and understanding of exactly how the framework performs its duties through its implementations.

Frameworks Should Be Extensible

Determining the extensibility of a framework is done by analyzing how the framework provides for specific uses in context. Extending a framework to accommodate a specific application involves implementing key abstractions or interfaces and plugging them into the framework context, thereby providing functionality more tailored to the application. To a lesser degree, specialization through subclassing can extend the current capability of framework objects by implementing abstracted functionality.

Other Characteristics

Other characteristics are important to framework design, such as safety, efficiency, simplicity, and completeness [Booch, 1994].

The *safety* of a framework ensures the developer or user that nothing alarming is going to result from using the framework. For example, I wouldn't expect a 3D modeling framework to erase documents on my hard drive! A framework that deals with sensitive or volatile data should clearly state the policy it employs for dealing with that data, and it should not compromise data integrity in the event of a system error condition or exception.

A framework should strive for optimum *efficiency* where possible. In a multi-threaded language like Java, there are plenty of facilities for thread control and management. Frameworks that utilize threads should ensure that appropriate thread-safe mechanisms are in place and that threads that do not need to block don't. This optimizes the thread flow within the framework and ensures that it runs efficiently. Aside from threads, it is a fundamental concept that any code segment should be optimized to run as efficiently as possible. This is more important in the area of frameworks because frameworks are intended to be reused across a wide range of efforts and therefore have to provide the highest quality.

Simplicity is often unachievable when targeting large, complex systems, but through techniques such as modeling and abstraction, functionally complex frameworks that expose very small and simple interfaces can be created. This should be something to strive for and will pay off in the long run.

The *completeness* of a framework refers to its capability to address the problem domain for which it was created. For example, if I create a framework that models the entities in a banking environment, I would not want to leave out the definition for Account. Doing so would render the framework incomplete and greatly reduce its capability to address the problems for which it was designed. This characteristic is the most difficult to achieve. You want to make sure your framework addresses a problem that is general enough so it can reused, but you also need to make sure the framework is complete enough so that it provides all the necessary tools to accurately solve the problems for which it is used.

Benefits

Some worthy benefits to framework adoption are pertinent to bring up at this point:

- Designing for frameworks maintains greater simplicity and reusability within and beyond your system.

- Frameworks create multiple levels of organization within your application architecture.

- Frameworks facilitate the plug and play of functionality at various levels within your system through interface definitions and implementation abstractions.

- Frameworks save time when used to solve application domain problems.

The key benefit here is savings. Developing a framework requires more time in design and construction than simply solving a particular problem through a brute force, direct approach. Using someone else's framework or one you've previously built will cut down on time and costs. The phrase "short-term pain, long-term gain" comes to mind when deciding whether to implement a system by building your own frameworks initially or not.

Depending on your particular situation, it may not be possible to take the extra time needed to identify the potential for framework use within your application. However, the long-term benefits of proper framework design on large systems are being realized now and deserve some up-front attention for any project you start. The question for any software organization for which designing mission-critical applications is the backbone of the business is not "Can we afford the extra time to develop frameworks?" but "Can we afford not to?"

Framework Considerations

One of the reasons frameworks exist as they do is to save developers the effort of reinventing complex solutions to problems that transcend applications. As most developers have done all too often, the "wheel" (insert mundane object of your choice) has been designed and redesigned many times to serve essentially the same purpose in a variety of different circumstances. When you design a framework, you do so knowing that the utility of the framework, much like the wheel, can be realized beyond the specific application at hand (if one exists at the time). But for this to occur, the problem domain the framework addresses must be closely analyzed. If the framework addresses too specific a problem domain, then its reusability becomes impaired. If the framework is too general, it may not contain enough utility to be useful or powerful enough for a particular domain. Frameworks need to be *sufficiently* generic, meaning neither too generic nor too specific.

Before you begin developing your framework, there are a few basic considerations to keep in mind:

1. *Define the boundaries your framework will address.* Try not to design the "kitchen sink" framework, by which I mean the tendency to include every needed capability except, maybe, the kitchen sink.

2. *Keep your framework small and simple [Taligent, 1995].* Complex frameworks will arise, but not before simple ones precede them. Grow into complexity; do not try to tackle it all at once.

3. *Test your framework as you build it.* Perform object-level testing on every object in your framework *before* you start defining the interactions between them. Although this is not always possible, it helps to eliminate the propagation of negative effects in your system. For example, if faulty code can be detected earlier in the development cycle, then additional faulty code that is dependent on the original faulty code can be avoided.

Likewise, approaching the design and implementation of frameworks within your project will require a few other considerations. Because the size of teams or projects varies, take time to decide how best to divide the work among team members. Properly identifying frameworks within your application design process will facilitate better organization among your fellow developers. When working with many people on a project, one of the first things I do is begin thinking about how the project can be broken into smaller, more efficient teams that can focus on one or a few subsets of the problem domain. This approach is good for a variety of reasons:

- No one knows everything, and more than likely each person on your team will have some useful knowledge he or she can apply to different areas of the project. Grouping people with similar knowledge about certain problems can yield effective and efficient results.

- Dividing large problems into subproblems allows groups of people to work at different paces and in parallel. That said, be aware that there are factors that violate this observation. For example, it is often the case that the manner in which a problem is decomposed involves many individuals competing for the same solution. This should be avoided if possible.

- Smaller teams of two or three people are less affected by political struggles and miscommunications that often plague larger groups. My motto is "Keep it small, friendly, and efficient."

In general, the focus and attention needed to effectively design and evolve a framework is best kept within smaller parties in the early stages. If designed properly, a framework can evolve into a much larger complex structure without requiring additional engineers. This evolution should not occur too rapidly, however. Because dramatic changes in your framework could alienate any clients that use it successfully in its present form, there are a few rules to follow once you've begun using or distributing your framework:

1. *Make bug fixes only as needed.* Because the interfaces and method signatures of your framework are not altered during this effort (or shouldn't be!), there is no threat of breaking existing applications that adopt the newly fixed framework.

2. *Add functionality to your framework incrementally and in moderation.* Add new classes and new methods to existing classes, but avoid altering previous methods, method names, signatures, and class names. Define subclasses to enhance the functionality of existing classes.

3. *In some cases, fundamental change to existing framework interfaces or classes cannot be avoided.* If this occurs, be sure to document those changes well and provide sample programs to assist users of your framework in the transition to the new definition.

Build versus Buy

In today's software world, the market for reusable components is growing. IT project managers and developers now must choose whether to engineer a component of their system from scratch or explore commercial components that satisfy the requirements. From the commercial side of the fence, components must be flexible and extensible so developers will find them useful and adaptable over time. It's a difficult task to predict the level of requirements for any given project ahead of time, making it difficult to find suitable components from a third party that meets all the needs of a given project. This is why such frameworks and components need to be small, extensible, and generic.

Types of Frameworks

Recall that a framework targets one type of problem domain. Targeting multiple discrete problems simultaneously would prevent the framework from being reused and make it unnecessarily complex. For this reason, there are three simple categories of frameworks that attempt to describe the role of a particular framework [Taligent, 1995]:

- Application frameworks
- Domain frameworks
- Support or utility frameworks

Application frameworks target horizontal functionality across a wide range of application clients [Taligent, 1995]. *Domain frameworks* encapsulate expertise in a particular problem domain such as financial or inventory. *Support* or *utility frameworks* target system-level types of services such as object persistence, memory management, or device drivers. Table 1.1 shows some examples of these types of frameworks.

Frameworks and Complexity

A framework can provide various *plug points* that allow implementation objects supplied by an application developer to be dynamically added to an application. The architecture of a framework is patterned in such a way that the framework's longevity is ensured through its capability to extend and adapt implementation details. For application developers, this is an attractive

Table 1.1   Types of Frameworks

FRAMEWORK TYPE	FRAMEWORK NAME	DESCRIPTION
Application	JFC	Provides a complete GUI class library and framework for developing user interfaces to any type of application.
	InfoBus	Provides an API and framework for connecting vendor-independent JavaBeans.
	Collections Framework	Provides interfaces and implementations to complex containers and collection objects.
Domain	San Francisco	Provides classes and frameworks for constructing complex financial applications.
Utility	TopLink	Layers on top of JDBC to provide object-relational database mapping.

feature because it saves the effort of redesigning portions of a complex system that are better suited to a generic architecture like the one provided by a framework. In terms of complexity, the less code the developer has to understand or write, the less complex his or her perceived effort.

Complexity of Design

Bar-Yam [1997] defines complexity as ". . . the amount of information needed to describe a particular system." Take an apple, for example. When placed on a table, it is relatively motionless and so can be described in relatively the same way no matter how often you look at it (over a reasonably short period of time). Its state is relatively static and does not change noticeably. A babbling brook, on the other hand, is a vastly complex system of interacting molecules, rocks, and debris all coming together, interacting, and changing rapidly and constantly over time. Defining the state of such a system could be summed up descriptively more easily than it could mathematically. The state of these real-world systems is defined as a mathematical continuity. In other words, there's no space between changes of state; or, there's no nonstate.

Complexity thrives on the interaction between particles or elements in a system. These interactions produce feedback effects that propagate and often amplify over time, where distant outcomes become largely unpredictable. This effect is known to chaologists as the *butterfly effect*. It states, simply, that somewhere a butterfly flaps its wings. The propagation of outcomes from that motion causes winds to stir and build up, and over time, possibly on the other side of the world, a hurricane occurs. Effects of this kind can be viewed as traveling between particles with which they come into contact, or passing along from particles from which they originate, to particles nearby. At certain junctures in a continuous system, effects may be absorbed or muted by other ones and hence go unnoticed or become unobservable in the system.

In a digital computer, state is maintained in its memory; and updates are registered on a short periodic basis called a *CPU cycle*. The difference here is that effects in a digital system can impact anywhere within the system and have unpredictable results almost immediately (e.g., a system crash).

When thinking about software applications, developers seldom address how complexity can arise in a system (possibly, in part, because no scientific methods exist in doctrine to do this), or, more specifically, how developers can control for complexity in design and implementation. One reason for this is the simple human limitation of coping with complexity. Humans can only juggle a few items accurately at any one time. Psychology tells us that this number is 7, plus or minus 2. When designing systems with objects that interact, special attention must be given to control the states of those objects. Certainly there are desirable states and, likewise, undesirable states an object can be in.

The State of a Complex System

Ultimately, the number of possible states of a system should fall into the domain of those states acceptable to the defined task of the system. To put it bluntly, an application should not do anything it isn't supposed to do at any particular time. Fortunately, controlling and determining the state of a digital system is a finite process, though not one that lends itself to practicality. You would not, for example, want to peer into computers and take a snapshot of the state of every logical gate. Supposing such a task could be done, it would yield enormous amounts of indecipherable information and detail that is not very useful to humans.

Instead, the preferable way to design software systems is to use a descriptive language that is readable and intuitive to human thought. Object-oriented languages like Java and C++ serve this purpose well because they allow for discrete entities (objects) to encapsulate their characteristics and behavior much like objects in the real world. The unions and interactions between vast arrays of objects comprise the complexity within the software system. Controlling for the state of such objects is key to controlling the complexity of the system.

There are, however, various levels of state within a software system. There's the state of individual objects, collections of objects, frameworks, applications, and devices. You need to be concerned with not only the micro states, but the macro states as well.

How do frameworks contribute to better understanding and control over complexity regarding the state of a system? When you consider the design of a large, possibly distributed system, your consideration of effort as applied to the complexity of the task forces you to decompose discrete portions into more easily handled and managed problem domains. These subproblem domains are likely to be less specific to the greater design goal of the system, and should be. The results are carefully created frameworks that address generic problem domains and become reusable across applications through time. In addition, the state management of these pieces can be accounted for in stages: the objects, patterns of objects, the framework as a whole, then frameworks together, and on to applications and clusters of applications.

This is an important design consideration that will be revisited throughout this book. In terms of state management and complexity, the concept of a framework that addresses a generic problem domain within a system becomes a powerful mechanism for controlling the state and complexity of that system and other systems built upon that framework.

Effects within a System

As mentioned earlier in this chapter, effects propagate within a complex system. Software applications are naturally complex systems. They contain a vari-

We find it easy to solve some problems by solving sections or pieces of the whole and fitting them together.

ety of interacting mechanisms and provide the user with a seemingly endless number of permutations of functionality. For example, the discrete steps I followed to write this chapter are numerous and varied. Though I interacted with my keyboard and word processor in a variety of ways, not always the same way or in the same order, my word processor behaved predictably (most of the time), no matter what order I chose to accomplish my tasks. Its internal state management is designed in such a way that it allows me to interact with it in varying degrees of complexity. Most of the operations it reveals to me are atomic, which means the side effect of initiating the operation is done at once or as a single unit (like an atom). Chaining together atomic operations provides higher levels of complex behavior. Although the atomic operations within my word processor are well defined, the higher-order complexity is difficult to define because of the vast number of permutations possible. Believe me, if there were a button called "finish the chapter," I would be finished in two seconds!

Grouping similar objects that perform a discretely definable set of tasks is what framework design is all about. Higher-order capabilities can be manifested through frameworks and better controlled and understood as separately defined structures that represent subdomains of a whole. The subdomains can be validated, most often, independently of their application context and therefore analyzed and constructed with greater confidence and fewer negative effects.

> **NOTE** If a subdomain cannot be solved or validated independent of the application whole, then it is not a likely candidate for a framework and would not be reusable. One of the compelling benefits of frameworks is solutions that are independent of specific application infrastructures.

Negative effects occurring within a complex software system can go unnoticed over a period of time until they propagate into larger, more destructive behaviors. I've seen systems built on top of some rather brave assumptions about available resources and how those resources would be managed. Some examples include applications allocating memory indefinitely; or eating up file system space, under the assumption that a human would eventually step in and clean things up. These sorts of runaway systems probably didn't impose any immediate concerns, but eventually they would cease to operate, the consequences of which were probably not considered at the time.

Pre- and Postconditions

One way of preventing the state of an object or system from drifting outside the acceptable bounds is to implement pre- and postconditions on atomic operations. The basic idea is that for each atomic operation, the current state of the system must be within the acceptable valid range of states for that operation. Subsequently, when the atomic operation has completed, the system must not be in an unacceptable state based on the operation performed. In order for preconditions to be tested, the language supports a feature called an *assertion*, which originated in the Eiffel programming language developed by Dr. Bertrand Meyer. Assertions identify what the acceptable preconditional states must be before an operation can occur. They also define the result of an operation, thereby providing the semantics for pre- and postconditionals. This type of programming is often referred to as *programming by contract* or *design by contract* (DBC), where the contract represents the acceptable conditions and obligations between callers and callees, including the behavioral semantics of operations occurring between them.

This methodology greatly reduces the amount of bugs or negative effects within your application because it accurately controls for the state of the system before and after certain operations. In this sense, the system efficacy is increased, as is its robustness and reliability.

> **NOTE** Unfortunately for Java, the language spec does not directly support assertions. One of the problems with implementing assertions that are not directly supported by the language syntax is that the code representing the assertions tends to be difficult to read and so consumes more time and effort.

Figure 1.5 shows pre- and postconditional blocks that surround an operation or series of operations that can be seen as atomic, in the sense that the conditional blocks either hold true or false for the states governed by the operation. That is, if the preconditional block allows the operation or operations to take place, then the postconditional should also ring true, indicating no unacceptable states were generated by the operations in between.

In the Complexity of Design section of this chapter, I discussed continuous systems and how effects propagate within a continuous system. Recall that sometimes effects get absorbed into the system and then become muted or unnoticeable. In terms of software design, the proper employment of exception handling is an attempt to produce a similar muting effect, as well as a systematic method for dealing with runtime conditions.

Frameworks designed to handle specific tasks, such as object persistence, object transference, and data visualization, should identify and isolate negative effectual conditions within their context. This allows errors originating in a particular framework to be noticed by systems utilizing that framework; thereafter, appropriate decisions about whether or how to propagate the exception (or effect) can be made. Chapter 2, "Java Framework Design" takes a close look at how exceptions can be handled within a framework context.

Figure 1.6 shows the generation of two types of exceptions that originate in different frameworks. The client of a particular framework should trap exceptions of the framework and decide whether and how those exceptions are to be relayed to other objects within the system.

Object Interactions

In the frame of object programming, you are building a system containing objects, each with its own behavior and interactions. As the number of objects increases, the amount of interaction and feedback also increases geometrically,

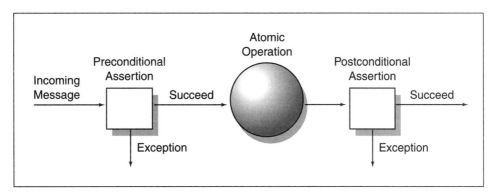

Figure 1.5 Pre- and Postconditional blocks surrounding an atomic operation managing exceptions.

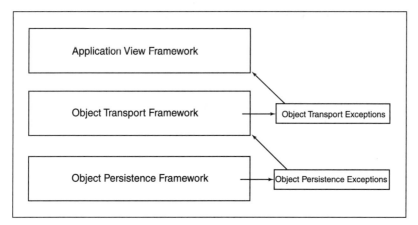

Figure 1.6   Simple exception propagation between adjacent frameworks.

rather than linearly. It is important to understand early how such a system will behave not with just a small number of objects, but with a large, possibly incomprehensible number of objects. You might be wondering, how is this possible? How is an individual supposed to control for complexity that cannot be fully grasped at one instance?

Grow your framework! Do not attempt to make it all-encompassing; define its boundaries and stay within those boundaries. This will allow you to effectively create scenarios to run through your framework and verify its efficacy. Doing this incrementally over time, as you build and extend your framework, will help you to better understand its models and processes, even though it has become much larger and far more complicated. These incremental growth periods represent delta enhancements to your framework that are more easily tracked, managed, and accounted for. Object interactions can increase over time without drowning your ability to grasp and understand the entire framework. If this is lost, the framework is not as useful.

Design Ordering and Classification

To begin to define higher-order behaviors in a system, as opposed to atomic operations, the mental model shifts away from the details of object-level complexity and into the relationships between higher-level structures and functionality. Through the process of analysis, the system can be defined on a variety of levels at the same time. Each level deals with a particular amount of information granularity.

One level is where the fundamental objects are defined and emulated by the system. Another has the organization or grouping of those models. On another, is the relationships those objects have to one another. The logical processes that affect the attributes of the objects can be analyzed, and finally, the ultimate purpose behind why these objects work together can be examined. Depending

Complexity can evolve from smaller simple systems.

on the approach you take, you might have to look through either a microscope or a telescope, figuratively speaking. There is no scientific method as to the order in which these should take place, and often they happen in parallel. It is important, however, to choose a design order methodology that is suitable to your particular application domain.

For example, let's begin thinking about design approaches to a hypothetical system. Let's say you are building an application system for a network of banks. There are a variety of domain-specific requirements that such a system would need to perform. At one level, you can study how the individual bank employee would utilize such a system. What are the kinds of gestures or operations he or she needs to perform his or her job? What types of things does he or she work with? What are the ultimate goals of the system? You might begin modeling your application around certain domain-specific objects that are familiar to bank employees. Some of these might include accounts, customers, transactions, and statements. This process is often referred to as *object modeling* or *domain modeling*. You can further your analysis by understanding the simple relationships between these objects. For example, a Customer has an Account. This kind of relationship is a HAS-A relationship; a Customer HAS-A Account. You can further your model by concluding that, an Account HAS-A Statement and an Account HAS-A Transaction. Figure 1.7 shows the HAS-A hierarchical relationship between the domain objects and includes an inheritance or class

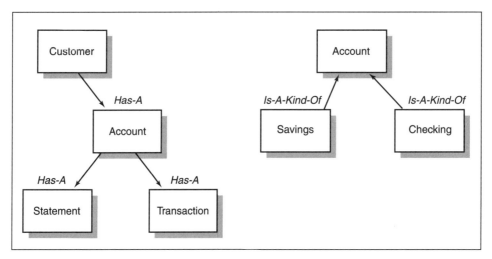

Figure 1.7   Entity-relation diagram.

hierarchy representation. These types of diagrams are referred to as *entity-relation* (ER) diagrams because they contain simple entities with connectors representing the type and direction of relationship between two entities.

These object definitions serve a common purpose that is centered around maintaining customer accounts common to all banks. To this end, a common objective or goal can be realized from these entities. Suppose you decide that your application needs a way to store groups of accounts together for an individual customer based on the type of the account. You could use a Hashtable extension (called AccountList) to provide this organizational model. The following code segment shows the simple AccountList Hashtable extension.

```
public class AccountList extends Hashtable {

    public void addAccount(Account account,String type)
    {
      put(type,account);
    }

    public void removeAccount(Account account)
    {
      remove(account);
    }

 ....

}
```

First, the domain objects are identified, then the focus turns to questions about the organization of those models. This order is not uncommon, but there is a distinct difference in the resulting development process for each classification of objects.

In terms of the domain problem addressed by the class list, the AccountList object appears to be of a different nature from the others. This object would seem to be useful in terms of organizing Account objects within the application, but is there a domain-specific counterpart to this category of object like the others?

There are operations that are performed on collection classes like AccountList that would not directly map to operations performed on Accounts specifically (e.g., sorting or ordering). Possibly, in some banks, an object called the AccountList is involved at some real-world level with customers performing transactions on their accounts, but in this hypothetical model let's assume that such a real document or object does not exist. Instead, you've discovered the utility of organizing your domain models in such a manner for a very good reason. You've provided a facility to gather, access, and order objects so that such needs would be used frequently by the application.

This is a rather simple concept that is common in object-oriented development. The point is not to emphasize the utility of this object model, but to realize that there is a distinctness among the domain objects first described. They relate to one another in a direct way. The organization abstraction of these objects seems to fall into another category of thinking, one more in tune with the development of the application itself and less to the real-world objects and processes. The design order followed in this micro example started with the definition of the domain constituents and followed with an organizational abstract model of one of those constituents. It's almost as if you began by looking under a microscope at the domain environment and slowly backed away and are now peering through a magnifying glass. By doing this, you see higher levels of organization that are not manifest in the object models themselves. In this approach, two major types of classification models arise:

- The object model
- The organizational model

Classifications

Determining how processes and objects you identify in your system relate involves classifying them. In this example, it was easy to see that the result was objects from the domain and objects organizing those objects, representing two essential classifications. In practice, you may discover other types of classifications. The primary goal of classification is to identify and, subsequently, group objects. This process exists in a variety of other scientific disciplines, and is in fact at the heart of almost all scientific endeavors. For example, in physics, there are different kinds of particles classified by name and characteristic, some of which assemble into larger particles. In this sense, there is a hierarchi-

Sometimes things appear to have qualities that would classify them in other categories.

cal relationship among different kinds of particles in physics. Electrons, protons, and neutrons assemble into atoms; atoms assemble into molecules. Quarks appear within neutrons and so on and so on.

Any attempt to classify objects will result in an ontology that defines fundamental relationships among them (e.g., containment, genealogy, or inheritance). In object-oriented design, classification is an important but somewhat ad hoc process, and there is no real structured methodology for carrying this process out other than experience. As much as we attempt to define the real world in terms of discretely defined objects, the real world will find a way to defy that structure. Consider some of these questions: Where does the sky begin? When is someone considered old? How tall is tall? The answers to these and similar questions will often be relative, but relativity is not something useful in practical engineering unless you're into artificial intelligence. The fact is, these questions are fuzzy in nature; that is, they do not always have concrete answers.

Abstraction and Chunking

Abstraction, a powerful mechanism for shielding complexity, is used throughout this book. Complexity abstraction contributes to grouping and organizing object models and processes into discretely usable frameworks. These frameworks can then be utilized and extended with far greater ease and understanding than the complexity details they have buried inside them. As framework composition is discussed, methods for exposing higher-order behaviors and complexities through abstractions and class organizations in your framework will be explored.

I first encountered the term *chunking* in Douglas Hofstadter's wonderful book *Godel, Escher, Bach. An Eternal Golden Braid* [1979]. His definition of chunking refers to how the human mind organizes and identifies complex objects. For example, the human mind is not particularly good at summing or grasping many different things at once, so compensates by understanding a multitude of similar objects together as a collective chunk.

Conversely, the mind is quite good at shifting perspective within a complex structure to isolate cross-sections that are relevant in the current thinking process. Consider for a moment a tree. When you identify a tree, you notice a trunk, branches, and leaves. Each part is distinct in its own right, but crucial to the notion of a tree. A trunk without branches and therefore without leaves is called a stump. It is no longer considered the same as a tree. However, you do not attempt to sum all the individual parts of a tree, namely each individual leaf, before identifying it as such. Instead, the countless pieces are chunked together and abstracted together as one collective unit.

In object-oriented software, good design directs us to chunk discrete pieces into collective bodies that are much easier to control and therefore understand (such as components). This natural tendency is a fundamental human thought process and crucial to designing and understanding large systems. Categorizing object collections that perform a common set of objectives is one of the primary goals of good framework design. When done properly, the complexity contained within the framework is abstracted. Your view of an application can be thought of as higher-level interactions between frameworks and the relationships those frameworks have to one another. This view represents a wider-angled lens than the object-level view, but serves as a useful way to understand the multilevel relationships certain object types have to one another and the system proper as a whole. Figure 1.8 shows how to visualize a collection of objects as standalone entities as part of respective frameworks. Each view represents a different perspective into the same object relationship. One is more object-centric, and the other shows us a framework view and how the interacting instances in each framework collaborate.

Encapsulation

By now you should be familiar with the concept of encapsulation. It is essentially what makes objects, well, objects. It's a powerful abstracting mechanism. For this reason, working with object-oriented systems is much easier for humans, and most programmers will testify to this. It's not by coincidence either, that the real world is heavily encapsulated. I wake up in the

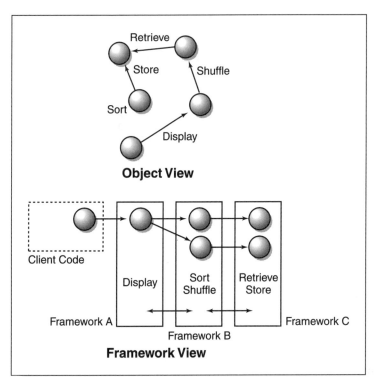

Object View

Framework View

Figure 1.8 Organization of objects from a free-form context into that of interacting frameworks.

morning, put bread in my toaster, and in a few seconds I have toast. I'm not really concerned with what goes on inside that tiny chrome box, as long as it produces the desired results. Simply put, the bread is its input and the toast is its output. I can reuse this object many times and get the same predictable outcome (most of the time). Also, because someone else has gone through the trouble to design and build it, I don't have to. Besides, I wouldn't know how to build a toaster. It's not something that should enter into my mind when I'm thinking about breakfast either. This simple analogy serves a powerful purpose: when you build objects, your intention should be to reuse them without worrying about how they operate. Like my microwave oven, an object can encapsulate a great deal of complexity, yet be easy to use and powerful at the same time.

Frameworks are collections of objects with defined interactions. They contain a great deal of complexity and should encapsulate it equally as well as its components. It's a tool, and using it saves the user the time and the headache of creating one from scratch every time it is needed.

Problem Decomposition

Software systems today are larger and more complicated than their predecessors, so much so that it becomes impossible for one person to break down all the components of a system and understand the purpose and role of every object. Coping with this problem involves segmenting it into smaller problem sets. It is a natural tool to view a large problem as a collection of smaller subproblems, each of which can be solved independently of the whole. Assembling the solutions to the subproblems together results in a solved whole. This can be viewed as deconstructing complexity into simpler pieces and reassembling those pieces, much as we were taught in high-school algebra. If your software system is designed as a set of interacting but separate pieces, you can define the acceptable domain of states (or solutions) for each piece independently much easier than the entire system at once. This is one of the core principles and goals of framework design and application engineering.

Although this is a commonly adopted approach to problem solving, in software engineering, the sum of the parts is not always equal to the whole. In other words, simply assembling working pieces together does not imply a fully working whole. In any complex system, there exists the behaviors of the individual constituents of the system and then the behavior of the whole system. This *emergent behavior* is manifest in the assembled system, not in the individual objects themselves. Although it is a great practice to begin constructing pieces into large applications, the emergent behavior of the application must be addressed as well, which is particularly difficult to predict and control. Figure 1.9 shows the abstract process of decomposing an entity into smaller subsets.

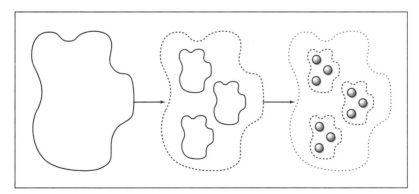

Figure 1.9   Decomposing an abstraction into embedded subset domains.

Emerging Behavior

The emergence of behavior, or traits, in a complex system is most noticeable in the Game of Life, a simulation consisting of species that breed and mutate. Their initial state contains small populations isolated across a map. As the species breed and multiply, they migrate and intermix with other slightly different species, possibly exchanging DNA and evolving into slightly different combinations of species. This cross-fertilization produces some interesting new behaviors and characteristics. The key concept here is not so much the nature of evolution of life, but how the logical program that manifested the diversity of action was implemented in nondiversified code. The logic that created the multitude of unusually evolving objects is, more or less, static. In other words, it is based on rules, and the rules do not typically evolve. Figure 1.10 illustrates the Game of Life. Each automata represents a heuristically based algorithm that interacts with nearby parties. The initial state and genetic algorithms used will cause a variety of emergent scenarios to occur.

It is not enough to decompose large tasks into smaller, solvable tasks. You must further analyze or study how the assembled elements interact with one another to provide a predictably functioning system. Fortunately, in computer programming, this is rarely a challenge. Programs tend to do exactly what they're programmed to do and seldom do they show signs of deviant behavior! It's more a matter of honing that behavior to a reasonably acceptable set.

The reality is that most end-user software applications emulate simple, controllable processes. My word processor is doing relatively nothing (arguably) unless I instruct it to; it does not evolve. An embedded system running a robotic arm in an auto factory, however, is constantly analyzing its environment and making calculations.

The level at which you should be concerned about chaos and emerging or evolving behavior depends upon how much feedback your system provides to itself and how it responds to that feedback. As discussed earlier, causal effects early in a feedback system can amplify over short periods into much larger, unpredictable effects. Where do frameworks enter into this picture? Determin-

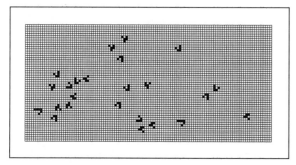

Figure 1.10   Game of Life initial state.

THOUGHTS Applications of the future will be larger, more complex, and smarter, and will have the capacity to learn, evolve, and improve over time. Naturally, there is a place in our lives for simple linear applications like word processors (although they, too, are becoming nonlinear!), but on a much larger scale. Software systems and, more specifically, distributed intelligent software systems, will emerge as an important part of our economics.

ing how your framework organizes information, propagates effects, and interacts with other frameworks will contribute to the design of the emergent behavior in your system. This is a rather abstract concept to consider, which Figure 1.11 attempts to illustrate.

Hierarchical Structures

Hierarchical structures are useful for representing objects that have cascading relationships between them. The object world is built upon *class hierarchy* and *composition*. This is a useful mechanism for containing the relationships seen in

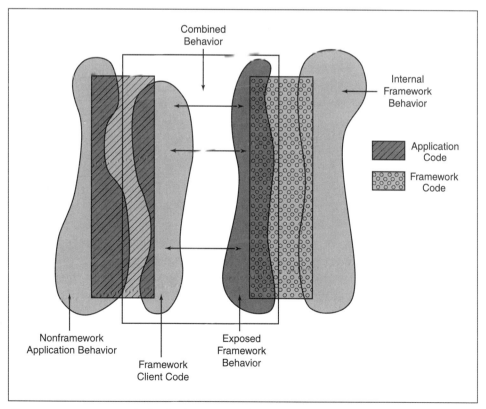

Figure 1.11 Emergent behavior intersection between two frameworks.

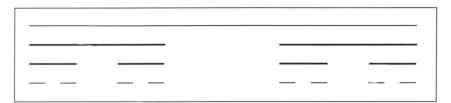

Figure 1.12   Cantor fractal set.

the real-world objects we attempt to model. It gives us the ability to create generalizations of objects and refine those generalizations as isolated descendants on the hierarchy. Much of what has been discussed thus far in this chapter lends itself to hierarchically organized structures. For example, problem decomposition views large problems as containers for smaller problems (similar to fractal sets built from repeated embedded structures. The Cantor fractal set in Figure 1.12 is the simplest example of this). Emerging behavior is evident in the organization of elements into clusters that scale hierarchically as well. The process of classification itself, relies on a hierarchy to represent taxonomies of entities. Abstracting or chunking complex things into simpler more discrete things is another form of clustering that is a hierarchical process.

The relationships between nodes in a hierarchy can vary depending on the nature of classification. For instance, a family tree is a hierarchy based on genealogy or ancestral relations. Most often in object decomposition, objects are looked at as being part of a common category, such as a car and a truck sharing the generalization of vehicle. They share characteristics, yet each has specific features the other lacks. This kind of relationship can be represented as IS-A-KIND-OF, where a car IS-A-KIND-OF vehicle. It has everything a vehicle has, along with some unique qualities that make it a car. This type of inheritance relationship is one of the foundations of object analysis. However, when discussing object organization on different levels (e.g., IS-A, HAS-A, IS-A-KIND-OF, BEGETS, etc.), there are multiple simultaneous hierarchies that possibly contain a heterogeneous mix of the same objects. This structural organization is often the most important aspect of a system, and certainly deserves consideration when designing systems using frameworks. Because a framework addresses a specific category of problem, it is important that the objects used within the framework be organized and structured in such a way that not only addresses the problem well, but facilitates reusability, extensibility, and scalability.

Orders of Magnitude

Orders of magnitude refers to the capability of something to provide multiple simultaneous levels of information depending on the current view, or *magni-*

tude. Consider the fractal nature of coastlines. As seen from space, the East Coast is jagged and varied to the same degree as it would appear to you flying in an airplane and viewing only a few miles at a time, or possibly walking along the shore where stretches are curved or jagged to the same effect. You can almost conclude through this simple observation that the East Coast is made up of smaller coastlines, which are made up of yet smaller ones, and so on, the sum of which cannot be completely digested as a whole. Instead, we find ourselves zooming in under the hood, so to speak, and zooming out again. It is this process that leads to a full understanding of the levels comprising something vast and complex.

As we think about designing complex software systems, we know they will contain a vast number of components, all of which will interact with one another at some level. The components designed for these systems are not created in isolation, but are a result of intense domain analysis of the problem being addressed. Similar components can be assembled into hierarchies or families once they have been properly classified. Also, the components can work together to perform a common function in the context of a framework. Now the framework becomes a composition of smaller individual pieces each of which addresses a specific task or goal. Again, these frameworks assemble and fit together to form working applications, and to provide the basis for families of applications as well. Hopefully, how the different orders of magnitude relate to one another is clear. The order progresses from the very small to the very large, composing or decomposing depending on the direction.

Each order of magnitude requires special attention in different ways from the other. For example, think about the objects you created in your banking application example: you were focused on the domain, that is, the real world from which the objects emulate. The relationships between those objects and their attributes could be found through analysis of the banking environment. But creating a banking application framework that can be reused in a variety of banking applications raises a different set of problems and considerations to address to properly reach that objective. Once you've done that, you step back even farther to address the immediate goals of the finished application, which intends to build upon your previous efforts. The implementation goals specific to your particular banking application will address yet even more specific criteria than the previous two levels.

Being able to effectively migrate from one level to another will enhance your ability to cope with the complexity of the evolving system, because at any one time, you are not trying to grasp the entire picture. Problems can only be solved a few at a time, so it is necessary that those problems reside in the same problem domain. It is difficult to think about two levels of problems, one of which may very well change as the other changes.

Framework Composition

"Composition" really means two things. On the one hand, it refers to what frameworks are composed of; on the other, it refers to the act of composing frameworks. In some ways, the elements that compose a framework are abstract; that is, they are more methodology- or approach-oriented. Recall from the previous example involving accounts, customers, and account lists that there are two types of modeling that occurred in the analysis: the *object model* and the *organizational model*.

The Object Model

The focus of the *object model* is on the domain. Because of this, objects used to model the domain are often referred to as *domain models*. The object model describes the class hierarchies utilized by your framework. Therefore, you must carefully consider which object definitions will be included in your framework. This process is not easy to master, and there are a variety of approaches to identifying when something becomes a class in your system.

Your object model will contain a variety of domain-related objects you've uncovered and classified during analysis. The model is not, however, limited to simply domain objects, but will likely contain other types of objects as well. Let's revisit the object model from the hypothetical banking application.

- Account
- Transaction
- Customer
- Statement

Because these classes are being created in the context of a framework, you must consider the range of applications suitable for this type of framework. It's important to ask two questions early and often:

1. What is the problem domain this framework will address?
2. How will this framework address the problems of the domain it was constructed for?

For this example, the answer to the first question is easy. The mini-framework provides the building blocks needed to construct banking applications. The second question is somewhat open ended and so is more difficult to answer, but so far the framework will provide the least common denominator of definitions required to model high-level domain elements that exist in almost all banking environments and possibly other environments as well (e.g., a video store account tracking system). For all intents and purposes, you are creating a simple wheel, useful only for applications requiring Customers, Accounts, and Transaction type objects, along with the supplied interactions among them.

Let's delve a bit deeper into the class models and see how they would operate inside your application. Each Customer object can have a number of Account objects associated with it. Each Account object has a list of Transactions. Each Account object can also have a Statement object, and each Statement object has a list of Transactions over a certain period. In order to establish an Account with a given customer (assuming Customers come first), Customer.addAccount() is invoked. Take a look at Listing 1.1 to see how Customer is implemented.

Listing 1.1 Customer class definition.

```java
// Customer.java
import java.util.*;

public class Customer {

    private Hashtable accounts = new Hashtable();
    private int ssn = 0;
    private String name = "";

    public Customer(String name, int ssn)
    {
        this.name = name;
        this.ssn = ssn;
    }

    public void addAccount(Account account)
    {
        accounts.put(new Integer(account.getAcctNum()),account);
    }

    public void removeAccount(Account account)
    {
        accounts.remove(account);
    }

    public Account getAccount(int acctNum)
    {
        return (Account)accounts.get(new Integer(acctNum));
    }

}
```

The Account object accepts two parameters in its constructor: the account number *acctNum* and the customer this account is associated with, *customer*. One of the things tellers would like to do in this system is find out who owns a particular account. Listing 1.2 shows the code for the Account object.

Listing 1.2   Account class definition.

```
// Account.java
import java.util.*;

public class Account {

   private int acctNum = 0;
   private Vector transactions = new Vector();
   private Customer customer = null;

   private float amount = 0;

   public Account(int acctNum,Customer customer)
   {
      this.acctNum = acctNum;
      this.customer = customer;
   }


   public void addTransaction(Transaction transaction)
   {
      transactions.addElement(transaction);
      amount+=transaction.getAmount();
   }

   public Vector getTransactions()
   {
      return transactions;
   }

   public float getAmount()
   {
      return amount;
   }

   public int getAcctNum()
   {
      return acctNum;
   }
}
```

NOTE A removeTransaction() method does not appear in the Account class because once money changes hands, it can't be undone. In case of error, the bank would simply issue another offsetting transaction to the account.

The process this example is attempting to model involves a new customer coming to a bank to open a new account. A Customer object is created within the system with that person's name and social security number (SSN) as attributes (much like the real person). The new account is associated with the customer by calling Customer.addAccount().

When a transaction occurs on an account, it can originate from sources other than the account owner. For example, your employer may deposit money in your account or a lender may debit money from your account. The Transaction object needs to associate an identification number with the originator of the transaction. If it is the account owner, this number may be his or her SSN. Listing 1.3 shows the code for the Transaction object.

Listing 1.3   Transaction class definition.

```
// Transaction.java
import java.util.*;

public class Transaction {
    private float amount = 0;
    private int originId = 0;
    private Date date = null;

    public Transaction(float amount, int originId)
    {
        this.amount = amount;
        this.originId = originId;
        date = new Date();
    }

    public Date getDate()
    {
        return date;
    }

    public float getAmount()
    {
        return amount;
    }
}
```

Listing 1.4 defines the Statement class, which will gather all the transactions from an Account object between the given start and end date.

Once the objects and methods for accumulating transactions on accounts have been established, periodically you'll want to issue statements on that account that detail the transactions over a specified date range. The Statement object allows for the specification of arbitrary date ranges. Typically, banks will issue statements quarterly, but in the spirit of flexibility, the Statement object has been designed to accept any range of dates. The Statement object uses a simple comparing algorithm to determine which transactions qualify for the statement. Other types of objects similar to Statement objects can be created that perform different algorithms on an account's transactions.

If you were to write a simple application that uses this mini-framework, a segment of it might look like this:

```
...
// Joe walks into bank and he is identified in the system.
Customer customer = new Customer("Joe",222112222);
```

Listing 1.4   Statement class definition.

```
// Statement.java
import java.util.*;

public class Statement {

    private Vector transactions = new Vector();

    public Statement(Account account,Date start,Date end)
    {
        Vector trans = account.getTransactions();
        for(int i=0;i<trans.size();i++) {
            Transaction transaction = (Transaction)trans.elementAt(i);
            Date tranDate = transaction.getDate();
            if((tranDate.equals(start) || tranDate.after(start))
&&
                (tranDate.before(start))) {
                transactions.addElement(transaction);
            }
        }
    }

    public Vector getTransactions()
    {
        return transactions;
    }
}
```

```
...
// He creates a new account.
Account account = new Account(1998,customer);
...
// Joe deposits $500 into his account.
Transaction transaction = new Transaction(500.00,222112222);
account.addTransaction(transaction);
...
// Joe's employer adds $2000 to his account.
Transaction transaction = new Transaction(2000.00,5467081234);
account.addTransaction(transaction);


..
// Joe's lender debits $400 from his account.
Transaction transaction = new Transaction(-400.00,8877124678);
account.addTransaction(transaction);


..
Statement statement = new Statement(account,new Date(12,15,1997),new
Date(4,15,1998));
Vector transactions = statement.getTransactions();
//Print the transactions
```

These code fragments are simple and straightforward (hopefully). The state management is handled internally by the framework objects. The Account object automatically calculates its balance. It also maintains all the transactions through time.

At the application level, the primary duties include interfacing with the user to gather information like names, SSNs, and transaction information, and forwarding it to the objects. If the framework is useful, the objects will be organized without the application developer knowing the semantics behind the framework. This level can be thought of as connecting the framework domain objects with information gathered from human interfaces. Once this information connection is made, the framework handles the rest.

> **NOTE** The framework classes currently reside more toward the class library end of the spectrum because they do not define any application plug points for which implementations can be plugged.

The Organizational Model

There are useful aggregations and collections of objects within a framework that more readily address the goal of the framework (or application) than simply the objects alone. The *organizational model* deals specifically with the arrangements and groupings of objects that fit with the processes and interactions defined in the problem domain, and represented, at least in default, by the framework.

Various levels of organization exist in a given problem domain. Addressing the organizational context of a particular level is important when considering the design and use of frameworks. Because they are more than class hierarchies, it's not enough for your framework to constitute only your object model. It's necessary to provide different levels of organization among the objects and data in your application as necessary to the specific application. The right organization will keep the complexity of your evolving system manageable. Also, this gives your framework flexibility to address organizational differences in similar domain environments.

Over time, you might discover other ways to organize your objects that do not involve interactions with them directly. In the application in this example, a few relationships are rooted within certain objects. A Customer object maintains a list of Accounts internally. Although this seems natural to conclude, any situations arising where this association is different or nonexistent would not be addressable by your framework or would be awkwardly implemented. When analyzing the organizational model, you must ask yourself whether a particular structure suits your needs and is also scalable and extensible. Another way to organize the relationship between Customers and Accounts is through the addition of organizational classes.

Listing 1.5 defines the CustomerAccounts class, which associates a specific account with its account number. Given the account number as the key, the respective account within this collection is returned.

Listing 1.5 CustomerAccounts class definition.

```java
// CustomerAccounts.java
import java.util.*;

public class CustomerAccounts extends Hashtable {


    public void addAccount(Account account)
    {
        put(new Integer(account.getAcctNum()),account);
    }

    public Account getAccount(int acctNum)
    {
        return (Account)get(new Integer(acctNum));
    }


}
```

If the CustomerAccounts object were added to the example framework, the domain objects would not impose any associations that could prevent them from being used by a variety of slightly different applications. In this case, the association link from Customer objects to Account objects is removed and handled separately. Because of this, your Customer object looks like Listing 1.6.

NOTE There are a number of interesting benefits to this type of organizational structure when applied to certain object relations, especially when dealing with object-oriented databases. Because certain object-oriented persistence mechanisms retrieve objects based primarily on reachability, retrieving a simple Customer object could result in a excess of Account and Transaction objects that may not be of interest. This consideration is covered in Chapter 7, "Java Application Architectures" under Data Access Models.

The way accounts for a particular customer are acquired has been altered. But in order to do this, you still need an index object, and in either scenario, you will continue to use Customer objects. Previously, you would start with a Customer object and invoke getAccount(acctNum) to acquire a particular account. Now you will do something like:

Listing 1.6 Revised Customer class.

```
// Customer.java

public class Customer {

    private int ssn = 0;
    private String name = "";

    public Customer(String name, int ssn)
    {
        this.name = name;
        this.ssn = ssn;
    }

    public String getName()
    {
        return name;
    }

    public int getSSN()
    {
        return ssn;
    }
}
```

```
CustomerAccounts customerAccounts = new CustomerAccounts(customer);
...
Account account = customerAccounts.getAccount(acctNum);
```

You now need to add an organizational construct that allows CustomerAccount objects to be identified based on a given Customer object. It's not unreasonable to think that somewhere a bank maintains a database of all its customers, and from there can find out information about each customer. For this example, create an object called CustomerDatabase, shown in Listing 1.7.

This second organizational model relieved the Customer class from having to provide the overhead of maintaining or organizing its own account objects. The Customer object reflects only the data attributes that describe customers and methods for inspecting those values. There are a few reasons why this is better for your framework:

■ Different organizational models can be built alongside the default one. Doing so does not disrupt the way the domain models behave internally.

Listing 1.7   CustomerDatabase class definition.

```java
// CustomerDatabase.java
import java.util.*;

public class CustomerDatabase extends Hashtable {

    public void addCustomer(Customer customer)
    {
        put(customer,new CustomerAccounts());
    }

    public Customer getCustomer(String name)
    {
        Enumeration customers = elements();

        while(customers.hasMoreElements()) {
            Customer customer = (Customer)customers.nextElement();
            if(customer.getName().equals(name)) return customer;
        }
        return null;
    }

    public CustomerAccounts getCustomerAccounts(Customer customer)
    {
        return (CustomerAccounts)get(customer);
    }
}
```

- Because of the first reason, you can reuse objects in your framework more often. For example, you can still use the Statement object as provided.

- When accessibility is a concern, you can tailor which objects are utilized systematically and dynamically rather than as mandated by the object model.

Given this new design approach, the client application code would look like this:

```
// Our teller gathers the name of her customer and retrieves
// the Customer object.
Customer customer = customerDatabase.getCustomer("Joe");
CustomerAccounts accounts =
customerDatabase.getCustomerAccounts(customer);

Account account = accounts.getAccount(acctNum);

// Joe deposits $500 into his account.
Transaction transaction = new Transaction(500.00,222112222);
account.addTransaction(transaction);
...
// Joe's employer adds $2000 to his account.
Transaction transaction = new Transaction(2000.00,5467081234);
account.addTransaction(transaction);

System.out.println("The amount of your account,"+customer.getName()+",
is: $"+account.getAmount());
```

Figure 1.13 shows the organizational model relating Customers and Accounts.

It might occur to you that the relationship previously established between Customers and Accounts, namely Customer HAS-A Account, no longer exists in

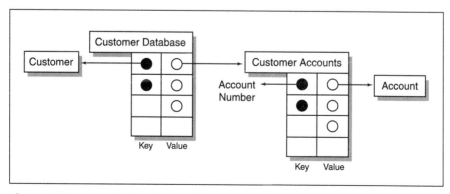

Figure 1.13 Organizational model for CustomersAccounts.

the object-oriented sense of the term. It would be invalid to construct an ER diagram showing a direct connection between Customers and Accounts, as done previously. However, this does not mean that, at some level, Account objects cannot be acquired given a Customer object. The organizational structure has been modeled or encapsulated in two new classes: CustomerAccounts and CustomerDatabase. Each organizational model deals with a particular level of organization. At the highest level, Customers are associated with CustomerAccount objects. CustomerAccount objects key Account objects off of their account numbers. This loose coupling between the domain models and their organization allows you to create interesting and adaptive new structures on top of the existing framework. Also, because CustomerAccount and CustomerDatabase are provided by your framework, a useful default organizational mechanism exists.

You might notice one difference between the domain objects (Customer, Account, Transaction, etc.) and the organizational models built with them (namely CustomerAccounts and CustomerDatabase): The organizational models extend the Hashtable data structure object. Structured objects, called *collections,* are the building blocks used to create complex and efficient organizational models. Collection classes do just that: they collect. They are designed to hold groups of objects in a specific manner like a tree structure, a list, or a queue. Also, collections open the door for the use of *iterator* objects that are used to sequence (or iterate) through the collection, performing some supplied operation on each object or restructuring the collection based on some Boolean logic operation. Iterators and collections are important concepts in frameworks because of their contribution to organization and their capability to accommodate scalability and state management. Chapter 2 spends a good deal of time looking at the Java 2 Collection classes and how they can be utilized in your frameworks.

Separating Interface and Implementation

By their nature, frameworks will provide a degree of separation between their interfaces and implementations of those interfaces. Clearly, this allows different implementations to be plugged into the framework. There are many ways to implement plug points within a framework [D'Souza et al., 1998]. As noted earlier, plug points are locations defined by, but not implemented by, the framework. In Chapter 2, "Java Framework Design," you'll see how you can provide plug points in framework classes.

Inheritance

Inheritance is a simple but rather stiff mechanism for reusing object templates by subclassing them. The basic inheritance manifesto states that subclassing allows for the overriding of base class methods. And, in theory, this seems natural, but caution must be exercised because the subclass must always adhere to the specification or type model of the base class. If the subtype overrides too much of the base class, then the hierarchy needs to be considered. Maybe it's not really a subclass, but a new class in itself. This question is compounded by time, as roles of objects possibly shift in different directions, resulting in invalidating an otherwise solid object model.

Interface

Interfaces provide a way to enforce a given set of behavior on a given class. In Java, stating that a class implements an interface means that the class will strictly provide implementations (empty or otherwise) for all methods defined on the interface. Furthermore, the object itself can now be represented as the type corresponding to any interfaces implemented by that object. This allows for very generically defined object models that are based solely (or partially) on interface types, deferring the actual implementations. Because a framework is a definition of an architecture, key implementations are thereby delegated to the application developer.

A New Mind-Set

Often, when constructing a new software system, developers look for the straightest path to take to create an application that meets the minimal set of program requirements. Typically, contract-based software engineering falls under this mind-set. It's no secret in software engineering that most large multi-effort software projects seem to go over budget and over schedule. There are a number of reasons why this might occur. Possibly, time schedules were unrealistic; unforeseen or unsolvable problems arose; or requirements kept changing, and the application either couldn't adapt or had to be rewritten. It would seem, regardless of the reason, that some new perspective is needed to correct the course of projects that are snowballing out of control. Some of this has to do with system complexity, managing that complexity, managing the organization of the resources for the project, and understanding the project goals. Although only certain of those concepts fall within the scope of this text, I hope to illuminate a slightly different and better philosophy behind design approaches to these systems. As pointed out earlier, when complex beasts are not properly bounded or grown incrementally, they can easily run amok.

One of the areas where new thinking will help contribute to stable, manageable systems is in their design structuring and approach. A poorly designed system will never achieve the goals of good scalability and extensibility; and the system will not be easily understood or reusable, for that matter. The field of framework design attempts to make applications easier to build, thereby reducing the time it takes to construct and extend them in the future. Framework design also facilitates easier modification and hence extensibility to existing systems built upon solid frameworks and foundations. Proper utilization of framework design in your application will enable you to remove obsolete implementations of certain abstracted layers and replace or update them through time, thereby extending the appeal of your software and ensuring that you will spend the minimal amount of time addressing evolving requirements and technical challenges that predictably will appear.

In order for these types of benefits to be realized, a new mind-set is required. The first question is no longer, "How do I build a banking application?" but rather "How do I *define* a banking application?" That definition is what gets embodied in your framework. The definition can be realized in a variety of different implementations. If you establish a framework that provides the core set of objects and definitions representing an account-driven banking system, you need only provide the appropriate wrapper on that framework. This is what the application represents. The key here is that the definition doesn't change, though the implementation may vary. In some frameworks, entity interfaces are defined and implementation is left for the developer. Operations on interface objects like this remain constant, but implementations will vary depending on the technical needs of the project. Certainly, these may change and can be replaced within your system with minimal effort and little or no redesign.

Figure 1.14 shows a simple layered model visualization of the relationship between base foundation classes and applications that are built on top of them.

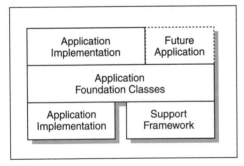

Figure 1.14 Framework layer visualization model.

Future Concepts

The future of computing is quite exciting to ponder. In terms of the kinds of software that will be prevalent, almost certainly it will be far more complex and distributed than today's systems. There is more to be discovered in the realm of software design and construction, and tomorrow's technologies will surely build and improve upon those of today. Where software companies currently are burdened with impossible deadlines and staggering inefficiencies, companies of tomorrow will discover new ways to leverage their entire enterprise efforts through accumulation and reuse of technological building blocks. These software companies will function with much higher efficiency and with less humanpower than today's resource-hungry corporations.

The concept of reuse can be viewed not only from the application or multi-application level, but from the enterprise level as well. Today's corporations are large distributed networks of people and machines. Harnessing the combined efforts of humans and machines for optimal reuse is where the companies of tomorrow will prosper. The point is, not only should you approach application design with reuse as a goal, but you must also consider how corporate reuse can be achieved as well.

Figure 1.15 shows what a layered model architecture might look like for a company with a unified strategic approach to designing and reusing frameworks across vertical applications. The uppermost segments could represent horizontal applications residing within a common domain. The key principle here is that the granularity scales from a small number of similar applications to a variety of dissimilar applications, all coexisting in the architecture.

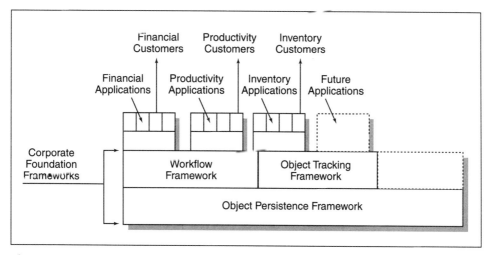

Figure 1.15 Projectwide strategic architecture based on layered framework components.

Summary

This chapter addressed some interesting ideas and principles that hopefully will help you approach the design of complex software systems from a new perspective. I discussed complexity in some detail: what it is, how it works, and how you can better control for it when approaching system designs. I also spent a good deal of time talking about the philosophy behind framework usage and design. I also presented some interesting concepts within frameworks that intersect with other topics, like abstraction, state management, and reuse.

To this point, some of the key benefits of framework adoption should stand out. To recap :

- Frameworks pave the path for higher levels of reuse for existing and future applications.

- Framework adoption can save developers a significant amount of time.

- Good problem decomposition can lead to larger reusable structures. These structures can evolve into frameworks and adapt to a variety of circumstances.

- Replacing framework implementations with newer or other implementations can increase the longevity of your application as it adopts new requirements or technologies.

The topics in this chapter were meant to tantalize your intellect by providing a somewhat high-level cross-section of principles in software engineering and frameworks. These principles will be revisited and explored at various intervals within the book, but with increasing levels of technical details.

References

Adair, Deborah: "Building Object-Oriented Frameworks" *http://www.developer .ibm.com:8080/library/aixpert/feb95/aixpert_feb95_boof.html*, Taligent Inc. Appearing in AIXpert February 1995.

Bar-Yam, Yaneer. *Dynamics of Complex Systems*. Reading, MA: Addison-Wesley, 1997.

Booch, Grady. *Object-Oriented Analysis & Design with Applications*. Reading, MA: Addison-Wesley, 1994.

da Fontoura, Marcus, M. C. Felipe, Edward H. Heausler, and Carlos Jose P. de Lucena. "Using Unification Rules to Derive Object-Oriented Frameworks." Computer Science Department, Pontifical Catholic University of Rio de Janeiro, Brazil.

D'Souza, Desmond, and Alan Cameron Wills. *Objects, Components and Frameworks with UML: The Catalysis Approach*. Reading, MA: Addison-Wesley, 1998.

Gamma, Erich, Richard Helm, Ralph Johnson, and John Vlissides. *Design Patterns: Elements of Reusable Object-Oriented Software*. Reading, MA: Addison-Wesley, 1995.

Hofstadter, Douglas. *Godel, Escher, Bach. An Eternal Golden Braid*. New York: Basic Books, 1979.

Johnson, Ralph. Frameworks Home Page, st-www.cs.uiuc.edu/users/johnson/frameworks.html, 1997.

Johnson, Ralph, and Brian Foote. "Designing Reusable Classes." Department of Computer Science, University of Illinois, 1992.

Lewis, Ted, Larry Rosenstein, Wolfgang Pree, Andre Weinand, Erich Gamma, Paul Calder, Glenn Andert, John Vlissides, and Kurt Shumucker. *Object-Oriented Application Frameworks*. Upper Saddle River, NJ: Prentice-Hall, 1995.

Meyer, Bertrand. *Object-Oriented Software Construction, 2nd Edition*. Upper Saddle River, NJ: Prentice-Hall, 1998.

Szyperski, Clemens. *Component Software*. Harlow, UK: Addison-Wesley Longman Limited, 1998.

Wirfs-Brock, Rebecca. *Designing Object-Oriented Software*. Englewood Cliffs, NJ: Prentice-Hall, 1990.

CHAPTER

2

Java Framework Design

Since its introduction, Java has made a great impact on the way developers think about and build applications. Java has changed the manner in which information is sent out and gathered across the Web, and has provided new methods for deconstructing applications, making applications simpler to design, construct, and enhance. Java has features that, although not entirely new, promote new levels of object organization and structure, which allow developers to build and reuse frameworks with greater ease (although it is still quite a difficult task). These features are discussed in some detail throughout this and the remaining chapters of this book.

The fact that Java is bundled with a plethora of prefabricated frameworks is testimony to the awesome power that both Java and frameworks can offer. This is evident in the rapidly increasing numbers of developers and IT managers who are realizing how the vision of openness, portability, and reuse can provide a truly cost-effective combination.[1]

Chapter 1, "Framework Concepts," introduced frameworks, ways to use them, and why they are important for large and complex projects. This chapter continues the discussion with a look at the design methodologies, model structures, building blocks, and techniques used to construct frameworks that

[1]The popularity of Java is rising rather geometrically and the reasons center on Java's openness, portability, and base frameworks and API's.

Good design always preceeds successful implementation.

> **NOTE** By now, you should be familiar with the concepts of object-oriented programming, design, and analysis, and some framework ideology. Many books are available that further detail the process of object-oriented analysis and design. There is much more to discuss on this subject, most of which is beyond the scope of this book. Cruise your local bookstore if you need more background on these subjects.

are understandable, scalable, reusable, and extensible. This chapter also explores the object-oriented concepts that facilitate these four traits in your frameworks, by implementing a useful framework that comes bundled with Java 2.

Abstraction

Ted Lewis [1995] defines abstraction as the ". . . concept of delegating the implementation of tailored functions to a lower class object. . . ." I would venture to add that, in Java, abstraction can be achieved by hiding the class-specific nature and implementation of an object by adhering to a well-known contract or interface, delegating implementation details and execution to outside classes.

Abstraction is vital to successful framework design. The key benefits of good abstraction are:

- Objects of different origins can communicate through interfaces (as a reliable protocol).

- Client objects and future class extensions are shielded from individual interface declarations. Client objects simply provide the necessary method blocks as required by the parent abstract class. This achieves the basic notion of *separating interface from implementation*.

- Functionality can be layered over time without compromising protocol integrity within the framework.

- Client objects can effectively provide their own application-specific behaviors, to be invoked within the framework processes through abstracted methods and interface declarations.

In Java, there are two mechanisms for achieving abstraction: *abstract classes* and *interfaces*.

Abstract Classes

Abstract classes provide the developer with a mechanism for defining the methods (or protocol) of a particular object in advance of the implementation in an abstract way. This is an important concept in frameworks because, as mentioned earlier, frameworks often enable client code through internal processes. The client code must adhere to the class definitions and protocol assumed by the framework; the developer maintains the ability to cater implementations of certain methods to best suit the application at hand. In many cases, a framework is unable to provide implementation to certain class methods, and doing so would limit the scope to which the framework could be used. When designing class hierarchies, it is generally better to base those hierarchies upon abstract classes. Specifically, it is better to initially inherit from an abstract class than from a concrete class [Johnson, 1992].

In Java, the abstract class can declare abstract methods whose implementation is deferred, as well as provide method implementations that are subsequently inherited by future subclasses. Abstract methods do not require an enclosing method block (e.g., {}) and are declared using the abstract keyword. For example, this construct mechanism:

```
public abstract boolean save();
```

forces the subclass to provide a needed implementation as defined by the abstract superclass. Listing 2.1 is an example of how this looks in Java.

Listing 2.1   DomainModel abstract class definition.

```java
// DomainModel.java

public abstract class DomainModel {

    // Member variable
    protected int objectId = 0;

    // Inherited method implementation
    public int getObjectId()
    {
        return objectId;
    }

    public void setObjectId(int id)
    {
        objectId = id;
    }

    // Abstract method that must be implemented in subclass
    public abstract boolean save();


}
```

NOTE   Throughout the code examples in this book, lines of particular interest to the discussion will appear in bold face to draw your attention.

In this listing, the DomainModel abstract class provides some base data and functionality. The abstract method save() is required by the client code that subclasses DomainModel. Because DomainModel cannot be directly instantiated, a client object subclass is required in order to utilize this class of the framework. A variety of different subclasses can provide different implementations of save(), depending on the technical needs. In other words, this duty is not provided by the framework, but may by *triggered* from within this framework. One implementation of DomainModel might look like Listing 2.2.

The subclass in this simplified example is designed to model an automobile. It does this by providing members that indicate the color and mileage of the automobile. The Automobile class inherits the methods setObjectId() and getObjectId(). As dictated by the rules of subclassing, any child of Domain-Model is also an object of type DomainModel.

Notice in the following example code that the invocation of model.save() will execute the implementation in Automobile because the object, model, is

Listing 2.2   Automobile class definition.

```java
// Automobile.java

import java.io.*;
import java.awt.*;

public class Automobile extends DomainModel implements Serializable {

    // The color of this automobile.
    private Color color = null;

    // The mileage
    private int mileage = 0;

    public Automobile(int id)
    {
        setObjectId(id);
    }

    public int getMileage()
    {
        return mileage;
    }

    public void setMileage(int mileage)
    {
        this.mileage = mileage;
    }

    public Color getColor()
    {
        return color;
    }

    public void setColor(Color color)
    {
        this.color = color;
    }

    public boolean save()
    {
        try {
            FileOutputStream file = new
                    FileOutputStream("Automobile"+objectId);
            ObjectOutputStream out = new ObjectOutputStream(file);
            out.writeObject(this);
            return true;
        } catch (Exception e) {
```

continues

Listing 2.2   Automobile class definition. *(Continued)*

```
        return false;
    }
  }


}
```

actually an abstracted superclass of the Automobile instance, auto. Calling model.save() will have the same effect as calling auto.save().

```
Automobile auto = new Automobile(12);
DomainModel model = (DomainModel)auto;
model.save();
```

A framework making use of abstraction techniques such as this one will not have knowledge about client subclasses like Automobile because the developer will have created the subclass as an extension to the framework. However, the method signatures important to the framework are, at least, defined by the DomainModel abstract class, through which the framework can access subclass implementations. In this example, the save() method contains a *concrete implementation*, but remains entirely accessible from the framework proper. Other methods in Automobile, such as setColor() or getMileage() for example, are not important to the DomainModel framework because they are application-specific and are not visible. It is possible that these methods would be utilized at the application level or by another framework. This is what abstraction provides: the ability to separate the declaration or interface of a future implementation.

Figure 2.1 shows a hypothetical framework defining a class called Domain-Model. The framework contains a simple organizational model that can be utilized by the application; it also defines a process that acts upon that organization. In Listing 2.2, the DomainModel abstraction is subclassed to provide key application-specific implementations, to which the framework calls out through its internal process. Because the framework maintains its own organizational model, the Automobile instance is ensured to function within the framework context. In addition, the application can interact with the Automobile instance.

Rules for Identifying and Using Abstract Classes

Ralph Johnson [1992] identified a few important rules of thumb that can be applied to help identify where abstract classes will be suitable within your framework hierarchy. These include the following items:

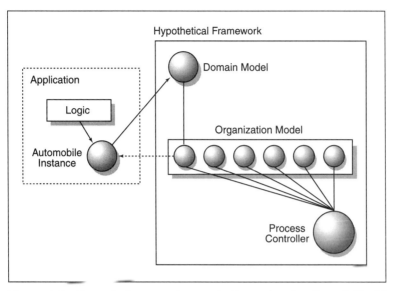

Figure 2.1 Example framework organization using the DomainModel abstraction.

- *Class hierarchies should be deep and narrow.* This means that a single superclass with a large number of subclasses residing at the same level is typically not good design. Thorough analysis of objects within a hierarchy should yield commonalties of protocol and functionality that can migrate to new superclasses, thereby enriching the hierarchy as a whole and improving the reusability of those newly generalized classes.

- *The top of the class hierarchy should be abstract.* Regarding frameworks, abstract classes provide a template model for a category of object where implementations can be deferred to subclasses. In this case, application developers can subclass a framework's abstract base class and provide only the slotted implementations that are utilized within the framework.

- *Accesses to variables should be minimized.* When defining access to variables in a base abstract class (or any class), you should choose to use messages or method wrappers to access such variables. This will allow the data representation to change or be changed within the base abstract class without affecting the protocol used to access the data.

- *Subclasses should be specializations.* Specialization (or subclassing) of abstract classes should provide refinement of base class operations. If a subclass chooses to override or alter behavior semantics to a great degree, the subclass should consider residing in a different or new hierarchy. Also, in this situation, a semantic protocol in the form of an interface may arise in which case two different classes (possibly in different hierarchies) may implement the key protocol in different ways.

Abstract classes offer a method of reuse and extensibility centered on class inheritance by providing a sort of template from which variations and application specific implementations can be provided while retaining the ability to provide default base class implementations. Another method of providing application specific behavior is through interfaces which rely more on object composition rather than inheritance.

Interfaces

Java interfaces define a series of method signatures that can be implemented by any class, regardless of the class hierarchy. This is because interfaces are not classes, and class definitions do not extend interfaces but, rather, implement them. Consider the following simple example:

```
public interface Persistable {
    public void store();
    public void fetch();
}


public class MyPersistableObject implements Persistable {

    // This method block is required for compilation
    public void store() {
       // Some implementation here
    }

    // This method block is required for compilation
    public void fetch() {
       // Some implementation here
    }
}
```

The implementation of interface methods is delegated to the implementing class. Any object that implements an interface must provide method blocks for each method defined in the interface. This type of abstraction provides protocol integrity within a framework. That is, a framework can verify the operations on objects before sending messages. In framework design, it is important to ensure that client objects adhere to the message protocol in given situations as expected by the framework. In other words, the framework must not allow runtime exceptions to occur on object interactions (message passing or method invocation). The InfoBus API is an example of a framework that provides interfaces that client objects must implement. InfoBus is discussed in more detail in Chapter 5, "Analysis of Java Frameworks."

Reliable Protocols and Type Morphology

A *reliable protocol* refers to the way a particular framework defines the interactions between itself and client objects. Remember, the term *client objects* refers to objects that extend or utilize the framework. They are not native in implementation to the framework, but rather provide some level of specificity unique to a particular object. The mechanisms through which a framework interacts with a client object should be well documented by the framework. Interfaces provide a mechanism for defining that interaction and for defining the morphology of an object. Specifically, the morphology of an object refers to its capability to be engaged in various polymorphic behaviors. Using the preceding example, objects of type MyPersistableObject also behave as the morphological type Persistable.

By default, objects that implement framework interfaces have the necessary morphology to interact with that framework in the manner defined by the interfaces that the object implements. By using mechanisms and guidelines such as these, any object can be plugged into a framework system without generating framework runtime exceptions because the object will only function in the context defined by the type of interfaces it represents. A reliable protocol places the burden of execution in the hands of the implementation. That is, because the protocol is provided by contract, it is guaranteed to be called; subsequently, the execution code represented by that protocol (or message, or method) is governed strictly by the particular implementation currently used.

Figure 2.2 is a simple interface called Sorter that defines a single method, sort(). Implementors of Sorter can provide the necessary implementation of sort() in a variety of ways. It shows that, given an interface protocol, multiple variations of implementations may exist without disrupting users of that protocol.

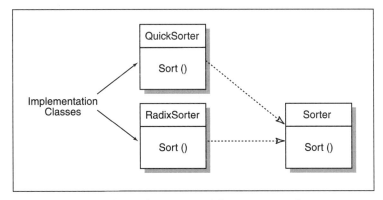

Figure 2.2 Multiple implementors of the Sorter interface.

Listing 2.3   Trackable interface definition.

```java
// Trackable.java

public interface Trackable {

    public String getKey();
    public String getItemType();
    public String getItemDescription();
    public boolean isThisYou(DomainModel model);
}
```

Recall the class DomainModel and the subclass Automobile, presented previously. Listing 2.3 introduces the Java representation for the interface Trackable, which provides unique, object-specific keys for use in a tracking system, along with some additional information specific to the object being tracked.

Trackable has four method declarations. To compile, any class implementing this interface will need to provide method blocks that implement each of these declared methods. A framework that uses Trackable objects can guarantee at runtime that any object it encounters of type Trackable will implement the declared methods and that no runtime exceptions of object type casting will occur. The results returned by each method are object-specific; that is, the implementor of Trackable decides what value is returned. Application-specific client objects will act as implementors, deciding how to respond to each type of message received. It is a reliable protocol because the message always goes through!

For all domain models in the mini framework example to be trackable, they could be required to implement the Trackable interface methods. Rather than putting the knowledge of the Trackable interface directly in the hands of subclasses, which would be more error-prone and an additional burden to the developer, it is simply placed in the abstracted parent class. Because all current subclasses automatically inherit the new requirements from the abstracted parent class, all current subclasses of DomainModel must adhere to the new interface definition. This prevents objects that do not conform to the protocol from slipping through the cracks. The Java compiler will catch culprits that do not provide the necessary method implementations. Listing 2.4 is the Domain-Model class abstraction with the addition of the Trackable interface.

In this listing, the method signatures of the Trackable interface in the abstract class are declared as abstract because the abstract class Domain-Model cannot provide the implementation for these subclass-specific methods. Because the methods have been declared abstract, the DomainModel class will compile properly as an implementor of Trackable; however, the executed implementation of these methods will occur in the subclass of DomainModel. It is the subclass that actually gets instantiated, because an abstract class cannot be instantiated.

Message delivery guaranteed!

The Automobile class in Listing 2.2 will no longer compile because it does not provide implementations for the abstract methods declared in Domain-Model. The altered code appears in Listing 2.5.

Notice that the alterations in Listing 2.5 now include implementations for the Trackable interface. Also notice that in the Automobile class, those implementations have been tailored to suit this particular class. Other subclasses of DomainModel (e.g., an Application object) would provide unique implementations to serve its type. By embedding interfaces in an abstract superclass and promoting implementation of those interfaces to descendants of that class, a template object is created, to which users of that template must adhere.

The internal framework processes in this example will interact with the new Automobile class as a DomainModel object and invoke the client code implementation of save() and those defined by the Trackable interface. In order for the new class to be a constituent of the framework, it must provide these implementations, otherwise it will not compile properly, and therefore will not be able to produce runtime violations within the framework during message delivery. A reliable protocol ensures that objects are properly typed and that the delivery of messages is guaranteed.

A good example of a framework that relies heavily on interface (protocol) and abstract representations is the JDK Collections Framework. A discussion of how this framework is constructed and various ways it can benefit your own framework and application development is up next.

Listing 2.4 DomainModel class implementing Trackable.

```java
// DomainModel.java

public abstract class DomainModel implements Trackable {

    // Member variable
    protected int objectId = 0;

    // Inherited method implementation
    public int getObjectId()
    {
        return objectId;
    }

    public void setObjectId(int id)
    {
        objectId = id;
    }

    // Abstract method that must be implemented in subclass
    public abstract boolean save();


    // Trackable interface methods. Subclasses are forced
    // to implement these.
    public abstract String getKey();
    public abstract String getItemType();
    public abstract String getItemDescription();
    public abstract boolean isThisYou(DomainModel model);

}
```

The JDK Collections Framework

A *collection* is a generic term used to describe an object that groups or collects other objects. Collections rely heavily on abstraction and client code implementation. This maximizes the utility of a collection and makes collections usable in a variety of situations. A *collections framework* provides interfaces and abstract classes as well as default implementations of common collection data structures for use in applications. There are three advantages to using a collections framework:

Listing 2.5 Revised Automobile class.

```java
// Automobile.java
import java.io.*;
import java.awt.*;

public class Automobile extends DomainModel implements Serializable {

    // The color of this automobile.
    protected Color color = null;

    // The mileage
    protected int mileage = 0;

    public Automobile(int id)
    {
        setObjectId(id);
    }

    public int getMileage()
    {
        return mileage;
    }

    public void setMileage(int mileage)
    {
        this.mileage = mileage;
    }

    public Color getColor()
    {
        return color;
    }

    public void setColor(Color color)
    {
        this.color = color;
    }

    public boolean save()
    {
        try {
          FileOutputStream file = new
              FileOutputStream("Automobile"+objectId);
          ObjectOutputStream out = new ObjectOutputStream(file);
          out.writeObject(this);
          return true;
        } catch (Exception e) {
          return false;
        }
```

continues

Listing 2.5 Revised Automobile class. *(Continued)*

```
    }

    // Implementations of Trackable interface. These methods are
    // required because they have been declared abstract in the parent
    // class even though they originate in the Trackable interface.
    public String getKey()
    {
        return mileage+""+color+""+getObjectId();
    }

    public String getItemType()
    {
        return "Automobile";
    }

    public String getItemDescription()
    {
        return "This is a "+color+" automobile with "+mileage+" miles.";
    }

    public boolean isThisYou(DomainModel model)
    {
        return this.equals(model);
    }

}
```

1. *Institutes standard data exchange structures.* Applications coded around a standard collections framework can share data structures. This is demonstrated with the InfoBus API.

2. *Provides commonly used structures and algorithms.* Common data structures like trees, stacks, and queues are standard collections elements. Algorithms such as binary searches or quicksorts are also typical in collection frameworks. Common structures and algorithms save the developer time by eliminating the need to reinvent these well-known capabilities.

3. *Facilitates reuse.* Coding applications or frameworks with collections increases the potential of future interoperability and longevity and promotes reusability.

The Collections Framework bundled with Java 2 is an excellent example of how collections foster good framework design. The JDK Collections Frame-

Various real-world containers.

work specifically handles generic object organizations, iterators, and algorithms such as searching and sorting. The JDK collection classes are broken down into six categories:

1. *Collection Hierarchy.* This facet represents the core collection interfaces such as sets, lists, and maps.

2. *Concrete Implementations.* Default implementations of the core collection interfaces.

3. *Anonymous Implementations.* Static factory methods that return Collection objects.

4. *Abstract Implementations.* Partial implementations of the core collection interfaces to facilitate custom implementations.

5. *Infrastructure.* Interfaces, such as iterators, that define the Collection Hierarchy.

6. *Algorithms.* Static methods, such as sorting, that perform polymorphic functions on objects.

The following sections explore the classes that make up the Java Collections Framework and how the framework is useful within other frameworks; they are not intended to be a primer for collections, but to serve as an instructional example of good framework design and useful framework building blocks.

Collection Hierarchy

The Collection Hierarchy provides the basic building blocks for a variety of unique Collection objects through simple interface definitions. The four basic collection interfaces are: Collection, Set, List, and Map.

Collection

The Collection interface is a root interface in the Collections Framework upon which other collection-type objects (such as Hashtables, Sets and Lists) are built. New and unique types of collections that are reusable in a variety of contexts and applications can be created by providing an implementation to the Collection interface. Depending on the implementation of the Collection interface, the objects contained in the collection can have characteristics at the group level, such as specific ordering, or rules governing uniqueness.

The interfaces that represent the various collection types are designed to allow the collections to be used and manipulated in an implementation-independent manner. Regardless of exactly how a particular collection implements its internal storage mechanisms or logic operations, the protocol is constant and the behavior semantics are presumed to follow the definition of the collection. These semantics may or may not be explicit in the interface definition itself. In some cases, the interface is identical to the Collection interface, but because the interface imposes further stipulations on the behavior of certain operations, it is suitable as a subinterface in the semantic sense. In other words, the reliable protocol or operations accepted would be identical to Collection, but the nature of the implementation will vary. The Set interface is an example of this; it stipulates that only one occurrence of the same object may exist within the collection.

Because the Collection interfaces have been designed in this way (specifically, common base interfaces), it is possible to easily insert and adopt new collections within a working framework or application. This is possible because the interface protocol is reliable and can be seen as a Collection object, regardless of the specific nature of the underlying implementation. Again, this notion is heavily dependent on the abstraction made possible through interfaces.

The Collection interface represents a very basic and fundamental definition of the functions of a collection. It is designed to be very generic, and maintains a strong link to the abstract concept of a container. Most of the methods defined in the Collection interface are natural behaviors common to real-life containers. Because a collection acts as a container for objects, it is possible to add and remove individual and groups of objects from the collection. In addition, it is possible to test for inclusiveness and to obtain simple metadata about the collection itself. For example, the method size() returns the size of the collection. The method isEmpty() returns the elements in the collection, if any exist. Table 2.1 lists the interface methods that define a generic collection.

Table 2.1 Collection Interface Methods

RETURN TYPE	METHOD SIGNATURE	DESCRIPTION
boolean	add(Object o)	Ensures that the collection will contain Object o.
boolean	addAll(Collection c)	Ensures that the collection will contain all of the elements in Collection c.
void	clear()	Removes all elements from this collection.
boolean	contains(Object o)	If the Object o is in this collection, return true.
boolean	containsAll(Collection c)	If all elements in Collection c are in this collection, return true.
boolean	equals(Object o)	Tests if Object o is this Collection object
Int	hashCode()	Returns the hashCode identified with this object.
boolean	isEmpty()	Returns true if this collection is empty.
Iterator	iterator()	Returns an iterator over the objects in this collection.
boolean	remove(Object o)	Removes object o from this collection, if it is present.
boolean	removeAll(Collection c)	Removes all elements in Collection c that coincide with elements in this collection.
boolean	retainAll(Collection c)	Removes all elements from this collection that are not in Collection c.
int	size()	Returns the number of elements in this collection.
Object[]	toArray()	Returns an array containing all the elements in this collection.
Object[]	toArray(Object[] a)	Returns an array containing all of the elements in this collection whose runtime type is that of the specified array.

Collections make it easy to store and retrieve objects.

Collecting objects so they can be grouped, ordered, and searched provides an organization that can be tailored per application. Organization using collections is useful and can be applied almost ubiquitously across applications. Consider an inventory control program that needs to provide multiple groupings of objects based on a variety of conditions. The items in the inventory can be

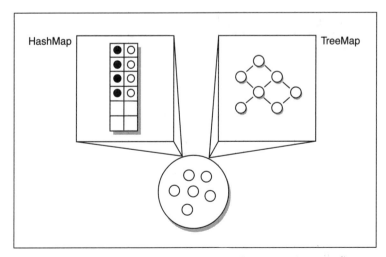

Figure 2.3. Multiple differing collections of the same object pool.

grouped by the type or subtype of item. In addition, they can be cross-grouped by tracking number or price. These different organizations can coexist within an application, offering easy immediate access to object organizations that can proliferate over time. The items themselves are not actually replicated across these collections. Different views into the domain can be achieved by using different types of collections. Collection organizations provide a convenient and dynamic way to group object associations that are cumbersome or difficult to capture within the object model. Figure 2.3 shows how two different collections of the same objects can be organized internally and independently of the object pool itself.

Set

The Set interface represents an unordered collection and is a subinterface of Collection. It has additional methods that separate the notion of a Set from a generic collection. A Set is a mathematical model that does not contain duplicate numbers or elements.

> **NOTE** In Java, the term Set means that no two elements, such as element1 and element2, will cause either element1.equals(element2) or element2.equals(element1) to return true. This comparison relies on the natural equality of the objects. In some cases, a special Comparator object can be used to provide the logical analysis of two objects to determine their equality.

Because of the rules that govern sets, implementors of Set must ensure that no duplicate items exist at any time in the Set collection. Add operations on Set objects must determine if a given object already exists in the collection, and, if so, disallow the addition of that object.

The interface for Set is nearly identical in protocol to Collection. The definitions of operations are similar in concept for both generic Collection objects and Sets. The primary difference is in the semantic implementation. As mentioned, Sets do not allow multiple occurrences of the same object. The definition given by both the Set and Collection interface is simplified and generic enough so that it too can be reused across semantically different entities. This is a rather interesting concept to consider. Objects that implement Set are easily distinguished by type from simple objects that implement Collection, but because Set forces additional stipulations on the implementation, Set resides as a descendant of the Collection interface. In other words, it is everything a Collection is, with some additional meaning.

The result is the ability to add semantically different objects that can respond to the same core set of messages. The benefit is that these new, semantically different, Collection objects can plug into existing frameworks and receive messages in the same fashion as their ancestors; in this case, the root

Table 2.2 Set Interface

RETURN TYPE	METHOD SIGNATURE	DESCRIPTION
boolean	add(Object o)	Adds Object o to this set providing it does not already exist.
boolean	addAll(Collection c)	See Collection.
void	clear()	See Collection.
boolean	contains(Object o)	See Collection.
boolean	containsAll(Collection c)	See Collection.
boolean	equals(Object o)	See Collection.
int	hashCode()	See Collection.
boolean	isEmpty()	See Collection.
Iterator	iterator()	See Collection.
boolean	remove(Object o)	See Collection.
boolean	removeAll(Collection c)	See Collection.
boolean	retainAll(Collection c)	See Collection.
int	size()	See Collection.
Object[]	toArray()	See Collection.
Object[]	toArray(Object[] a)	See Collection.

ancestor is simply the Collection interface. Table 2.2 summarizes the Set interface methods.

THOUGHTS It's interesting to consider that, in addition to implementation details, object behavior semantics can be encapsulated and abstracted using interfaces and abstract classes. The Collection interface represents a semantic definition of an object container. The difference between a simple container and a container of type Set is subtle and not evident in the definition itself. The implementation must provide the object behavior semantics. Also, because of the morphology of the Set interface (it descends from Collection), Set can also be seen as simply a Collection object. This facilitates the plugability and reusability of objects of these types within a variety of application contexts. This is also a good example of abstraction.

List

The List collection is referred to as an *ordered collection*. Simply, an ordered collection maintains the order or sequence of the object members. For this reason, ordered collections are sometimes referred to as *sequences*.

The List collection object is not much different from everyday lists, such as your to-do list. In either case, each contains a linear sequence of items that may be prioritized or rearranged at different times. The List collection object performs these familiar duties.

The List interface is an extension of Collection. In addition to providing additional semantics on interface methods inherited from Collection, the List interface adds method definitions suitable to the behavior of lists. Table 2.3 shows all of the interface methods defined by List. The first half of the table replicates the methods defined in Collection and indicates the methods that differ semantically from Collection. The bottom half of the table shows the methods added by the List interface.

Map

A Map, shown in Figure 2.4, is a type of collection abstraction that maps keys to values. A Hashtable is an example of a Collection object that performs the function of a map. Hashtables use a simple key-hashing algorithm to store values in buckets with the Hashtable. Typically, one key maps to one value. The CAT (Customer-Account-Transaction) framework classes introduced in Chapter 1, "Framework Concepts," used Hashtables in their *organizational model* to associate account numbers with the Account objects they represented and Customer objects with their CustomerAccounts. In that example, the account number was the key and the Account was the value. Likewise, the Customer object represented a key and the CustomerAccounts object was the associated value. Knowing a particular key allows the associated value to be retrieved in a single call. Keys cannot be duplicated.

The Map interface offers multiple Collection views that allow the contents of a Map to be retrieved in different ways. A Map can return the following views:

- *A Set object containing the keys of the Map.* Because keys must be unique, the Set collection ensures one key, one value.

- *A Collection object containing the values of the Map.* Numerous different keys may contain the same object; therefore, the values of the Map do not need to be maintained as a Set.

- *A Set object containing key-value mappings.* As stated, there cannot be two identical key-value pairs; therefore, a Set is the only collection to contain these pairings.

Table 2.4 summarizes the Map interface methods.

Table 2.3 List Interface

RETURN TYPE	METHOD SIGNATURE	DESCRIPTION
boolean	add(Object o)	Adds Object o to the end of this list.
boolean	addAll(Collection c)	Appends the objects contained in Collection c to the end of this list in the same order as provided by the iterator of c.
void	clear()	See Collection.
boolean	contains(Object o)	See Collection.
boolean	containsAll(Collection c)	See Collection.
boolean	equals(Object o)	See Collection.
int	hashCode()	See Collection.
boolean	isEmpty()	See Collection.
Iterator	iterator()	See Collection.
boolean	remove(Object o)	See Collection.
boolean	removeAll(Collection c)	See Collection.
boolean	retainAll(Collection c)	See Collection.
int	size()	See Collection.
Object []	toArray()	See Collection.
Object []	toArray(Object[] a)	See Collection.
void	add(int index, Object o)	Inserts the specified Object o into the list at position index.
boolean	addAll(int index, Collection c)	Appends all the elements contained in Collection c to the end of this list in the order provided by the iterator returned from c.
int	indexOf(Object o)	Returns the index of the first occurrence of Object o in this list, or −1 if the object does not exist.
int	indexOf (Object o, int index)	Returns the index of the first occurrence of Object o after the specified index, or −1 if it does not exist.
int	lastIndexOf(Object o)	Returns the index of the last occurrence of Object o in this list, or −1 if no such object exists.

Table 2.3 *(Continued)*

RETURN TYPE	METHOD SIGNATURE	DESCRIPTION
int	lastIndexOf (Object o,int index)	Returns the index of the last occurrence of Object o in this list at or before the specified index, or −1 if no such object exists.
ListIterator	listIterator()	Returns a ListIterator of the elements in this list in sequence.
ListIterator	listIterator(int index)	Returns a ListIterator for this list, starting with the elements after the specified index.
Object	remove(int index)	Removes the element at the specified position.
void	removeRange (int *from*, int *to*)	Removes the range of elements starting at *from* up to, but not including the element at position *to*.
Object	set(int index,Object o)	Replaces the element at the specified position with Object o.

SortedSet

A SortedSet is an extension of the Set collection; it guarantees that its elements will be in a determined ascending order as defined by the iterator returned by this type of object. In addition, a special type of object called a Comparator can be supplied to provide the logic used to determine the *natural ordering* of the objects in the Set. All objects inserted into a SortedSet must implement the Comparable interface or be recognized by the Comparator supplied in the SortedSet constructor. Four defined constructor types are recommended for

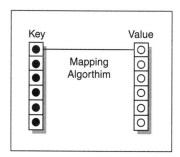

Figure 2.4 Map object.

Table 2.4   Map Interface

RETURN TYPE	METHOD SIGNATURE	DESCRIPTION
void	clear()	Removes all mappings from this Map.
boolean	containsKey(Object key)	Returns true if this Map contains a mapping for the key.
boolean	containsValue (Object value)	Returns true if this Map contains one or more keys to the specified value.
Set	entries()	Returns a Set view of the mappings represented in this Map.
boolean	equals(Object o)	Compares Object o with this Map and returns true if they are the same.
Object	get(Object key)	Returns the value mapped to the supplied key.
int	hashCode()	Returns the hash code value for this Map object.
boolean	isEmpty()	Returns true if this Map object contains no mappings, false otherwise.
Set	keySet()	Returns the keys contained in this Map object as a Set collection.
Object	put(Object key, Object value)	Creates a new mapping between the specified key and value and places it in this Map.
void	putAll(Map map)	Copies all the key-value mappings from map to this Map.
Object	remove(Object key)	Removes the mapping represented by key (if it exists).
int	size()	Returns the number of key-value mappings in this Map.
Collection	values()	Returns a Collection view of the values contained in this Map.

objects implementing this interface (note, however, that because interfaces cannot define constructors, these recommendations are left to the discretion of the developer):

- An empty constructor, which provides a default natural ordering algorithm to its elements.

- A single argument constructor, which accepts a Comparator that will determine the ordering of the elements.

- A single argument constructor of type Collection. The contents of the Collection become the contents of the new SortedSet and the ordering defaults to the elements natural ordering.

- A single argument constructor that accepts a SortedSet collection where a new SortedSet is created based on the elements and ordering of the supplied SortedSet.

Table 2.5 summarizes the SortedSet interface methods.

NOTE Iterators provide a mechanism for cycling through the elements in a collection. Because not all collections are sequences, iterators are a necessary mechanism to explore and examine the objects in a collection in a linear or systematic fashion.

Table 2.5 SortedSet Interface

RETURN TYPE	METHOD SIGNATURE	DESCRIPTION
Comparator	comparator()	Returns the Comparator used by this SortedSet, or null if none exists, in which case the elements' natural ordering is used.
Object	first()	Returns the first element in the SortedSet.
SortedSet	headSet(Object toElement)	Returns a view into this SortedSet containing only the elements that are strictly less than toElement.
Object	last()	Returns the last element in this SortedSet.
SortedSet	subSet (Object fromElement, Object toElement)	Returns a ranged view of this SortedSet, which contains all elements between fromElement and toElement, including fromElement but excluding toElement.
SortedSet	tailSet(Object fromElement)	Returns a view into this SortedSet containing only the elements that are strictly greater than fromElement.

SortedMap

A SortedMap is the Map analogue of the SortedSet. It guarantees that its keys will be in ascending order, depending on the optionally provided Comparator object. In the event a Comparator is not used, the natural ordering of the elements take effect. Like elements of a SortedSet, restrictions exist for elements of SortedMaps; specifically, objects entering into a SortedMap must also implement the Comparable interface or be well known to the supplied Comparator object.

Objects in either SortedMaps or SortedSets must be mutually comparable. That is, when these collections determine the placement of objects, they use the following conditional tests:

```
element1.compareTo(element2);
```

or, if a Comparator is being used:

```
comparator.compare(element1,element2);
```

Regardless of the objects tested, a return value of true from either method call will deem both objects equal from the collection's perspective.

Similar to SortedSets, general-purpose implementations of SortedMaps will also provide four basic constructor types:

- An empty constructor, which provides a default natural ordering algorithm to its elements.

- A single argument constructor, which accepts a Comparator that will determine the ordering of the elements.

- A single argument constructor of type Collection. The contents of the Collection become the contents of the new SortedMap and the ordering defaults to the elements natural ordering.

- A single argument constructor that accepts a SortedMap collection where a new SortedMap is created based on the key-value mappings of the supplied SortedMap.

Table 2.6 summarizes the SortedMap interface methods.

Figure 2.5 shows the interface hierarchy for the Java Collections Framework.

As you can see from the interfaces presented thus far, the Collections Framework provides a set of abstractions that define what a collection object should do. Various implementations of the behavior semantics of these interfaces produce a variety of useful and specialized collections. This is an important concept with dual implications to the framework designer. On the one hand, the collections themselves prove a useful tool for implementing solid, reusable, and extensible organizational models within frameworks. In addition, it clev-

Table 2.6 SortedMap Interface

RETURN TYPE	METHOD SIGNATURE	DESCRIPTION
Comparator	comparator()	Returns the Comparator used by this SortedMap, or null if it uses its keys' natural ordering.
Object	firstKey()	Returns the first key in the SortedMap.
SortedSet	headMap(Object toKey)	Returns a view into this SortedMap containing only the keys that are strictly less than toKey.
Object	lastKey()	Returns the last key in this SortedMap.
SortedSet	subMap(Object fromKey, Object toKey)	Returns a ranged view of this SortedMap, which contains all keys between fromKey and toKey, including fromKey but excluding toKey.
SortedSet	tailMap(Object fromKey)	Returns a view into this SortedMap containing only the keys that are strictly greater than fromKey.

erly demonstrates how a well-defined abstraction can facilitate multiple, possibly semantically differing implementations. The goal of any framework design effort is to use well-defined abstractions, as the Collections Framework demonstrates. Well-defined abstractions allow the user of a framework to tailor those definitions by adding application-specific logic and behavior without violating the protocol of the framework proper.

NOTE Remember from Chapter 1, "Framework Concepts," that frameworks do not just provide abstract classes and interfaces, but also general-purpose default implementations that make them usable "out of the box." This is important because developers can begin using the framework quickly. In addition, a framework should be extensible so that more specific implementations can be created and used seamlessly within the framework.

Collection Implementations

As part of the utility of a good framework, it must not only be reusable in variety of ways, but it must be readily *usable*. I emphasize the word usable because a framework should provide application-ready objects or implementations that are sufficient for general-purpose use. Default implementations exist for

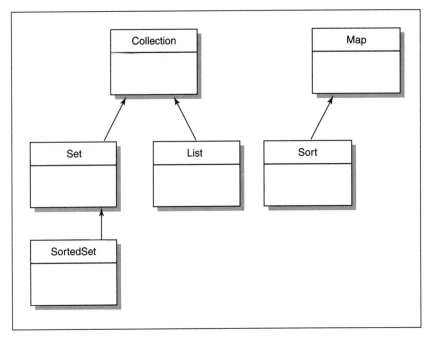

Figure 2.5 Interface hierarchy.

the major collection interfaces of the Collections Framework. This gives the developer the flexibility to implement his or her own specialized collection classes or to use the default implementations to begin to use the framework quickly.

The concrete implementations included in the Java Collections Framework include the following class types:

HashSet

TreeSet

ArrayList

LinkedList

Vector

HashMap

TreeMap

Hashtable

Most Java developers are familiar with the Vector and Hashtable collection objects, which were part of the early core JDK. Vectors and Hashtables are collections widely used for organizing sequences and key-value pairs, respectively. The other implementations address the primary collection bodies represented in the Collections Framework, namely, Lists, Maps, and Sets.

HashSet. The HashSet collection implements the Set interface and backs it with a HashMap (or Hashtable). It does not make any guarantees as to the iteration ordering of its elements, which may change internally over time. One of the important considerations for this containment object is that it offers constant time performance. This means that for the fundamental operations such as add, remove, contains, and size, the time to process the invocation will be constant between them due to the Hashing algorithm provided by the HashMap. Iterating over this structure will be proportional to the size of the HashMap.

TreeSet. Similar to the HashSet, this class implements the Set interface and backs it with a tree structure. It guarantees an ascending order to the keys contained within the Map. This sequence is based on the natural ordering of the key Class or the ordering supplied by a Comparator. This implementation provides a time cost of log(n) on the fundamental operations add, remove, and contains.

ArrayList. The ArrayList collection object provides a resizable array implementation of the List interface. Each ArrayList object has two attributes for managing its size and resize policies. The *capacity* parameter provides the basis for the initial size of the list, while the *capacityIncrement* tells the ArrayList how much to grow when capacity has been reached.

LinkedList. A LinkedList is a special kind of List object that allows for the creation and use of specialized list-type data structures. The current common data structures that can readily be created with a LinkedList are Stacks, Queues, and Dequeues (Double-Ended Queues).

The LinkedList provides a uniform definition of the operations of linked lists, namely get, remove, and insert, at either the beginning or end of the list. LinkedList objects appear and behave as would any double-linked list.

For simple structures like a stack, which is FILO (first in last out), the order of operations on a LinkedList collection would resemble the following code snippet:

```
LinkedList list = new LinkedList(10,5);

list.addFirst(objectA);    // Push objectA onto top of stack
list.addFirst(objectB);    // Push objectB onto top of stack

Object obj = list.removeFirst();    // Pop top most object
                                    // from stack = objectB
```

Queues operate on a FIFO (first in first out) basis. Therefore, a map of this sort of behavior using a LinkedList would look something like this:

```
LinkedList list = new LinkedList(10,5);

list.addFirst(objectA);    // Push objectA into Queue
list.addFirst(objectB);    // Push objectB into Queue behind objectA
```

```
Object obj = list.removeLast();    // Remove last object from queue

// obj is now equal to objectA
```

It doesn't matter to which end objects are added or removed; as long as they're opposite one another, the queue will behave like a queue. A double-ended queue simply supports the adding and removing of objects from both ends. The implementation would be similar to the previous code snippet, reversed depending on which side you chose to manipulate.

Simply stated, there are two basic rules to remember when dealing with LinkedList structures :

1. Stacks add and remove from the same end.
2. Queues add on one end and remove from the other.

Vector. Vector behaves much like ArrayList. It stems from earlier versions of Java, and with Java 2, has been properly retrofitted to implement List as well as the previously maintained methods from the original Vector class. In earlier versions of Vector, methods for adding and removing elements appeared as addElement() and removeElement(). These have been maintained for convenience and backward compatibility.

HashMap. HashMap is an implementation of a Hashtable based on the Map interface. It is nearly identical to the Hashtable structure except that it is unsynchronized (i.e., not thread-safe) and allows null objects to exist within it.

TreeMap. A TreeMap is an implementation of the SortedMap interface and imposes a balanced binary tree structure to its elements. The elements are placed in their default natural ordering or ordered based on a Comparator object provided at the TreeMap creation time. TreeMap is, by default, not synchronized. A synchronized version can be obtained by making the associated static call in the Collections class like this.

```
Map m = Collections.synchronizedMap(new TreeMap(...));
```

Hashtable. Hashtable is similar to Vector in that it predates the collections provided by Java 2. It remains backward compatible by implementing all previous methods in addition to those defined by the Map interface.

Iterators returned by the collection implementations described as follows are *fail-fast*. If the collection is modified at any time after the iterator is created in a manner other than through the iterator itself, the iterator will throw a ConcurrentModificationException. This allows an iterator to fall out of its processing due to a corruption of the enumeration it is operating on. This dilemma occurs partly because these implementations are not thread-safe (meaning not synchronized).

NOTE The Java Collections Framework also provides factories for creating thread-safe versions of the core interfaces. Refer to the Java 2 documentation for more on how to acquire synchronized versions of collection objects.

Anonymous Implementations

The Java Collections Framework has a facility for providing anonymous implementations of interfaces through public static methods of the Collections class. This facility is rather interesting, not only from a framework user perspective, but from a framework developer perspective as well. The basic idea behind an anonymous implementation is that the class-specific details are kept hidden and only the interfaces are exported. In this sense, it can offer the developer a solid, reliable mechanism for accessing or requesting certain object instances where the implementing classes may change or evolve over time. In this sense, it acts much like a factory that obscures implementation details and simply provides the interface object as requested.

For example, to request a synchronized version of a List object, you would not want to hard-code a class name such as synchronizedList into the application. This might violate some of the abstraction guidelines and bind some of the application code to this particular class definition. Instead, you would request a class that implements List. Consider the following line of code:

```
List list = Collections.synchronizedList(new LinkedList());
```

The List object is of type List, but it is thread-safe. The same algorithms and operations can be performed on this List object without declaring it as anything other than a List. Since List is an interface, there is no need to be concerned about implementing class details. The call to Collections.synchronizedList() initializes and returns a synchronized version of the provided object instance type. The exact class name representing the synchronized class is encapsulated and can change independent of a request.

This technique can be used for other purposes. For example, if you have an object interface (DataRepository) that defines methods for talking to and from a data repository, you could have a public static method that provides implementations that deal with relational or object databases, depending on the request or some other logical constraint:

```
DataRepository repository =
  DataRepository.newRelationalRepository("rdbms://host");
```

or

```
DataRepository repository =
  DataRepository.newObjectRepository("odbms://host");
```

The actual class implementations of the interface DataRepository might be called RelationalDataRepository or ObjectDataRepository, but the application may not have specific knowledge about these classes, or this information may be have been provided at a later time and now need to be integrated with the finished product. The point to remember is that the access point to these particular classes does not need to change to accommodate new class definitions that adhere to a given interface. Depending on the request mechanism, various classes can be loaded on demand to serve a particular request, possibly through a generic method such as:

```
DataRepository repository =
  DataRepository.newObjectRepository("rdbms://host");
```

The method newObjectRepository() can perform a check on the supplied database host and determine whether the appropriate DataRepository class definition is available (e.g., RelationalRepository, ObjectRepository) and return it once it has been loaded.

Figure 2.6 shows how a factory method can supply different object instantiations possibly loaded dynamically.

Table 2.7 shows the Collections class, which contains a number of useful static methods for performing generic algorithms, operations, and factory operations.

Abstract Implementations

Sometimes, raw interfaces require significant effort and overhead to implement common objects, like collections. This is due, in part, to the complexity of collections in general. Also, a complex interface can define a multitude of behaviors (through method signatures), which the developer is then responsible for implementing. However, most of the interface methods are well-enough defined so that default implementations can be provided in a skeletal fashion by using an abstract base class. The developer can then focus on the

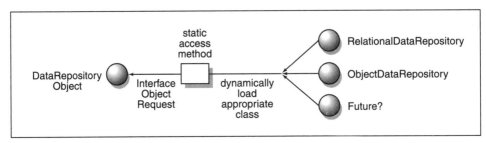

Figure 2.6 Dynamic class provision factory method.

Table 2.7 Collections Class Static Methods

RETURN TYPE	METHOD SIGNATURE	DESCRIPTION
static int	binarySearch(List list, Object key, Comparator c)	Searches the list for object key, using Comparator c and a binary search algorithm.
static int	binarySearch(List list, Object key)	Searches the list for object key, using a binary search algorithm.
static void	copy(List dest, List src)	Copies elements from one list to another.
static Enumeration	enumeration(Collection c)	Returns an enumeration over the specifed collection c.
static void	fill(List list, Object o)	Replaces all the elements of the specified list with object o.
static Object	max(Collection coll, Comparator comp)	Returns the maximum element in the collection based on the ordering provided by the specified Comparator.
static Object	max(Collection coll)	Returns the maximum element in the collection based on the natural ordering of the elements.
static Object	min(Collection coll, Comparator comp)	Returns the minimum element in the collection based on the ordering provided by the specified Comparator.
static Object	min(Collection coll)	Returns the minimum element in the collection based on the natural ordering of the elements.
static List	nCopies(int n, Object o)	Returns an immutable List containing n copies of the specified object o.
static void	reverse(List l)	Reverses the order of the elements in the specified list.
static Comparator	reverseOrder()	Returns a Comparator that imposes the reverse of the natural order of the collection of Comparable objects.
static void	shuffle(List list, Random rnd)	Shuffles the order of the given list based on the supplied random seed.
static void	shuffle(List list)	Shuffles the order of the given list using the default random seeding.
static Set	singleton(Object o)	Returns an immutable Set containing only the specified object.

continues

Table 2.7   Collections Class Static Methods *(Continued)*

RETURN TYPE	METHOD SIGNATURE	DESCRIPTION
static void	sort(List list, Comparator c)	Sorts the specified list based on the order induced by using the specified comparator.
static void	sort(List list)	Sorts the list based on the elements natural ordering.
static Collection	synchronizedCollection (Collection c)	Returns a thread-safe Collection backed by the specified collection c.
static List	synchronizedList(List list)	Returns a thread-safe List backed by the specified list.
static Map	synchronizedMap(Map m)	Returns a thread-safe Map backed by the specified map.
static Set	synchronizedSet(Set s)	Returns a thread-safe Set backed by the specified set.
static SortedMap	synchronizedSortedMap (SortedMap m)	Returns a thread-safe SortedMap backed by the specified sorted map.
static SortedSet	synchronizedSortedSet (SortedSet s)	Returns a thread-safe SortedSet backed by the specified sorted set.
static Collection	unmodifiableCollection (Collection c)	Returns an unmodifiable view of the specified collection.
static List	unmodifiableList(List list)	Returns an unmodifiable view of the specified list.
static Map	unmodifiableMap(Map m)	Returns an unmodifiable view of the specified map.
static Set	unmodifiableSet(Set s)	Returns an unmodifiable view of the specified set.
static SortedMap	unmodifiableSortedMap (SortedMap m)	Returns an unmodifiable view of the specified sorted map.
static SortedSet	unmodifiableSortedSet (SortedSet s)	Returns an unmodifiable view of the specified sorted set.

subclass-specific behavior he or she wants to change for the implementation. For this reason, the Collections Framework supplies a set of usable abstract classes that take care of much of the tedious implementation for the various collections. Of course, these classes cannot be instantiated directly. They are designed for developers to extend and plug in method implementations, which are likely to vary [D'Souza et al., 1998]. D'Souza refers to locations within the abstracted class where implementation is deferred as *plug points.* The following list identifies the abstract implementations provided by the Collections Framework.

AbstractCollection

AbstractSet

AbstractList

AbstractSequentialList

AbstractMap

Maximizing the utility of a framework for use by potential developers is an important goal, but one that is not always achievable. Depending on your specific situation, it may not be practical to address usability to this extreme. Most developers face strict schedules and cannot afford the luxury of providing ample abstractions for all situations. Luckily, the designers at JavaSoft realize how important these decisions are to the Java developers who use and depend on these frameworks.

Iterators

Iterators are objects that allow client objects to iterate over or review the elements of a particular collection. As mentioned, not all collections are sequences, or ordered, collections. Some, such as Bags, are unordered and require a reliable protocol or interface for iterating over the elements in either a particular or arbitrary order. This stable mechanism is provided by iterator objects.

The are two key reasons why iterators are useful as separate objects:

1. The same iterator can operate on multiple collections, providing the specific ordering as dictated by the iterator's conditionals.

2. Likewise, multiple iterators can act upon the same collection, thereby providing different ordered views on the same set of elements.

This type of separation seems quite natural, because objects themselves are not aware of their placement within a grouping; placement is *imposed* on the object collection by some external process. The result is that these external processes can be tailored to specific tasks independent of the collection body it acts upon. Listing 2.6 shows a simple example involving a HashSet:

This listing creates two Automobile objects and adds them to the HashSet called carlot. If you wanted to find the black Automobile from the carlot, you would have to iterate through each Automobile and locate the correct one. More complex collections will provide custom iterators that present the objects contained within the collection in a particular order useful to users of the col-

Listing 2.6 HashSet example.

```
HashSet carlot = new HashSet(10,5);

Automobile car1 = new Automobile();
car.setObjectId(1);
car.setMileage(46000);
car.setColor(Color.blue);
carlot.put(car1);

Automobile car2 = new Automobile();
car2.setObjectId(2);
car2.setMileage(20000);
car2.setColor(Color.black);
carlot.put(car2);

// Get an iterator object from our HashSet collection.
Iterator iterator = carlot.iterator();

// Cycle the iterator, retrieving each Automobile object
// until the iterator has finished.
while(iterator.hasNext()) {
    Automobile auto = (Automobile)iterator.next();
    if(auto.getColor()==Color.black) {
      System.out.println("I found the black car! It has
        "+auto.getMileage()+" miles on it.");
    }
}
```

lection. For example, any ordered list, such as LinkedList, will return an iterator that exposes the collections objects in the order in which they are currently placed. For collections like the HashSet, there is no specified order and no guarantee the order will remain the same. It is simply undefined in this case. The point is that different iterators can operate on the same collection, irrespective of the manner in which the collection organizes the objects internally. This is useful for frameworks that utilize collections, because application developers can use those collection entities in different forms and capacities (which are likely application-specific).

Enumerators

Enumerators are simplified iterators that were part of Java prior to the advent of the Collections Framework. In the past, it was useful in some cases to acquire an enumeration of an arbitrary collection of objects. For example, consider a Hashtable where object values are associated with keys. The only access mechanism for retrieving values is through keys. It is conceivable that

Listing 2.7 Enumeration example.

```
Hashtable hashtable = new Hashtable();

hashtable.put(new Integer(1),new String("One"));
hashtable.put(new Integer(2),new String("Two"));
hashtable.put(new Integer(3),new String("Three"));
hashtable.put(new Integer(4),new String("Four"));

Enumeration tableEnum = hashtable.keys();

while(tableEnum.hasMoreElements()) {
    System.out.println(hashtable.get(tableEnum.nextElement()));
}
```

you would want to cycle through all the keys in a given Hashtable similar to the previous example.

In Listing 2.7, a Hashtable is populated with the English equivalent value of the first four counting numbers, with the Integer objects as keys.

Given a particular Integer value, the language equivalent can easily be found. However, cycling through all the keys in the Hashtable requires an Enumeration object, which is likely to return a sequence identical to the order in which the key-value pairs were added to the Hashtable. As you can see in the listing, you can then loop through the enumeration and acquire each value of the Hashtable without knowing the individual keys. Typically, an enumeration provides the natural ordering of a given collection of objects, whereas iterators can provide different orderings of the same generic collection (i.e., iterators can contain logic about how to present the order).

Algorithms

The Java Collections Framework provides some basic generic algorithms that are easy and practical to use. Most developers are familiar with the variety of algorithms available for searching and sorting. Because these algorithms are generic in nature, they are presented as static invocations on the Collections class. The Collections Framework provides a simple and reusable application-neutral method for searching, sorting, and reorganizing. This frees the developer from repeatedly implementing these algorithms. Table 2.8 outlines the algorithm-based static methods of the Collections class.

Generic Programming

The concept of generic programming refers to designing and implementing structures and algorithms that behave consistently and apply to certain very

Table 2.8   Collections Class/Algorithm Methods

RETURN TYPE	METHOD SIGNATURE	DESCRIPTION
static int	binarySearch(List list, Object key, Comparator c)	Searches the list for object key, using Comparator c and a binary search algorithm.
static int	binarySearch(List list, Object key)	Searches the list for object key, using a binary search algorithm.
static void	reverse(List l)	Reverses the order of the elements in the specified list.
static Comparator	reverseOrder()	Returns a Comparator that imposes the reverse of the natural order of the collection of Comparable objects.
static void	shuffle(List list, Random rnd)	Shuffles the order of the given list based on the supplied random seed.
static void	shuffle(List list)	Shuffles the order of the given list using the default random seeding.
static void	sort(List list, Comparator c)	Sorts the specified list based on the order induced by using the specified Comparator.
static void	sort(List list)	Sorts the list based on the elements natural ordering.
static void	fill(List list, Object o)	Replaces all the elements of the specified list with object o.

generic types of problem areas. Abstracting concepts like object collections or algorithms enables developers to create logical operations within frameworks and applications that can behave on different object classes in a consistent (or generic) way. You can specify an organizational structure and define, in abstract terms, operations permitted by that structure. The constituents of those structures can be typed and determined at runtime and do not directly influence how the generic pattern or algorithm operates.

Framework Development

The techniques and considerations important during framework development can be categorized into three basic categories:

1. Defining the framework.

2. Analyzing and designing the framework.

3. Documenting the framework.

Let's take a look at each of these categories in more detail.

Defining the Framework

Framework construction begins with defining the framework. The framework must address a particular problem set and encapsulate specific knowledge of the problem. A framework can address a wide range of problem sets, problems that are ubiquitous and uniform across applications, such as those addressed by utility frameworks, or more refined problem domains, such as those specific to financial applications.

It is crucial to define the domain and scope of problem set you intend to address before you begin constructing your framework. This context and definition establishes a guide for you to follow during development. As mentioned in Chapter 1, you want to avoid creating a "kitchen-sink" framework—one that includes everything except the kitchen sink. Proper definitions early in development will help keep the scope from expanding.

If you discover after building a large complex application that certain implemented traits of the application can best be defined as a framework, you can reverse-engineer the framework definition from an existing application for future reuse by a new application [da Fontoura et al.]. Determining the cost effects of either approach is not well defined, and needless to say the benefits of framework adoption are not always immediate, but they are bound to provide more of a payoff in the long run.

Generalization

Remember that whatever your framework attempts to address, your goal is to create a framework that can be generalized for other types of applications. For the framework to be truly useful and reusable, it must be flexible in more than one application setting. The point is, be careful not to make the definition too specific, to address a very specific problem. The reusable trait of your application will be affected by how general your framework definition is.

A good technique to use is *generalization* [Booch, 1994]. This involves taking a given problem domain and providing the key constructs of the problem without the application-specific pieces. Because these pieces are application-specific, and cannot be generalized for every problem domain, their implementation is deferred to the application developer, who can best address the application-specific contexts with his or her own client code. As demonstrated in a previous example, there were facilities the DomainModel class defined,

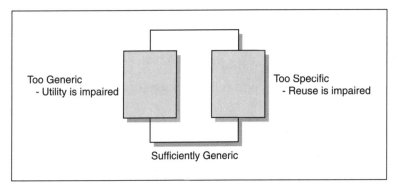

Figure 2.7   Sufficiently generic.

but did not provide. In essence, there are missing pieces to the solution of the problem, because these pieces cannot be generalized across applications and so must be addressed on a case by case basis. This is the key to adding flexibility within your framework.

NOTE This is also what has been referred to as *plug points,* places within the framework that applications plug code into.

The process of generalization involves refining the definition of your framework to make it *sufficiently generic* (see Figure 2.7). If your framework is too generic, the application developer will have to reproduce common elements that could have been included in the framework. If your framework is too specific, its use will be limited to certain situations, which will discourage developers. Determining when your definition is sufficiently generic is difficult to quantify.

Analyzing and Designing the Framework

A framework also should be *decomposable;* that is, it should be able to be broken down into a few, well-defined areas. The process of framework analysis involves (among other things) breaking the framework down into parts.

Through analysis, three distinct parts (or models) can be isolated within the framework design: the *object model,* the *organizational model,* and *the collaboration model.* Each of these constructs serves a distinct purpose.

- The object model represents the domain models, classes, and interfaces defined by your framework.

- The organizational model provides a means of relating and grouping objects within the framework. Not all frameworks will require this provision, but it provides a mechanism of composing objects in a flexible and dynamic way that may be beneficial.

- The collaboration model diagrams the object collaborations or processes that occur between the framework proper and application client code.

Let's look at each of these in more detail.

The Object Model

A framework's object model identifies the major object constituents of the framework in the form of class hierarchies and interfaces. For domain model frameworks, the object model represents the domain objects (models if you prefer) that were extracted through the process of domain analysis and object decomposition. The object model construct is the result of defining classes, which are to be used by the framework, and the class associations at a fundamental level.

When creating an object model, it is important to determine where to institute default behavior and where to abstract it. In the example in Listing 2.5, the Automobile class inherited a few abstract methods, one of which was save(). Functionality that you intend for application developers to provide (à la plug points) should be made abstract. That is, you provide the definition or slot for which future implementations will implant themselves. Figure 2.8 shows a simple object model class hierarchy.

One drawback to forcing each subclass to implement abstract methods is that other sibling classes that also inherit from DomainModel will have to provide implementations as well. If an identical implementation exists for both

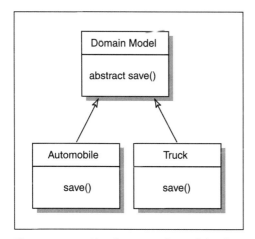

Figure 2.8 Simple DomainModel class hierarchy.

classes, it would be erroneous and cumbersome to force the developer to reimplement save() for each new class. For example, if you decide to create another subclass of DomainModel called Truck, it too would have to implement save(). The implementations for Truck and Automobile would inevitably be the same, and therefore, you'd have some redundant code.

Another liability is that the save policy for subclasses of DomainModel is defined at compile time. Subclasses of DomainModel provide their own implementations, which cannot be changed at runtime.

Where the framework designer can provide default implementations of save() that delegate the task to another object instance, the implementation of save() can be swapped in and out for the entire hierarchy (this is similar to the Bridge pattern [Gamma et al., 1995] which will be discussed in Chapter 3, "Using Design Patterns"). This allows the same object instance to act on behalf of other object instances that invoke save() from a different hierarchy, (see Bridge pattern on page 137). To illustrate this technique, let's modify our DomainModel class to delegate this task to another object, possibly in an accompanying utility framework, separate from the evolving domain model framework. The altered code is shown in Listing 2.8.

In this listing, notice the new class called ObjectArchiver (this class could be a part of another third-party framework or possibly of the current framework). Regardless, the current domain model framework interacts with an object of this type by delegating to it the storage of object instances. Users of the domain model framework, however, need not be concerned about ObjectArchiver objects if they're happy with the default implementation. Currently, the DomainModel class will instantiate an ObjectArchiver that will provide a default serialization facility for storing objects. The flexibility of this object model is expanded by allowing the framework user to plug in his or her own ObjectArchiver instance. Because all objects of type DomainModel delegate their save() methods to the same ObjectArchiver, the save policy for all of the DomainModel objects can be changed simply by providing a different implementation of an ObjectArchiver by calling DomainModel.setObjectArchiver(). This can be accomplished through simple subclassing.

But notice that when subclassing ObjectArchiver, a method implementation inherited from the base class is overridden. This is not efficient object-oriented programming. Instead, make a clean separation of definition and implementation of ObjectArchivers. From this, an interface is extrapolated that defines the reliable protocol or method declarations for objects of class ObjectArchiver. In addition, the framework will provide a general-purpose implementation class of this interface to make it readily usable. As would be expected, future implementations can be layered into existing applications and architectures with little modification.

Listing 2.9 shows the Java source code for the ObjectArchiver interface and a concrete implementation in SerialObjectArchiver.

Listing 2.8 ObjectArchiver and DomainModel class definitions.

```java
// ObjectArchiver.java
import java.io.*;

public class ObjectArchiver {

    public boolean save(Object object, int id)
    {
        // Save object
      try {
        FileOutputStream file = new
                 FileOutputStream(id+"");
        ObjectOutputStream out = new ObjectOutputStream(file);
        out.writeObject(object);
        return true;
      } catch (Exception e) {
        return false;
      }
    }

}


// DomainModel.java

public abstract class DomainModel implements Trackable {

    // Member variable
    protected int objectId = 0;

    // Object Archiver used to save objects.
    static ObjectArchiver archiver = new ObjectArchiver();

    public static void setObjectArchiver(ObjectArchiver arch)
    {
        archiver = arch;
    }

    // Inherited method implementation
    public int getObjectId()
    {
        return objectId;
    }

    public void setObjectId(int id)
    {
        objectId = id;
    }
```

continues

Listing 2.8 ObjectArchiver and DomainModel class definitions. *(Continued)*

```
    public boolean save()
    {
        return archiver.save(this,objectId);
    }



    // Trackable interface methods. Subclasses are forced
    // to implement these.
    public abstract String getKey();
    public abstract String getItemType();
    public abstract String getItemDescription();
    public abstract boolean isThisYou(DomainModel model);


}
```

Listing 2.10 shows a version of DomainModel that includes a default implementation of an ObjectArchiver, namely, SerialObjectArchiver.

A couple of modifications were made in Listings 2.9 and 2.10. First, an interface was defined to represent all ObjectArchivers, now called ObjectArchiver. This allows multiple, differing implementations to be represented simply as ObjectArchiver objects. Second, the previous ObjectArchiver class was renamed as SerialObjectArchiver, because it now provides a serialization implementation to the interface ObjectArchiver. Third, the declaration within DomainModel was changed to instantiate a specific ObjectArchiver, namely, a SerialObjectArchiver.

If I invented a new ObjectArchiver and wanted it to define the policy for all DomainModels used by my framework, the result might be code that looks like Listing 2.11.

By delegating the responsibility of storing objects away from the class hierarchy rooted by DomainModel, various ObjectArchiver implementations can be plugged in and used, without altering or recompiling existing code that utilizes the DomainModel hierarchy. This method is referred to as *object composition,* in contrast to using the inheritance method in the initial approach. In many cases, *inheritance* is not flexible enough to define behaviors that apply uniformly to an entire family of objects. In these situations, object composition is the best approach [Coad et al., 1996].

Figure 2.9 shows the new object model that includes the interface definition ObjectArchiver with two implementing classes: ODBObjectArchiver and SerialObjectArchiver. The method invocation of save() takes place in DomainModel because the method is no longer abstract, and the subclasses Automobile and

Listing 2.9 ObjectArchiver interface and SerialObjectArchiver implementation.

```
// ObjectArchiver.java

public interface ObjectArchiver {

    public boolean save(Object object, int id);
}



// SerialObjectArchiver.java
import java.io.*;

public class SerialObjectArchiver implements ObjectArchiver {

    public boolean save(Object object, int id)
    {
        // Save object
        try {
          FileOutputStream file = new
                FileOutputStream(id+"");
          ObjectOutputStream out = new ObjectOutputStream(file);
          out.writeObject(object);
          return true;
        } catch (Exception e) {
          return false;
        }
    }

}
```

Truck do not override this method. The default implementation of this method is to invoke the current instance of ObjectArchiver. The precise handling of the objects passed is entirely implementation-dependent. Now, the DomainModel subclasses can individually choose when the default implementation of save() is not satisfactory and override it as appropriate.

In most cases, solid relationships will be identified between the classes defined in the framework, but to maintain the spirit of flexibility, it is important to refrain from mandating nebulous or undetermined organizations within the framework proper. Instead, it is necessary to have a separate model that logically organizes or associates object instances that meet the needs of the application when the future adaptability of a certain object model is unclear. The organizational model serves this purpose.

Listing 2.10   DomainModel revision including default initialization of an ObjectArchiver.

```
public abstract class DomainModel implements Trackable {

    // Member variable
    protected int objectId = 0;

    // Object Archiver used to save objects.
    static ObjectArchiver archiver = new SerialObjectArchiver();

    public static void setObjectArchiver(ObjectArchiver archiver)
    {
       this.archiver = archiver;
    }

    // Rest of DomainModel definition see previous listing.
    ...
}
```

The Organizational Model

If you are familiar with the organizational model, you are already aware how it can be applied to the Java Collections Framework. When you consider organizing object instances within a framework, you should provide the application developer with a convenient and appropriate mechanism that is also flexible. Collections act as flexible building blocks from which you can construct and define a variety of organizational constructs for a framework, as well as reliable iterators and algorithms that act on those collections and maintain the framework's internal consistency and integrity.

When analyzing the relationships between classes, there is a tendency to embed object associations within classes that seem, at the time, to be logical. These associations can also seem logical for the application at hand, but if the goal is to develop a framework that has adaptive qualities, some object relationships or associations need to be organized outside of the related class definitions. That is, they need to be *mutable*.

Consider the following example. Suppose you are developing a domain model framework for a particular application. The object model contains a class called Party. A party is typically a person or company involved in a type of transaction or agreement with another person or company. Two or more parties are common. In this particular application, each Party object requires an association to particular CreditUnion object. A simple Party can be defined as shown in Listing 2.12.

The domain analysis of this application can indicate that all Parties engaging in transactions or agreements will have a corresponding CreditUnion associated with them. It is natural to embed this association with Party because the

Listing 2.11 Setting ObjectArchiver policy using a different implementation.

```
// Instantiate an implementation of ObjectArchiver that talks
// to an object-oriented database.
ObjectArchiver odbArchiver = new ODBObjectArchiver();

// Set the save policy for all DomainModels to this particular
// ODBObjectArchiver instance.
DomainModel.setObjectArchiver(odbArchiver);

Automobile auto = new Automobile();
auto.setObjectId(69);
auto.setColor(Color.green);
auto.setNumWheels(4);

// Actually delegates to our ODBObjectArchiver instance within
// DomainModel
if(auto.save()) {
   System.out.println("Successful save!");
} else
   System.out.println("Save failed.");
```

direction of the association is from Party to CreditUnion, not necessarily vice versa. However, if, in the future, you wanted to associate a given Party instance with another object, such as a Bank object, you would discover a flaw in the object model: The object model does not compose Party objects and Bank objects together. Thus, you would likely be forced to compensate in an inefficient manner or redesign the object model to account for Bank objects, both somewhat undesirable.

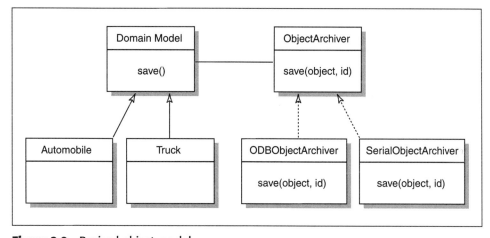

Figure 2.9 Revised object model.

Listing 2.12 Party class definition.

```java
// Party.java

public class Party extends DomainModel {

    private String address = "";
    private String name = "";
    private String telephone = "";

    private CreditUnion creditUnion = null;

    public void setAddress(String address)
    {
       this.address = address;
    }

    public String getAddress()
    {
       return address;
    }

    public void setName(String name)
    {
       this. name = name;
    }

    public String getName()
    {
       return name;
    }

    public void setTelephone(String telephone)
    {
       this. telephone = telephone;
    }

    public String getTelephone()
    {
       return telephone;
    }

    public void setCreditUnion(CreditUnion creditUnion)
    {
       this.creditUnion = creditUnion;
    }

    public CreditUnion getCreditUnion()
    {
       return creditUnion;
```

continues

Listing 2.12 Party class definition. *(Continued)*

```
    }

    // Trackable interface implementations
    // class even though they originate in the Trackable interface.
    public String getKey()
    {
        return name+address+telephone;
    }

    public String getItemType()
    {
        return "Party";
    }

    public String getItemDescription()
    {
        return "A Party involved in a transaction.";
    }

    public boolean isThisYou(DomainModel model)
    {
        return this.equals(model);
    }

}
```

An organizational model can provide view associations between disparate objects in a way that does not require modification of the associated objects. To do so, refrain from embedding associations that are questionable or subject to change. Instead, allow other organizing or collecting objects to handle the linkage. An example is shown in Listing 2.13.

This listing shows a collection object that allows CreditUnion objects to be associated with specific Party object instances. The nature of this association can be tailored according to the needs of the application. In this example, a CreditUnion needs to be associated with a Party and be able to retrieve a CreditUnion object given a particular Party. This organization does not, however, support the retrieval of Party objects given a CreditUnion.

Because this approach does not require modification to the object model, organizational structures can be created as needed. For example, you may discover a need for many different organizations that create interesting mappings between object instances, where each mapping may serve a different purpose.

Listing 2.13 CreditUnionList class definition.

```
//CreditUnionList.java
import java.util.*;

public class CreditUnionList extends Hashtable {

    public void addCreditUnion(Party party,CreditUnion creditUnion)
    {
        put(party,creditUnion);
    }

    public CreditUnion getCreditUnion(Party party)
    {
        return (CreditUnion)get(party);
    }
}
```

Notice in Figure 2.10 that the central class Party is associated with a variety of different classes through an organization supplied by a Map collection. Acting as the key, the Party object can determine associations to Bank, CreditUnion, and future Class objects. Although this method of creating associative mappings requires more overhead and effort, it eliminates the burden of reprogramming the object models over time and allows for interesting and dynamic relationships to be established between object instances.

THOUGHTS Some of the problems with object modeling in general revolve around the static nature of the definitions. When you determine the nature of the classes you intend to use during your analysis and design phases, you must make decisions that are more or less immutable once laid out into a class hierarchy. But in the real world, there are always exceptions to rules, and there are certainly members of a particular class that exhibit additional or temporal behavior or attributes yet still are valid members of their class. Accounting for these exceptions in a dynamic way is an ongoing problem in object-oriented modeling.

Sorting and Searching

Sorting collections can be a relatively trivial task. You can simply invoke interface methods on your collection to sort it in a natural order or use a provided Comparator object that determines the ordering of two compared objects. With this kind of flexibility, you can accommodate just about any sorting or ordering problem you might encounter.

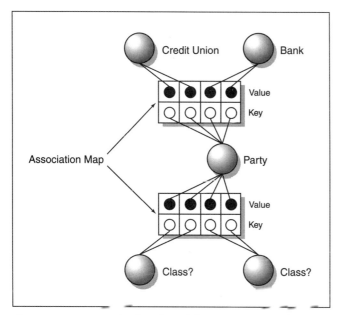

Figure 2.10 Organizational model using a Map collection.

Recall that iterators provide a mechanism for cycling through collections and for performing uniform operations or algorithms along the way. Depending on the type of object organization, different types of searching are possible and useful. In the previous example, CreditUnion objects were keyed off of existing Party instances. From this, you can determine that there will always be a given Party object with which to acquire the necessary association. However, in some situations you might want to have more free-form organizational models that do not key off existing objects, but instead, contain pieces of information. In this case, it useful to adopt searching patterns within the framework to match object instances with pieces of information. Specifically, you might want to find the set of objects whose attributes match a set of attributes or ranges.

As is the case with algorithmic searches, determining the length of time needed to find a given key requires that the keys be ordered in some way. For example, binary searches require that the collection being searched be ordered. Binary searches can operate effectively on indexed array lists or binary tree structures. Searching a binary tree involves navigating each node and determining which child node (there are a maximum of two children per node) is less than or equal to the key being searched. The other child node is pruned and simply not navigated.

The organizational parts of the framework specifically address extensibility and adaptability. Independent of the attributes and associations between classes provided by the object model, you should be able to easily create organizational structures on top of those classes without undoing or overriding critical behavior or associations already established by the framework. As pointed out, associations and mappings that are not mandated as final by the framework should be implemented as organizational models to give the developer the option of using the framework out of the box or providing a tailored organization more akin to his or her application. If this can be done without compromising the framework's process control, then optimum flexibility can be achieved.

The Collaboration Model

Knowing that a framework defines not only object classes but also an interaction process leads to the final model structure that requires careful consideration when designing a robust framework. The collaboration model describes the interactive behavior semantics between the instances of your framework. The instances within a framework refer to objects that have been inserted into your framework by the client developer (these are also referred to as client objects). Because frameworks often interact with application code, you need a solid way to model, document, and communicate how the framework abstractions facilitate usable behavior among cooperating instances.

It should be clear to the developer using your framework product exactly how his or her application code should react to framework events and messages. Unfortunately, there are no real scientific methods for creating good collaboration models. Much depends on the goal at hand, personal preference, or required degree of specificity. Whatever the case may be, a practical approach is always a prudent one. Consider these four guidelines when thinking about the process your framework may adopt:

1. *Create a rigid and robust set of interfaces through which your framework can establish reliable protocols for message delivery between instances.* This does not strictly imply using Java interfaces, but the methods used between important process-driven objects in your system should not change frequently. The processes within your framework should be generic in the sense that the protocols or interfaces with which they deal remain static while implementations can be supplied by developers to suit their needs.

2. *Establish documentation that identifies the major components of the framework that require developer intervention.* How these components interact is important to the developer if the framework is going to help save time and be useful.

3. *Remember that a collaboration model simply defines how objects interact and react to one another.* This can be a relatively high-level description, in which case some form of modeling language like the Unified Modeling Language (UML) might be suitable to express object interactions in addition to time and space definitions.

4. *Use patterns where possible and document how the patterns work.* By under-standing the generic patterns adopted by the framework, the developer can work through scenarios for his or her application.

The mini-CAT (short for Customer/Account/Transaction—the classes we introduced in Chapter 1) framework toolkit has a very simple collaboration model. Recall that whenever a transaction is added to an Account, any current Statement objects governing a date range that includes the current Transaction would automatically be updated. This is handled within the framework, and to properly use it, the developer only needs to know that this process occurs. This simplified example demonstrates the process definition of interactions within the mini-framework.

Exception Handling

Managing error conditions within your framework is vital to maintaining the normal state of operation and integrity of the running system. Older methods of error handling involved checking return codes from function calls. This proves highly inadequate as the onus is on the developer to understand and subse-quently check each and every significant return code resulting from an error condition within the function call. Even with object languages like Java, using return values to signal error conditions is bad practice for the same reasons.

An exception is the result of a method invocation that does not complete. This could be because a severe condition has occurred that prevents the exe-cution from continuing or because immediate notification of the results of the invocation needs to be transmitted to the invoking context.

Essentially, there are four primary reasons an exception is thrown in Java [Haggar, 1998].

1. You made a programming error.

2. An internal error in Java (or the JVM) has occurred.

3. You called a method that has thrown an exception.

4. You explicitly threw an exception using *throw*.

In addition, there are three basic categories of exceptions that fall into these four situations:

- Error exceptions
- Runtime exceptions
- Caught (or checked) exceptions

Error exceptions are unchecked exceptions that typically originate within the Java Virtual Machine (JVM) such as OutOfMemoryException or similar.

Runtime exceptions are typically thrown in the event of a fatal condition that occurs within your application or framework (reasons 1 and 2). For this reason, these exception types do not have to be accounted for (or caught) by an invoking context. A good example of this is NullPointerException, which will be thrown whenever an object being accessed is equivalent to null. If you were forced to use try-catch clauses whenever this might occur, it would consume more code than the application itself!

Caught exceptions, on the other hand, can be thrown to notify invoking contexts of certain conditions or events as they occur. Caught exceptions *must* be caught. That is, the invoker of a method that explicitly declares and throws an exception must explicitly account for that exception.

> **NOTE** Regardless of the type of exception being thrown, when an exception is thrown, any statements appearing after the throw point will not be executed, because control is given back to the invoking context.

There are two courses of action that can be taken when an exception is thrown. The invoking context must either catch the exception or pass it along by throwing it yet again. Listing 2.14 is a simple example of trapping caught exceptions.

This listing traps for two kinds of exceptions. In each try-catch clause, a specific exception is trapped by the object methods that throw them. In Java, whenever a method throws an exception, the invoking context must either catch the exception directly or throw the exception to the method's invoking context. If an invoking context fails to catch a particular exception, it will fall out, and the current executing thread will cease to execute. The rationale behind this process is that if a condition occurs that prevents the application from continuing in a reliable way, the application is required to take an approach to resolve the situation. Requiring certain exceptions to be caught to prevent unusual states from arising within your framework or application is a robust way to improve the reliability of your application.

Try-Catch Clauses

In Java, exceptions are handled by *try-catch* (and, optionally, *finally*) clauses. Listing 2.14 contains one try-catch clause embedded in the other. Depending on which other calls are enclosed in the topmost clause, the segment could have been rewritten as shown in Listing 2.15. This example simply demonstrates that you can create embedded or consolidated invoking contexts to watch for a range of exceptions that may be thrown between the try-catch clauses. No single method of implementing these clauses will suffice for all circumstances, thus knowing different ways to do this will prove useful in the long run.

> **TIP** As previously stated, older methods of checking return codes are prone to human error and oversight. Java forces the compiler to catch the class (or superclass) of a caught exception, thereby reducing the margin of error before program execution.

Listing 2.14   Example of caught exceptions.

```
try {
    // This line of code throws a FileNotFoundException
    FileInputStream file = new FileInputStream ("myfile");

    try {
        // This line of code throws an IOException
        while(file.read());

    } catch (IOException e) {

    }
    // Some actions can proceed here after the inner exception
    // occurs
} catch (FileNotFoundException e) {

}
```

The code in Listing 2.16 forces the catching of a newly created exception class by appending a throws clause to the setObjectId() method. The first part of Listing 2.16 shows the source code for InvalidIdException, which extends the Exception base class. It is highly recommended that any new exception classes always extend the Exception base class.

Listing 2.15   Single context Exception handling.

```
try {
    // This line of code throws a FileNotFoundException
    FileInputStream file = new FileInputStream ("myfile");

    // This line of code throws an IOException
    while(file.read());

    // Any code residing here will not get executed
    // in the event of an exception within the above
    // while loop assuming the new FileInputStream statement
    // succeeds.

} catch (FileNotFoundException e) {

} catch (EOFException f) {

}
```

Listing 2.16 InvalidIdException class and DomainModel revision.

```java
// InvalidIdException.java

public class InvalidIdException extends Exception {

    public InvalidIdException(int id)
    {
        super("ID["+id+"] is not a valid id.");
    }
}


//DomainModel.java
import java.util.*;

public abstract class DomainModel {

    // Statically maintained list of all
    // instantiated and id'd DomainModels.
    static Hashtable allModels = new Hashtable();

    // Member variable
    protected int objectId = 0;

    // Inherited method implementation
    public int getObjectId()
    {
        return objectId;
    }

    // Now we've added a throws clause for a
    // new class of exception we created for
    // this framework.
    public void setObjectId(int id)
    throws InvalidIdException
    {
        // If this id is already in our
        // collection of DomainModels, then
        // throw an exception.
        if(allModels.get(new Integer(id))!=null) {
          throw new InvalidIdException(id);
        } else {
          // Since the id is unique, set it
          // to this object and store the
          // association in our static hashtable
          objectId = id;
          allModels.put(new Integer(id),this);
        }
```

Listing 2.16 InvalidIdException class and DomainModel revision. *(Continued)*

```
    }

    // Rest of class omitted for brevity

}
```

A static Hashtable collection has been added to DomainModel to store any DomainModels that have their object IDs set to a specific unique value. No duplicate keys are allowed in the collection; otherwise, the setObjectId() operation is not permitted and the invoking context must trap the InvalidIdException thrown exception.

Listing 2.17 shows a simple example of accounting for the exception defined in Listing 2.16. In the first invocation to setObjectId(), success is expected; however, the second attempt to setObjectId() should throw an InvalidIdException, which must be provided in order for the sample code to compile.

Exceptions that are explicitly stated in a methods declaration (using throws) are expected to be caught by invokers of that method. Likewise, subclasses

Listing 2.17 Example of trapping InvalidIdException exception.

```
Automobile ford = new Automobile();

try {
    ford.setObjectId(1);
    System.out.println("Success!");
} catch (InvalidIdException e) {
    System.out.println("Could not setObjectId for "+ford);
    System.out.println(e.getMessage());
}


DomainModel chevy = new Automobile();

try {
    // We know this will generate an exception
    chevy.setObjectId(1);
    System.out.println("Success!");
} catch (InvalidIdException e) {
    System.out.println("Could not setObjectId for "+chevy);
    System.out.println(e.getMessage());
}
```

that override methods throwing an exception object must either throw the same exception object or a descendant thereof (i.e., a derived exception).

You must design exceptions carefully into your system. Give special attention to areas within your framework where irrecoverable events or events for which only client code would have a logical recourse can occur. These areas are targets for heavy use of an exception hierarchy. Because it was explicitly stated that the setObjectId() method (see Listing 2.16) would throw a specific kind of exception, any Java code that invokes that method must catch the specified exception in order to compile. This forces the exception condition to be explicitly dealt with by the developer.

Substrate Propagation

Visualizing applications built using a variety of specialized frameworks is similar to layering, in that the flow of control initiates at a particular point and traverses instances contained in different layers whose process and implementations are buffered or subsequently abstracted from adjacent layers. For example, I might instruct an ObjectArchiver object to save an object. It in turn might communicate to a database connectivity layer (e.g., JDBC) to finish its tasks. My initial interaction with the ObjectArchiver object is (should be) completely shielded from the process within. When thinking of different object layers (whether frameworks or not) within your application, you should design your exception hierarchy in such a way that each layer or *substrate* generates a specific family of exceptions. Each layer specializes in its particular task, and there are exceptional conditions unique to each layer that must be caught and addressed.

Interfacing with a particular framework layer involves not only utilizing the interfaces and abstractions it provides, but interpreting conditions it throws to your running application. When your final application is built upon multiple layered hierarchies of classes or frameworks, you must ensure that the state management and integrity of a given framework or layer does not unknowingly affect or alter another. Exceptions provide a strict mechanism for identifying the critical *hot spots* within a framework, which must be accounted for either directly by your application or by objects of another framework.

Figure 2.11 shows the absorption and propagation of exceptions through joined frameworks as a simple layered model.

Recall the ObjectArchiver class that represented possibly part of a larger *data access framework*. The following example expands this object to include a small family of exceptions and broadens its interface definition.

Notice the changes to the ObjectArchiver interface in Listing 2.18. Another method—load(int id)—was added, and clauses are thrown to each method in the interface. Accompanying this new interface is a small class hierarchy of exceptions specific to ObjectArchiver objects, as shown in Figure 2.12.

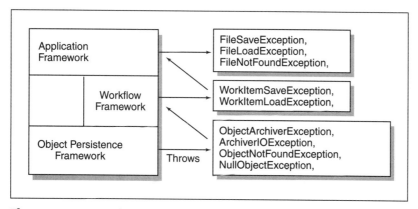

Figure 2.11   Exception propagation through framework substrate layers.

When designing a modular framework, you should consider how exceptions are both handled and propagated by your framework. As a general rule, any framework objects that interact with application-specific code or client objects should always throw *individual* exception classes rather than generalized superclasses, such as the base Exception class. Given the exception family created in Listing 2.18, generate specific exceptions depending on the type of event that occurs. Again, invoking contexts should trap specific classes of exceptions to deal with the different conditions that each represents, rather than simply catching the base class (in this case, ObjectArchiverException).

Notice in the new ObjectArchiver interface that specific classes of exceptions are thrown on the save() and load() methods. The invoking context must catch these exceptions and address them explicitly. At the developer's discretion, the

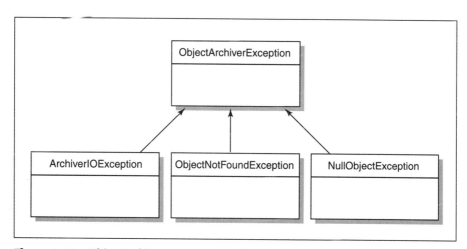

Figure 2.12   ObjectArchiver exception family.

Listing 2.18   Enhanced ObjectArchiver interface definition with Exception family classes.

```
// ObjectArchiver.java

public interface ObjectArchiver {

    public boolean save(Object object, int id)
        throws ArchiverIOException, NullObjectException;
    public Object load(int id)
        throws ArchiverIOException, ObjectNotFoundException;
}

// ObjectArchiverException.java

public class ObjectArchiverException extends Exception {

}

// ArchiverIOException.java

public class ArchiverIOException extends ObjectArchiverException {

}

// ObjectNotFoundException.java

public class ObjectNotFoundException extends ObjectArchiverException {

}

// NullObjectException.java

public class NullObjectException extends ObjectArchiverException {

}
```

family of exceptions produced by ObjectArchivers (name: ObjectArchiverEx-
ceptions) can be caught on all invocations against ObjectArchiver objects. In
other words, the developer may opt to catch the family of exceptions, thereby
handling all subclasses of the family in a reasonably identical manner. This
gives the developer the choice of simplicity or specificity, depending on his or
her application needs. Also, it is important to note that even though exceptions
are specified to be thrown against methods belonging to an interface, it is still
up to the implementation class to account for internal conditions that map
onto the exception types mandated by the interface. This helps maintain con-

sistency within your framework; as developers plug in implementations of key interfaces, they must still provide the necessary state management and exception notification that allows applications to operate with a given confidence and reliability.

In some situations, however, it might not prove as useful to track the exact exception instances that originate at a particular level within your application substrates, which may end up being handled or muted by another substrate, which would throw an exception from its particular family of exceptions. In this case, it would prove more useful for developers to grab an exception generated by a particular subsystem and peer inside it to uncover any other exceptions that may have been trapped within that subsystem and embedded within the exception object (this can occur at many embedded levels as well).

To accommodate this capability, create an exception base class that encapsulates one other exception object. At each point in your application where an exception is caught and another possibly more generic exception is thrown, the first exception can be embedded in the second and recursively uncovered if needed at a high-level invocation context. Consider the exception class to handle this in Listing 2.19.

This listing contains a simple exception class that holds one other exception rooted by the base class Exception. If the application has multiple isolated layers, frameworks, or components, and at some level an exception originates and is propagated to the invoking context of another framework, it can subse-

Listing 2.19 BaseException class definition.

```
public class BaseException extends Exception {

    Exception embeddedException = null;

    public BaseException(String message, Exception exc)
    {
        super(message);
        embeddedException = exc;
    }

    public Exception getEmbeddedException()
    {
        return embeddedException;
    }

}
```

quently be embedded in an exception of another type, indigenous to that layer. When an application object receives notification of the exception, it can opt to peel away the layers to gather useful information. Whether or not exceptions are embedded and passed along between layers is handled by the layers themselves. Depending on your system, you may decide to do this in some places and not in others.

Exceptions Guidelines

Creating exception hierarchies, managing and controlling exceptions, and enforcing their accountability are difficult tasks and so require focus, insight, and thought. It is easy to overlook the importance of exception handling in a system, because easier, faster routes exist (such as trapping everything as Exception). For most simple, practical purposes, trapping only the Exception class might prove sufficient, but for framework or component development, it's better to categorize a family of exceptions that reflects the operations performed by said framework or component.

When coding exception classes, here are some additional points to consider [Haggar, 1998].

1. *Use exceptions for all error conditions.* If the conditions are simple, error codes (e.g., true or false) may prove easier to wield.

2. *Do not use exceptions to control flow.* When this is the case, use if/then/else statements.

3. *Always extend the Exception class.* Doing so guarantees proper operability within Java and between Java APIs and possibly other frameworks or libraries.

4. *Propagate exceptions between interacting frameworks or subsystems.* This will allow conditions occurring at a low level within your system to be mapped cleanly to higher-level conditions. For example, a Banking framework may throw a BankAccountNotFoundException, which ultimately originated from an IOException when trying to access a file. IOException has a less specific meaning to developers using a Banking framework.

5. *Use exceptions for conditions outside that of expected behavior.* In other words, exceptions should most often occur when improper states arise in your framework or application; hence, they can be dealt with in a strict manner.

6. *Don't overuse try catch clauses.* If necessary, group similarly related exception classes by a common base class if possible.

7. *Attempt to restore your objects to a proper functioning state after receiving an exception.* Even if you intend to pass an exception along, ensure that any

given object receiving or throwing an exception is not left in a negative state, where it might be reused and compromise the integrity of your system. Often, this simply means to leave the object in the state it was before the exception occurred (this may involve using the *finally* clause).

Framework Integrity

One of the challenges of framework design is properly addressing a specific problem domain in a seemingly general or reusable way. In addition, the framework developer must consider providing a rigid set of abstractions that represent a sufficiently generic description of the problem addressed by the framework. There will always be pieces of the framework that the application code must provide, and it is an important step to identify which pieces can be extended, enhanced, or replaced, and which cannot. If the developer using your framework can replace or modify key pieces of your process or object model, then your framework may no longer solve the problem for which it was created. In other words, the integrity of the framework has been compromised.

Fortunately, Java provides a mechanism to prevent the subclassing or modification of classes. By using the *final* keyword, a particular class cannot be subclassed, which means that its internal methods cannot be overridden. In Java, a final class is declared as follows:

```
public final class Controller implements ProcessHandler {
    ...
}
```

Likewise, static class and instance variables can also be made final so they cannot be changed or overshadowed in subclasses. Similarly, individual methods can contain the *final* keyword with the same effect. Listing 2.20 shows a variation on the previously defined final class Controller. In this situation, the class is not final, but important static member variables and the readDuplex() method are defined as final and cannot be changed or overridden.

By properly utilizing final declarations on critical pieces within your framework, you can increase the integrity of your system by ensuring that key processes will operate according to design and that only designated objects within your framework will allow subclassing and adaptation.

Rules for Factoring Frameworks

Often, when designing class hierarchies or object models for large projects, the potential exists for frameworks to distill. Ralph Johnson [1992] defines a few

Listing 2.20 Controller class definition.

```
public class Controller implements ProcessHandler {

    public static final int FDUPLEX = 0;
    public static final int HDUPLEX = 1;

    public final String readDuplex(int duplex)
    {
        switch(duplex) {
            case FDUPLEX:
                    return "Full Duplex";
                    break;
            case HDUPLEX:
                    return "Half Duplex";
                    break;
        }
    }
}
```

useful rules to apply for facilitating the existence of frameworks from existing class hierarchies.

1. *Split large classes.* The concept of a class defines a set of specific attributes and operations. If too many attributes or operations are present, probably more classes should be used.

2. *Factor implementation differences into subcomponents and interfaces.* If differences exist between implementations of methods and the protocol for those methods, then using interfaces or a third-party component is useful to further separate the definition of the operation from the class hierarchy, where the semantics of operations provided by the hierarchy should remain as constant as possible.

3. *Send messages to components instead of to self.* Classes that perform multiple operations may define that behavior, which can then be inherited. The execution of that behavior can reside within the class or within another class, in which case the actual implementation is bridged (See the Bridge pattern discussion in Chapter 3, "Using Design Patterns") between the abstraction and implementation, allowing each to vary independently.

4. *Reduce implicit parameter passing.* If a case arises where two methods that should belong in separate classes cannot be split because they access the

same instance variable, determine whether that instance variable (or implicit parameter) should be an explicit parameter to each, thereby allowing them to reside in different classes.

Unification Rules for Deriving Frameworks

In addition to rules and guidelines for facilitating frameworks within a complex object hierarchy, there are some useful rules to apply for successfully extracting frameworks from these object hierarchies [da Fontoura et al.]. These rules include the following:

1. *Identical concepts should use identical names or terminology.* When creating a framework from an existing system, ensure that concepts driving the framework have been properly unified through a consistent set of terms; for example, if the concept of an automobile is defined as both Auto and Automobile in different applications, for the resulting framework, simply choose one and map the common attributes and behavior to both.

2. *Attribute types must be consistent.* Attributes referring to the same conceptual idea should be typed accordingly in the resulting framework.

3. *Cyclic hierarchies must be avoided.* In systems where framework decomposition is taking place, avoid the situation where structures in one hierarchy promote structures in another hierarchy, and vice versa.

Documenting Your Framework

One of the key considerations in developing and evaluating a framework for usage in your own projects is understanding what it does, how it works, and how to use it. Like any other software system or program, a framework should be well documented and thoroughly tested. If you intend your framework to be reusable and to truly realize its benefits, document it thoroughly.

In today's world, it is not only developers who make technical decisions; IT managers and project managers must also have the information they need to make accurate and beneficial decisions about adopting new technologies. Three types of documentation can be used for your framework: *overview, external,* and *internal documentation.*[2]

Overview Documentation

Overview documentation identifies the major goals of the framework in the form of an executive summary. It provides enough high-level information

---

[2] Categorizing documentation came from the template approach used in the GoF (*Gang of Four*) patterns book.

for anyone to quickly analyze the problem domain addressed by the framework and determine if the framework is appropriate for his or her application.

Table 2.9 shows a list of important topics to consider when delivering overview documentation for your framework. This type of documentation is less targeted for developers, but gives everyone a quick and easy method for understanding what your framework product is and what it does.

External Documentation

External documentation addresses how to interface with your framework from a coding standpoint. It provides useful text on the contracts, abstractions, and solutions provided by the framework, as well as examples on how to use the framework in an application context. Essentially, the external documentation supplies information a developer needs to use the framework. It does not necessarily include details about the inner workings of the framework; that is covered by internal documentation.

Table 2.10 lists some important criteria that should be considered for your external documentation. Each criterion should be well described within the documentation.

Table 2.9 Overview Documentation Criteria

TYPE	DESCRIPTION
Terminology	Identifies the name of the framework and the important terms it conveys to the reader.
Specific Knowledge	Identifies the specific or special knowledge that the framework encapsulates, possibly, the domain-oriented expertise that results in time savings.
Problem Intent/Motivation	Describes the reason or situation where the framework should apply. Identifies the problem the framework addresses.
Value Proposition	Includes a high-level statement of the value the framework brings to the user or developer; itemizes the savings benefits and emphasizes the flexibility and longevity of the framework.
Description	Describes the framework in high-level terms; doesn't attempt to address areas covered in other categories.

Table 2.10 External Documentation Criteria

CRITERIA	DESCRIPTION
API/Contracts	Documents all the external interfaces and contracts or abstractions provided by the framework for client applications to utilize.
Specialization Process	Outlines the rules or guidelines useful to developers who wish to extend the functionality of the framework in key areas (which may have been predetermined and need to be documented as such).
Solution	Details how the framework solves a particular class of problems. Gives details on the collaboration among objects (i.e., the collaboration model), the objects themselves (the object model), error handling policies, example code, and configuration.

Internal Documentation

A framework should attempt to encapsulate specialized knowledge and processes to be presented to a developer in a less complex manner. Sometimes, however, it is important for a developer to dig into that complexity to understand how a framework accomplishes its internal tasks. That is the purpose of the internal documentation bundled with your framework. The criteria is similar to external documentation, but takes on a likeness most related to your particular framework. A good example of internal documentation is commenting through JavaDoc. This tool comes bundled with Java and allows for insertion of formatted comments within your code. The following snippet shows a simple example of JavaDoc comments.

```
/**
 * This method returns an employee's name based on their ID
 * @param id The employee's id number
 * @return The employee's name
 ********************************************************/
public String getName(int id)
{
    // Useful code goes here
}
```

The JavaDoc tool will automatically generate HTML pages from your Java class files and insert formatted comments where you have applied them in your code.

Following good coding and documentation guidelines and standards will improve the overall appeal of your framework code to developers, who ultimately will be using it. Scott Ambler [1998] has established a set of nice Java coding styles, standards, and conventions that are quite usable.

Summary

This chapter explored techniques for designing and implementing frameworks in Java. It covered the basic approach to abstraction and the importance it has in separating key implementations from interfaces provided by a framework. You saw how to bridge an abstraction with an implementation (which is revisited in Chapter 3, "Using Design Patterns"). You also were introduced to the Java Collections Framework, a good example of a framework that provides characteristics such as flexibility and usability, and discovered how it can be useful for your own purposes. In addition, this chapter explored concepts involving exception handling within your frameworks, including methods, implementations, and guidelines.

Applications of tomorrow will rely more heavily on frameworks as the basis of construction and evolution over time. Because of the loose coupling characteristics and abstractions frameworks provide, new technologies can be assimilated into existing system architectures with far less redesign required than in the past. Java has emerged as a splendid object-oriented language and runtime facility for developing truly reusable frameworks. This chapter covered only some of the interesting design aspects of framework design in Java; there are many more interesting technologies that factor into this blossoming approach to application design. The following chapters discuss in more detail the impact of design patterns, components, and various architectural patterns to facilitate solid system designs, including distributed architectures and application and enterprise frameworks.

References

Ambler, Scott. "100% Maintainable Java: Component Strategies." OOPSLA '98 midyear workshop, Denver, CO, July 1998.

Arnold, Ken, and James Gosling. *The Java Programming Language*. Reading, MA: Addison-Wesley, 1996.

Booch, Grady. *Object-Oriented Analysis and Design with Applications*. Reading, MA: Addison-Wesley, 1994.

Coad, Peter, and Mark Mayfield. *Java Design: Building Better Apps and Applets*. Upper Saddle River, NJ: Yourdon Press, 1996.

da Fontoura, Marcus, M. C. Felipe, Edward H. Heausler, Carlos Jose P. de Lucena. "Using Unification Rules to Derive Object-Oriented Frameworks," Computer Science Department, Pontifical Catholic University of Rio de Janeiro, Brazil.

D'Souza, Desmond, F. Wills, and Alan Cameron. *Objects, Components and Frameworks with UML: The Catalysis Approach.* Reading, MA: Addison-Wesley, 1998.

Haggar, Peter. "Java Exception Handling." Lecture at Software Development East '98, Washington, DC. 1998.

Johnson, Ralph, and Brian Foote. "Designing Reusable Classes." Department of Computer Science, University of Illinois, 1992.

Lewis, Ted, Larry Rosenstein, Wolfgang Pree, Andre Weinand, Erich Gamma, Paul Calder, Glenn Andert, John Vlissides, and Kurt Shumucker. *Object-Oriented Application Frameworks.* Upper Saddle River, NJ: Prentice-Hall, 1995.

Using Design Patterns

Framework design attempts to promote the reusability of software by providing packaged functionality (in the form of a collection of classes) that addresses a particular goal. The typical end user of the framework is an application developer who uses it to solve a particular class of problem. The framework solves the problem in a *sufficiently generic* way, enabling the developer to realize the value by virtue of not having to invent a solution of his or her own.

The philosophy of framework reuse applies equally well to the constructs within it. Christopher Alexander, an architect, is credited with recognizing useful constructs in architecture that could be reused to solve recurring problems in his buildings [Alexander, 1977]. He suggested that applying useful and reusable constructs, or patterns, could reduce design and construction time and promote consistency. In addition, he promoted the idea of using patterns to define and describe recurring structures in buildings and towns, thereby creating a lexicon of useful constructs that could be reapplied in later contexts.

The field of object-oriented software design refers to these reusable patterns as *design patterns*, simply, solutions to recurring problems in software development. The book *Design Patterns: Elements of Reusable Object-Oriented Software* [Gamma et al., 1995], whose authors are commonly referred to as the "Gang of Four" or "GoF," is considered the definitive source on this subject and catalogs a variety of design patterns implemented with C++. This chapter looks at some of those design patterns, and how they can be implemented with Java. And for more information on this subject check out *Patterns in Java* by Mark Grand [1998].

Characteristics of Patterns

Design patterns capture important relationships between abstract kinds of objects that can collectively be applied to accommodate a particular problem in object-oriented design. Experienced software developers are often confronted with the same types of problems in different projects. Applying a known solution to these problems makes them easier to solve and promotes reliability in their application. By naming and cataloging these patterns, developers have a common library of solutions from which to choose.

Patterns have three distinguishing characteristics:

- *Patterns are reusable.* A pattern's only purpose is to be reused. And because a pattern is implementation-independent, it is suitable for inclusion in a framework. Patterns typically provide micro-architectural solutions to common recurring problems. Many of these problems may be embedded in a framework, which addresses a larger-scale domain problem. Hence, the patterned approaches can surely be reused across frameworks as well.

- *Patterns are context-free.* The context, or surrounding implementation, in which a pattern can be applied is generally not a constraint. Given a specific type of problem, if a pattern exists to address that type of problem, it can be applied generically, meaning that the application specific objects or components of the pattern are supplied by the application developer and the behavior mechanics are dictated by the pattern.

- *Patterns have granularity.* Design patterns are fundamental structures and are not intended to scale into larger domain aspect types of problems. They represent useful reusable micro-architectures that developers can apply to a given problem of an equally minute granularity. This is not to suggest that design patterns do not exist at many levels within a complex system. Actually, a variety of patterns can be extracted during the development of large applications and then reapplied in similar situations. It would seem that the reusability of aggregated design patterns diminishes as the complexity and specificity of the pattern rises. For the sake of our discussion, however, we will cover some of the fundamental design patterns as presented by the Gang of Four.

THOUGHTS These characteristics reflect the *fractal nature* of architecting complex systems from reusable and embedded structures. Chapter 1 introduced the concepts of replication, scale, and complexity. I prefer the affectionate moniker *fractacality* to refer to these three concepts combined. If you take a completed system and decompose it into discrete pieces, and then take each discrete piece and decompose it, you can identify certain patterns. Typically, it would be by design that such patterns would exist, or rather such pattern-levels would manifest from combinations of granular patterns. When you need a gear to complete the job, you use a gear. Your architecture can contain gears of various sizes; sometimes many gears behave as a system to turn another gear. In a single architecture, they all work together to produce the result.

The Gang of Four defines a pattern as having four essential traits, used to distinguish the patterns from one another. The four traits are:

- *Name.* A word or two that describes the pattern. After developers conceptualize abstract solutions to problems, it is convenient and efficient to be able to refer to these abstractions by name. This makes it much easier to communicate with other developers who understand the encapsulated concept; there is no need to describe it.

- *Problem.* The problem the pattern addresses. Similar to the goal of a framework, each pattern is designed to address a specific problem or situation that frequently occurs in object-oriented development. However, patterns are much finer-grained and address smaller domain-neutral types of problems. The information under this heading describes exactly the circumstances in which the pattern is useful, including any special conditions or constraints that must be present before implementing the pattern.

- *Solution.* The solution to the problem. The solution statement describes the content of the pattern in terms of objects, definitions, and interfaces, and the relationships between them. The solution is like a template that organizes the key abstractions of the pattern, which can then be applied to a particular problem independent of implementation details.

- *Consequences.* The results of applying the pattern. As with most things in software development (and the world in general) there are always trade-offs when choosing a particular path. That is, there is seldom a solution to a problem that doesn't have consequences, foreseen or otherwise. The consequences narrative of a pattern attempts to convey any trade-offs that are known for that particular pattern. This information allows the developer to make informed decisions about choosing that pattern or selecting another with the less negative side effects, if multiple patterns provide the same solution.

NOTE These descriptions are an overview for the four traits of a pattern. For a more detailed description of these traits, refer to the GoF book or Grand's, *Patterns in Java.*

Understanding the characteristics of design patterns will help you better include them in your framework design.

Patterns and Frameworks

It is important to consider using patterns when designing and implementing your framework. Your framework architecture should not only represent smart, robust design, but be able to pass the benefit of that design on to the user. Proper use of abstraction and reusable patterns in your framework will reflect its true power and usefulness. A framework that does not provide extensible abstractions and does not expose interfaces or classes that snap together into reusable patterns and micro-architectures will not meet the needs of today's complex applications.

Pattern adoption in framework design is essential for four reasons:

■ *The value of reusable patterns is passed along to the other developers through exposed pattern constructs within your framework.* In addition, if your framework provides a solution via a pattern, it facilitates the dynamic inclusion of application objects into the pattern, relieving the developer from implementing the pattern him- or herself. Because the pattern achieves a high degree of reusability, this degree of reusability is passed to the framework.

■ *Basing any architecture, whether framework or otherwise, on documented and proven design patterns is considered good programming.* This doesn't mean that these pattern constructs must be part of the exposed API of the framework. The framework's own internal construction can be built on proven solutions and methods.

■ *The value of using frameworks mirrors the value of applying patterns to design efforts.* Patterns and frameworks provide the ability to plug and play object implementations. This buffers objects from one another and hides the protocol traffic or implementations details. Well-documented object organization also reduces complexity and chaos.

■ *Developers familiar with the patterns will find it easier to work with a framework that is built using popular design patterns, which are covered in framework documentation.* Also, using a framework should speed up their learning curve about the mechanics of such a framework if it is not entirely black boxed, meaning that only its interfaces are revealed.

Before you embark on any significant framework development, you should conduct a thorough analysis of the types of objects and services your framework will address, then attempt to distill categories of problems within the framework that map neatly to the types of available patterns for solving these categories. There is no strict methodology for mapping domain types of problems to patterns that may apply, and in practice, you will find that more than one pattern can be used to solve the same general problem. For this reason, as mentioned, the GoF book has provided details about the trade-offs and consequences of each pattern.

Overview of Design Patterns

There are a variety of patterns that can be useful in your development efforts. Table 3.1 provides a quick overview of the patterns discussed in this section.

This section takes a look at each of these patterns, and provides code segments showing how partial implementations in Java will look.

Table 3.1 Design Patterns

PATTERN NAME	BRIEF DESCRIPTION
Factory Method	Using the same creation process (for varieties of instances) allows subclasses of an abstraction to provide their own object instantiations.
Abstract Factory	An abstraction whose subclasses implement a common protocol for creating families of related objects.
Adapter	Allows two objects that normally cannot exchange messages to communicate by adapting one object's messages to the interface of the other.
Bridge	Decouples the implementation of an abstraction from the hierarchy in which the abstraction resides, thereby allowing the two to vary independently.
Builder	Decouples the representation of a complex object from its construction process, allowing the two to vary independently.
Observer	Defines an Observable object upon which many Observer objects will receive notification of state changes.
Model/View	Separates the data and visual portions of an object so that multiple views may be linked with the same model.
Iterator	Provides a consistent interface for cycling through a series of objects in an order defined by the particular iterator or collection upon which it iterates.

Factory Method

The Factory Method pattern [Gamma et al., 1995] defines an interface method used to return new instantiations of a specific type of object. The type of object returned by a Factory Method is not known by the factory base class or interface. The responsibility of instantiation is deferred to specific subclasses that implement the Factory Method.

Discussion

Within the context of a framework, the Factory Method provides an interface for encapsulating application-specific instantiation yet can be utilized by the framework proper. This mechanism allows applications to plug in subclasses of factories that have knowledge about class implementations of which the framework is unaware (e.g., application objects). Through polymorphic mechanisms, the framework can still interact with the subclass implementations. Acquiring instances to classes not provided by the framework in this manner is typically done in the framework process model. Interactions occur within the framework between its native classes, even though the instances themselves are application-specific subclasses. The amount of interaction with custom application-side subclasses your framework provides is at your discretion.

This pattern is used to extend a framework. By exposing key framework classes and interfaces through the Factory Method, the framework can create instances of objects originating outside the framework proper. It is this linking to outside objects that makes the framework useful to developers, because much of the process and architecture is already designed into the framework. Figure 3.1 shows a simple diagram of the Factory Method.

Example

Suppose I have two classes, FormApplication and Form. FormApplication represents an application that creates and manages Form objects. It does this through two basic methods: createForm() and openForm(). A Form

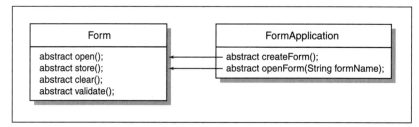

Figure 3.1   Factory Method diagram.

Listing 3.1 FormApplication class definition.

```
// FormApplication.java

public abstract class FormApplication {

    public abstract Form createForm();
    public abstract Form openForm(String formName);

}
```

object represents a simple form, like a loan application you might fill out at a bank. A Form is a user-interface counterpart to a real-world paper form. The Form class has a few basic method declarations: open(), store(), clear(), and validate().

In the FormApplication framework, you would not expect to know exactly what types of Forms a developer would implement, nor exactly how he or she intended to implement the behavioral aspects provided in your protocols. Your framework is aware only of objects descendant from FormApplication and Form, and can only send messages that are defined strictly in those classes.

Listing 3.1 and 3.2 are the abstract class definitions for FormApplication and Form, respectively. Subclasses of FormApplication will implement create-Form(), which is a Factory Method for Form objects. The returned Form instance will be a subclass of Form.

Listing 3.3 shows an example subclass of FormApplication called Loan-FormApplication. This subclass is written outside of the framework. It implements the Factory Method createForm() that returns a new instance of LoanForm, which is itself a subclass of Form. Because the framework abstract

Listing 3.2 Form class definition.

```
// Form.java

public abstract class Form {

    public abstract void open();
    public abstract void store();
    public abstract void clear();
    public abstract void validate();

}
```

Listing 3.3 LoanFormApplication class definition.

```
// LoanFormApplication.java

public class LoanFormApplication extends FormApplication {

    public Form createForm()
    {
        return new LoanForm();
    }

    public Form openForm(String formName)
    {
        Form aForm = null;

        // Load a form from a database or somewhere
        // Details omitted for brevity
        return aForm;
    }

}

// LoanForm.java
```

classes are abstract, they cannot be instantiated directly; they require nonabstract subclasses for proper instantiation. In addition, Listing 3.4 shows the LoanForm class.

Both LoanFormApplication and LoanForm (in Listing 3.4) are *concrete classes*; they extend abstract base classes and provide concrete implementations to the abstract methods defined in their superclasses. Figure 3.2 shows the relationship established between the framework-defined classes and the concrete subclasses.

Remarks

As mentioned previously, including the Factory Method in frameworks is useful because it decouples the creation of object instances from their declaring abstract hierarchies. Keeping the logic that defines the complete LoanFormApplication outside of the framework increases the reusability of the framework. Other types of FormApplication can easily be provided because the abstraction is well defined beforehand.

The Factory Method pattern promotes the coupling of similar class hierarchies. In the example, the LoanFormApplication and the LoanForm object were each a single descendant of their respective base classes. It would also be

Listing 3.4 LoanForm class definition.

```
public class LoanForm extends Form {

    public void open()
    {
        // some useful implementation here
    }

    public void store()
    {
        // some useful implementation here
    }

    public void clear()
    {
        // some useful implementation here
    }

    public void validate()
    {
        // some useful implementation here
    }

}
```

possible to have a DriverLicenseFormApplication and a DriverLicenseForm object, though a LoanFormApplication would not act as a factory for a DriverLicenseForm. If this were to occur, the efficacy of your application would be compromised. There should always be a reasonable degree of similarity between the class hierarchies of objects providing Factory Methods and the objects they provide.

THOUGHTS Consider other types of object pairings, such as such as Application–Document or Model–View that would benefit from the Factory Method pattern.

Abstract Factory

The Abstract Factory pattern [Gamma et al., 1995] allows you to interface to a particular factory implementation without knowing the exact nature of that implementation, that is, its class. A client object can request objects provided by a specific factory implementation that is unknown until runtime. This allows client objects to be coded in a generically identical manner.

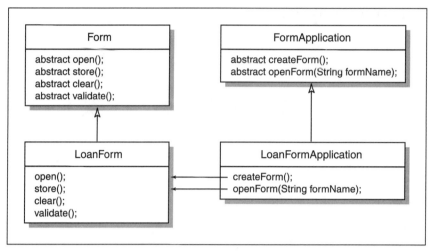

Figure 3.2   Relationship between framework-defined classes and concrete implementations.

Discussion

The Abstract Factory pattern is useful in frameworks because of the way it hides implementation details. A client object residing outside the framework can make requests through an Abstract Factory included in the framework. The framework can then make intelligent decisions about which factory implementation to use to service a particular request. Additional factory implementations can be provided over time and even loaded into a system at runtime (how this is done is discussed in more detail in Chapter 8, "Enterprise Frameworks").

These implementations are called *concrete implementations* because they implement the abstract class representing the Abstract Factory.

> **NOTE** Chapter 2, "Java Framework Design," demonstrated how the Java 2 Collections Framework provides for abstract and concrete versions of classes and interfaces.

Objects provided through an Abstract Factory can also masquerade as abstractions within their own hierarchy. This means that the implementation and class details of both factories and the objects they provide can be completely hidden. By doing this, you not only hide the complexity and knowledge about the nature of these objects, but you provide a stable, single mechanism for client objects to acquire objects through a single factory interface (or abstraction). This reduces the amount of change needed in the client

Listing 3.5 AbstractFactory class definition.

```
// AbstractFactory.java

public abstract class AbstractFactory {
    public abstract AbstractObjectA createObjectA();
    public abstract AbstractObjectB createObjectB();
}
```

system and isolates any necessary expansion beyond the factory interface within your framework (where it should be!).

Example

The following listings show the Java code for implementing an Abstract Factory class along with concrete implementations. Abstract and concrete classes for the objects provided by the factories are also shown. They are generic classes and serve only to illustrate the pattern. The factory example will service A and B type objects belonging to either the "1" or the "2" family. This terminology is used simply to illustrate how the objects relate to one another.

Listing 3.5 shows an abstract definition of the AbstractFactory class. It defines two methods, one for creating objects of type AbstractObjectA and one for creating objects of AbstractObjectB.

Listings 3.6 and 3.7 show concrete implementations of AbstractFactory that provide a common family of objects. ConcreteFactory1 provides object classes

Listing 3.6 ConcreteFactory1 class definition.

```
// ConcreteFactory1.java

public class ConcreteFactory1 extends AbstractFactory {

    public AbstractObjectA createObjectA()
    {
        return new ConcreteObjectA1();
    }

    public AbstractObjectB createObjectB()
    {
        return new ConcreteObjectB1();
    }

}
```

Listing 3.7   ConcreteFactory2 class definition.

```
// ConcreteFactory2.java

public class ConcreteFactory2 extends AbstractFactory {

    public AbstractObjectA createObjectA()
    {
        return new ConcreteObjectA2();
    }

    public AbstractObjectB createObjectB()
    {
        return new ConcreteObjectB2();
    }

}
```

ConcreteObjectA1 and ConcreteObjectB1, both belonging to the 1 family. ConcreteFactory2 similarly provides objects belonging to the 2 family.

Listings 3.8 and 3.9 represent abstract definitions of a basic object with one method. In this case, AbstractObjectA defines a method called getMessageA(), while AbstractObjectB defines one called getMessageB().

Listing 3.10 shows two concrete class definitions for AbstractObjectA, namely ConcreteObjectA1 and ConcreteObjectA2. Each provides a different implementation for getMessageA().

Likewise, Listing 3.11 provides class definitions for concrete implementations of AbstractObjectB. The implementation of getMessageB() is different for each concrete implementation.

Listing 3.12 generates an instance of an AbstractFactory in the call to new ConcreteFactory1(). Hypothetically, that reference is returned to an object out-

Listing 3.8   AbstractObjectA class definition.

```
// AbstractObjectA.java

public abstract class AbstractObjectA {
    public abstract String getMessageA();
}
```

Listing 3.9 AbstractObjectB class definition.

```
// AbstractObjectB.java

public abstract class AbstractObjectB {
    public abstract String getMessageB();
}
```

side the framework that interprets it as an AbstractFactory and does not have any knowledge about the class ConcreteFactory1.

When the client code invokes the method createObjectA(), an object of type AbstractObjectA is returned. At that point, it is uncertain which type of factory provided which type of object. The client is concerned only that an object of type AbstractObjectA is now acquired. The acquired object could be either ConcreteObjectA1 or ConcreteObjectA2. Through polymorphism, any messages sent to this object are received by the appropriate instance class. Figure 3.3 shows the AbstractFactory class relationship diagram.

Remarks

The Abstract Factory pattern ensures that families of related objects are obtained through a single entry point in an abstracted, reliable manner. It

Listing 3.10 ConcreteObjectA1, ConcreteObjectA2 class definition.

```
// ConcreteObjectA1.java

public class ConcreteObjectA1 extends AbstractObjectA {
    public String getMessageA()
    {
        return "This is an AbstractObjectA :: ConcreteObjectA1! ";
    }
}

// ConcreteObjectA2.java

public class ConcreteObjectA2 extends AbstractObjectA {
    public String getMessageA()
    {
        return "This is an AbstractObjectA :: ConcreteObjectA2! ";
    }
}
```

Listing 3.11   ConcreteObjectB1, ConcreteObjectB2 class definition.

```
// ConcreteObjectB1.java

public class ConcreteObjectB1 extends AbstractObjectB {
    public String getMessageB()
    {
        return "This is an AbstractObjectB :: ConcreteObjectB1! ";
    }
}

// ConcreteObjectB2.java

public class ConcreteObjectB2 extends AbstractObjectB {
    public String getMessageB()
    {
        return "This is an AbstractObjectB :: ConcreteObjectB2! ";
    }
}
```

allows the framework designer to utilize families of objects provided by the application developer. For the application developer, adhering to this relationship constraint makes it easier to use the framework in different contexts, because different families of objects can be provided through the same AbstractFactory interface. Ensuring that the proper objects in the same family are referenced in the same context is a useful constraint. It would not be possible to acquire a reference to an object in the 2 family in Listing 3.12 because the factory acquired only service objects belonging to the 1 family. By doing this,

Listing 3.12   Example use of AbstractFactory.

```
// Possibly, somewhere in our framework a proper instance
// is created and returned as a reference.
AbstractFactory af = new ConcreteFactory1();

// In our client code we acquire a reference to an
// AbstractFactory of some sort. Either, ConcreteFactory1
// or ConcreteFactory2.

AbstractFactory abstractFactory = af;

// I get a ConcreteObjectA1 from the "1" family.
AbstractObjectA objA = abstractFactory.createObjectA();
System.out.println(objA.getMessageA());
```

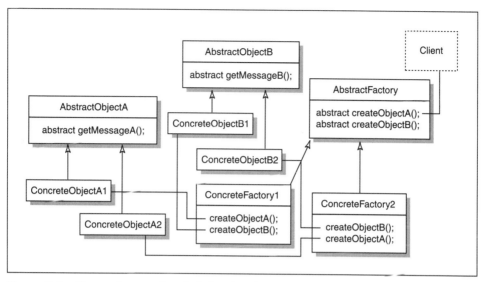

Figure 3.3 AbstractFactory class/relationship diagram.

you can ensure the integrity of operations within your system because you know that this pattern will not inadvertently provide an implementation that is not appropriate to a given family of objects.

Adapter

The Adapter pattern [Gamma et al., 1995] delivers a message to two objects that cannot communicate directly because their interfaces are incompatible. The adapter conforms an incoming message to that of the target object without the source object knowing about that transformation. As the adapter receives messages through the expected interface of one object, it forwards a translated message to the target. It adapts two distinctly different interfaces or methods by conforming to one or the other or both. The adapter is said to have a direction. It can adapt in one of three possible directions: from object A to object B, from object B to object A, or to both object A and object B.

Discussion

Adapters are useful for connecting two seemingly unrelated objects that contain incompatible interfaces and therefore cannot identify one another directly. In a framework, this situation can arise when you intend to utilize an object that does not descend from the framework hierarchy. In this situation, you use an adapter to act as liaison for the new object. The adapter is recognized by the framework as a valid recipient of messages conforming to a protocol provided by the framework. Your adapter, however, would forward appropriate messages to your target object, with which the framework cannot communicate directly. Figure 3.4 shows a simple diagram of the Adapter pattern.

Example

The Java AWT contains a number of classes suffixed with Adapter:

> ComponentAdapter
>
> ContainerAdapter
>
> FocusAdapter
>
> KeyAdapter
>
> MouseAdapter
>
> MouseMotionAdapter
>
> WindowAdapter

Each adapter is an abstract class containing empty methods that represent the interface expected by GUI components with Java. Coupled with each adapter abstract class is an interface representing the protocol definition.

Table 3.2 shows types of adapter classes found within Java (specifically, the AWT). Each adapter object implements what is called a *listener interface*. This separation of adapter implementation and listener interface allows developers to code their own adapter objects that adhere to a well-defined interface as expected by the internals of the AWT toolkit or framework.

> **NOTE** Because each adapter class is backed by an appropriate interface, the developer can choose to implement the interface directly, eliminating the need for an adapter class. Using the adapter class, however, allows for implementation subclassing, which can save some overhead time otherwise spent providing implementations to an entire interface when only one type of interface method is important.

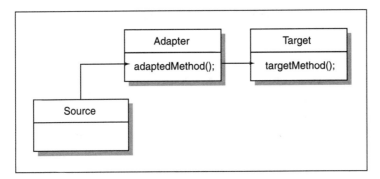

Figure 3.4 Adapter pattern diagram.

Table 3.2 AWT Adapters and Listener Interfaces

ADAPTER CLASS	LISTENER INTERFACE
ComponentAdapter	ComponentListener
ContainerAdapter	ContainerListener
FocusAdapter	FocusListener
KeyAdapter	KeyListener
MouseAdapter	MouseListener
MouseMotionAdapter	MouseMotionListener
WindowAdapter	WindowListener

Listing 3.13 shows the Java code for the ComponentAdapter class. Notice that the method implementations are blank. This allows a subclass of ComponentAdapter to choose which methods need implementations, thereby eliminating redundant empty method blocks. If these methods were declared abstract, subclasses would be forced to provide method blocks (empty or otherwise) for all declared methods.

The ComponentAdapter is registered as a ComponentListener against GUI objects within Java (Swing, AWT, or otherwise). GUI objects that receive ComponentListener objects will invoke the appropriate method when a certain event occurs, such as moving or resizing a component. Another class wishing to respond to these events would either have to implement ComponentListener or create an adapter of type ComponentAdapter and provide specific behavior in the desired methods. Listing 3.14 shows an example of how this works.

Although the example code in Listing 3.14 doesn't do anything useful, it serves to illustrate how these objects are created and connected. In this example, ApplicationComponentAdapter adapts ApplicationObject to Button because there are no interface discrepancies between Button and Application-

Listing 3.13 ComponentAdapter class definition.

```
public abstract class ComponentAdapter implements ComponentListener {

    public void componentHidden(ComponentEvent e) {}
    public void componentMoved(ComponentEvent e) {}
    public void componentResized(ComponentEvent e) {}
    public void componentShown(ComponentEvent e) {}


}
```

Listing 3.14   ApplicationObject class definition with custom adapter.

```java
// ApplicationObject.java
import java.awt.*;
import java.awt.event.*;

public class ApplicationObject {

    ApplicationComponentAdapter aca = null;

    public ApplicationObject()
    {
        aca = new ApplicationComponentAdapter(this);

        Button button = new Button("Hello");
        button.addComponentListener(aca);
    }

    public void objectWasHidden(ComponentEvent e)
    {
        Object source = e.getSource();

        // Some useful code would go here
    }

}


// ApplicationComponentAdapter.java
import java.awt.event.*;

class ApplicationComponentAdapter extends ComponentAdapter {

    ApplicationObject appObject;

    public ApplicationComponentAdapter(ApplicationObject ao)
    {
        appObject = ao;
    }
    // No need to override methods we are not concerned
    // about

    // Here we adapt componentHidden to objectWasHidden by
    public void componentHidden(ComponentEvent e)
    {
        appObject.objectWasHidden(e);
    }

}
```

ComponentAdapter. Invocations originating in Button find their way to ApplicationObject through the adapter.

Remarks

Adapters will come up again in the discussion on Java Foundation Classes in Chapter 5, "Analysis of Java Frameworks." Adapters are useful for enabling disparate objects to communicate, thereby making it possible for some objects to be reused in newer or different contexts. This is possible because the adapter essentially joins a source and target object. Because either the source or target may change, parts of the trio (adapter, source, and target) can be reused in other contexts.

Creating an adapter to connect two disparate objects does not warrant any changes in the adapted object—ApplicationObject in the example. This gives the developer some future flexibility in his or her system design choices. New types of adapters can be created, or existing adapters changed, without altering the objects they connect

Bridge

The Bridge pattern [Gamma et al., 1995] is useful for larger systems where key abstractions of framework constructs need to be completely separated from implementation class hierarchies. Bridge allows an abstraction hierarchy, provided by a framework, and its implementation hierarchy to vary independently.

Discussion

The Bridge pattern is used to provide implementations to complete and disparate subsystems within a framework architecture without binding classes of the implementation within the abstraction hierarchy. Why is this useful? Sometimes, it is easier to develop a family of classes based on an abstraction hierarchy by rooting the family in a single class implementation that is subsequently inherited from within the family. Other implementation classes do not extend from this base implementation class, but would have their own base implementation class. This creates a completely isolated class hierarchy that represents an implementation of an abstraction provided by a framework. If the framework were to change details about the abstractions, you would not have to change a multitude of classes that directly extend the abstractions. Because you've separated your hierarchy by rooting it in a common ancestral class, only the ancestral class would require significant change. Furthermore, because you've rooted your implementations in a class hierarchy, you do not need to duplicate similar behavior among variations within your class family.

The bridge occurs within the abstraction, which obtains a reference to a particular implementation root that you can provide. By obtaining a reference, the abstraction is delegating its method implementations to the provided root and executes on it directly. Figure 3.5 shows a diagram depicting what the Bridge pattern looks like.

Example

Suppose you had an application that utilized a variety of technologies for creating, managing, and accessing remote objects. For example, it could use Remote Method Invocation (RMI), serialized objects, or Java Naming and Directory Interface (JNDI) to look up and acquire references to remote objects. Because each technology implements object references and messaging differently, you would need to know which method you intended to use prior to implementing your system. However, within the abstraction hierarchy, you would not have to determine which method you intended to use, as this is dictated by the implementation hierarchy. The system is coded against these key abstractions; implementations for RMI, serialized objects, and JNDI could be plugged in or swapped out as needed.

In the abstraction hierarchy, you declare a root abstract class called Object-ReferenceFactory, which will act as a factory for providing objects of type Object, based on the name of the objects.

NOTE In this example, assume that objects are identified by a name of type String. In practice, you could use any criteria you wanted for determining when the desired object is found. The nice thing about the factory is that it encapsulates this logic, thereby freeing the user of the factory from the specific details about how the object is created. In this case, the object is searched for over a network and returned through the Factory Method.

ObjectReferenceFactory will implement the interface ObjectFinder, which declares a single method findObject(). Implementations of findObject() outside of our abstraction hierarchy will be handled by the interface ObjectFinderImpl and subsequent implementations of it.

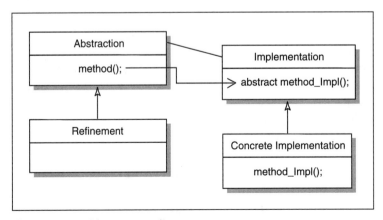

Figure 3.5 Bridge pattern diagram.

Listing 3.15 ObjectFinder and ObjectFinderImpl interface definitions.

```
// ObjectFinder.java

public interface ObjectFinder {
    public Object findObject(String name);
}


// ObjectFinderImpl.java

public interface ObjectFinderImpl {
    public Object findObjectImpl(String name);
}
```

Implementors of ObjectFinder return Object class types based on a String identifier. How an object is created is up to the implementor, given the String ID. Listing 3.15 shows the code for the interface ObjectFinder and ObjectFinderImpl.

Listing 3.16 shows ObjectReferenceFactory, which is declared an abstract class. This means this class cannot be instantiated and is intended to be refined through subclassing. ObjectReferenceFactory has a member variable *objectFinderImpl*, which is the real implementation of ObjectFinderImpl to which it intends to delegate. Refined subclasses within the abstraction hierarchy rooted by ObjectReferenceFactory inherit only the delegation logic within findObject(), not the particular implementation provided by *objectFinderImpl*. This allows for different ObjectFinderImpl objects to be used with the same abstraction hierarchy without modification.

Listing 3.16 ObjectReferenceFactory class definition.

```
// ObjectReferenceFactory.java

public abstract class ObjectReferenceFactory implements ObjectFinder {

    static ObjectFinderImpl objectFinderImpl;

    public Object findObject(String name)
    {
        return objectFinderImpl.findObjectImpl(name);
    }

    public static void setObjectFinder(ObjectFinderImpl of)
    {
        objectFinderImpl = of;
    }

}
```

The static method setObjectFinder() sets a particular ObjectFinder implementation for all ObjectReferenceFactory objects. If this were an instance method, the implementation policy would then apply only to particular instances of ObjectReferenceFactory.

Listing 3.17 shows a refined ObjectReferenceFactory. ObjectManager provides additional methods for storing objects. The ObjectArchiver interface discussed in Chapter 2, "Java Framework Design," is used. Notice that an identical class policy for ObjectArchiver is implemented as for ObjectFinder. The class ObjectManager inherits implementations of ObjectFinder and provides implementation delegation to ObjectArchivers. It also exposes the method storeObject(), which delegates to the instance of ObjectArchiver that has been set for the class ObjectManager.

Notice in Listing 3.17 that instances of ObjectManager can find objects with findObject() and store them with storeObject(), albeit possibly in different locations (the implementation is up to you). In addition, you can change the ObjectArchiver freely, thereby altering the storage policy for all instances of ObjectManager. Likewise, you can change the ObjectFinder with the same effect. The logic and duties within a refined abstraction, including the hierarchy itself (e.g., ObjectReferenceFactory and ObjectManager), do not need alteration and could contain additional unrelated functionality that operates separately from the bridged objects (in this case, ObjectFinders or ObjectArchivers). Note that this loose coupling eliminates compile time dependencies between abstraction and implementations.

Listings 3.18 and 3.19 show implementations of the ObjectFinderImpl interface. Instances of these classes act as delegates on behalf of ObjectManager

Listing 3.17   ObjectManager class definition.

```
// ObjectManager.java

public abstract class ObjectManager extends ObjectReferenceFactory {

    static ObjectArchiver objectArchiver;

    public void storeObject(Object ob, int id)
    {
        objectArchiver.save(ob,id);
    }

    public static void setObjectArchiver(ObjectArchiver oa)
    {
        objectArchiver = oa;
    }

}
```

Listing 3.18   RMIObjectFinder & SERObjectFinder class definitions.

```
// RMIObjectFinder.java
import java.rmi.*;
import java.rmi.registry.*;

public class RMIObjectFinder implements ObjectFinderImpl {

    Registry registry;

    public RMIObjectFinder(String registryName)
    {

        try {
            // Acquire the registry we intend to use for
            // object lookups
            registry = LocateRegistry.getRegistry(registryName);
        } catch (Exception e) {
            // possibly throw an exception here
        }
    }

    public Object findObjectImpl(String name)
    {
        try {
            Remote remote =
                (Remote)registry.lookup(name);
            return remote;
        } catch (RemoteException e) {
            return null;
        } catch (NotBoundException e) {
            return null;
        }

    }

}

// SERObjectFinder.java
import java.io.*;
import java.util.*;

public class SERObjectFinder implements ObjectFinderImpl {

    public SERObjectFinder()
    {

    }

    public Object findObjectImpl(String name)
```

continues

Listing 3.18   RMIObjectFinder & SERObjectFinder class definitions. *(Continued)*

```
    {
        // Load the serliazed file containing the object
        // then pass the object back
        try {
            File file = new File(name);
            FileInputStream f = new FileInputStream(file);
            ObjectInputStream oos = new ObjectInputStream(f);
            Object obj = (Object)oos.readObject();
            oos.close();
            return obj;
        } catch (Exception e) { return null; }
    }

}
```

instances, albeit unknowingly to the ObjectManager because the delegation implementation is nestled nicely within ObjectReferenceFactory.

Listing 3.20 shows the pattern in action. For brevity's sake, snippets of code are presented that are not part of the same lineage of execution. These are noted where applicable. Finally, Figure 3.6 on page 145 shows the class diagram for the bridge example.

> **TIP** If you wanted more rigid error handling, you could cause findObject to throw an ObjectNotFoundException exception. Because it would be a *caught* exception, callers of findObject would be forced to address that scenario, making their code more robust.

Remarks

The Bridge pattern is very useful in frameworks. Loose coupling between the abstraction hierarchy and an implementation hierarchy provides high degrees of separation, which can increase the longevity of a system as new technologies and their implementations are weaned into a system. This separation facilitates extensibility by allowing either hierarchy to change and evolve independently. Delegation details about implementation objects can be well hidden from refined subclasses within the abstraction hierarchy. This bodes well for framework developers who want to code classes quickly, knowing that implementations for important functionality already exists or that refined implementations can be provided to suit their needs.

Listing 3.19 JNDIObjectFinder class definition.

```
// JNDIObjectFinder.java
import javax.naming.*;
import java.util.*;

public class JNDIObjectFinder implements ObjectFinderImpl {

    Context context;

    // This object would be properly instantiated
    // before being set to ObjectReferenceFactory
    public JNDIObjectFinder(String url)
    {
        // Initialize the context for the url so we can
        // do lookups on the context.

        Hashtable env = new Hashtable(11);
        env.put(Context.INITIAL_CONTEXT_FACTORY,
                "com.sun.jndi.fscontext.RefFSContextFactory");
        env.put(Context.PROVIDER_URL,url);
        try {
            context = new InitialContext(env);
        } catch(NamingException e) {
        }
    }

    public Object findObjectImpl(String name)
    {
        try {
            // Look up the object name within the JNDI context
            Object obj = (Object)context.lookup(name);
            return obj;
        } catch (Exception e) { return null; }
    }

}
```

Builder

The Builder pattern [Gamma et al., 1995] separates the construction process of
a complex object from its representation. This allows the same construction
process to be used against different representations, thereby reducing the
amount of code you would change in order to add new class representations.
Because the same construction process is used, additional representation
objects called *builders* can be added to your system.

Listing 3.20 Example of bridged abstractions in action.

```
// The following section of code would occur
// in some initialization section of your application
//***********************************************************

// This value could originate anywhere and could
// be one of the three types we assume in this
// segment
String theFinder = "RMI";

if(theFinder.equals("RMI"))
   ObjectReferenceFactory.setObjectFinder(new
                           RMIObjectFinder("localhost"));
if(theFinder.equals("SER"))
   ObjectReferenceFactory.setObjectFinder(new
                           SERObjectFinder());
if(theFinder.equals("JNDI"))
ObjectReferenceFactory.setObjectFinder(new
                           JNDIObjectFinder());

// Now the ObjectFinder policy has been set throughout
// the application.
//***********************************************************

// Here we've chosen our SerialObjectArchiver as the
// storage policy
ObjectManager.setObjectArchiver(new SerialObjectArchiver());

//***********************************************************
ObjectManager objectManager = new ObjectManager();

// Assumes an object "object1" exists somewhere and can
// be found by the current ObjectFinder
Object object1 = objectManager.findObject("object1");

// Maybe do some stuff with object1

// Now store our object with the current
// ObjectArchiver
objectManager.storeObject(object1,1999);
```

Discussion

The objects within the Builder pattern play four roles: Builder, Concrete-Builder, Director, Product. The Builder role is represented as an abstract class from which ConcreteBuilders can be derived to contain a construction process for assembling parts of the Product object. The ConcreteBuilder rep-

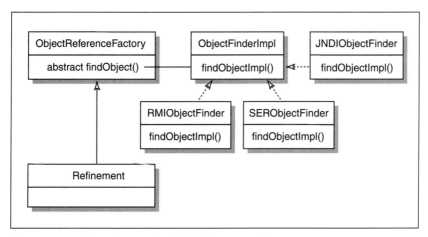

Figure 3.6   Class diagram for the bridge example.

resents the actual implementation class. The Product is a representation from which the desired Product object will be created. The Director object delegates the assembly of complex objects to the builder abstraction for acquiring assembled complex objects. Figure 3.7 shows a simple diagram of the Builder pattern.

Example

You are no doubt familiar with the HyperText Markup Language (HTML), the set of tags used to create Web pages. An evolution of HTML, called XML (eXtensible Markup Language) is expected to usurp HTML to become the document and object display language of choice. XML, like HTML, is based on tagged phrases that format data for the Web.

You can define your own XML tags capable of defining any type of object. For this example, we'll define a tag called <OBJECT>. Interpretation of this tag and its parameters depends on the particular XML renderer and what it recognizes and can display. For example,

```
<OBJECT objectType="Java/Widget" ClassName="myWidget.class"
param1=value1 ~>
```

Let's say you are writing a simple XML viewer that recognizes and displays various types of <OBJECT> tags. For each <OBJECT> type that your XML-Reader class understands, there is an appropriate class that can interpret the <OBJECT> tag and return an XMLObjectView object that is used to render that XML object inside the viewer. Regardless of what the specific <OBJECT> tag

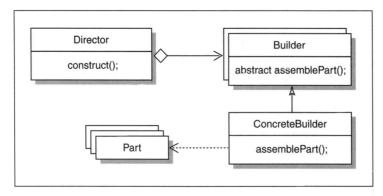

Figure 3.7 Builder pattern diagram.

represents, all XML objects are represented by XMLObjectView in your XML-Reader. Therefore, XMLObjectView is an abstraction that is represented as an abstract class. Listing 3.21 defines the XMLObjectView class that will be used to render a given <OBJECT> tag for display by an XMLReader.

Each XMLObjectView object receives an XMLTag object from which it extracts the appropriate parameters and renders the object defined by XML-Tag. Specific subclasses of XMLObjectView will only receive objects of type XMLTag that they are designed to decode and for which they will provide appropriate views. Listing 3.22 shows the class definition for the XMLTag.

Listings 3.23 and 3.24 show two subclass implementations of XMLTag. Each subclass implements the abstract method getObjectView() by instantiating the

Listing 3.21 XMLObjectView class definition.

```java
// XMLObjectView.java
import java.awt.*;

public abstract class XMLObjectView {

    Component view;

    public Component getViewComponent()
    {
        return view;
    }

    public abstract void renderView(XMLTag tag);

}
```

Listing 3.22 XMLTag class definition.

```
// XMLTag.java
import java.util.*;

public abstract class XMLTag {

    private Hashtable parameters = new Hashtable();

    /**
     * This is a Factory method that chooses an appropriate
     * XMLTag subclass. Realistically, you would want
     * this somewhere else, but for our example, we placed it
     * here.
     **/
    public static XMLTag createXMLTag(String tagString)
    {
        // Create a Hashtable representing the
        // key value pairs in the XML tagString
        Hashtable params = new Hashtable();

        // XML parsing would go here.

        // Get the type of object this tagString
        // represents
        String objectType = (String)params.get("objectType");

        XMLTag xmlTag = null;

        if(objectType.equals("OBJECT/WIDGET")) {
            xmlTag = new XMLWidgetTag();
        }
        if(objectType.equals("OBJECT/WIDGET")) {
            xmlTag = new XMLImageTag();
        }
        xmlTag.setParameters(params);

        return xmlTag;
    }

    // This method will return the subclass of XMLObjectView
    // that is appropriate for the subclass of XMLTag represented
    // by this object.
    public abstract XMLObjectView getObjectView();

    public void setParameters(Hashtable params)
    {
        parameters = params;
    }
```

continues

Listing 3.22   XMLTag class definition. *(Continued)*

```
    public Hashtable getParameters()
    {
        return parameters;
    }

    // This method returns the value associated with
    // a key represented in the XML tag string.
    public String getValue(String key)
    throws KeyNotFoundException
    {
        try {
            String value = (String)parameters.get(key);
            return value;
        } catch (Exception e) {
            throw new KeyNotFoundException();
        }
    }
}

class KeyNotFoundException extends Exception {

}
```

correct XMLObjectView for its type, passing itself (XMLTag) to the renderView() method and finally returning the complete XMLObjectView object.

Listings 3.25 and 3.26 are the subclass implementations of XMLObjectView that correspond to each of the XMLWidgetObjectView and XMLImageObjectView subclasses for XMLTag.

Listing 3.23   XMLWidgetTag class definition.

```
// XMLWidgetTag.java

public class XMLWidgetTag extends XMLTag {

    public XMLObjectView getObjectView()
    {
        XMLWidgetObjectView view = new XMLWidgetObjectView();
        view.renderView(this);
        return view;
    }

}
```

Listing 3.24 XMLImageTag class definition.

```
// XMLImageTag.java

public class XMLImageTag extends XMLTag {

    public XMLObjectView getObjectView()
    {
        XMLImageObjectView view = new XMLImageObjectView();
        view.renderView(this);
        return view;
    }

}
```

The XMLReader class will direct the process of reading and displaying the XML text document. For each <OBJECT> tag appearing in the XML text, the appropriate XMLObjectView builder will be used to decipher the XMLTag and provide a constructed Component object that is suitable for display on-screen. Listing 3.27 shows the class definition for the XMLReader object.

Notice in the code for XMLReader that it only knows about the XML abstraction classes, not the actual implementations for the various XMLTags that may be encountered. Knowledge about which subclass to provide is encapsulated in the Factory Method createXMLTag() within XMLTag. It is a

Listing 3.25 XMLWidgetObjectView class definition.

```
// XMLWidgetObjectView.java

public class XMLWidgetObjectView extends XMLObjectView {

    public void renderView(XMLTag widgetTag)
    {
        // Code here would parse key value pairs
        // in XMLWidgetTag and render it correctly
        // on component. The key names will be known
        // to both XMLWidgetTag and XMLWidgetObjectView
        // so the keys may vary from object type to type.

    }

}
```

Listing 3.26 XMLImageObjectView class definition.

```
// XMLImageObjectView.java

public class XMLImageObjectView extends XMLObjectView {

    public void renderView(XMLTag widgetTag)
    {
        // Code here would parse key value pairs
        // in XMLImageTag and render it correctly
        // on component. The key names will be known
        // to both XMLImageTag and XMLImageObjectView
        // so the keys may vary from object type to type.
    }

}
```

public static method that returns an appropriate implementation of XMLTag based on knowledge about the object's type. Therefore, any extensions to the XMLReader would require altering the XMLTag class to include additional instantiations of XMLTag to service new objects.

TIP **The Bridge pattern can be useful in relieving this modification burden from XMLTag.**

The call to xmlTag.getObjectView() satisfies this requirement. It performs the construction process on XMLObjectView that is encapsulated and hidden from the request. In this example, XMLTags are, in fact, builders for their own views, XMLObjectView. Figure 3.8 shows the class diagram for our XML-Reader Builder example.

Remarks

The power of the Builder pattern is its capability to associate the appropriate subclass representation based on the same construction process. It resembles the Factory Method pattern in that calls to getObjectView return instances that are subclasses of XMLObjectView, and the details behind the class remains hidden. Factory Method will behave in the same manner, depending on the subclass of the abstraction being used. Think of the Builder pattern as a form of evolved factory whose responsibility is to assemble or build complex objects. In this example, the Builder object returned class representations of XMLTag in the form of either XMLImageTag or XMLWidgetTag, which themselves were responsible for directing the construction of their views.

Listing 3.27 XMLReader class definition.

```java
// XMLReader.java
import java.util.*;

public class XMLReader {

    // Contains all tags in XML document
    Vector xmlTags = new Vector();

    // Contains all <OBJECT> tags in XML document
    Vector objectTagStrings = new Vector();

    // Contains all XMLTag objects
    Vector objectTags = new Vector();

    // Contains all rendered Component views for
    // our object tags.
    Vector objectViews = new Vector();

    // This method assumes the XML file has been
    // read into a String for scanning.
    public void parseDocument(String xmlDoc)
    {
        tokenizeTags(xmlDoc);
        renderObjects();
    }

    public void tokenizeTags(String xmlData)
    {
        // Scan the xmlData string and place
        // all tokenized <OBJECT> tags into objectTagStrings
    }

    public void renderObjects()
    {
        for(int x=0;x<objectTagStrings.size();x++) {
            // Depending on the nature of the tag string
            // we will get back an appropriate XMLTag class
            // suitable for the appropriate viewer.
            XMLTag xmlTag = XMLTag.
                createXMLTag((String)objectTagStrings.elementAt(x));

            // Add this xmlTag object to our internal list of
            //  XMLTag objects.
            objectTags.addElement(xmlTag);
            XMLObjectView objectView = xmlTag.getObjectView();
            objectViews.addElement(objectView);
```

continues

Listing 3.27   XMLReader class definition. *(Continued)*

```
                    // How the actual rendering happens is non-specific
                    // I could simply add the Component view objects to
                    // my XMLReader's display Panel object if I chose.
            }

      }
}
```

Observer

The Observer pattern [Gamma et al., 1995] defines a relationship between two objects—that is, the observer and the observed. This pattern is quite intuitive, and its usefulness is widespread. Basically, an object whose state is being observed by Observer objects is said to be *observable*. Changes in state to the observable object cause change notification messages to be sent to any and all Observer objects.

Discussion

In Java 2, there is an interface and class used to represent the basic model-view paradigm: Observer and Observable. Objects wishing to have their state changes monitored would extend the Observable class. Objects wishing to observe the Observable objects would implement the corresponding Observer interface. Combined, this interface/class combination allows for a flexible, extensible, and scalable implementation of this pattern. Listing 3.28 shows the Java code for the Observer interface and the Observable class.

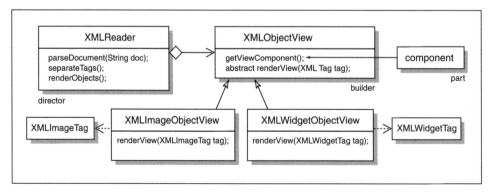

Figure 3.8   Class diagram and object relationships for XML example.

Listing 3.28 Observer Interface and Observable class.

```
// Observer.java

public interface Observer {
    public void update(Observable obs, Object obj);
}

// Observable.java

public class Observable {
    protected void clearChanged();
    public int countObservers();
    public void deleteObserver(Observer o);
    public void deleteObservers();
    public boolean hasChanged();
    public void notifyObservers();
    public void notifyObservers(Object arg);
    protected void setChanged();
    public void addObserver(Observer observer);
}
```

NOTE This type of pattern is used as the primary basis for the JavaBean event model. Adaptations on the Observer interface and Observable class are used to link change notifications between JavaBean components. Chapter 4, "JavaBean Components" takes a look at this in more detail.

Example

Consider a basic clock program that declares a class called ClockModel to hold the numeric information of the current time. Another class called ClockView is declared that is responsible for displaying the numeric time information. Listings 3.29 and 3.30 show the code for ClockModel and ClockView.

The following snippet registers a ClockView as an observer of a particular ClockModel.

```
ClockView clockView = new AnalogClockView();
ClockModel clockModel = new ClockModel();

clockModel.addObserver(clockView);
```

Whenever clockModel.setTime() is invoked, all subsequent Observers (in this case clockView) are notified by calling their corresponding updateClock()

Listing 3.29 ClockModel class definition.

```java
// ClockModel.java
import java.util.*;

public class ClockModel extends Observable {
    int hours;
    int minutes;
    int seconds;
    Vector observers = new Vector();

    public void setTime(int h,int m,int s)
    {
        hours = h;
        minutes = m;
        seconds = s;
        for(int x=0;x<observers.size();x++)
            ((Observer)observers.elementAt(x)).update(this,this);
    }

    public void addObserver(Observer observer)
    {
        observers.addElement(observer);
    }

    public void removeObserver(Observer observer)
    {
        observers.removeElement(observer);
    }

    public int getHours()
    {
        return hours;
    }

    public int getMinutes()
    {
        return minutes;
    }
    public int getSeconds()
    {
        return seconds;
    }

}
```

Listing 3.30 ClockView class definition.

```
// ClockView.java
import java.util.*;

public abstract class ClockView implements Observer {

    public void update(Object obj) {
        updateClock((ClockModel)obj);
    }

    protected abstract void updateClock(ClockModel model);

}
```

method. The generic nature of the Observer pattern is abstracted in the Clock-View class into something more specific to clocks. Subclass implementations of the ClockView must implement the updateClock() method. This method is called (through polymorphism) through the inherited method implementation for update() in the base class ClockView. This restriction is provided to ensure that only ClockModels notify ClockViews of state changes. If an object of another type were to send a change notification to a ClockView, a ClassCastExaception would occur. Additional steps could be taken to discourage this, such as creating different interface types and following the paradigm presented by Observer and Observable. In this case, adding observers of a strict object type would only be allowed, in contrast to the example where ClockModel accepts any object of type Observer; but this is sufficient for the example.

Remarks

This simple example clearly demonstrates how Observer works. You could easily have a number of ClassView observers all observing the observable ClockModel. You can create your own declaration names and interfaces that mimic this pattern. You are not required to use the Observer and Observable interfaces bundled with Java. You could provide any meaningful name set to interfaces you create that behave in the same manner. Many interfaces within Java (some of which are discussed throughout this book) behave identically to the Observer pattern, but use interface and method names more appropriate for the context they are provided.

Within a framework, the Observer pattern addresses scalability and adaptability. Application client objects can register themselves as observers of framework-based model components. The objects can react to state changes driven from within the framework architecture in an application-dependent manner, without affecting the model or observable component of the framework or its environs.

Model/View

The Model/View pattern [*Journal of Object-Oriented Programming*, 1988] is a commonly used pattern resembling Observer, but with an implicit visual or GUI context.

Discussion

This pattern was originally called the MVC pattern, for Model View Controller when it appeared in the context of SmallTalk. The *model* represented the underlying data that the *view* subsequently used for rendering to the screen (like ClockModel in the Observer pattern example). The *controller* implemented the mechanics behind the view, that is, the interactions with a view that would affect the values contained in the model. For example, dragging the arms on an analog clock is an interaction with the view that would change the time. There have been many debates and discussions on this particular pattern. It is often asserted that the controller and view are so closely bound that they seldom, if at all, vary independently from one another. Therefore, they should be viewed collectively as one unit: *the view*. Hence, MVC pattern is often referred to as MV or Model/View or Modified MVC. This book refers to it simply as Model/View.

Example

I intentionally presented the ClockModel and ClockView classes in Observer to show how similar Observer and Model/View are in nature. Observer and Observable do not imply the presence of a visual component, whereas MV implies that a view exists.

The Observer pattern made a ClockView an observer of a ClockModel. Realistically, there could be many such views. Suppose you have two view implementations of the ClockView. Listings 3.31 and 3.32 show implementations of ClockView, one for each type of clock.

Given the classes AnalogClockView and DigitalClockView, you can represent ClockModel objects in two distinctly different ways. To attach each view to a single model, you would do something like the following code snippet depicts.

```
ClockModel clockModel = new ClockModel();

ClockView analogView = new AnalogClockView();
ClockVIew digitalView = new DigitalClockView();
```

Listing 3.31 AnalogClockView class definition.

```
// AnalogClockView.java

public class AnalogClockView extends ClockView {

    public void updateClock(ClockModel model)
    {
        // Draw an analog clock based on values in model
    }

}
```

```
clockModel.addObserver(analogView);
clockModel.addObserver(digitalView);
```

Remarks

If you wanted to conceal the fact that an Observer interface underlies the Model/View, you could wrap the Observable methods addObserver() inside other methods such as addClockView(). Then you could only expose the fully clock-based API if you wanted to. This simply means that you can tailor the naming convention used to indicate the special nature of the implementation. For example:

```
clockModel.addClockObserver(analogView);
```

Linking the Observer and Model/View patterns in the example is important. You could implement the Model/View example without the underlying

Listing 3.32 DigitalClockView class definition.

```
// DigitalClockView.java

public class DigitalClockView extends ClockView {

    public void updateClock(ClockModel model)
    {
        // Draw a digital clock based on values in model
    }

}
```

Observer pattern, and any subsequent changes in the ClockModel would not cause the appropriate views to be notified; hence, they wouldn't change. This may be appropriate for some objects, but not for clocks!

Iterator

The Iterator[pattern [Gamma et al., 1995] defines a method for iterating through a collection of objects without knowing the details of how objects within the collection are actually stored. Iterators were introduced in Chapter 2, "Java Framework Design," in the discussion about collections and organizational models.

Discussion

If your framework adopts an organizational model and exposes it to the developer, it is useful for the developer to take advantage of iterators provided for your framework collection classes. At its simplest level, the iterator cycles through each object in a collection. Remember, a collection may be a vastly complex structure with various levels of object redundancy. In cases like this, you might choose to provide an iteration policy that presents the objects in the collection in a particular, but meaningful order. For example, objects stored in a Hashtable are paired as key-value; that is, one object serves as the key to retrieve the other. The Hashtable collection does not define an order to the keys or values that may be returned by the Hashtable. Consider the following code segment:

```
HashSet hashSet = new HashSet();

hashSet.add(new Integer(3));
hashSet.add(new Integer(1));
hashSet.add(new Integer(2));

Iterator iterator = hashSet.iterator();

while(iterator.hasNext()) {
    Object obj = iterator.next();
    System.out.println(obj);
}
```

This code snippet would not display the objects added to the hashset in any guaranteed order. It may be, in fact, that the order is predictably the sequence in which the objects were added to the hashset; but it is strictly warned that any particular ordering imposed by the implementation of HashSet is subject to change without notice. Do not assume that the hashset is in any particular order. Iterator objects exist to guarantee a particular ordering of a collection of objects. Any given set of ordered objects can be iterated in different ways; ascending or descending are just two examples.

TreeSet implements the OrderSet interface, which is part of the Java Collections Framework discussed in Chapter 2. The following code demonstrates the use of an iterator with a well-defined policy.

```
TreeSet treeSet = new TreeSet();

treeSet.add(new Integer(3));
treeSet.add(new Integer(1));
treeSet.add(new Integer(2));

Iterator iterator = treeSet.iterator();

while(iterator.hasNext()) {
    Object obj = iterator.next();
    System.out.println(obj);
}
```

This code snippet displays the Integer objects 1, 2, 3, in that order, because the default Comparator object assures that objects added to the collection fall into the proper ordered organization using the default, or natural, ordering, which is ascending. You can provide your own Comparator object to indicate a different iteration order. Only collections that impose a strict ordering require that a Comparator object be used to judge the order of two given objects. The iterator in this case simply iterates over the already ordered set of objects. The Iterator interface in Java is defined in Listing 3.33.

Example

Suppose you wanted to store information about people in a given collection. You could create a class and call it Person, as in Listing 3.34.

Listing 3.33   Iterator interface definition.

```
public interface Iterator {

    public boolean hasNext();
    public Object next() throws NoSuchElementException;

    public void remove() throws UnsupportedOperationException,
        IllegalStateException;
}
```

Listing 3.34 Person class definition.

```
// Person.java

public class Person {

    String name = "";
    int age;

    public Person(String name, int age)
    {
        this.name = name;
        this.age = age;
    }

    public String getName()
    {
        return name;
    }

    public int getAge()
    {
        return age;
    }

}
```

You could then create and add Persons to a given collection. To do so, you would define a new collection class called AgeOrderedCollection that is specifically designed to hold Person objects. AgeOrderedCollection would return an iterator that presents the Person objects ordered from youngest to oldest. Listing 3.35 shows this AgeOrderedCollection class. Because Vector provides a facility for indexing objects directly, this is a convenient way to store objects; it is subclassed in this example.

Listing 3.36 shows the Iterator that goes with AgeOrderedCollection.

Remarks

In this example, the order placement of objects was performed during add operations on the collection. The iterator was really a generic indexing class that provided a reliable protocol over the collection of Person objects. As another consideration, you could retain the ordering in which Person objects were added to your collection by delegating the sorting of the Person objects in a location other than the add operation. In fact, you could write another iterator object that duplicates the collection it receives and orders the duplicate appropriately. In this case, you could retain one object ordering and expose

Listing 3.35 AgeOrderedCollection class definition.

```java
// AgeOrderedCollection.java
import java.util.*;

public class AgeOrderedCollection extends Vector {

    public AgeOrderedCollection(int size)
    {
        super(size);
    }

    public void add(Person person)
    {
        int x=0;
        // Use insertion sort to find the ordered
        // slot for object person
        for(x=0;x<size();x++) {
            Person p = (Person)elementAt(x);
            if(p.getAge()>person.getAge()) break;
        }
        super.add(x,person);
    }

    public Iterator iterator()
    {
        return new AgeOrderedIterator(this);
    }
}
```

another. Through interfaces other than those provided by the Collections Framework, your classes could implement other similar methods, such as getYoungFirst(), which could return an ascending iterator. Someone else might use getSalaryOrdered() and receive a different iterator that provides a different ordered and duplicated version of the same collection. These techniques, however, are not recommended for use in frameworks because they breach the standard interfaces provided by the Java 2 collection mechanisms. You must evaluate the impact and decide for yourself.

Summary

This chapter introduced a number of common and useful patterns that will come in handy when you begin thinking about architectures for your frameworks. The Java code in the examples for each pattern showed how the pro-

Listing 3.36 AgeOrderedIterator class definition.

```java
// AgeOrderedIterator.java
import java.util.*;

public class AgeOrderedIterator implements Iterator {

    Object elements[];

    int index = 0;
    int size  = 0;

    public AgeOrderedIterator(AgeOrderedCollection persons)
    {
        elements = persons.toArray();
        size = elements.length;
    }

    public boolean hasNext()
    {
        if(index<(size)) return true;
        else return false;
    }

    public Object next()
    throws NoSuchElementException
    {
        if(index>=size || index <0) throw new NoSuchElementException();
        return elements[index++];
    }

    public void remove()
    {
        // Implementation not pertinent for our example
    }
}
```

gramming language embodies the concept of the pattern. By now, the value of patterns should be evident.

The concept of scale is reflective in the scale of patterns themselves. The granularity of patterns falls into a medium where they're neither too specific nor too generic or simple. Similar to frameworks in general, patterns solve a certain type of problem. The problem is not necessarily specific, but has only a few elegant and reusable solutions. The pattern designed for a particular problem fits the mold and should appeal to developers looking to solve that type of problem. Likewise, the framework is a scale of magnitude higher than a pattern. A framework could contain many specialized patterns that collectively provide a reusable solution to a more complex or involved problem domain (one that the functions of the framework address). The problems that frameworks best suit can vary in their granularity and specificity, and this trait sets them at a higher level than patterns.

Other than utilizing patterns, frameworks can benefit from adopting a universal component model paradigm. The combination of a component model and patterns makes developing frameworks easier in that both patterns and components of the JavaBean variety address reusable problems and object models respectively. The next chapter explores the JavaBean component model in Java and highlights some key issues in using them for frameworks.

References

Alexander, Christopher. *A Pattern Language: Towns, Buildings, Construction.* Oxford University Press, 1977.

Gamma, Erich et. al. *Design Patterns: Elements of Reusable Object-Oriented Software.* Reading, Massachusetts: Addison Wesley, 1995.

Grand, Mark. *Patterns in Java.* New York: John Wiley & Sons, 1998.

Johnson, Ralph. Documenting Frameworks using Patterns. Department of Computer Science, University of Illinois, 1991.

The Model/View pattern *Journal of Object-Oriented Programming*, 1(3):26-49, August/September,1988.

Schmidt, Douglas C., Ralph E. Johnson, Mohamed Fayad. *Software Patterns, Communications of the ACM*, Special Issue on Patterns and Pattern Languages, Vol. 39, No. 10, October 1996.

Patterns Home Page, http://hillside.net/patterns/patterns.html

CHAPTER

4

JavaBean Components

In the fast-paced development world of Java, in which millions of developers are designing and creating new solutions to problems, there is a need for a simple, standardized model for building reusable objects. This chapter focuses on JavaBeans, Java's model for building components. It describes the characteristics of components, presents a brief tutorial on JavaBeans, and uses an example of building a television and remote control using the concepts presented in this chapter.

A *component* is an object with defined inputs and outputs; it can be individually tested and used with other simple components to provide a complex solution. It is similar to the black boxes referred to in Chapter 1, "Framework Concepts." When a software component is well designed and simple to manage, it makes the testing process easier. Because these component black boxes can be tested individually and have well-defined inputs and outputs, developers should not have to worry about the logic of the internals of each component when they are testing a complex enterprise application. Instead, they can focus testing on *interactions* with each component. Using a standardized method for building components increases an object's reusability, scalability, and extensibility.

NOTE Sun Microsystems and Java engineers refer to JavaBeans as *components*, and to JavaBeans as a *component model.* This means that the

JavaBeans spec offers a standard object-oriented software component architecture for building object modules with a standard API. Throughout this chapter, JavaBeans are referred to as components and adopt this component model. Keep this definition in mind.

TIP Those of you who are familiar with the television series *Star Trek, The Next Generation* will recognize the similarity between components and the Borg. The Borg is a group of cyber-human drones who work together in a parallel, distributed network to assimilate other species. Each Borg drone is made up of simple, smaller components that work together. Each drone also acts as a component working with drones to form a network of knowledge.

As the software engineering process matures, more developers are building component-based systems. In the fast-paced world of development, it is necessary to have an arsenal of well-tested and proven modules to use in software applications. Component development grows a reusable code base, which can be implemented to develop complex frameworks.

Software components are the building blocks of frameworks; they can be used to achieve the characteristics of good frameworks. But adopting a component model is important whether you're building a framework or not, and therefore, the framework designer is well advised to learn this information thoroughly. So before discussing why and how components are useful for framework or toolkit development, let's study the details behind JavaBeans.

Most things around us behave like black boxes.

What Is a JavaBean?

The Sun Microsystems JavaBeans specification is Java's answer to software components. It defines JavaBeans as "a reusable software component that can be manipulated visually in a builder tool." JavaBeans are reusable, platform-independent objects, commonly referred to as "beans."

A bean can be considered a "self-describing" object. One of a bean's descriptive characteristics is that it allows introspection; that is, other objects and builder tools can see the ins, outs, and attributes of beans. Although introspection does not distinguish beans from other Java classes, the JavaBeans API provides descriptor classes that allow visual builder tools to easily use and manipulate beans. The basic characteristics of beans are events and properties. Different beans can listen for and trigger certain events, based on certain inputs, enabling beans to communicate and collaborate. At the same time, beans have properties that can be visible to and changeable by other beans and objects, making them easily customizable. Beans also have persistence, which means the complete state of a bean can be saved at runtime to an output

Beans are components, too!

stream and be re-created at any time. This is especially powerful when a developer is using many JavaBean components to build a larger application in a visual development tool. The state of each bean can be saved in the software development cycle, allowing developers to change the interactions and property values at design time as they revise their project.

Developers use software builder tools to create beans that work together with other beans. At the time of this writing, there were several tools on the market: Sun's BDK, Sybase's PowerJ, Borland's JBuilder, IBM's Visual Age for Java, SunSoft's Java Workshop, and Symantec's Visual Café. These tools provide developers with a visual environment in which they can see the properties and events for each bean (just like playing with the black box!). These visual builder tools let developers drag beans into their Java applications and applets and connect beans to each other.

Before exploring the technical details, let's take a look at a simple example of how beans interact. Figure 4.1 shows a television and a remote control, two objects that are made up of smaller components. The television has a display screen, an On/Off button, and channel buttons. The remote control also has an On/Off button, channel buttons, and a keypad for entering channel numbers. The components on the television and remote control in this example represent JavaBeans. These components are objects that can have properties. Some components generate events when pressed; for example, a red light could illuminate when you press the on button. The on state is a property of

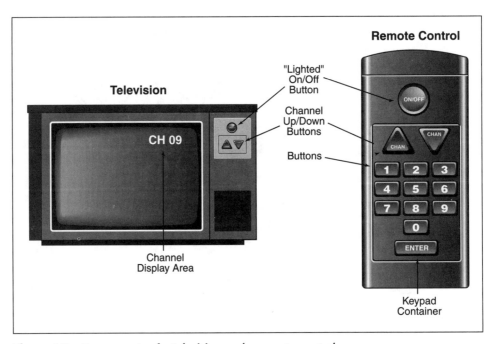

Figure 4.1   Components of a television and a remote control.

the remote control. The On/Off button generates an event to change the on property of the television. Keying in a channel on the remote control sends an event to the television to change the channel. These are simple, but basic, characteristics of remote controls and televisions.

As just stated, some of the components on the remote control can also exist on the television. For example, the On/Off button on the remote control can be used as the On/Off button on the television. As long as the button does what buttons usually do, an engineer could build the television and the remote control with some of the same parts.

At the same time, the remote control and the television can be built as components that are utilized by other things. With a little customization, the keypad in the remote control could be used as a component of a calculator. Components are customized easily by editing their properties and actions.

If these concepts sound simple, great! Components are, and should be, inherently simple. The TV-remote control example demonstrates the basics of components and how they work together. This example also can be built with JavaBeans. We'll return to the TV-remote control example later to develop simple JavaBeans components as the chapter unfolds.

JavaBean Basics

To repeat, the two primary characteristics of JavaBeans are:

- *Properties.* The changeable attributes of a bean. Beans contain properties.
- *Events.* The "triggers" that are generated by beans as a response to a certain action. Beans can both generate and listen for events.

A standard API is used to specify JavaBean properties and events. There are different types of properties and events, and Java has standard naming conventions associated with developing beans. The following sections define the types of properties and events, and show the naming conventions and coding standards for creating beans.

Properties

Properties determine the tangible characteristics of a JavaBean. In the television and the remote control example, the on state of the television can be defined by a property. Changes in properties can affect the state and the behavior of beans, depending on the property type.

There are four types of properties: *simple, bound, indexed,* and *constrained.*

Simple. Simple properties are those properties with simple data types. For example, a speedRate property on a speedometer can have an integer value, and a displayLabel property can have a string value.

Bound. Bound properties notify other objects when their values change. A property in one bean can be bound to a property in another bean. For example, the remote control's on property can be bound to the television's on property, if you want to notify the remote control that the television is on. Changes to bound properties generate propertyChange events. These are discussed in the next section.

Indexed. Indexed properties are an array of possible values. For example, a stateName property could have an array of the 50 states of America.

Constrained. Constrained properties are similar to bound properties. The difference is that constrained properties notify objects of impending changes. These properties give the notified object the power to veto the change. For example, if someone using the remote control tried to change the television station's channel number to a bogus channel (say 999999), the television object could overrule the property change; in this case, the television's "channel" property would not change.

Properties of beans are visible and settable by other beans and objects. When a bound or constrained property of a bean is set, the bean generates an event.

Events and Listeners

One of the greatest results of the evolution of Java from its original to current version (Java 1.1. and later) is the *event model*. Java's event model allows developers to create objects that generate and listen to specific types of events. An object that generates events is typically referred to as an *event source*, and an object that wants to listen for events is called an *event listener*. Event listeners must register to receive events from an event source. When an event source generates, or "fires," an event, the event listener is notified. Beans use this event model to generate and respond to events. [Flanagan, 1997]

NOTE Java's event model is the framework that drives JavaBeans and gives JavaBeans its power. Understanding this framework is crucial for understanding and developing JavaBeans. Once beans are well-tested and deployed, a designer only needs to concentrate on the beans' event connections to guarantee correct functionality. This gives the designer the opportunity to treat beans as black boxes!

Beans interact with each other by triggering, or "firing," events. Beans implement listener interfaces that correspond to the specific events fired by other beans. For example, beans with bound properties send Property-ChangeEvents. Another bean must implement the PropertyChangeListener interface in order to listen for and register and deregister to receive these events. Beans with constrained properties send VetoableChangeEvents. In order for another bean to listen for an impending property change, it must implement the VetoableChangeListener interface for the easy registration and deregistration of events.

Coding Principles and Conventions

Visual development programs use introspection to determine the properties and events that beans support. In order to cooperate with these programs, you must use classes in the java.beans package and the naming conventions defined in the following section.

Using these naming conventions enables beans to talk to each other, and allows for quick and easy development and "plug and play" with various builder tools.

Getter and Setter Methods

All properties are accessed via getter and setter methods. *Getter methods* retrieve the value of a property. The names of getter methods begin with "get" and end with the property name:

```
public <PropertyType> get<PropertyName>();
```

Setter methods set the value of a property. The names of setter methods begin with "set" and end with the property name:

```
public void set<PropertyName>(<PropertyType> value);
```

When the type is Boolean, the getter method could look like:

```
public boolean is<PropertyName>();
```

When using indexed properties (arrays), the developer not only can specify the getting and setting of the entire array with getter and setter methods, but can also get and set elements of the indexed property, as follows:

```
public <PropertyType> get<PropertyName>(int index);
public void set<PropertyName>(int index, <PropertyType> value);
```

With constrained properties, the method call for the getter is the same as in regular properties, but the setter has to throw a PropertyVetoException:

```
public void set<PropertyName>(<PropertyType> value) throws
  PropertyVetoException
```

Table 4.1 lists getter and setter methods, with examples.

Table 4.1 Getter and Setter Methods for Property Types

PROPERTY TYPE	GETTER AND SETTER METHODS	EXAMPLE
Simple properties	`public <type> get<name>();` `public void set<name>(<type>value);`	`public int getNumber();` `public void setNumber(int value);`
Boolean properties	**Same as simple, but getter could be** `public boolean is<name>();`	`public boolean isOn()` `public void setOn(boolean value);`
Bound	**Same as simple**	`public int getName();` `public void setName(String value);`
Constrained	`public <type> get<name>();` `public void set<name>(<type> value)throws PropertyVetoException`	`public int getChannel();` `public void setChannel(int value) throws PropertyVetoException`
Indexed	**Same as simple, but could set and get indexed elements:** `Public <type> get<name>(int index>` `Public void set<name>(int index, <type> value>);`	`Public String[] getStates(); Public void setStates(String[] states); public String getStates(int index); public void setStates(int index, String statename);`

Event Handling and Registration

As mentioned previously, property changes generate events. A JavaBean with bound properties generates a PropertyChangeEvent. If beans want to know about the property change to be able to listen to this event, they must be able to register and unregister as a listener.

For bound properties, the bean implementing the property must supply listener methods, so that other beans or objects can register to listen. The bean implementing the property must use this naming convention:

```
public void addPropertyChangeListener(PropertyChangeListener pcl);
public void removePropertyChangeListener(PropertyChangeListener pcl);
```

A JavaBean with constrained properties generates a VetoableChangeEvent. Similar to bound properties, other beans that want to know about the property changes must listen. The event registration methods for constrained properties are:

```
public void addVetoAbleChangeListener(VetoableChangeListener vcl);
public void removeVetoableChangeListener(VetoableChangeListener vcl);
```

A bean could also trigger a customized event for a specific property. In order to do this, the bean must register and deregister for the events in the same manner, and there must be a listener method that handles the event when an object triggers the customized event. The registration and deregistration methods are as follows, where *<PropertyName>* is the name of the property:

```
public void add<PropertyName>Listener(<PropertyName>Listener vcl);
public void remove<PropertyName>Listener(<PropertyName>Listener vcl);
```

For a customized event, the object handling the event must have a method that handles <PropertyName>Event, as follows:

```
public void <methodName>(<PropertyName>Event e);
```

Rules for registering and deregistering a bean are summarized in Table 4.2.

Helper Classes Naming Conventions

Other so-called helper classes can be associated with a bean. Some of these classes are BeanInfo, Customizer, and BeanDescriptor. When a class is associated with a bean, it must be named <Beanname><RestofClassName>. For example, if I am creating a BeanInfo class for the Television bean, the class should be named TelevisionBeanInfo. This is discussed later on in the chapter in more detail.

Table 4.2 Event Handling and Registration

EVENT TYPE	REGISTRATION AND DEREGISTRATION
PropertyChangeEvent (for bound properties)	```Public void addPropertyChangeListener (PropertyChangeListener pcl); Public void removePropertyChangeListener (PropertyChangeListener pcl);```
VetoableChangeEvent (for constrained properties)	```Public void addVetoableChangeListener (VetoableChangeListener vcl); Public void removeVetoableChangeListener (VetoableChangeListener vcl);```
<Custom>Event	```Public void add<Custom>Listener (<Custom>Listener cl); Public void remove<Custom>Listener (<Custom>Listener cl);``` **Also:** A <Custom>Listener interface or class must contain a method that handles the custom event with a method in the following syntax: ```Public void <methodName>(<CustomEvent> ce);```

Packaging Beans

To enable beans for use in a visual design environment, they need to be *packaged*. The Java Development Kit (JDK) comes with a jar packager that packages beans into a Java archive, or *jar file*. A jar file can contain beans, images, and other files.

To specify which classes in the jar file are actually beans, the developer creates a *manifest file* similar to the following:

```
Name: beandemo/Television.class
JavaBean: True

Name: beandemo/RemoteControl.class
JavaBean: True

Name: beandemo/TelevisionIcon.gif
```

This file is then packaged with the Java classes into a MyJar.jar jar file using the following command:

```
% jar cfm MyJar.jar manifest.mine beandemo/*.class beandemo/*.gif
```

Once this jar file is created, the bean is ready for import into a visual development environment.

TIP For more information about packaging beans, go to java.sun.com/beans.

Visual Development

JavaBeans components allow developers to create applications simply and easily using visual developer tools. For the rest of this chapter, Sun's BDK BeanBox is used as an example of how developers can use these tools to develop applications and applets.

NOTE This section briefly discusses visual development using the BeanBox that comes with Sun Microsystems' Bean Development Kit (BDK). Usage of other builder tools may vary, but they interact similarly. For more information, visit Sun's JavaBeans home page at java.sun.com/beans/.

Developing beans for a visual environment is fairly easy. Once a bean is developed, it is packaged into a jar file that identifies the component as a Java-Bean, as discussed in the last section. When the .jar file is moved into the "jars" of the BDK (in this case, c:/bdk/jars directory), it appears in the Toolbox window with the other components. Components are simply dragged and dropped from this window onto the BeanBox, where events and properties of beans can be connected easily in the visual environment. As a developer creates beans, he or she can save his or her work, because beans are serializable.

The BeanBox environment is shown in Figure 4.2. Using the BDK, it's a simple matter to drag a few objects to the Toolbox. From here you can modify the beans by altering the Properties style sheet. Using the BDK's Edit dialog, you can attach events of components to others. Good examples are listed in the directions that come with the BDK. Before you move on to the next section, play around with some of the existing components. The example that follows uses the OurButton bean, one of the components that is included in the BDK.

Advanced Features

The JavaBeans API offers classes that allow you to customize your beans in a visual environment. This section discusses JavaBeans' features of introspection and customization, along with the classes associated with each feature.

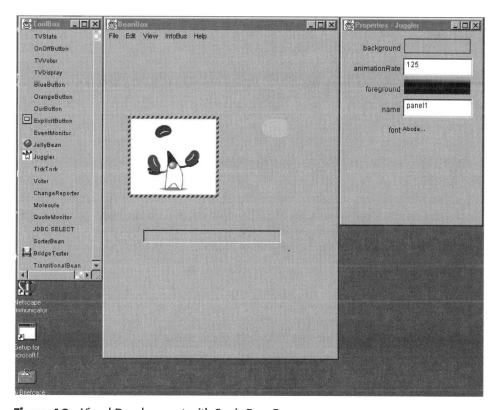

Figure 4.2 Visual Development with Sun's BeanBox.

Introspection

Developer tools use introspection to discover information about beans. The visual development kit uses the Java Reflection API (located in the java.lang .reflect package) to determine the attributes about beans at runtime. To provide more information to the visual development tool, a developer can create BeanInfo to explicitly define a bean in more detail. BeanInfo classes implement the interface java.beans.BeanInfo, or simply extend the java.beans.SimpleBeanInfo class. The bean developer then packages that BeanInfo class with the bean to provide extra information to the visual developer tool.

The developer creates a class that inherits from the java.beans.Simple-BeanInfo class to specify more information, such as descriptions of methods, properties, the class itself, and an icon for use with visual development. SimpleBeanInfo is a trivial class that implements the BeanInfo interface, and is provided so that it can be extended by the developer to provide more information to the visual development environment.

The SimpleBeanInfo class has the following syntax:

```
public class SimpleBeanInfo implements BeanInfo
{
        public BeanInfo[] getAdditionalBeanInfo();
        public BeanDescriptor[] getBeanDescriptor();
        public int getDefaultEventIndex();
        public int getDefaultPropertyIndex();
        public EventSetDescriptor[] getEventSetDescriptors();
        public Image getIcon(int iconKind);
        public MethodDescriptor[] getMethodDescriptors();
        public PropertyDescriptor[] getPropertyDescriptors();
        public Image loadImage(String resourceName);
}
```

The developer can implement one or more of the methods listed in the class (by overriding the methods) to provide more information about his or her bean. As mentioned in the "Coding Principles and Conventions" section, the name of the BeanInfo class that the developer writes is very important. The name of the BeanInfo class for the bean must be <beanclassname>BeanInfo. The syntax for naming the class for, say, the bean Television, would be class TelevisionBeanInfo.

The BeanInfo class facilitates the ease with which the component can be used, especially if the component is complex and not very intuitive. For example, the developer could write a BeanInfo class that overrides the getMethod-Descriptor() method to provide a detailed description of each method. The developer could override the getPropertyDescriptors() method to provide a more detailed description of each property. The developer could override the getBeanDescriptor() method to add a Customizer, which is discussed in the next section. This class also allows the developer to provide an icon associated with the bean by overriding the getIcon() method. The visual development tool uses the BeanInfo classes to provide more detail at design time. When developing JavaBeans, it is customary to provide this class.

Customization

Although visual development environments are usually intuitive, the Java-Beans API gives the developer the opportunity to add features to the bean builder tools as he or she uses your bean. The Customizer interface and the PropertyEditor interface are two classes in the java.beans package that let you customize the use of the bean in the visual development environment. This can provide much-needed support to designers using your bean.

The Customizer Interface

The Customizer interface lets you offer automated assistance to developers using your beans at design time. This is especially helpful if the functionality of the bean is difficult to understand. This interface creates a wizard that gives the designer step-by-step instructions for using the bean. The bean developer can create this customizer and package it with the bean. From there, the visual development environment does the rest: it utilizes the Customizer class as the developer manipulates the bean!

The Customizer interface is simple:

```
public interface Customizer
{
public abstract void addPropertyChangeListener(PropertyChangeListener);
public abstract void
            removePropertyChangeListener(PropertyChangeListener);
public abstract void setObject(Object);
}
```

The most important method in Customizer is setObject(). It is called when a designer selects the component, and acts as the "design wizard" that can give the designer step-by-step instructions.

The bean developer creates a customizer by implementing the Customizer class. As discussed in the "Coding Principles and Conventions" section, the naming scheme for the customizer is important. In order for the visual development tool to understand which bean the customizer supports, a Customizer should be named in the format <BeanName>Customizer. For example, a customizer for a RemoteControl class might be RemoteControl-Customizer.

The PropertyEditor Interface

Another arsenal in the developer's toolbox is the ability to create individual *property editors*. A property editor is a tool for changing a property's value in the visual environment at design time. For example, a property editor for a label in a builder tool's property sheet must allow the user to change the label's value. Although visual design tools come with a property sheet with default property editors for properties with simple values such as integers and Booleans, the JavaBeans API gives the bean developer the opportunity to provide new editors for complex types. For example, most tools include the option to select colors and change labels for components at design time; but some properties need special property editors. The PropertyEditorManager class allows the bean to determine, at runtime, the available property editors and the supported property types. If the bean finds that a certain necessary type is not supported by the default property editor, the bean can use a PropertyEditor class packaged with the bean. A programmer uses the PropertyEditor interface to add a property editor that supports a typed property.

To develop a property editor, you extend the PropertyEditorSupport class. It extends the PropertyEditor interface, which has the following syntax:

```
public class PropertyEditorSupport implements PropertyEditor
{
    protected PropertyEditorSupport();
    protected PropertyEditorSupport(Object source);
    public synchronized void
        addPropertyChangeListener(PropertyChangeListener l);
    public void firePropertyChange();
    public String getAsText();
    public Component getCustomEditor();
    public String getJavaInitializationString();
    public String getTags();
    public Object getValue();
    public boolean isPaintable();
    public void paintValue(Graphics g, Rectangle r);
    public synchronized
        voidremovePropertyChangeListener(PropertyChangeListener l);
    public void setAsText(String text) throws IllegalArgumentException;
    public void setValue(Object value);
    public boolean supportsCustomEditor();
}
```

Developers subclass from PropertyEditorSupport to create custom property editors, and reference this property editor by setting the PropertyDescriptor value in the bean's BeanInfo class.

TV-Remote Control Example

Now that we've gone through some fundamental principles of JavaBeans, let's expand the initial discussion of the TV-remote control example to demonstrate properties, events, and visual development. The steps in this example are: first, to determine the functionality of each element; second, design the beans at the object level; third, write the code; and finally, build a project using the beans with a visual interface.

Overview

Refer back to Figure 4.1 to review the remote control and television used in this example. The remote control has a numeric keypad, channel up/down buttons, and a light signifying the on/off state of the television. The television has an On/Off button, channel up/down buttons, a television screen, and a channel display area. (For simplicity reasons, let's just pretend that volume control is not needed—this can be added in a later exercise.) The channel display area is similar to that on most new televisions and flashes the channel number on the bottom of the screen after a channel change, then disappears after a few seconds.

Now, let's talk beans. How should the beans be designed? Let's begin by determining what properties a television and remote control could have. The remote control has two properties: lightOn and channelNumber. The lightOn property can be a Boolean, and the channelNumber can be an Int. The lightOn property can be a simple property, because it doesn't have to notify other objects of a change. The channelNumber property, on the other hand, can be a Constrained property, because the television needs to be informed of an impending change. Table 4.3 summarizes the properties of the remote control.

The television has three properties: tvOn, channelDisplay, and channelNumber. The tvOn property can be a simple Boolean, and the channelDisplay and channelNumber properties can be simple Ints. Because the television has the last word on which channel it displays, channelNumber is a bound property; that is, the remote control should not be able to veto a change. Table 4.4 summarizes the properties of the television.

Table 4.3 Properties of the Remote Control

PROPERTY	TYPE	DATA STRUCTURE
LightOn	Simple	Boolean
ChannelNumber	Constrained	Int

Table 4.4 Properties of the Television

PROPERTY	TYPE	DATA STRUCTURE
TvOn	Simple	Boolean
ChannelDisplay	Simple	Int
ChannelNumber	Bound	Int

Object Decomposition

Now that we have identified the general properties of the television and remote control, we need to break down the television and the remote control into JavaBeans components and decide which properties to give each component.

Components of the Remote Control

The remote control element can be broken into four beans, as shown in Figure 4.3:

- *OnOffButton.* The on/off switch that lights up when the television is on.
- *KeyPadBean.* The object with the numeric keypad.
- *Channel Button.* Used for incrementing the channel value.
- *Another Channel Button.* Used for decrementing the channel value. Notice that this bean can be reused for two different functions.

NOTE The remote control in this example is built with very simple components. It is possible to create one RemoteControl bean, but the purpose of this example is to demonstrate customizability. A developer could create his or her own remote control with some of the components. For example, a developer could add volume buttons to the remote control or replace the lighted On/Off button with a plain button bean. If that were the case, then the same bean could be used for the channel buttons and the On/Off button.

The events and property changes of the remote control connect to the television. Table 4.5 lists those events and properties of the remote control objects that are relevant to the TV-Remote control example.

Figure 4.3 is an inheritance diagram of the remote control components. As with Sun's BDK, a few beans are already included that could be helpful in building this remote control. Because we do not want to reinvent the wheel, the Sun's OurButton can be reused for the channel up/down buttons.

Table 4.5 Remote Control Properties and Events

OBJECT	PROPERTIES	EVENTS GENERATED
OnOffButton	On	ActionEvent (button press)
Each Channel Button	None	ActionEvent (button press)
KeyPad	Value	PropertyChangeEvent

As you can see from Figure 4.3, the KeyPad is the most complex object; it contains the buttons for entering channels, as well as a display for the channel the user is entering. Because of this, the KeyPad will handle its own events relating to the number buttons and the display. The Enter button will trigger the propertyChange event.

Components of the Television

Now, let's decide how to design the television. As shown in Figure 4.4, the television is broken down into multiple components:

- *Channel Button beans.* These are the two buttons that increment and decrement the channels on the television. You can use the same buttons as those used with the RemoteControl.

- *OnOffButton.* This is the switch that turns the television off and on. The same button used for the remote control will be used here.

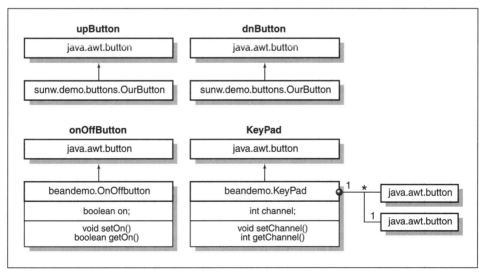

Figure 4.3 Components of the remote control.

- *TVDisplay Bean.* This bean shows the display of the television. It also displays the current channel for a few seconds after a channel change.

- *TVState Bean.* This is an invisible bean that maintains the current state of the television. This bean may be the most important, because many of the beans will interact with it as properties change.

- *TVVoter Bean.* This bean is also invisible. It handles VetoableChange events. Why do you need this bean? The channel number is a constrained property. This bean votes on issues such as vetoing a channel change.

TVVoter inherits from TVState, as shown in Figure 4.4. Why? It concerns the events that each object will throw. Because TVVoter has the last word on vetoing a channel, TVVoter can inherit the setChannel() and getChannel() methods, so that it when it accepts a channel property change, it can send a propertyChange event directly to the TVDisplay. Table 4.6 defines the objects, properties, and events generated by each bean.

The next section hooks the beans together to see how they interact.

Events and Event Listeners

Now that the components have been identified, the next step is to determine how to tie events to these beans. The general properties of the television and

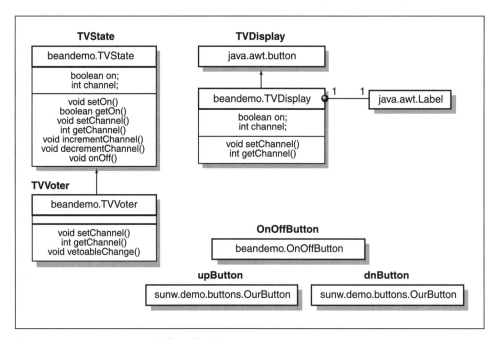

Figure 4.4 Components of the Television.

Table 4.6 Television Properties and Events

OBJECT	PROPERTIES	EVENTS GENERATED
OnOffButton	On	ActionEvent (button press)
UpButton, dnButton	None	ActionEvent (button press)
TVState	Channel On	VetoableChangeEvent (channel) PropertyChangeEvent(on)
TVVoter	Channel On (inherited)	PropertyChangeEvent(channel)
TVDisplay	Channel On	PropertyChangeEvent

remote control were determined in the last section. Now let's delve deeper into which beans generate events and which beans need to listen!

Figure 4.4 shows how these beans interact. Each event is designated with an arrow. You can link the events of the television and remote control bean components with each other. Figure 4.5 lists three types of events: propertyChangeEvents, vetoableChangeEvents, and actionEvents.

The components use the TVState object as the main interface for communication. Pressing the On/Off or the up/down buttons creates an actionPerformedEvent. To allow this event to be handled by TVState, create an onOff()

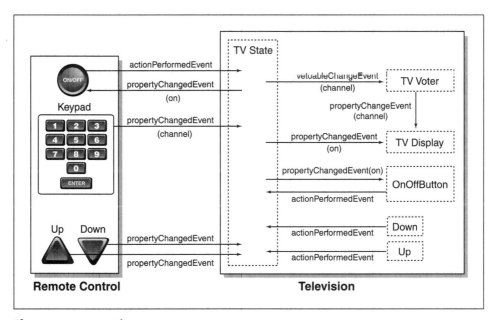

Figure 4.5 Interacting events.

method, a channelDecrement() method, and a channelIncrement() method on the TVState bean. As the user of the visual development kit uses the beans in the BDK, he or she can connect these events to the corresponding TVState method. When the TVState's channelIncrement() and channelDecrement() methods are called, the TVState will set its own channel property. When the onOff() method is called, the TVState will set its own on property.

In this example, an actionEvent (button press) on the On/Off button generates an actionEvent, which calls the TVState's onOff() method. As mentioned in the last paragraph, the TVState sets its own on property when the onOff() method is called. The TVState's on property is bound to the On/Off button's on property, so when this occurs, a propertyChange event is received by the On/Off button, and the light in the On/Off button can be turned on or off, depending on the value of on. The TVDisplay's on property is also bound to the TVState's on property. When the property changes, the display of the television should turn on or off to reflect that change.

The KeyPad bean binds its "value" (or channel) property to TVState. When this occurs, the TVState will fire a VetoablePropertyChange, which is handled by the TVVoter component. If the KeyPad has entered a correct value, the channel property will change. The TVVoter is in charge of the decision to veto or accept the property change. If the TVVoter accepts the change, it sets its own channel property to the accepted value. Because the TVDisplay's channel property is bound to the TVVoter's channel property, the TVDisplay's channel will change as the TVVoter's channel property changes. If the value entered by the KeyPad is incorrect, the TVVoter can veto the property change, and nothing will happen to the television's display.

If you can understand the event diagram in Figure 4.5, you will be able to connect the beans after writing the code. Changes in properties trigger events, which propagate the changes to the connected beans. A designer using the BDK or another visual builder tool can connect the beans in this manner to create a television and remote control application.

Creating the Beans

Let's write the first bean. The On/Off button is very simple to create because it will inherit most of its functionality from java.awt.Button. We'll build this button in a package called beandemo. This code is shown in Listing 4.1.

Notice the PropertyChangeSupport object. This object will do a lot of the work when tied to other objects. It allows other objects to listen to the events and notifies the listening objects when a property change is fired. The registration and deregistration methods for property changes are added for this reason.

NOTE Why is the actionEvent not handled in the OnOffButton class? This object is designed to let the TVState object handle the actionEvent. When the OnOffButton is hooked to the TVState, the TVState will handle the event, fire

Listing 4.1 OnOffButton class definition.

```
/******************************************************************/
/*  Filename:    OnOffButton.java                           */
/*                                                          */
/*  Description: A button for the TV & Remote Control Demo, */
/*               Lights up when the state is on!            */
/******************************************************************/
package beandemo;

import java.awt.*;
import java.beans.*;
import java.io.*;

public class OnOffButton extends Button
implements Serializable, PropertyChangeListener
{

   protected boolean on; //Our "on" property
   protected PropertyChangeSupport pcs;

   //constructor
   public OnOffButton()
   {
      //Every bean needs a default () method
      super("On/Off");
      pcs  = new PropertyChangeSupport(this);
      on   = false;
   }

   //Getter method for on property
   public boolean getOn()
   {
      return (on);
   }

   // Setter method for on property
   public void setOn(boolean o)
   {
      // Let's fire the change!
      pcs.firePropertyChange("on", new Boolean(on), new Boolean(o));
      on = o;
      changeLight();
   }

   // Method to "Turn the light on/off"
   private void changeLight()
   {
      if (on)
```

continues

Listing 4.1   OnOffButton class definition. *(Continued)*

```
        setBackground(Color.red);
    else
        setBackground(Color.gray);
}


// If this is the listener for another bean's ON property,
// then we need this propertyChange method!
public void propertyChange(PropertyChangeEvent pcEvent)
{
    String changedProperty = pcEvent.getPropertyName();
    Object newval = pcEvent.getNewValue();

    if (changedProperty.equals("on"))
    {
        Boolean b = (Boolean)newval;
        this.setOn(b.booleanValue());
    }
}

// Listener registration method
public void addPropertyChangeListener(PropertyChangeListener l)
{
    pcs.addPropertyChangeListener(l);
}

// Listener deregistration method
public void removePropertyChangeListener(PropertyChangeListener l)
{
    pcs.removePropertyChangeListener(l);
}
}
```

a property change and, because TVState's on property is bound to the OnOffButton's on property, the light will change. You should explore other ways this could be designed.

This bean is designed to interact with the TVState bean, so let's write the code for TVState. This will be a little different, because a constrained property—channel—is added to TVState. This code is found in Listing 4.2.

Notice that a couple of things are different from Listing 4.1. In addition to the PropertyChangeSupport object from the OnOffButton in Listing 4.1, a VetoableChangeSupport object, as well as registration and deregistration methods for the VetoableChangeListener, are added. This object will fire the event

Listing 4.2   TVState class definition.

```
/*****************************************************************/
/*  Filename:    TVState.java                                    */
/*                                                               */
/*  Description: This bean has state info for the TV.            */
/*****************************************************************/

package beandemo;

import java.beans.*;
import java.io.*;

public class TVState implements Serializable
{

   protected int channel; //property
   protected boolean on;  //property

   protected PropertyChangeSupport pcs;
   protected VetoableChangeSupport vcs;

   //constructor
   public TVState()
   {
      pcs = new PropertyChangeSupport(this);
      vcs = new VetoableChangeSupport(this);
      channel = 0;
      on = false;
   }

   //getter for On property
   public boolean getOn()
   {
      return (on);
   }

   //setter for On property
   public void setOn(boolean o)
   {
      if (o != on) {
         pcs.firePropertyChange("on", new Boolean(on),
               new Boolean(o));
         on = o;
      }
   }

   //getter for Channel property
   public int getChannel()
```

continues

Listing 4.2 TVState class definition. *(Continued)*

```
{
   return (channel);
}

//setter for Channel property
public void setChannel(int cn) throws PropertyVetoException
{
   vcs.fireVetoableChange("channel", new Integer(channel),
        new Integer(cn));
   // If vetoed, this next statement is not reached.
   channel = cn;
}

//increments channel..
public void incrementChannel()
{
   int newchannel  = channel + 1;
   try
   {
     setChannel(newchannel);
   }
   catch (PropertyVetoException pve)
   {
      System.out.println("Vetoed!");
   }
}

//decrements channel..

public void decrementChannel()
{
   int newchannel = channel - 1;
   try
   {
     setChannel(newchannel);
   }
   catch (PropertyVetoException pve)
   {
      System.out.println("Vetoed!");
   }
}

//onOff toggle function
public void onOff()
{
   if (on)
      setOn(false);
```

Listing 4.2 *(Continued)*

```
       else
           setOn(true);
   }

   //propertyChange registration
   public void addPropertyChangeListener(PropertyChangeListener l)
   {
       pcs.addPropertyChangeListener(l);
   }

   //propertyChange deregistration
   public void removePropertyChangeListener(PropertyChangeListener l)
   {
       pcs.removePropertyChangeListener(l);
   }

   //vetoableChange registration
   public void addVetoableChangeListener(VetoableChangeListener l)
   {
       vcs.addVetoableChangeListener(l);
   }

   //vetoableChange deregistration
   public void removeVetoableChangeListener(VetoableChangeListener l)
   {
       vcs.removeVetoableChangeListener(l);
   }

}
```

that talks to the TVVoter object, to make sure that the channel is a valid entry.

Now that we have gone this far, we can test a few things. Let's package these objects into a jar file, copy them in the BDK's jars directory, and load up the BDK BeanBox. When we run the BeanBox builder tool, we should be able to see the two beans we just created.

We'll drag the TVState and the OnOffButton objects into the BeanBox, then bind the TVState's on property to the OnOffButton's on property, as shown in Figure 4.4. Next, we'll connect the OnOffButton's actionPerformedEvent to the TVState's onOff() method. We begin by clicking on the OnOffButton, and see the color of the button changing from off to on.

Now let's continue programming the example. The next step is to create the TVVoter object so that the channel changes can be tested. This bean, shown in Listing 4.3, is designed so that it inherits from TVState.

Listing 4.3 TVVoter class definition.

```
/****************************************************************/
/*  Filename:    TVVoter.java                                   */
/*                                                              */
/*  Description: Votes on the channel and fires an exception if */
/*               the channel is not in bounds.                  */
/****************************************************************/

package beandemo;

import java.beans.*;
import java.io.*;

public class TVVoter extends TVState
implements VetoableChangeListener, Serializable
{
    //constructor
    public TVVoter()
    {
        super();
    }

    //is it valid?
    public boolean isValidChannel(int c)
    {
        return (c > 0 && c < 100);
    }

    //setter method for channel - will connect with the display
    //This overrides TVState's setChannel method, so that we
    // can bind the property to the display's channel property.
    public void setChannel(int cn)
    {
        pcs.firePropertyChange("channel", new Integer(channel),
                               new Integer(cn));
        channel = cn;
    }

    //vetoableChange - this has the logic of accepting/rejecting
    //                 the channel change!
    public void vetoableChange(PropertyChangeEvent channelChanged)
    throws PropertyVetoException
    {
        Integer proposed = (Integer)channelChanged.getNewValue();
        String reason;
        if (!isValidChannel(proposed.intValue()))
        {
            reason = "Channel out of bounds!";
            throw new PropertyVetoException(reason, channelChanged);
```

Listing 4.3 *(Continued)*

```
        }
        else
        {
            setChannel(proposed.intValue());
        }
    }
}
```

The TVState's vetoableChange() property is connected to the vetoable Change() method. At the same time, TVVoter overrides the TVState's setChannel() method to fire a property change event. This allows the TV Display to get the correct channel property. Why isn't the TVDisplay connected to TVState? The TVState's channel property could be set to a bad value. It is the TVVoter's responsibility to set TVState straight.

The next object is the KeyPad, shown in Listing 4.4. This will be a little bit more complicated, because it handles its own events for the number button presses.

KeyPad's code isn't too complicated. Like the other beans, it has property registration and deregistration methods, and it also handles the actionEvent. This sets the property value when the user clicks the Enter button or updates the display for every keypress.

Finally, let's develop the code for the television's display, found in Listing 4.5. For simplicity, this bean will display the current channel number and change the color of the screen to show its on or off property.

The TVDisplay inherits from java.awt.Canvas, which allows us to "draw" the display in the paint() method.

Testing with the BDK

Now let's load the beans into the BeanBox development environment. To do this, we'll create the jar file with the classes, and a manifest file that describes the classes as beans, and put the jar file in the BDK\jars directory. As you load the BeanBox, the beans should be listed in the toolbox. As you drag each bean to the BeanBox window, you can change properties of the beans by editing the fields in the Property window. Figure 4.6 shows visual development with this example.

The next step is to connect the beans, as shown in Figure 4.4, in the following manner:

1. Drag the On/OffButton, the TVState, and the KeyPad from the BDK's Toolbox to the BeanBox frame.

Listing 4.4   KeyPad class definition.

```
/****************************************************************/
/*  Filename:    KeyPad.java                                    */
/*                                                              */
/*  Description: A keypad bean for use on the Remote Control!   */
/****************************************************************/
package beandemo;

import java.awt.*;
import java.awt.event.*;
import java.beans.*;
import java.io.*;

public class KeyPad extends Container implements ActionListener
{

   protected int value = 0;       // This is the bean's property
   private   int temporaryValue; // temporary # on label

   protected PropertyChangeSupport pcs;
   private Button enterButton = new Button("ENTER");
   private Label  displayLabel = new Label("");

   //constructor
   public KeyPad()
   {
      pcs = new PropertyChangeSupport(this);
      Panel p = new Panel();
      p.setLayout(new GridLayout(2,5));
      setLayout(new BorderLayout());

      //Create all buttons
      for (int i = 0; i < 10; i++)
      {
         Button b = new Button(Integer.toString(i));
         p.add(b);
         b.addActionListener(this);
      }
      enterButton.addActionListener(this);
      add ("South",enterButton);
      add ("Center", p);
      add ("North", displayLabel);
      displayLabel.setAlignment(Label.CENTER);
      temporaryValue = 0;
   }

   //getter for value
   public synchronized int getValue()
```

Listing 4.4   *(Continued)*

```
{
   return value;
}

//setter for value
public synchronized void setValue(int v)
{
   pcs.firePropertyChange("value",
             new Integer(value), new Integer(v));
   value = v;
   temporaryValue = 0;
   displayLabel.setText("");
}

//changes the label on the remote
public void changeTemporaryValue(String v)
{
   try
   {
       String newStr = String.valueOf(temporaryValue) + v;
       temporaryValue = Integer.parseInt(newStr);

       //Only allow three digits..
       if (temporaryValue > 999)
          temporaryValue = Integer.parseInt(v);

       displayLabel.setText(String.valueOf(temporaryValue));
   }
   catch (NumberFormatException nfe)
   {
       nfe.printStackTrace();
       return;
   }
}

//registration method
public void addPropertyChangeListener(PropertyChangeListener l)
{
   pcs.addPropertyChangeListener(l);
}

//deregistration method
public void removePropertyChangeListener(PropertyChangeListener l)
{
   pcs.removePropertyChangeListener(l);
}

// handles the "buttonPress" event
```

continues

Listing 4.4   KeyPad class definition. *(Continued)*

```
public void actionPerformed(ActionEvent ae)
{
   if (ae.getSource().equals(enterButton))
     setValue(temporaryValue);
   else
     changeTemporaryValue(ae.getActionCommand());
}
}
```

2. Connect OnOffButton's actionPerformedEvent to the TVState's onOff() method.

3. Bind TVState's on property to OnOffButton's on property.

4. Bind KeyPad's value property to TVState's channel property.

5. Drag two OurButton beans provided with the BDK to the BeanBox frame. Change the labels of the buttons to Up and Down, respectively. These beans are referred to as the UpButton and the DnButton.

6. Connect the UpButton's actionPerformedEvent to TVState's increment-Channel() method.

7. Connect the DnButton's actionPerformedEvent to TVState's decrement-Channel() method.

8. Connect TVState's vetoableChangeEvent to TVVoter's vetoableChange() method.

9. Bind TVState's on property to TVDisplay's on property.

10. Bind TVVoter's channel property to TVDisplay's channel property.

Now, we can test the functionality of the buttons. Because the beans are connected, everything should be working. When the OnOffButton is pressed, the TVDisplay should change color (to either on or off), and the OnOffButton should change color. When the channel is changed, the value should appear in the TVDisplay (unless it is vetoed). If the correct functionality does not occur, go over the steps again, and consult the BDK's user manual. It's easy to accidentally connect a wrong event!

If the correct functionality does not occur, it is simple to test each bean individually. The BDK comes with a ChangeReporter bean, and when you connect your bean's different change events to the ChangeReporter, the ChangeReporter's reportChange() method will display the property change. As I developed each bean, I tested it individually with the ChangeReporter. That way, I could more easily find in the code a simple mistake I made, such

Listing 4.5   TVDisplay class definition.

```
/********************************************************************/
/*  Filename:    TVDisplay.java                                   */
/*                                                                */
/*  Description: A simple display for a television.               */
/********************************************************************/
package beandemo;

import java.awt.*;
import java.beans.*;
import java.io.*;

public class TVDisplay extends Canvas
    implements PropertyChangeListener, Serializable
{

    protected int channel; //property
    protected boolean on;   //property

    protected PropertyChangeSupport pcs;
    private Color current; //represents off/on

    //constructor
    public TVDisplay()
    {
        super();
        pcs = new PropertyChangeSupport(this);
        channel = 0;
        on = false;
        current = Color.gray;
    }

    //paint()
    public void paint(Graphics g)
    {
        int height = getSize().height;
        int width  = getSize().width;
        int x      = 0;
        int y      = 0;
        int offset = 1;
        g.setColor(Color.black);
        g.drawRect(x,y,width-offset,height-offset);
        g.setColor(current);
        g.fillRect(x+1,y+1,width-offset-1,height-offset-1);
        g.setColor(Color.red);
        g.drawString(String.valueOf(channel),width/2, height/2);
    }

    //getter method for on
```

continues

Listing 4.5 TVDisplay class definition. *(Continued)*

```java
public boolean getOn()
{
   return (on);
}

//setter method for on
public void setOn(boolean o)
{
   if (o != on)
   {
     pcs.firePropertyChange("on", new Boolean(on),
             new Boolean(o));
     on = o;
   }
   if (on) current = Color.white;
   else    current = Color.gray;
   repaint();
}

//getter for channel
public int getChannel()
{
   return (channel);
}

//setter for channel
public void setChannel(int cn)
{
   pcs.firePropertyChange("channel", new Integer (channel),
             new Integer(cn));
   channel = cn;
   repaint();
}

//handles property change of channel of another bean
public void propertyChange(PropertyChangeEvent pcEvent)
{
   String changedProperty = pcEvent.getPropertyName();
   Object newval = pcEvent.getNewValue();
   if (changedProperty.equals("channel"))
   {
             Integer i = (Integer)newval;
             this.setChannel(i.intValue());
   }
   if (changedProperty.equals("on"))
   {
      Boolean b = (Boolean)newval;
```

Listing 4.5   *(Continued)*

```
        this.setOn(b.booleanValue());
    }
}

//propertyChange registration
public void addPropertyChangeListener(PropertyChangeListener l)
{
    pcs.addPropertyChangeListener(l);
}

//propertyChange deregistration
public void removePropertyChangeListener(PropertyChangeListener l)
{
    pcs.removePropertyChangeListener(l);
}
}
```

as a missed naming convention, and figure out why an event had not been triggered.

NOTE How does the BeanBox connect the beans? Like other visual development tools, the program generates and compiles adapter classes—the "glue" that connects the beans. From this point on, you could save your project file, and because the beans are all serializable, the next time you reloaded your project, the beans would still be connected.

Using visual development to test beans can eliminate simple mistakes. After testing each bean for correct functionality, you can begin developing a software version of a television and a remote control.

Putting It All Together

To this point, you have seen how a developer could use a visual development program to manipulate, customize, and design a project using beans. However, you have not seen how to load beans in a program or in another bean. Java allows us to do this via instantiation.

It is sometimes useful to separate functionality from the GUI to make your code as reusable and flexible as possible. For this example, you will create two classes: a RemoteControlGUI class that extends Frame, loads the beans, and adds the GUI components, and a RemoteControl class that will handle the events and communication with the television. The RemoteControl inherits from RemoteControlGUI. The code is shown in Listing 4.6.

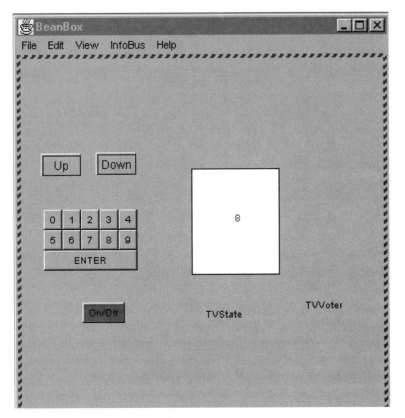

Figure 4.6 The TV-Remote example in the BeanBox.

> **NOTE** In this subsection, you will begin writing the code for the **RemoteControl. Due to space restrictions, only the necessary steps are shown. A good exercise would be to finish the code for the remote control and the television. A further extension of this example would be to use a distributed architecture, like CORBA or RMI, to demonstrate "true" remote control-television functionality. This example is shown in Chapter 8, "Enterprise Frameworks."**

In Listing 4.6, the Beans.instantiate() method loads the beans. The return value from Beans.instantiate() must be cast to the right object. The Remote-ControlGUI class is simply a container for the beans. You can add functionality by subclassing it to perform the communication interaction with the television. This final class, Remote.java, will act as a client, and will talk to the television. This class should be written as a bean, as shown in Listing 4.7.

Listing 4.6   RemoteControlGUI class definition.

```
/*****************************************************************/
/*  Filename:     RemoteControlGUI.java                        */
/*                                                             */
/*  Description: Handles setup of the GUI for the remote!      */
/*****************************************************************/

package beandemo;

import java.awt.*;
import java.awt.event.*;
import java.beans.*;
import java.io.*;
import sunw.demo.buttons.*;

public class RemoteControlGUI extends Frame
{
    //Our beans
    protected KeyPad keypad;
    protected OurButton up, down;
    protected OnOffButton onoff;

    //constructor
    public RemoteControlGUI()
    {
        loadBeans();
        setUpGUI();
    }

    //instantiates the beans!
    private void loadBeans()
    {
        try
        {
            keypad = (KeyPad)Beans.instantiate(null,
                          "beandemo.KeyPad");
            up     = (OurButton)Beans.instantiate(null,
                          "sunw.demo.buttons.OurButton");
            down   = (OurButton)Beans.instantiate(null,
                          "sunw.demo.buttons.OurButton");
            onoff  = (OnOffButton)Beans.instantiate(null,
                          "beandemo.OnOffButton");
        }
        catch (ClassNotFoundException noSuchBean)
        {
            System.out.println("Could not be found: " + noSuchBean);
            System.exit(-1);
        }
```

continues

Listing 4.6 RemoteControlGUI class definition. *(Continued)*

```
            catch (IOException beanIOerror)
            {
                System.out.println("I/O error while loading bean!");
                System.exit(-1);
            }
        }

        //sets up the GUI interface.
        private void setUpGUI()
        {
            up.setLabel("Up");
            down.setLabel("Down");

            Panel updownpanel = new Panel();
            updownpanel.setLayout(new BorderLayout());
            updownpanel.add("West", up);
            updownpanel.add("East", down);

            setLayout(new BorderLayout());
            add("North", onoff);
            add("Center", keypad);
            add("South", updownpanel);
            setSize(new Dimension(120,180));
            setVisible(true);
        }
    }
```

The communications with the TV object are commented out in this listing. A developer could implement the communications using CORBA or RMI. The final design is shown in Figure 4.7.

You could design the television to act as a container of the beans, as shown in Figure 4.7. As a matter of fact, both the remote control and the television could be beans themselves. Another option is to replace the TVState bean with the television bean, which would contain the rest of the beans, controlling all of the connections internally, but talking directly to the remote control bean.

What Did the Example Leave Out?

As mentioned, a lot was left out of this example in the interest of space and simplicity. Here's what was left out:

- *BeanInfo classes were not created.* By creating a class that inherits from Java's SimpleBeanInfo class, or by creating a class that implements

Listing 4.7 Remote class definition.

```
/*******************************************************************/
/*  Filename:      Remote.java                                     */
/*                                                                 */
/*  Description: This class is the main remote control that        */
/*               acts as a client talking to the television!       */
/*               This class could be implemented in CORBA or       */
/*               RMI, and is not yet finished. The commented       */
/*               code shows what needs to be done.                 */
/*******************************************************************/

package beandemo;

import java.awt.event.*;
import java.beans.*;
import java.io.*;

public class Remote extends RemoteControlGUI
implements PropertyChangeListener, ActionListener
{
    Television tv = null;
    protected boolean on;  //property
    protected PropertyChangeSupport pcs;

    //constructor
    public Remote()
    {
        super();

        pcs = new PropertyChangeSupport(this);
        //Listen to the beans!
        keypad.addPropertyChangeListener(this);
        up.addActionListener(this);
        down.addActionListener(this);
        onoff.addActionListener(this);

        /*Here, we can instantiate a television using
          RMI or CORBA. We'll see this in Chapter 8! */
        tv = (some lookup for TV with CORBA/RMI)
    }

    //This will change the channel on the TV..
    public void propertyChange(PropertyChangeEvent pcEvent)
    {
        String changedProperty = pcEvent.getPropertyName();
        Object newval = pcEvent.getNewValue();
        Integer i = (Integer)newval;
        tv.setChannel(i.intValue());
    }
```

continues

Listing 4.7 Remote class definition. *(Continued)*

```java
// This handles all of the remote control's buttonpress
// events.
public void actionPerformed(ActionEvent ae)
{
    Object source = ae.getSource();

    if (source.equals(up))
        tv.incrementChannel(); /*Increment the TVs Channel! */
    if (source.equals(down))
        tv.decrementChannel(); /*Decrement the TVs Channel! */
    if (source.equals(onoff))
        tv.onOff();             /*Call the onOff() method on TV! */
}


//setter for on property
// - the television sets this to
//    light up the remote control's display.
public void setOn(boolean value)
{
    onoff.setOn(value);
}


//propertyChange registration
public void addPropertyChangeListener(PropertyChangeListener l)
{
    pcs.addPropertyChangeListener(l);
}


//propertyChange deregistration
public void removePropertyChangeListener(PropertyChangeListener l)
{
    pcs.removePropertyChangeListener(l);
}
}
```

java.beans.BeanInfo, the beans can explicitly describe themselves, their properties, events, and icons, for their representation in a builder tool.

■ *Because these beans were fairly simple, a Customizer was not implemented.* The Customizer would give online assistance to anyone using the beans.

■ *A customized property editor was not created.* Because the properties were fairly simple (Int and Boolean), the BeanBox's property editors were used to edit the properties. If you develop complex properties, it would be necessary to add a new property editor—implementing the interface java.beans.PropertyEditor.

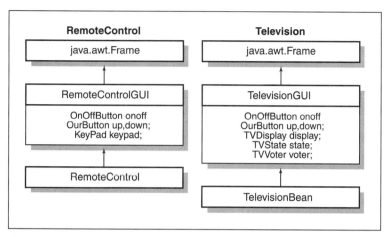

Figure 4.7 Final design.

Hopefully, the example showed you that beans are very powerful tools for Java developers. For more information on the capabilities of beans, visit java.sun.com/beans/ on the Internet.

Designing Good Components

There are so many tips for designing good components that to include them all would have made this section a chapter in itself. Therefore, I've narrowed them down to three important rules:

1. *Components should be simple.* As long as a developer keeps each component simple, other developers using these components can treat them as black boxes. If you want a component to perform more than one task, perhaps it should be two components.

2. *Components should be intuitive.* If the component is difficult for a user or designer to understand, it's probably not a good component. If a Java-Bean is less than intuitive, there should be a corresponding BeanInfo class that describes the object very well.

3. *Components should only interact with others via events and public methods.* In designing components, remember this. Only allow objects to generate events, and offer public methods to interact with other objects.

If you follow these rules, the JavaBeans event model can ensure that components within a framework maintain their state properly and effectively by reacting to state changes in other objects. This cause/effect model allows state changes to be multicast to an arbitrary number of listeners. Because these listeners are usually components plugged into the framework by the developer, the process driving the framework is hidden, and the developer shouldn't have to worry about the details.

Components in Frameworks

Now that you know what a component is and how to construct one, you may be wondering why they are useful to include in your framework design efforts. The reusable (a.k.a. black box) properties of beans make them attractive for a reusable framework. Frameworks emphasize abstractions through mechanisms like interfaces, abstract classes, and patterns. Frameworks also provide default or concrete implementations to those key abstractions that give it some core or basic out-of-the-box functionality. Depending on the type of framework you're designing, a useful set of JavaBeans will make your framework easy to use right away.

Recall that frameworks can reside at different levels within your application. That is, there are application level frameworks like *presentation frameworks* and *domain frameworks* in addition to *utility* or *support frameworks* that can offer services like data access or memory management. Also, it is at the discretion of the developer to determine how the framework exposes objects and behaviors for use within an application. This decision is often not obvious. On the one hand, you want applications to plug in as much code as is required for maximum flexibility; on the other hand, you want to provide some useful implementations that applications can use right away.

As an example, consider the loan application system mentioned. As part of a complete suite of frameworks or class libraries provided to build applications for banks to track their internal documents (like loan applications), the developer would find a useful set of JavaBeans representing various common forms. Each of these form beans could easily be visually modified and configured to serve the needs of a particular application. In addition, the beans could be extended and their behavior modified if necessary. The value in reusing those components even within the same project or application is quite high. The following list summarizes some key points about the use of components in frameworks.

- Because beans are self-contained black boxes, they can be used in a variety of different contexts more easily than simple objects. Beans are designed to be reusable.

- Beans provide an attractive and universal model for coding concrete objects that you may have in your framework. Because the bean model is a standard for Java, you can interact with other beans in an application in a standard and predictable manner.

- Because the JavaBean component model is an industry standard, developers can use a variety of tools to take advantage of the beans your framework provides in new and interesting ways. Developers can combine your beans with other beans and harness the power of your framework by linking different components together quickly and visually.

- The idea of visual and runtime design is the future trend for dynamic application evolution and similar concepts. Exposing bean components in your framework makes it attractive to that community and to the future of application design and development as well.

Summary

In this chapter, you learned how to build simple JavaBean components. By now, the idea of a standard component model should have quite an appeal. Basing your design and development efforts on these new universal standards is a wise approach, whether you are designing applications or frameworks. Simply put, components are the wave of the present *and* the future! They provide nicely encapsulated data objects that can be dropped into various containers and edited using visual bean builder tools. The fact that such beans are also linked to elaborate frameworks that you can harness through these simple components is a value-added feature that has yet to be fully realized. As the popularity of components and frameworks rises, you will see interesting combinations of the two, and software development will take another step forward.

In the next chapter, "Analysis of Java Frameworks," we will further explore some of the concepts presented in this and the previous chapter. Specifically, we will take a look at two interesting Java frameworks to understand how they are designed, including which patterns they adopt and how they incorporate various JavaBean techniques.

References

Flanagan, David. *Java In A Nutshell*. Sebastopol, CA: O'Reilly, 1997.

Vanhelsuwe, Laurence. *Mastering JavaBeans*. Alameda, CA: Sybex, 1997.

CHAPTER

5

Analysis of Java Frameworks

Most programmers will confess that learning through example is a great instructional method, so in this chapter, you'll take a look at two exciting and powerful real world Java frameworks—the Java Foundation Classes (JFC) [java.sun.com/products/jfc] and the InfoBus [java.sun.com/beans/infobus/]—that demonstrate the techniques you've mastered so far.

Both of these frameworks exhibit some of the important qualities and techniques covered in this book so far, such as design patterns, abstractions, component-based objects (JavaBeans), and interfaces. This chapter illustrates the architecture of each framework and how it accommodates some of the techniques and qualities discussed, such as:

- Flexibility/adaptability
- Pattern usage
- Component usage
- Abstraction through interface
- Exception handling
- Style and naming convention

> **NOTE** This chapter is not intended to be a comprehensive primer on these technologies, but rather to reveal the inner workings of two important and useful Java frameworks to help you understand how their design techniques can be applied to your frameworks.

Each of these frameworks represents a different category and magnitude: the JFC is a large comprehensive framework that focuses more on user interfaces for applications, while the InfoBus, a much smaller framework, deals with data objects and event passing between JavaBean component objects. Together, these two frameworks form a good cross-section of functionality and size from different domains. Each also clearly demonstrates many of the design elements presented in this book so far, and therefore, they are interesting to explore at this point.

Java Foundation Classes

The Java Foundation Classes (JFC) are a set of specialized packages and classes that elevate the technological foundation of Java from its prior versions. These classes enable such advanced capabilities as pluggable look and feel for user interfaces, drag-and-drop functionality, bean-based visual component sets (also known as Swing, the part of JFC that is the focus of this chapter) and 2D graphics algorithms and objects. JFC attempts to set the new standard upon which Java applications of today and tomorrow will be developed. JFC represents an extended effort of many industry partners, each adding valuable input to the design and functionality of the JFC in order for it to meet the needs of a demanding community.

Overview

As just mentioned, the presentation framework portion of JFC is called *Swing*. Swing is the nickname for the component of JFC that deals with the user interface, or GUI. It is composed of a number of packages that contain graphical JavaBean components (or widgets). All of Swing is based on the JavaBean standard and includes a number of popular design patterns, which are discussed later in this chapter.

The Swing components are built "on top of" the older Advanced Windowing Toolkit (AWT). This means that each Swing component is, at some level within its class hierarchy, also an AWT component. Typically, however, AWT components are not mixed with Swing components; instead, AWT acts as a foundation upon which Swing is developed.

Swing has components that are very similar in nature to the objects in the AWT packages, but with a few key differences:

- All Swing components adhere to the JavaBean spec and appear and behave as beans.

- All Swing components are lightweight and are responsible for drawing themselves; whereas AWT components have native peers that are drawn by the local operating system.

- Because Swing components draw themselves, they look the same regardless of the platform on which they're running. In addition, the look and feel of Swing components (that is, how they are drawn) can change dynamically.

The goal for Swing was to represent a comprehensive set of fundamental application building blocks for creating user interfaces. Therefore, the Swing team had to identify and address some major design goals if it was going to succeed in this effort.

The Goals of Swing

As stated in Chapter 1, "Framework Concepts," a framework always addresses a specific goal. Swing is an application GUI, or *presentation framework,* whose goal is to enable the quick and easy development in a flexible and extensible manner of advanced user interfaces for applications. The following list contains some of the primary design goals considered by the Swing team during its development [Fowler, 1997].

- Implement it entirely in Java to promote cross-platform consistency and easier maintenance.

- Allow for multiple looks and feels to be utilized by the same application code without internal or external changes or modifications.

- Enable the power of model-centric design patterns without requiring them at the highest level of the API.

- Adopt and adhere to the JavaBean design principles to ensure future interoperability with other beans, builders, and environments that support JavaBeans.

The Swing designers responded to the Java community's functionality requests and strived to achieve the goals they set.

Naming Conventions

Many frameworks choose a naming convention that uniquely identifies objects as part of that framework to prevent naming confusion. For example, in Swing, most UI-related components begin with the letter J. Though there are a number of reasons Swing designers might have chosen this, most likely it was to prevent naming conflicts with AWT counterparts.

NOTE Objects of the same class name may reside in different packages and be used within the same scope, providing each class name appearance is accompanied by a qualified package name that identifies, specifically, the definition to which you're referring. If at all possible, however, avoid using different classes with the same name.

Take a look at the following code segment.

```
// Old AWT button
Button button = new Button("Hello");

// Swing button
JButton button = new JButton("Hello");
```

The Swing JButton in this listing is the analog to the AWT Button object. The object names are different so that you can use either or both comfortably within a given context. Knowing whether you're using a Swing component is relatively trivial!

General Architecture

The Swing architecture, based on robust patterns and Java standards, is complex, but very powerful; it enables greater flexibility and control for the developer. First and foremost, Swing components are JavaBeans and so adhere to the methods and conventions mandated by the JavaBean spec (refer to Chapter 4, "JavaBean Components" for more on JavaBeans) such as representing properties, using getter and setter methods, and allowing for various listeners.

In addition to using JavaBeans, the designers of Swing have allowed the data representation of their components to be separate from the visual or actual representation of the component itself. That is, for each component there is a *view,* and a *model* that drives that view. To this extent, they facilitate proper data-centric design techniques.

REFERENCE Recall that the idea of MVC (model-view controller) was introduced in Chapter 3, "Using Design Patterns." Swing does not mimic the idea of a Controller object specifically. Rather, the view delegate also behaves as the controller. Because it is unlikely that there will be multiple controllers operating on a common view, the notion is often discarded and the pattern referred to as simply MV (model view), or modified MVC.

Data-Centric Design

The concept behind data-centric design is that the application data gives rise to the user interface, not the other way around (although there is certainly some synergy between the two). It is generally considered good practice to design the constructs of an application around the important data elements or domain models before determining how those elements will be presented in the user interface. There are two good reasons for this:

- Typically, the domain data is more readily available to a software engineer before he or she begins the architecture design; hence, it will influence the architecture more closely.

- Solidifying the requirements for the domain data of your application will reduce the amount of regressive change once front-end interfaces have begun to be developed. Certainly, it would be a chore to recode user interfaces regularly to account for a domain model that is in constant flux.

Once the data elements have been "frozen," it is much easier to follow through with visualization of those elements. This approach and technique is addressed in Chapter 7, "Java Application Architectures."

Each Swing component has an accompanying data model abstraction that is separate from the rendering, or view portion, of the component. Separating these parts of the component allows the developer to substitute different implementations of a particular model for a given component. In addition, Swing components also delegate their rendering to a view that draws the component, including information contained within the supplied model, on the screen. The basic concept is that either the model or the view can change (to some degree) independent of one another.

Another important concept to derive from this design technique is that application data can be coded in advance of the GUI elements. Furthermore, it can live (or be stored) independently and separately from any user interface components, which typically do not (but certainly could) constitute important persistent data within an application.

Listeners and Adapters

Because Swing components are usually interactive GUI-level objects, they often invoke some behavior at various levels. They contain, within themselves, individual component behavior, such as the scrolling of a table or a list. They can also make invocations on trapped events into client code supplied by the developer. In other words, a Swing component can call back to an application object or an object that is not inherently part of the Swing framework. For this reason, this processing is referred to as *calling back*, and the method or object that receives events from the framework component is referred to as a *callback* method or object.

Recall from the definition of a framework that a framework often will engage application code directly by interacting with client objects (developer-supplied objects), which are designed specifically for the application and are not directly supplied by the framework. One method of accomplishing this task is through callback objects or methods.

The latest Java event model (also defined in the JavaBean spec) includes the concept of listeners and adapters. Swing has maintained this architecture within its design. A *listener* is an interface object that registers itself with a target object and receives specific messages about certain events when they occur on the target object. This is closely related to the Observer pattern discussed in Chapter 3, "Using Design Patterns."

Adapters are implementations of listeners that listen for specific events on a given target, and subsequently respond by invoking methods on another object, typically the object implementing the callbacks. This chapter takes a closer look at the kinds of adapters provided by Swing. Figure 5.1 depicts an adapter interfacing two objects together.

Core Classes and Interfaces

Swing offers a variety of useful classes and interfaces for the application developer. This section looks at a subset of those classes and interfaces, and explores some of them by revealing their individual designs, patterns, and models. Exploring the classes and interfaces not only serves to introduce you to how the JFC framework can be used, but offers some design insight that can be applied to your own framework design efforts or projects.

Table 5.1 is a listing of the primary Swing bean components, along with the model interface and model type. The model interface represents the type of model that a particular component uses. The view portion of the Swing component is delegated to a particular look and feel through the L&F (look and feel) manager that manages the look and feel (by setting it to a particular style) for a running Java application. The model type indicates the nature of the model.

Swing Models

Swing employs the use of two distinct kinds of models: *GUI-state models* and *application-data models,* both of which are relatively transparent to the general-purpose programmer.

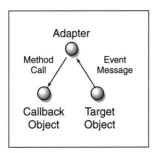

Figure 5.1   An adapter interfaces two objects.

Table 5.1   Swing Component Model Type Mapping

COMPONENT	MODEL INTERFACE	MODEL TYPE
JButton	ButtonModel	GUI
JToggleButton	ButtonModel	GUI/data
JCheckBox	ButtonModel	GUI/data
JRadioButton	ButtonModel	GUI/data
JMenu	ButtonModel	GUI
JMenuItem	ButtonModel	GUI
JCheckBoxMenuItem	ButtonModel	GUI/data
JRadioButtonMenuItem	ButtonModel	GUI/data
JComboBox	ComboBoxModel	data
JProgressBar	BoundedRangeModel	GUI/data
JScrollBar	BoundedRangeModel	GUI/data
JSlider	BoundedRangeModel	GUI/data
JTabbedPane	SingleSelectionModel	GUI
JList	ListModel	data
JList	ListSelectionModel	GUI
JTree	TreeModel	data
JTree	TreeSelectionModel	GUI
JEditorPane	Document	data
JTextPane	Document	data
JTextArea	Document	data
JTextField	Document	data
JPasswordField	Document	data

GUI-State Models

A GUI-state model holds the state information that is local to a particular component, such as the depressed state of a toggle button, the items selected in a list, or the position of a scroll bar. Manipulating GUI-state models directly is not required by Swing, which would be cumbersome to the developer. Instead, Swing components interact with their models directly through their exposed top-level methods. Let's look at an example.

JToggleButton has a model of type ButtonModel that contains the state of the toggle button—that is, whether it is depressed or not. When you want to programmatically control the state of the JToggleButton, you certainly would not want to first set values within a separate model. Specifically, you do not want to have to interact with both the model and view of a Swing bean separately. By specifying values directly with JToggleButton using the provided convenience methods, the model is changed for you. Consider the following code segments. Listing 5.1 shows how the state of a toggle button can be altered by manipulating its model; this also affects its visual representation.

NOTE Throughout the code examples in this book, lines of particular interest to the discussion will appear in bold face to draw your attention.

Listing 5.2 achieves the same result as Listing 5.1, except that, conveniently, the object's model can be affected without really knowing about it directly. For most general purposes, this method is sufficient.

Figure 5.2 shows the relationship between the GUI-state and its model.

The Swing designers realized that they had to provide for complex extensibility, control, and ease of use. Don't forget one of our axioms about frameworks: "If the perceived time of learning something new seems longer than doing it your own way or another way, the new way will seldom be used." This is especially true for frameworks that intend to appeal to the general public. If you had to code Swing components as presented by Listing 5.1, you would simply abandon Swing and use the old AWT instead. Realizing this, the designers embedded the model interaction within the components and exposed only methods to the developer, should they opt to use them. As Listing 5.2 shows, it is much easier to code this way and makes Swing appealing for both simple and complex applications.

Listing 5.1 Manipulating an object's state through its model.

```
JToggleButton toggle = new JToggleButton();

// Acquire the model associated with this button
ButtonModel model = toggle.getModel();

// Set the button model state to "selected."
// Interacting with the model in this way
// notifies the view to draw itself appropriately
model.setSelected(true);
```

Analysis of Java Frameworks   215

Listing 5.2   Manipulating an object's state through itself.

```
JToggleButton toggle = new JToggleButton();

// This is much easier.
toggle.setSelected(true);
```

THOUGHTS It's interesting to consider how JFC and other frameworks
achieve two levels of complexity. On one level, JFC can be used and understood
very easily because the constructs are simple, clear, and disconnected from the
developer. However, there are vastly more complex structures essentially
hidden from view that also provide flexibility and capability to those wishing to
uncover it. This idea is very similar to the discussion in Chapter 1, "Framework
Concepts," in which the fractal nature of object compositions and the
complexity of design was discussed. Throughout this text, I'll touch on the
parallel notions of engaging complexity through simplicity, which is similar to
the JFC context. Frameworks should make an attempt to conceal their
complexities so that the developer or user can engage it through a refined and
simpler set of constructs.

Application-Data Models

An application-data model is an interface that represents some portion of
application-specific data, that is, data whose meaning is useful in the application context rather than strictly within the GUI context. A good example of
application data supported by application-data models are the values in the
cells of a table or the elements in a list or tree. The application data displayed
by the Swing GUI components would likely be considered useful to humans
rather than widgets.

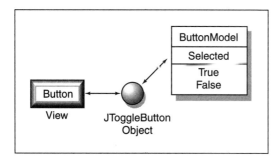

Figure 5.2   GUI-state model depiction.

As mentioned, separating data or logic and visualization (the GUI) is important to developers. It facilitates easy change and modification of these discrete pieces within an application, with few negative side effects throughout your framework or application. Useful conditions under which this is true include the following:

- *Often, an application can undergo various cosmetic changes throughout development.* The changes should not have a great impact on the domain models that encapsulate the application data. The benefit of maintaining a clear model-view relationship is realized only when the data and view are sufficiently separate and distinct.

- *Data requirements can change or be added during development.* In certain circumstances, adding data requirements should not cause unrelated objects or user interface components to be redesigned. Consider a scenario in which you have two user interface views: viewA and viewB. ViewA calls out to viewB. If viewB's data model changes, viewB may need to be updated. ViewA should not be affected, however, because it has its own data model. Another example scenario is one in which viewA's data model is extended to include more information. A new view called viewA1 is created to show this information. ViewA should continue to operate using its piece of the data model because none of its data requirements has been removed. In addition, viewA1 can also display its piece of the same data model, which contains different pieces of the data.

- *Application logic is a vital piece of any software system.* Separating the visual display of data from the logic that operates on it is also a valid way to improve the flexibility of your architecture by making it easier to modify the data or the logic independently, without serious effects to the other. User interface components should not try to act intelligently (by housing business logic), but instead display their data models completely and invoke logic control objects through callbacks. This allows each portion to change easily over time.

Figure 5.3 shows a simple diagram with two views attached to the same model. Figure 5.4 shows a view and data-model with logic callbacks attached.

Model Event Notification

In order for both the GUI-state and the application-logic models to be truly useful to their view counterparts, they must be able to inform interested listeners (which could be multiple views of various types) of internal changes. Swing models adhere to the JavaBean event mechanisms to achieve this. There are two primary methods for notifying a listener:

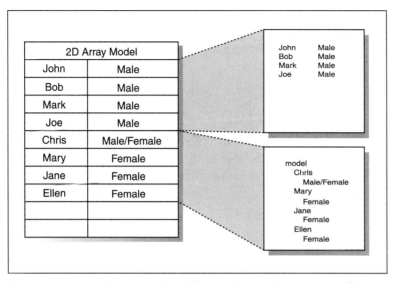

Figure 5.3 Two views exposing different slices of the same model.

1. A *lightweight notification* is sent to all registered listeners indicating that a change has taken place; however, it is at the discretion of the listener object to retrieve the desired changes from the target.

2. A *stateful notification* describes how the model has changed by providing an instance of the appropriate event object containing valid data regarding the transition state of the target object.

Notifying listeners by either method allows Swing models to ensure state consistency between their internal values and their visual representation by their view delegates or other interested objects.

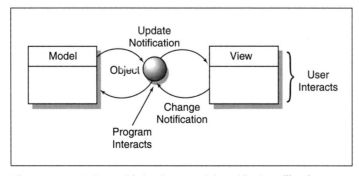

Figure 5.4 A view with its data model and logic callbacks.

Default Model Behavior

Remember that one of the goals of frameworks is that it be readily usable; to that end, it should provide the developer with default implementations of their primary interfaces or services. The Swing designers have ensured that the components in Swing are readily usable, while retaining the advance capability of having new model objects supplied to them.

Consider the following listings extracted from the Swing Architecture document on the Swing Connection Web site at www.javasoft.com/products/jfc/swingdoc-current/. Listing 5.3 shows how the JSlider interacts with its model within its constructor. This saves the developer from having to know about the DefaultBoundedRangeModel that JSlider uses for its model. Nevertheless, the developer has the ability to substitute his or her own specialized model into the JSlider class.

Listing 5.4 shows the creation of a JSlider and an inner class implementation of the BoundedRangeModel interface, which is the type of model used by JSlider. The new BoundedRangeModel is then set to a previously created JSlider instance, which will then carry the new model class from that point.

It is up to the model to respond appropriately when internal changes occur. The class DefaultBoundedRangeModel already contains this capability. Any custom model implementations should ensure the proper notification of listeners through the standard JavaBean mechanisms. Refer to Chapter 4, "JavaBeans Components," for more information.

Patterns and Designs

The JFC employs the use of a variety of design patterns and models within its architecture. Some of these have been introduced or discussed previously in this book, including Model-View and Listener. Let's take a closer look at exactly how Swing utilizes these and other patterns, and how the patterns contribute to the overall usefulness of the framework. It's very appealing to see

Listing 5.3 Example constructor showing default model construction.

```
public JSlider(int orientation, int min, int max, int value)
{
    checkOrientation(orientation);
    this.orientation = orientation;

    // This ensures that a default model is provided when this
    // instance is created.
    this.model = new DefaultBoundedRangeModel(value,0,min,max);
    this.model.addChangeListener(changeListener);
    updateUI();
}
```

Listing 5.4 Setting a substitute model class.

```
JSlider slider = new JSlider();
// I know my slider now has a default model.

BoundedRangeModel myModel =
        new DefaultBoundedRangeModel() {
          public void setValue(int n) {
            System.out.println("JSlider.model: setValue "+n);
            super.setValue(n);
          }
        }); // Inner class

// Now set the new model
slider.setModel(myModel);
```

how successfully these techniques contribute to the important qualities of a framework, such as extensibility, reusability, and scalability.

Abstract Implementations

Abstract implementations were introduced in Chapter 2, "Java Framework Design," (in the discussion about the design of the Java Collections Framework. They represent abstract classes that provide interface implementations, thereby creating a base class for an abstraction hierarchy that can be easily refined. This concept appears in the Swing framework as well. Because much of Swing and JFC are founded on interfaces, there should be workable abstract classes that implement these interfaces, from which useful implementation classes can be derived with much less effort than by reimplementing an entire interface. The idea behind the abstract implementation is to provide a root or base class that contains generic implementations of the interfaces it represents. By doing this, the application developer can then choose which methods need overriding in a subclass to provide the desired behavior without reimplementing the represented interfaces. In addition, abstract implementations can add numerous methods in both implementation and abstract form to further provide class-level functionality to future subclass implementations. As an example of this, let's look at the Border interface.

Border Interface

Most Swing components can have a border drawn around them. The border is delegated out to a Border object, an object that implements the Border interface. This form of delegation is quite similar to object persistence through delegation, as discussed in Chapter 2, "Java Framework Design." Listing 5.5 shows the Border interface declaration.

Listing 5.5 Border interface.

```
public abstract interface Border {
    public Insets getBorderInsets(Component c);
    public boolean isBorderOpaque();
    public void paintBorder(Component c, Graphics g, int x, int y,
            int width, int height);
}
```

NOTE Recall the example in Chapter 2. It began by requiring subclasses of the base class DomainModel to directly implement a save() method. Later, it was redesigned so that the DomainModel provided an implementation that actually delegated this action to an ObjectArchiver interface object. This is similar the border for Swing components. If Swing components provided implementations of a border drawing, it would be repetitious across classes. Instead, a separate object that performs this action on any given bean is required.

As indicated by its name, the AbstractBorder class provides an abstract implementation of the Border interface. A standard convention when naming abstract classes of this nature is to prefix them with the word Abstract. Because AbstractBorder is an abstract class, you cannot create instances of it directly. This class is designed for the developer to subclass. Listing 5.6 shows the class definition header for AbstractBorder.

Table 5.2 shows the complete AbstractBorder class with method signatures and descriptions.

In addition to the required interface methods of Border, AbstractBorder has provided some additional methods suitable to Borders. There's no actual rule specifying whether some methods should be kept at the abstract class level or incorporated into the base interface. In this case, the method getInteriorRectangle() is declared and implemented solely at the class level. It could very well have been at the interface level; it is up to the developer to decide how he or she wishes to provide this functionality.

ItemSelectable Interface

Another interface similar to Border is the ItemSelectable interface. It is designed for objects that represent one or more possible selections. The Swing/AWT classes that implement this interface are:

AbstractButton

CheckBox

CheckBoxMenuItem

Choice

Listing 5.6 AbstractBorder class header.

```
public abstract class AbstractBorder extends Object implements
Border, Serializable {

    public Insets getBorderInsets(Component c) {
        // Implementation left out for brevity
    }
    public Insets getBorderInsets(Component c, Insets is) {
        // Implementation left out for brevity
    }
    public static Rectangle getInteriorRectangle(Component c, Border b,
        int x,int y, int width, int height) {
        // Implementation left out for brevity
    }
    public Rectangle getInteriorRectangle(Component c, int x, int y,
        int width, int height) {
        // Implementation left out for brevity
    }
    public boolean isBorderOpaque(){
        // Implementation left out for brevity
    }
    public void paintBorder(Component c, Graphics g, int x, int y,
        int width, int height){
        // Implementation left out for brevity
    }

}
```

JComboBox

List

Figure 5.5 shows the class hierarchy diagram stemming from the ItemSelec-table interface.

Unlike the Border interface, ItemSelectable can be applied to a variety of abstract class types and therefore should not have a name that implies a specific class. Rather, this interface name should describe generically the *kind of* objects that would implement it. As an example implementation, let's look at AbstractButton.

NOTE It would be awkward for the root interface of this class to be called Button because it is utilized by other nonbutton classes. Though this can be cumbersome or inconsistent to deal with, it allows the greatest level of reuse within your application.

Table 5.2 AbstractBorder Class

SCOPE	METHOD	DESCRIPTION
public Insets	getBorderInsets(Component C, Insets insets)	Reinitializes the *insets* parameter with this Border's current Insets.
public Insets	getBorderInsets(Component c)	Returns the value of getBorderMargins (the default implementation).
public static Rectangle	getInteriorRectangle(Component c, Border b, int x, int y, int width, int height)	Returns a rectangle using the arguments, minus the insets of the border.
public Rectangle	getInteriorRectangle(Component c, int x, int y, int width, int height)	A convenience method that calls the static method.
public boolean	isBorderOpaque()	Returns false (the default implementation).
public void	paintBorder(Component c, Graphics g, int x, int y, int width, int height)	This default implementation does no painting.

Similar to AbstractBorder, AbstractButton implements a set of base interfaces and provides method implementations to those interfaces, in addition to other methods useful to the abstract notion of a button. Bear in mind that there is a clear separation between what the interface ItemSelectable captures and what is considered a button. Specifically, the idea of a button encapsulates the

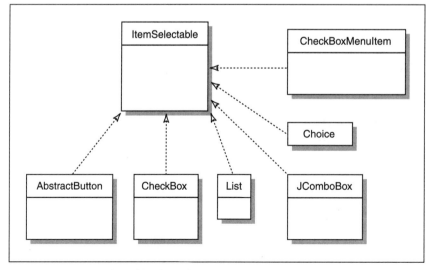

Figure 5.5 ItemSelectable class diagram.

Listing 5.7 AbstractButton class header.

```
public abstract class AbstractButton extends Object implements
  ItemSelectable, SwingConstants, Serializable {

// Refer to Table 5.3 for method descriptions.
// Omitted here for brevity.


}
```

characteristics captured by the interface ItemSelectable. Listing 5.7 shows the
AbstractButton class definition header.

TIP Because other characteristics in the form of interfaces can be combined
in different ways within a given abstraction class or notion, do not associate a
one-to-one correlation between these abstract classes and their root interfaces.
Although often it does exist, it is not implied.

Table 5.3 identifies all the methods provided for by AbstractButton.

At first glance, the list of methods seems overwhelming for something as
simple as a button. Therein lies an important concept about framework
design and usability: Most of the complex work has been done already. The
abstract concept of a button is more complex than expected, but how that
functionality is utilized is entirely up to the developer. For most cases, the
developer isn't concerned with the majority of the functionality provided to
buttons. For example, you can easily add an action listener to a JButton by
doing the following:

```
JButton button = new JButton("Hello");
button.addActionListener(new ActionListener() {
    public void actionPerformed(ActionEvent event) {
            System.out.println("Button pressed!");
    }
});
```

The complexities within JButton (a subclass of AbstractButton) remain well
hidden from everyday use but are there to serve the needs of developers
should they require it.

Default Implementations

Any useful framework will, of course, provide some ready-to-use implementations of its key interfaces. These are called *default implementations*. Default
implementations provide basic functionality useful to initial development.

Table 5.3 AbstractButton Class

METHOD	DESCRIPTION
addActionListener(ActionListener l)	Adds an ActionListener to the button.
addChangeListener(ChangeListener l)	Adds a ChangeListener to the button.
addItemListener(ItemListener l)	Adds an ItemListener to the checkbox.
checkHorizontalKey(int key, String exception)	Ensures that the key is valid.
checkVerticalKey(int key, String exception)	Ensures that the key is valid.
createActionListener()	Creates and returns an ActionListener object for this component.
createChangeListener()	Creates and returns a ChangeListener object for this component.
createItemListener()	Creates and returns an ItemListener object for this component.
doClick()	Programatically performs a "click."
doClick(int pressTime)	Programatically performs a "click."
fireActionPerformed(ActionEvent event)	Sends the ActionEvent event to all registered ActionListeners.
fireItemStateChanged(ItemEvent event)	Sends the ItemEvent event to all registered ItemListeners.
fireStateChanged()	Notifies all state change listeners about the new component state.
getActionCommand()	Returns the String action command currently used in ActionEvents.
getDisabledIcon()	Returns the ImageIcon used for the disabled state.
getDisabledSelectedIcon()	Returns the ImageIcon used for the selected disabled state.
getHorizontalAlignment()	Returns the horizontal alignment.
getHorizontalTextPosition()	Returns the horizontal text position.
getIcon()	Returns the icon associated with this button.
getMargin()	Gets the current margin settings.
getMnemonic()	Gets the key mnemonic currently associated with this button.

Table 5.3 *(Continued)*

METHOD	DESCRIPTION
getModel()	Returns the model being used.
getPressedIcon()	Returns the icon used when this button is pressed.
getRolloverIcon()	Returns the icon used during mouse rollovers.
getRolloverSelectedIcon()	Returns the icon used during selected mouse rollovers.
getSelectedIcon()	Returns the selected Icon.
getSelectedObjects()	Returns an array (length 1) containing the label, or null if the button is not selected.
getText()	Returns the button's text.
getUI()	Returns the button's current UI.
getVerticalAlignment()	Returns the vertical alignment of the text and icon.
getVerticalTextPosition()	Returns the vertical position of the text relative to the icon Valid keys: CENTER (the default), TOP, BOTTOM.
init(String text, Icon icon)	Initializes the button with text and image.
isBorderPainted()	Returns whether the border should be painted.
isContentAreaFilled()	Checks whether the content area of the button should be filled.
isFocusPainted()	Returns whether focus should be painted.
isRolloverEnabled()	Checks whether rollover effects are enabled.
isSelected()	Returns the state of the button.
paintBorder(Graphics g)	Paints the button's border if BorderPainted property is true.
removeActionListener (ActionListener l)	Removes an ActionListener from the button.
removeChangeListener (ChangeListener l)	Removes a ChangeListener from the button.

(continues)

Table 5.3   AbstractButton Class *(Continued)*

METHOD	DESCRIPTION
removeItemListener(ItemListener l)	Removes an ItemListener from the button.
setActionCommand(String actionCommand)	Sets the action command for this button.
setBorderPainted(boolean b)	Sets whether the border should be painted.
setContentAreaFilled(boolean b)	Sets whether the button should paint the content area or leave it transparent.
setDisabledIcon(Icon disabledIcon)	Sets the disabled icon for the button.
setDisabledSelectedIcon(Icon disabledSelectedIcon)	Sets the disabled selection icon for the button.
setEnabled(boolean b)	Enables (or disables) the button.
setFocusPainted(boolean b)	Sets whether focus should be painted.
setHorizontalAlignment(int alignment)	Sets the horizontal alignment of the icon and text.
setHorizontalTextPosition(int textPosition)	Sets the horizontal position of the text relative to the icon.
setIcon(Icon defaultIcon)	Sets the button's default icon.
setMargin(Insets m)	Sets space for the margin between the button's border and the label.
setMnemonic(char mnemonic)	Specifies the mnemonic value.
setMnemonic(int mnemonic)	Sets the keyboard mnemonic on the current model.
setModel(ButtonModel newModel)	Set the model that this button represents.
setPressedIcon(Icon pressedIcon)	Sets the pressed icon for the button.
setRolloverEnabled(boolean b)	Sets whether rollover effects should be enabled.
setRolloverIcon(Icon rolloverIcon)	Sets the rollover icon for the button.
setRolloverSelectedIcon(Icon rolloverSelectedIcon)	Sets the rollover selected icon for the button.
setSelected(boolean b)	Sets the state of the button.
setSelectedIcon(Icon selectedIcon)	Sets the selected icon for the button.
setText(String text)	Sets the button's text.

Table 5.3 *(Continued)*

METHOD	DESCRIPTION
setUI(ButtonUI ui)	Sets the button's UI.
setVerticalAlignment(int alignment)	Sets the vertical alignment of the icon and text.
setVerticalTextPosition(int textPosition)	Sets the vertical position of the text relative to the icon.
updateUI()	Gets a new UI object from the default UIFactory.

They are often used as base classes to further specify application behavior through proper subclassing. In Swing, there are many derived implementations to key interfaces and abstract classes. Let's continue to use Borders and Buttons to demonstrate these concepts.

Border Classes

Given the base abstract class AbstractBorder, there are a number of common Border implementations that subclass AbstractBorder with slight variations. These include:

BevelBorder

CompoundBorder

EmptyBorder

EtchedBorder

LineBorder

TitledBorder

Figure 5.6 shows the breakdown of classes and interfaces stemming from Border.

Each implementation provides a richer set of methods than those defined in AbstractBorder because each border type may contain properties unique to that implementation. For example, BevelBorder comes in two flavors, RAISED and LOWERED. The variation to use is specified through the BevelBorder constructor. Table 5.4 shows the various constructors used by BevelBorder. Table 5.5 highlights the methods provided by BevelBorder.

The Border interfaces and classes are quite extensive and thorough, and as a result are contained in their own package (javax.swing.border). Through proper representation of interface and separation of implementation the

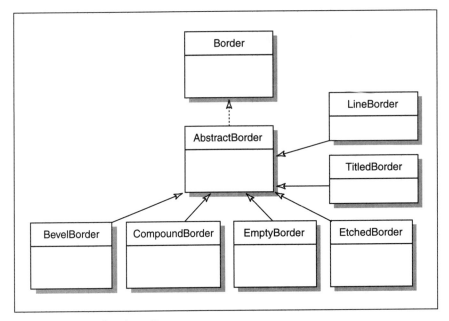

Figure 5.6 Border class diagram.

Swing designers have ensured that the border facilities of Swing are both extensible and flexible.

Button Classes

There are also some useful button classes that directly derive from Abstract-Button. Note: JCheckBox and JRadioButton are indented to show their hierarchical relationship to JToggleButton.

Table 5.4 BevelBorder Constructors

METHOD	DESCRIPTION
BevelBorder(int bevelType, Color highlightOuter, Color highlightInner, Color shadowOuter, Color shadowInner)	Creates a bevel border with the specified type and highlight shadow colors.
BevelBorder(int bevelType, Color highlight, Color shadow)	Creates a bevel border with the specified type, highlight, and shadow colors.
BevelBorder(int bevelType)	Creates a bevel border with the specified type and whose colors will be derived from the background color of the component associated with this border.

Table 5.5   BevelBorder Class Methods

SCOPE	METHOD	DESCRIPTION
public int	getBevelType()	Returns the type of the bevel border.
public Insets	getBorderInsets (Component c, Insets insets)	Reinitializes the *insets* parameter with this Border's current Insets.
public Insets	getBorderInsets (Component c)	Returns the insets of the border.
public Color	getHighlightInnerColor (Component c)	Returns the inner highlight color of the bevel border.
public Color	getHighlightOuterColor (Component c)	Returns the outer highlight color of the bevel border.
public Color	getShadowInnerColor (Component c)	Returns the inner shadow color of the bevel border.
public Color	getShadowOuterColor (Component c)	Returns the outer shadow color of the bevel border.
public boolean	isBorderOpaque()	Returns whether or not the border is opaque.
public void	paintBorder(Component c, Graphics g, int x, int y, int width, int height)	Paints the border for the specified component with the specified position and size.
protected void	paintLoweredBevel (Component c, Graphics g, int x, int y, int width, int height)	Paints a lowered bevel border.
protected void	paintRaisedBevel (Component c, Graphics g, int x, int y, int width, int height)	Paints a raised bevel border.

JButton

JMenuItem

JToggleButton

   JCheckBox

   JRadioButton

Figure 5.7 shows the basic class hierarchy diagram stemming from Abstract-Button.

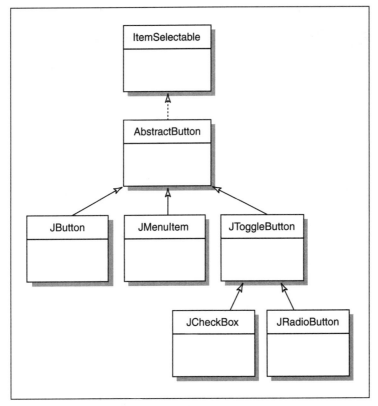

Figure 5.7   AbstractButton class diagram.

This segment of the class hierarchy is a good example of how proper generalization and classification is carried out. That is, JButton, JMenuItem, and JToggleButton are fundamentally different types of AbstractButton. JToggleButton, however, forms the base type for both JCheckBox and JRadioButton, which encapsulate the state-driven model of JToggleButton (i.e., selected or unselected), but have different views driving them. In Swing, checkboxes appear with a checkmark inside (possibly varying depending on the current L&F), while radiobuttons appear as a circular border that is either filled or empty. Each specialized subclass conveniently encapsulates the appropriate view delegate. Without separate classes to handle this, the developer would have to choose the appropriate view delegate and link it to the button class, an unnecessary and repetitive step.

Formatting the subtle variations of view and type of button in appropriate subclasses is a good method for giving the developer using your framework a clean and simple way to access functionality immediately. It also provides key root objects from which future class extensions can be linked. For example, I could create my own version of JCheckBox or JToggleButton without affecting the existing framework class structure.

Because Swing makes proper use of general abstractions of its key components, the developer can extend the capabilities of existing structures or create entirely new objects that adhere to the reliable protocols established by the framework collaboration model (in this case, it would be the Swing event model). The rich set of interfaces, abstract classes, and implementations offer the maximum number of options to the developer who wants to accomplish very demanding or refined objectives without impeding the everyday programmer, who'd rather work quickly and simply within the basic constructs of the framework and explore the complexities only as needed. This is a valuable concept to apply to other framework design efforts.

THOUGHTS Chapter 1, "Framework Concepts," talked a bit about complexity and the notions of *zooming* and *chunking*, the ability to manuever through various levels of complexity at will. Much of how the human mind grasps complexity involves chunking discrete pieces into larger more abstract ones. If developers do not have to grasp all the complexities of a large framework at once, they can more readily solve problems with it. Their perception of effort will be reduced and the value of the framework system will be realized. When larger, more complex problems arise, the complexity used to solve the problem within the framework can be revealed. Moving between the complex and the simple is necessary to improve mental efficiencies.

Factories

Chapter 3, "Using Design Patterns," discussed how the Factory Method [Gamma et al., 1995] pattern operates. Factory objects (and their subsequent Factory Methods) are useful in their own right and common among Java frameworks and APIs. To review, Factory Methods create instances of a particular class (or sometimes multiple classes) of object, based on static (or common) invocations often involving parameter passing. For example, I might ask a Factory object to give me an instance of a particular class, and I would supply certain parameters useful in determining the nature of the instance returned by the Factory without knowing details about the instance.

There are various Factory objects in Swing that provide convenient ways to institute implementations of key interface objects, such as Border (just when you thought we were through with borders!).

BorderFactory

The BorderFactory object in Swing contains a number of convenience methods for acquiring specialized instances of Border objects. The following code snippet shows how to acquire some Borders from BorderFactory.

```
Border bevel = BorderFactory.createBevelBorder(BevelBorder.RAISED);
Border empty = BorderFactory.createEmptyBorder();
Border etchd = BorderFactory.createEtchedBorder();
```

ViewFactory

A somewhat more compelling and appropriate use of the Factory Method (sometimes a class whose only methods represent Factory Methods is referred to as simply a Factory) [Gamma et al., 1995] pattern is with the ViewFactory interface. This interface defines a Factory object with a single method, as seen in Listing 5.8.

Without getting into the gritty details behind the text-processing facilities of JFC, it is worthwhile to mention how factories implementing this interface would behave. Because ViewFactory is an interface, multiple various implementations can exist, each seen as simply a ViewFactory. The framework text engine will ask ViewFactory objects to return Views based on dynamic elements present in a document. It is up to each factory implementation to load and instantiate the appropriate View object relating to the element. The reliable protocol is well defined, and any number of ViewFactories can be inserted transparently and seamlessly into your framework-based application.

This methodology is critical to a framework's ability to *evolve*. If new capabilities are required from a system, appropriately defined interfaces and factories can accommodate new implementation objects that can plug in and perform their given roles within the framework or application context. Figure 5.8 shows a View factory with possibly different types of View instances returned by the factory.

Listeners

Since the introduction of the JavaBeans event model, the concept of listeners has become quite important to Java development. As you know, Swing components are JavaBeans, and therefore provide adequate facilities for implementing the appropriate listener model for a given component. This is especially important because Swing is based on the *model* approach to object design. Because each model may have an arbitrary number of views or listeners, it is crucial to the proper functioning of Swing models that they maintain and notify specific listeners interested in changes to the model.

For most of the default model implementations provided in Swing, this notification is handled automatically. That is, if changes occur in a components

Listing 5.8 ViewFactory interface.

```
public interface ViewFactory {
    public View create(Element el);
}
```

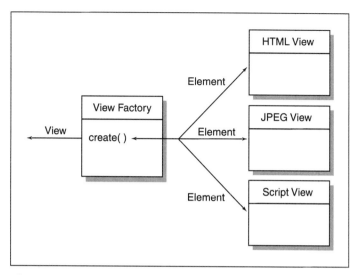

Figure 5.8   A factory and its implementations.

model, the components view will subsequently update to reflect the current GUI/data state of the model.

There are other places where listeners play an important role. The event model associated with the visual interaction between users and components is based entirely on certain types of listeners. This paradigm is not necessarily new with JFC or Swing, but it does represent key utilization of the pattern. Listing 5.9 shows how two types of listeners acting on the same object can be used.

TopView represents a relatively useless class, but is included mainly to show two common uses of listeners that occur through JFC and the standard Java AWT event model. In this example, a button is created, then a MouseOverListener is added as a MouseListener object on the button. Because MouseOverListener extends MouseAdapter (which in turn implements MouseListener), MouseOverListener will receive certain mouse events as they occur on the target component. In this case, something happens when a mouseEnter event occurs. In addition, the TopView class is added as an ActionListener (as it implements the interface ActionListener). Certain Swing components will notify ActionListeners about ActionEvents when they occur. JButton notifies its ActionListeners when it is pressed.

These components are designed so that appropriate listeners can be plugged in, supplying the necessary callback functionality on a given component wherever it is needed. Table 5.6 lists the types of listener interfaces defined in Swing.

Listing 5.9   Swing listeners example.

```java
import javax.swing.*;
import java.awt.event.*;

public class TopView implements ActionListener {

    class MouseOverListener extends MouseAdapter {
        public void mouseEntered(MouseEvent event)
        {
            JButton button = (JButton)event.getSource();

            System.out.println("Mouse entered "
                    +button.getText());
        }
    }

    public TopView()
    {
        JFrame frame = new JFrame("TopView")

        JButton button = new JButton("MyButton");

        button.addMouseListener(new MouseOverListener());
        button.addActionListener(this);

        frame.getContentPane().add(button);
        frame.show();
    }

    public void actionPerformed(ActionEvent event)
    {
        JButton button = (JButton)event.getSource();

        System.out.println("Button pressed "+button.getText());
    }
}
```

Adapters

Adapters are implementations of listener interfaces. They are commonly called adapters because the listener objects themselves act on behalf of an object that will ultimately receive the callback invocation. That is, the listener acts as an adapter or a go-between from the target object (the one being listened to) to the callback object. In this sense, the adapter "plugs" together

Table 5.6 Swing Listener Interfaces

LISTENER INTERFACE	DESCRIPTION
AncestorListener	Supports notification when changes occur to a JComponent or one of its ancestors.
CaretListener	Listens for changes in the caret position of a text component.
CellEditorListener	Defines the interface for an object that listens to changes in a CellEditor.
ChangeListener	Defines an object that listens for ChangeEvents.
DocumentListener	Allows an observer to register to receive notifications of changes to a text document.
HyperlinkListener	Notified when a hyperlink is updated.
InternalFrameListener	Interface for receiving internal frame events.
ListDataListener	Receives events about complex changes in List data.
ListSelectionListener	Notified when a list selection value changes.
MenuDragMouseListener	Defines a menu mouse-drag listener.
MenuKeyListener	Notified when a menu key is pressed.
MenuListener	Defines a listener for menu events.
MouseInputListener	Implements all the methods in both the MouseListener and MouseMotionListener interfaces.
PopupMenuListener	A popup menu listener.
TableColumnModelListener	Defines the interface for an object that listens to changes in a TableColumnModel.
TableModelListener	Defines the interface for an object that listens to changes in a TableModel.
TreeExpansionListener	Notified when a tree expands or collapses a node.
TreeModelListener	Defines the interface for an object that listens to changes in a TreeModel.
TreeSelectionListener	Notified when the selection in a TreeSelectionModel changes.
TreeWillExpandListener	Notified when a tree expands or collapses a node.
UndoableEditListener	Implemented by a class interested in hearing about undoable operations.

Listing 5.10 MouseListener interface.

```
public abstract interface MouseListener implements EventListener {

    public void mouseClicked(MouseEvent event);
    public void mousePressed(MouseEvent event);
    public void mouseReleased(MouseEvent event);
    public void mouseEntered(MouseEvent event);
    public void mouseExited(MouseEvent event);


}
```

these two disparate object types (or adapts them). Theoretically, the same adapter can be used to adapt different objects in other contexts. If the callback object itself acted as its own listener, and therefore acted upon itself when trapping events, there would be no intermediary object between it and the target; no true adapter would be present.

MouseInputAdapter

One example of an adapter in Swing is MouseInputAdapter, an abstract class that implements both MouseListener and MouseMotionListener interfaces. The aggregate interface MouseInputListener extends both MouseListener and MouseMotionListener. Therefore, any class implementing MouseInputListener must provide implementation methods for those defined in both MouseListener and MouseMotionListener.

MouseInputAdapter provides a convenient mechanism for catching any of the events thrown to listeners of type MouseListener and MouseMotionListener in a single place or object. Listings 5.10 through 5.13 show the source code for the various listeners involved in creating an object of type MouseInputAdapter.

Because you cannot instantiate MouseInputAdapter, subclassing it is required. If, for example, I needed to create an adapter that listened only for mouse-drag and mouse-clicked events, I would create a subclass like Listing 5.14.

Listing 5.11 MouseMotionListener interface.

```
public abstract interface MouseMotionListener extends EventListener {

    public void mouseDragged(MouseEvent event);
    public void mouseMoved(MouseEvent event);


}
```

Listing 5.12   MouseInputListener interface.

```
public abstract interface MouseInputListener extends
MouseListener, MouseMotionListener {

}
```

It is much easier to create a class like MyMouseAdapter and only provide the method blocks I want. If I were to declare this class as a direct implementor of MouseListener or MouseMotionListener, I would have to provide method blocks (empty or otherwise) for each and every method declared by those interfaces. This would quickly become cumbersome and time-consuming.

Characteristics

There are a few high-level characteristics worth mentioning about the Swing/ JFC framework. When analyzing a framework, there are some basic questions to ask regarding some valuable characteristics. Specifically: Is it easy to use and understand? Does it scale? Is it extensible and reusable?

Understandable. Many things contribute to understanding a framework, but it's important that a framework contain ample documentation that describes how the components operate. JFC provides a rich set of javadocs distributed with Java 2. The javadoc API documentation describes every class in detail, including their methods, fields, hierarchy, and cross-references. This is *internal documentation,* as described in Chapter 2, "Java Framework Design."

Listing 5.13   MouseInputAdapter abstract class.

```
public abstract class MouseInputAdapter implements
MouseInputListener {

    public void mouseClicked(MouseEvent event) {}
    public void mousePressed(MouseEvent event) {}
    public void mouseReleased(MouseEvent event) {}
    public void mouseEntered(MouseEvent event) {}
    public void mouseExited(MouseEvent event) {}
    public void mouseDragged(MouseEvent event) {}
    public void mouseMoved(MouseEvent event) {}

}
```

Listing 5.14   MyMouseAdapter subclass.

```
public class MyMouseAdapater extends MouseInputAdapter {

    public void mouseClicked(MouseEvent event)
    {
        // Do something useful here since I received a
        // mouseClick event from one of my target objects.
    }
    public void mouseMoved(MouseEvent event)
    {
        // Do something useful here since I received a
        // mouseMoved event from one of my target objects.
    }

}
```

Scalable. The scalability of a set of classes or framework is a bit difficult to quantify outside the context of a scenario or application. When you think about the scalability of something like Swing, consider how the components behave among one another, and consider any limitations that can arise when interactions and/or components increase in number and complexity. Scalability is more important to frameworks that deal with resources than presentation frameworks like Swing. JFC imposes no astonishing limitations on its components; however, the rendering speeds of complex Swing components can be negatively affected if there are many of them visible at once.

Extensible. Most of the classes provided for in JFC and Swing are designed to be easily extended. Swing relies heavily on interface objects, and substituting interface components into Swing is not only simple, but encouraged by Swing's design. Whether through the use of listeners or models, objects of these types can be used in many places throughout the framework. This allows the developer to plug in his or her own implementations, thereby extending the functionality of the framework *into* the application context through its client code.

Reusable. Reusability is the primary goal of any framework. The JFC is part of the Java 2 development kit and is, therefore, highly reusable. For generally the same reasons that JFC and Swing are extensible, they are also reusable. That is, they provide basic abstractions and default implementation upon which further refinements can be made. The constructs provided are generic enough that any type of application will find them useful in some context or another.

When writing your own Java-based framework, ask yourself how it reflects some of these characteristics and whether they're important to your programming needs. In general, it's a good idea to provide ample documentation, and simple generic abstractions that promote reusability and extensibility.

The InfoBus

Another Java-based framework is the InfoBus, a set of classes that facilitate the dynamic and generic exchange of data elements between JavaBeans. Its design implements some of the key patterns and topics discussed thus far and will further your understanding of framework design methods and useful programming aids as well. InfoBus is a significantly smaller framework than Swing/JFC, but nevertheless provides some identical design techniques just as well.

Overview

If you were to dissect the term "IntoBus" to gain some insight into its meaning, you could conclude that an InfoBus is an "information bus" or a conduit whereby information "gets on" and "gets off." In practice, that's precisely what InfoBus is.

There are three primary entities in the InfoBus system: *producers of data, consumers of data*, and *data items*. A producer will place data items on an InfoBus, at which point interested consumers are notified and can retrieve the data item and process it. The key concept here is that neither the producer nor the consumer is aware of the other. The InfoBus acts as a liaison between a producer of data and a consumer of that data so that consumers and producers can come and go as needed. In this sense, InfoBus provides a rendezvous mechanism.

The Goals of InfoBus

InfoBus was created so that developers of bean components could share and exchange data in an application- or bean-neutral way. For example, if I wrote a graphing bean that plots two-dimensional data in a variety of views, I could have written it to act as an InfoBus consumer. Another company could provide a data access bean that fetches table formatted data from a data base, and as an InfoBus producer, publish it over InfoBus where my graphing bean could identify it and plot the data. Neither developer has to be aware of the other during design and implementation of either kind of bean, yet both are able to plug them together and create a useful mini-application with little or no (post-development) effort. Also, because both objects are JavaBeans, a designer could, without coding, easily use a visual builder to assemble or attach these two beans over a common InfoBus to create the result.

Naming Conventions

As with the Swing classes, the InfoBus classes loosely follow a naming convention. Objects within InfoBus are prefixed with the same name if they belong to the same genre of objects. For example, there are three types of notification events associated with data items:

InfoBusItemRequestedEvent

InfoBusItemRevokedEvent

InfoBusItemAvailableEvent

Each event type object is prefixed by InfoBusItem and suffixed by Event to accurately identify the family of objects it belongs to and its specific classification. This naming convention is used consistently in the InfoBus framework, making it easier for developers to relate to the classes with which they are building. Furthermore, you will see a direct correlation between how events, notification methods, and exceptions are all named to clearly identify their relationship to one another.

Architecture

The InfoBus represents the rendezvous point where consumer and producer objects can exchange data items in an interface-driven, application-independent manner. The InfoBus API provides the necessary classes and interfaces for developers to write InfoBus-aware beans. Producers and consumers can add and remove themselves from any given InfoBus instance. They can also create new InfoBus instances by name. When a bean joins an InfoBus, it is said to be a *member* of that InfoBus. There can be many InfoBus instances in a given application, each with its own set of members, producers, and consumers.

Those Influential Beans

Most of InfoBus is based on the JavaBeans event model. Key interfaces and event objects of InfoBus are direct subclasses of JavaBean interfaces and events. The philosophy behind the JavaBeans component model is very similar to the philosophy behind InfoBus, and that is that objects can interact and exchange data dynamically and, in the case of InfoBus, do not even need to know about specific data types during implementation.

The Collaboration Model

InfoBus has a well-defined *collaboration model* that determines the internal order in which actions are carried out. This is important to understand as a

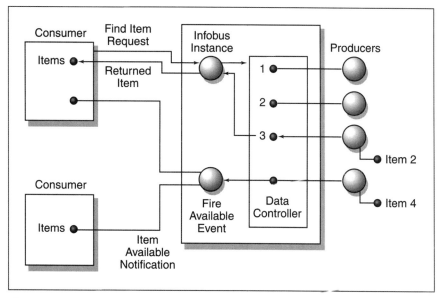

Figure 5.9 InfoBus internal process and organization.

developer. Consumers and producers can join an InfoBus and exchange information. Producers can fire off notifications about item availability, and consumers will receive these notifications. Consumers interested in the newly
available item can request it directly. The method through which InfoBus car-
ries out this ordered operation is its collaboration model.

The object that controls this process is the InfoBus class. All notification
events are submitted to an instance of this class. An InfoBus object responds to
a notification message by subsequently signaling every consumer currently
joined to it. InfoBus delegates this iterative task to a DataController object. The
DataController will sequence through an ordered enumeration of either producers or consumers (depending on which end initiates a notification event)
and construct and deliver the appropriate event object. Figure 5.9 shows how
objects fit together in this process.

Core Classes and Interfaces

InfoBus is a powerful framework for connecting beans and objects in an application-neutral manner. There are a good number of classes and interfaces, but
for the sake of brevity, Table 5.7 lists only those classes and interfaces that represent the core of InfoBus.

Let's start by looking at the InfoBus class, the core functional piece in this
framework.

Table 5.7 InfoBus Core Classes and Interfaces

NAME	TYPE	DESCRIPTION
InfoBus	Class	The primary process-controlling class.
InfoBusMember	Interface	Objects wanting to join an InfoBus implement this interface.
InfoBusDataConsumer	Interface	Objects wanting to acquire data items from an InfoBus implement this interface.
InfoBusDataProducer	Interface	Objects that can supply data items to an InfoBus implement this interface.
InfoBusDataController	Interface	An object that controls the order and delivery of notification events to and from consumers and producers implements this interface.
InfoBusItemAvailableEvent	Class	Sent to consumers informing them an item is available.
InfoBusItemRequestedEvent	Class	Sent to producers informing them an item is requested.
InfoBusItemRevokedEvent	Class	Sent to consumers informing them a particular item is no longer available.
InfoBusMemberSupport	Class	A support class that implements the InfoBusMember interface as a convenience.

InfoBus

Not surprisingly, the InfoBus class is the heart of InfoBus. It acts as the operator and overseer of InfoBus operations within a single virtual machine (VM). Through the use of static methods, this class will create, manage, and return instances of InfoBus. Each InfoBus instance is held within the class scope of the InfoBus class and tracked by name. That is, when I want to create a new InfoBus to join, I request it from the InfoBus class, which manages it closely. The following code snippet shows how to acquire a named InfoBus instance.

```
InfoBus myInfoBus = InfoBus.get("Channel 1");
```

The InfoBus class will maintain the reference returned from this call and free resources associated with it when all members have abandoned it.

Adding Members, Consumers, and Producers

Once an InfoBus instance is obtained, you can add members, consumers, and producers to it, as illustrated in the following code.

```
InfoBus myInfoBus = InfoBus.get("Channel 1");

try {
    myInfoBus.join(someMemberInstance);
} catch (PropertyVetoException pve) {
    // my setInfoBus() method must have rejected the
    // property set.
}
myInfoBus.addDataProducer(someProducerInstance);
myInfoBus.addDataConsumer(someConsumerInstance);
```

Removing these components is a simple matter of calling the appropriate analogous remove method.

```
myInfoBus.removeDataProducer(someProducerInstance);
```

When members request to join an InfoBus instance, that member's infobus property is set to the newly joined InfoBus. A failure to properly set the infobus property will cause that member to not be joined to the InfoBus instance, and a PropertyVetoException will be thrown.

Event Notification

The other important task of the InfoBus class is to generate event objects and deliver them to its members. In the case where a consumer is requesting a data item of a particular type, an appropriate event will be created and delivered to all producers. Producers that can provide the data will respond to the event, and the originating message will return appropriately. Listing 5.15 shows a code snippet on how a producer would generate an item available event notification.

Listing 5.15 Producer generates item-available notification.

```
InfoBus infoBus = InfoBus.get("NewInfoBus");

try {
    // Assume for brevitys sake that "this" is implements
    // InfoBusMember and InfoBusDataProducer
    infoBus.join(this);
    infoBus.addDataProducer(this);

    infoBus.fireItemAvailable("mars.rover",this);

} catch (PropertyVetoException e) {
    // Since it is a constrained property, another bean
    // could disallow this operation.
} catch (InfoBusMembershipException e) {
    // We have a stale infoBus handle
}
```

Listing 5.16 Consumer searches for data item.

```
InfoBus infoBus = InfoBus.get("NewInfoBus");

try {
    // Assume for brevity's sake that "this" implements
    // InfoBusMember and InfoBusDataConsumer
    infoBus.join(this);
} catch (PropertyVetoException e) {
    // Since it is a constrained property, another bean
    // could disallow this operation.
}


DataItem dataItem = infoBus.findDataItem("mars.rover",null,this)

if(dataItem != null) {
    // I have received the data item I requested from
    // some producer
} else {
    // No producers currently joined to the InfoBus could
    // provide the data item I requested.
}
```

Listing 5.16 shows how a consumer finds a data item that may be provided by a producer currently joined to the same InfoBus.

The call to infoBus.findDataItem() will block until the appropriate data item is found or it is determined that no producers can provide the data type requested. Subsequent calls to findDataItem() can produce desired results as new InfoBus producers join the same InfoBus instance.

InfoBusMember

The InfoBusMember interface is used by the InfoBus class to control objects that wish to join and leave InfoBus instances. Implementors of this interface are treated as JavaBeans with a single property, InfoBus, that points to the current InfoBus to which the bean is joined. By adhering to the JavaBean model for properties in this fashion, InfoBusMember objects can be conveniently used in bean-builder environments, where they can have their InfoBus properties manipulated accordingly. Listing 5.17 shows the Java code for the InfoBusMember interface.

Because InfoBusMember implementations represent JavaBeans and can be used in JavaBean builder environments, you can manipulate the InfoBus property of such beans, thereby connecting them to various other InfoBus beans on

Listing 5.17   InfoBusMember interface.

```
public interface InfoBusMember {

    public abstract void setInfoBus();
    public abstract InfoBus getInfoBus();
    public abstract void
        addInfoBusVetoableListener(VetoableChangeListener vcl)
    public abstract void
        removeInfoBusVetoableListener(VetoableChangeListener vcl)
    public abstract void
        addInfoBusPropertyListener(PropertyChangeListener pcl)
    public abstract void
        removeInfoBusPropertyListener(PropertyChangeListener pcl)

}
```

your bean-builder palette. The latest release of the Bean Development Kit (BDK) adds InfoBus support, allowing you to create InfoBus bean applets and applications within a visual environment. (The BDK can be downloaded from java.sun.com/beans/.)

InfoBusDataConsumer

An object wishing to receive notification events from the InfoBus about item availability will implement the InfoBusDataConsumer interface. The methods in this interface are not called openly from other application objects, but instead represent a protocol that is defined and expected by the InfoBus controller class. The collaboration model of InfoBus recognizes objects of this type and will send only the messages within this interface to objects wishing to consume data items. Listing 5.18 shows the source code for this interface.

Listing 5.18   InfoBusDataConsumer interface.

```
public interface InfoBusDataConsumer extends InfoBusEventListener {

    public abstract void dataItemAvailable(InfoBusItemAvailableEvent
        event);
    public abstract void dataItemRevoked(InfoBusItemRevokedEvent
        event);

}
```

The InfoBusDataConsumer interface contains two notification methods that are triggered when certain events occur within InfoBus. In this case, when data items become available and are subsequently revoked. Notice how the naming convention used clearly identifies the notification methods and their corresponding event objects.

InfoBusDataProducer

InfoBusDataProducer objects represent the other end of the sequence involving data consumers and producers. Data items only become available to consumers through a Producer object joined to the same InfoBus. Identical in nature to the InfoBusDataConsumer interface, the methods defined by this interface are not openly called from outside the InfoBus control process. There is only a single method in this interface, and it is invoked on behalf of a requesting Consumer object. Listing 5.19 shows the source code for the InfoBusDataProducer interface.

The InfoBusDataProducer interface has a single notification method that accepts an appropriately named event object from the family of InfoBus events. In this case, an InfoBusItemRequestedEvent object is delivered to InfoBusDataProducer listeners on an InfoBus. This methodology is in strict concordance with how JavaBeans operate and how they associate event and listener nomenclature.

Error Handling

A good framework will provide a family of well-defined exceptions. InfoBus has a number of exceptions you will need to trap within your application code, depending on which InfoBus constructs you are interacting with. Table 5.8 identifies the exceptions generated within InfoBus and what each does.

Some of the interfaces within InfoBus enforce the strict adoption of exception throwing. For example, the abstract method setInfoBus() defined by InfoBusMember, requires the catching of PropertyVetoException from the invoking context.

Listing 5.19   InfoBusDataProducer interface.

```
public interface InfoBusDataProducer extends InfoBusEventListener {

    public abstract void dataItemRequested(InfoBusItemRequestedEvent
      event)

}
```

Table 5.8   InfoBus Exception Family

NAME	DESCRIPTION
ColumnNotFoundException	Thrown by a RowsetAccess object when a specified column does not exist.
DuplicateColumnException	Thrown by a RowsetAccess object when more than one column exists that matches a given name.
InfoBusMembershipException	May be thrown if the InfoBus being joined is "stale"—no longer on the system's set of active InfoBusses—or because membership is not permitted for the joiner.
InvalidDataException	Thrown by a DataItem when a method attempting to change its contents (like addItem or setValue) has failed because the proposed new value is illegal.
RowsetValidationException	Thrown by a RowsetAccess DataItem when a method that modifies values fails. This base class should be extended by data providers to return more information via the getProperty method.
StaleInfoBusException	May be thrown if the InfoBus instance involved is stale (removed from active list). It indicates a bug in the caller's code.
UnsupportedOperationException	May be thrown if the InfoBus participant or data item does not support a method called. (To be replaced by java.lang.Unsupported-OperationException after Java 2.)

```
public abstract void setInfoBus(InfoBus newInfoBus) throws
  PropertyVetoException
```

Some exceptions can be caught optionally; that is, they are not strictly thrown from a given method, but will "fall through" the running thread if not handled properly. Such a method is InfoBus.join(). Though it is not required to catch the StaleInfoBusException, if it should occur, the current running thread would cease to execute. The reason StaleInfoBusException does not have to be caught is because it *should* never occur. If it does, it means there is a bug somewhere in the application where it creates and joins InfoBus instances. Having your program halt and dump trace is a reasonable and useful way of notifying the developer.

Characteristics

Like JFC, InfoBus has various framework characteristics.

> **Understandable.** The InfoBus API classes, like JFC, come with a set of nicely compiled javadoc HTML files that index the classes and interfaces. Also like JFC, there are example programs included with the InfoBus distribution. Combined, these provide the developer with a good foundation for understanding the framework. This is enhanced by the conformance to the well-documented and widely used JavaBean architecture and good internal naming conventions.

> **Scalable.** InfoBus is designed to allow for arbitrary numbers of beans to join and dismiss themselves at runtime. In addition, multiple InfoBus instances can be generated dynamically. InfoBus provides for crucial internal resource tracking to ensure that unused objects are discarded and that previously created objects are reused when appropriate. These sorts of internal behavior increase the robustness of the system and allow it to scale well under greater demands. Additionally, provisions within key InfoBus interfaces dictate the proper releasing of resources should they be allocated (e.g., dataItem.release()). This instructional and programmatic approach to resource tracking makes for a solid and scalable architecture.

> **Extensible.** InfoBus is not necessarily designed for heavy specialization or extension. The InfoBus class itself cannot be extended, and this is neither a good nor a bad feature; rather, it is a design consideration by the architect. Because of the crucial tasks the InfoBus class carries out, subclassing it could comprise the functionality of the system and diminish its reusability. For the most part, the InfoBus classes and interfaces were designed to interact within the InfoBus framework solely, so specialization is not necessary. Instead, the client objects themselves would contain the necessary functionality beyond the posting and retrieving of data items.

> **Reusable.** Because InfoBus is founded on interfaces and events, it is highly generic, and hence highly reusable. The primary constituents of the InfoBus API are in the form of interfaces. Most of the actual objects are simply events. Interfaces are highly reusable because they provide only a description of the protocols needed to interface with framework components. Descriptions are highly reusable, because the implementations may vary from application to application.

NOTE There are rules for implementation procedures of key interfaces in InfoBus. The behavioral semantics of these interfaces should not be comprimised by the implementor. Access the latest InfoBus spec (at java.sun.com/beans/infobus/index.html) for more information.

Summary

This chapter examined two popular and interesting examples of good Java frameworks: the Swing/JFC and the InfoBus. By now you're aware how these frameworks effectively represent some of the traits and techniques introduced in previous chapters, which are recapped in the following list:

- The proper use of abstraction through interfaces and abstract classes.
- The ability to substitute application objects into the framework.
- The ability to extend or enhance key objects already defined within the framework through abstract and default implementations.
- The presence of sufficient default implementations to make the framework readily usable.
- Well-defined objective or intent.

Certainly, there are more frameworks than the two discussed here, and it is always useful to see how other successful frameworks are put together and how they meet the needs that developers demand from a useful framework, so I recommend you visit the JavaSoft Web site at www.javasoft.com for updates and new releases.

The next chapter explores ways to organize, layer, and package frameworks in Java. Building large framework- or component-based systems involves defining an architectural approach that permits for the layering and abstracting of discrete functional components. We'll look at some interesting tools and methods that assist in the compositing of framework foundations within a larger system, as well as ways to optimize reuse.

References

Fowler, Amy. "Swing Architecture Overview." java.sun.com/products/jfc/tsc/archive/what_is_arch/swing-arch/swing-arch.htm. JavaSoft, 1997.

Hoque, Reaz. *Connecting JavaBeans with InfoBus.* New York: John Wiley & Sons, Inc., 1999.

Composite Foundation Architecture

Previous chapters have presented many instances of reuse. From JavaBean components to patterns to complete architectures, there is a movement toward reuse of objects and frameworks. Given the sheer volume of objects, frameworks, and components of an evolving complex system, there also must be a supporting architecture and methodology to govern the complexity and better maintain and manage its growth.

The *Composite Foundation Architecture* (CFA) is a methodology and architecture for organizing and developing frameworks, components, and subsystems within a larger complex system. It works by promoting the construction of architectural foundations in the form of class and framework interactions. In addition, it adopts a layered model approach to visualizing a system as a stratified set of interacting or derived frameworks (or foundations). This approach to framework composition makes it possible to buffer a system's top-level abstractions from various interconnected underlying abstractions. This then facilitates modular change and evolution of the various strata developed to represent a system supporting a variety of similar applications.

A complex system cannot be fully understood as a whole; it must be broken into detailed parts that are easier to understand [Hofstadter 1979]. Object-oriented techniques help you do this. Objects themselves form larger con-

Various entomological systems arranged in sized ordered linear fashion.

structs: objects are grouped into micro-architectures and frameworks, which also can be grouped to interact to form larger, more specialized constructs. These are ultimately instantiated as applications. By deconstructing a complex system into smaller subsystems,[1] components, and frameworks, problem domains can be better isolated, implemented, and evolved over time. The collective subsystems are often candidates for frameworks because they frequently contain specialized knowledge and address a specific goal or task. Each subsystem can be as small or as large as is needed.

When embarking on massive coding projects, securing a lengthy investment in time and effort is always a concern. Developing such a system often requires teams of developers and years of commitment. Therefore, any such project should be prefaced by an intense analysis into the various functional domains of the system, to identify the major functional domains that are eligible for framework components. By identifying discrete areas of your system and making them framework- or component-based, you can afford the future luxury of changing a given implementation without altering the architecture of your system. This can increase the longevity of your system architecture even as you find newer and better implementations to plug in.

---

[1] In this context, the term subsystem refers to a discretely defined functioning part of a larger system. Generally, a given subsystem is represented as a component of a greater system.

Development Strategy

To successfully streamline and optimize development efforts across projects involving teams, time, and money, you need a strategy. Basing your development strategy on fundamental principles leads not only to better, more stable systems, but longer-living applications that can be updated with minimal coding. The following subsections introduce these principles, methods, and practices:

- Configuration management
- Growth capability and scalability
- Deployment and maintenance
- Visualization models

Then we'll explore the Composite Foundation Architecture and present some interesting concepts and procedures for managing diversity and complexity in large, evolving systems using the Java platform, along with some key design concepts and mental tools (or things to help us think about things). Together, these provide a useful set of methods and tools for addressing the design and development of object-oriented scalable systems using Java.

Configuration Management

Configuration management concerns how a system moves through the various stages of its life cycle, such as development, testing, and deployment. Although each area is of vital importance to the success of any project, this discussion focuses on the development stage, specifically, how the code base of an evolving system is managed and controlled.

As a developer, I've worked with all types of systems using varying degrees of configuration management. I have found that the systems with better defined configuration management were not only more successful, but easier to understand and maneuver. Working on large projects with other team members often implies various communication and configuration dilemmas, and configuration management (CM) intends to improve and/or help solve these dilemmas.

Object-oriented technology makes an interesting suggestion for managing the developmental configuration of a large system. I've worked on successful projects in which isolating object components and modules of a system demanded the attention of a dedicated core team or an individual. The point is, if a system can be subdivided into discrete modules that act as well-interfaced black boxes, then these components, regardless of their size, can be better developed independently of the overall system. If your system architecture facilitates the objectifying of components in this manner, these components become easier to manage irrespective of their contained complexities, because they are dealt with in a repetitive microcosm of the overall system.

Segmentation Control

Configuration management provides procedures or facilities to manage the segments of a large application or suite of applications. These segments can be complete applications, frameworks, or class libraries unto themselves, but because they are separated from the whole in this regard, they have some independence within the system proper. This independence permits the localization of changes over time for individual or separate framework components. Obviously then, it is important that the configuration management of a large system be able to properly contain, isolate, and track how these segments evolve.

When designing a framework for use in your own projects or as a standalone product, you should treat the framework as if it were a separate product. That means: pay equal attention to the major areas of concern as if they were a whole application. These areas, as previously mentioned, include:

- Development
- Testing
- Deployment
- Maintenance

Proper segmentation control within your configuration management system facilitates the development and adoption of frameworks and components within your project.

The key principle of configuration management is controlling the evolution of your system. There are well-documented procedures and guidelines that will assist you in managing the complexity of your system through proper configuration management. Although these procedures are beyond the scope of this text, this discussion should give you the context through which these ideas can be investigated.

Growth Capability and Scalability

Unlike the monolithic applications of yesterday, today's applications are composed of many interlocking and interacting components, often distributed across a network—or even the world! The ability to evolve, grow, and scale is a primary concern for developers of large-scale systems, so during the design phase of a system, developers must pay close attention to the application architecture and ensure that it allows for growth and evolution over time.

Any complex system comprises a multitude of interacting elements that react to one another in specific ways. But over time, the expectations for the system can change due to outside forces such as new user requirements, new technologies, or even failed technologies. Developers should quantify and control the entities within a system and monitor the system's evolution and growth to ensure it continues to behave as expected. This includes altering behavior over time to meet the inflow of user requirements, feature requests, and bug fixes in a timely manner.

Because system requirements are constantly changing, large systems developed today must be able to effectively adopt tomorrow's new technologies that replace obsolete or inadequate ones. This increases the longevity of the application system and ensures positive return on the time invested in its initial design and implementation. Figure 6.1 shows the trend in application complexities over the years.

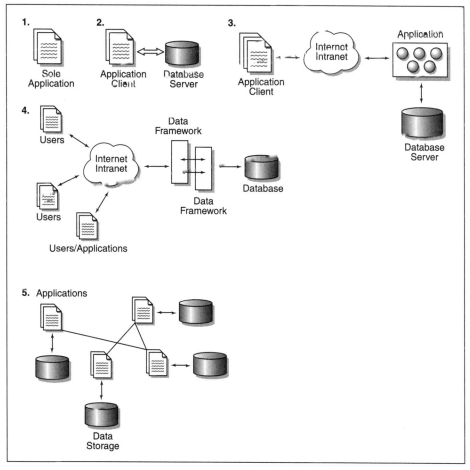

Figure 6.1 Evolution of application systems.

The cost investment in today's systems is enormous; and it continues to grow as application demands and user bases continue to expand. For these reasons, static monolithic systems cannot meet changing customer demands. Today's systems must be composed of parts that can be replaced, upgraded, or expanded throughout the lifetime of the system.

The *growth capability* of a system defines its inherent capability to adapt, change, and grow over time. These traits must be carefully designed for. To determine the growth capability of a system ask the following questions:

1. How many users will this system have initially? In the future?

2. What technologies does this system currently rely on? In the near future? Long-term?

3. Must this system meet ongoing requirements? How often will they change?

The answers to these questions will help you to determine how volatile and demanding the components and resources of a system are, which will influence the overall architecture.

As stated, the Composite Foundation Architecture presents a methodology for developing a system by deploying and reusing framework-based components. By interlocking framework components in various ways, a wide range of systems can be constructed in far less time than it takes to reinvent or redesign solutions across applications and systems.

Well-defined and designed frameworks should enable the plug-in of various implementations. In doing so, behaviors of domain problems addressed by your system can be replaced as newer and better solutions become available. The ability to do this seamlessly and easily is critical to the long-term success of future systems. The rate at which improved technologies become available is not in our control, but enabling for their quick and easy adoption is.

Deployment and Maintenance

Deploying a system solution to a heterogeneous customer base is a growing concern, due, in part, to the ever-fluid ocean of requirements that drives these systems. It is difficult to design, develop, and deploy a large system; it is even more difficult to ensure that such a system (if commercial bound) meets the needs of a wide range of customers, each having similar but different requirements. Any architecture that can address these concerns would have to facilitate the peaceful coexistence of modular interface components, which must have the capability to be handled, managed, upgraded, and developed independently of other modules, frameworks, or components.

Visualization Models

This book employs diagrams to help you to visualize the concepts and architectures we're discussing. An encapsulated polygon, like a square or rectangle, for example, has been used to depict a framework. Illustrating complex object hierarchies, frameworks, or components as simpler, more abstract entities assists the designer by providing an easy-to-wield semantic tool to describe a much more complex system. Subsequently, semantic information can be extracted more readily, depending on the visualization or mental model you choose. A variety of views into a complex system can expedite the understanding about the system's organization.

One of the reasons a framework is useful to an application designer is that the complexities of the framework's functioning is not immediately visible (or exposed) to the framework user (i.e., it is black-boxed). The interfaces exposed by the framework hide the framework's complex object patterns and hierarchies. Using frameworks eliminates the time-consuming decomposition and analysis usually necessary to solve a particular task from scratch. The semantic understanding of what the framework tool (or building block) provides is, therefore, easier, making using the framework more attractive than reinventing a solution set. Using a simple visualization model enhances a designer's ability to describe behaviors at a higher level within a system. The high-order problem domains of a system architecture, such as data storage, visualization, and object transportation, can be translated into equally large architectural components and depicted simply as interconnecting blocks. Operating at such a level defers concern for implementation details. When you design architectures and frameworks in terms of patterns, essentially that is what you're doing.

One method of designing and representing a system is as a series of interrelated and interconnected framework components, or *foundations*. They are referred to as foundations because refined variations are built on top of them to provide newer, more specific domains of behavior. As these foundations grow and proliferate, forming the basis for systems along the way, they give the developer a simple way to visualize such systems, using a *layered model* approach that shows which foundations are built from others.

The Layered Model

A complex and distributed application architecture can be depicted as a series of interrelated frameworks or hierarchies that have strictly defined relationships with one another. These relationships are represented as the contracts and interfaces in place between these interacting frameworks. Such contracts are not bilateral, in the sense that they are equal or symmetrical between two instances of adjacent foundations. There is strictly imposed directionality in the nature of the contracts between two frameworks. How one framework or foundation utilizes another does not imply the converse. In fact, in a layered model, the goal is to enforce the nature of hierarchy. That is, lower-level foundations are not cognizant of refinements or frameworks built on top of them. For this reason, upper-level foundations represent refined variations of underlying ones. Figure 6.2 shows a simple flow control diagram within a simple layered model.

If you think of a framework as an abstracted pattern or architecture with a predefined purpose, then you can think of an application that uses the framework as an *instance* of that framework. Just like instances of a class may carry different states, different applications will represent different instances of a framework in the same regard. If you advance this by viewing a framework as a possible refinement or collective abstraction of yet other frameworks, you begin to see how viewing such relationships in a simple progressive manner is useful. That is, you would like to know upon which frameworks a given application is built, and from which frameworks other frameworks are built, interact with, or otherwise rely on [Baumer et al., 1997].

The layered model attempts to show the linearity of dependency between such entities, and forces you to think about creating linear relationships between future instances. That is not to say that there is a strict one-to-one mapping between layers in the model, rather that this visualization tool represents a linear notion of specificity or genealogy between reusable structures used to define an application instance or many applications. In practice, many frameworks and components will relate in various hierarchical ways. It is the sum of these components and relationships that defines an overall strategic approach to reuse and systems design.

This layered model also indicates the path of interactions to and from applications. Using this approach, you can assemble large, complicated architectures that indicate:

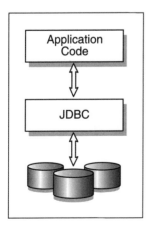

Figure 6.2 Layered model flow control.

- Which frameworks and components address which services and domains.
- Which frameworks and components collaborate with which applications.
- The level at which this collaboration occurs.

Remember, even at this level of detail, you are still not concerned with the details behind the individual framework subsystems. The focus is on how each high-order problem domain is collected in the governing architecture. Because this type of mental model illustrates these high-order relationships among architectural components, it is not intended to be descriptively rich. Figures 6.3 and 6.4 show simple representations of single and multiple application architectures, respectively, using the layered model.

Vertical Orientation

Similar to traditional architecture, where structures are built vertically upon foundations, application architectures can be seen as a set of vertical relationships whose events propagate between layers. Lower layers act as foundation components for upper layers by providing abstracted services and event propagation. Events or information passed between adjacent layers are usually not visible within nonadjacent layers unless otherwise propagated.

Figure 6.5 shows how events generated between two adjacent layers can be buffered from subsequent layers in your system. This is important when you

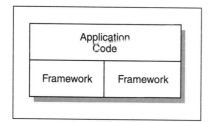

Figure 6.3 Single application layered model.

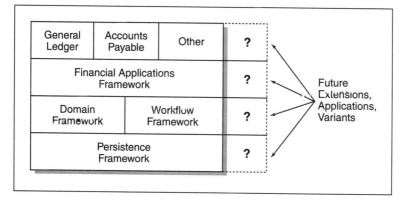

Figure 6.4 Multiapplication layered model.

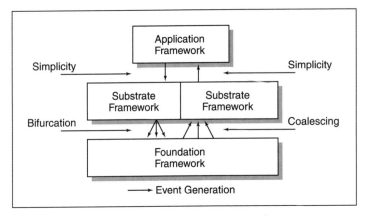

Figure 6.5 Buffered framework event propagation.

want to coalesce events, exceptions, or message traffic as it propagates to different levels within your application. Doing this can reduce the apparent complexity of a given application framework. Even though events triggered by an application may ripple through various layers (framework components) in the architecture, they have a point of origin that is typically based on some single event. (See the discussion in Chapter 1, "Framework Concepts," about atomic operations, perceived complexity, and state management.)

Architectural Framework Concepts

To begin to construct an architecture that, at some level, involves frameworks, it is useful to use the layered model approach to visualize the problem domains the architecture must support. This approach makes it easier to systematically identify the problem domains that occur (or may occur) within your system. This is similar to the method of problem decomposition discussed in Chapter 1, "Framework Concepts." Each domain can be further broken down into more detailed segments as the semantics of the problem become clearer and more refined. In addition, solutions to problem domains can be encapsulated as segments, and qualify for a useful framework in that regard. In addition, at the higher levels of system architecture, we can reason about system behavior in advance of problem implementations, which tend to be more fine-grained and require more detailed analysis and visualization.

Figure 6.6 is a chunk view of a system with a high-order visualization of the system's domain components. At this stage of design, the major areas of concern and possible candidates for framework usage have been identified. Figure 6.7 shows a magnified section of Figure 6.6 with solutions designed into the higher-order problem domains.

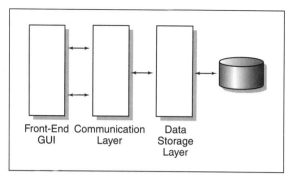

Figure 6.6   High-order domain visualization.

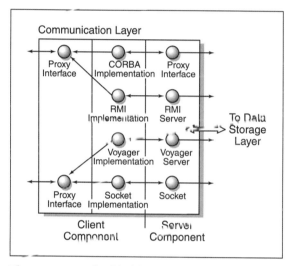

Figure 6.7   Embedded layer visualization.

Interacting Frameworks

In a layered model of a framework-based architecture, two adjacent frameworks that utilize, but do not extend or specialize, the classes of another framework are known as *interacting frameworks*. One framework interacts with another if it propagates an event or formally engages in message passing. Interacting frameworks do not necessarily imply a symmetrical relationship. Instances of one framework may invoke instances of another, not vice versa. Because of this, there is a strict dependency between object instances that control the flow of messages and events to and from instances in another framework, making a given framework and all of its dependent frameworks inseparable. However, this is not true in the reverse direction if there is no established form of messaging or interaction.

NOTE As a good example of this, you would find it normal that a GUI framework made use of a data storage framework, whereas it would sound a little weird to you if a data storage framework made use of a GUI framework.

This concept permits various groups of object hierarchies to be layered and abstracted, whether they are frameworks or slight variations thereof. As shown in Figure 6.6, the complexities involved in controlling flow within a nonadjacent framework or layer are not relevant beyond the utilizing layers. Therefore, nonadjacent object instances that do not directly utilize or interact with instances of another framework are simply unaware of message traffic that does not originate locally (and is subsequently not propagated). This is an important concept to consider when the goal is to manifest complex systems as well-abstracted, encapsulated, and reusable micro-architectures and frameworks.

Interacting frameworks are utilized primarily through object composition rather than inheritance (as with derived frameworks). In object composition, message passing occurs between two disparate objects (because one is composed of the other), whereas deriving a subclass from a given class in a framework does not assume any particular user of the inherited class. Typically, the design or use of a particular framework does not exclude either manifestation. It's not an either-or situation, rather a practical issue. Depending on the actual application framework, extension and specialization may simply not be needed, or the framework could restrict extension for various reasons. Through composition of objects from different frameworks, dependencies between them can reside in only one object which can be cleanly separated through the appropriate framework interface; that is, the frameworks bind together through a well-defined interface or protocol [Taligent, 1995]. Furthermore, messaging that occurs between interacting frameworks can be easily represented as atomic events indicating that a state change has occurred with the original framework or possibly that a state change is about to occur [D'Souza, 1998]. The JavaBeans event model (see Chapter 4, JavaBean Components) highlights the type of JavaBean events that support this form of interactive communication (namely PropertyChangeEvents). Given the type of listener, the change notification can be received and processed or vetoed thereby prohibiting the state change from occurring.

Figure 6.8 shows two simple frameworks in which instances within each deliver messages between them.

Derived Frameworks

A *derived framework* is one whose class hierarchy is a specialization (or derivation) of another framework (or subset thereof). Object definitions in a derived framework are strictly inherited from another framework. This results in a more specific representation of a particular framework. Later in this chapter, using the banking foundation classes as an example, you'll see how this con-

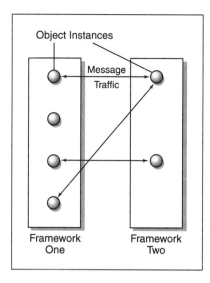

Figure 6.8 Object instances between interacting frameworks.

cept works. The banking foundation classes will be extended to provide secure versions of the originals. The result will be a newly packaged set of classes that extend the base framework classes to provide security enhancements.

Depending on the level of specialization of a particular framework, only certain components in a framework need refinement. This is one reason why frameworks are useful. Their components can be specialized to meet the needs of individual applications. But what if the specialization is not application-specific? What if the specialization is, itself, a reusable construct? It may not make sense to incorporate such a component into the original framework proper or its definition because this extension is not usable outside of the base framework classes. Semantically, it is a new framework that can be used separately from the original base framework, but it cannot be used independently from the base framework; it would depend on how a particular application utilizes such extensions.

Figure 6.9 shows a framework with some class extensions that represent a specialization of the framework. Because the specialization is inherently separate from the base framework (in that it specifically does not alter the base

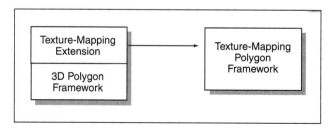

Figure 6.9 Framework extension and composite visualization.

framework), two frameworks, or two views, of the same framework result. The base framework is unaltered. Instead, the base framework's functionality is extended or specialized by creating subclasses that enhance, alter, or override its existing functionality. These new specializations cannot function on their own; they require the rest of the base framework to complete their class hierarchy. You can choose to use one of two possible frameworks: the base framework or the variation of the base framework that includes the new specializations and the remaining classes provided by the base framework. This decision would depend on whether you require the specialized variation of the base framework or not.

You can distinguish between the two frameworks by identifying each as a distinct unit in your visualization model. This is possible because the framework will exist in one form or the other, but not both simultaneously. Separating these forms makes it easier to indicate which version of the framework you are using in your design efforts. Figure 6.9 also shows this separation in view.

It is important to include any emerging complexity and "abstract away" redundant or erroneous details in your visual model. Figure 6.10 shows two applications based on a particular foundation. In both cases, the root foundation is the same, but one application inherits an extension to the root foundation.

Framework Abstraction

In Chapter 2, abstraction was defined as representing the delegation of method execution to lower-level classes. This means that method implementations at the subclass level would supply the execution of declarations existing

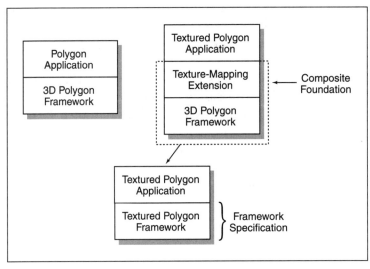

Figure 6.10   Framework-based application.

within the super-structure of the class hierarchy. Chapter 2 also mentioned that abstraction hides the implementation details by providing a consistent interface to that implementation.

When working with frameworks, abstraction goes beyond the boundaries specific to the strict object-oriented sense of the term: A definite scalability in abstracting behaviors, implementations, and entire object structures exist. In the case of object inheritance, methods declared in superclasses can be over-ridden. These specialized subclasses can also masquerade within your object framework as any of their class ancestors, while retaining the capability to execute subclass-specific methods. This is possible through polymorphic method calls into abstract classes (see Chapter 2 for more information on using abstract classes and polymorphic method calls).

This manner of abstraction can be manifest upon collections of objects as well as individual objects. At the framework level, you can provide specialized services and abstracted behaviors by buffering layers within the architecture from one another. The term *buffer* is used (as a verb) to identify a relationship between two instances of different frameworks by way of an interface protocol, object composition, or another delegate object.

To better understand what this means, consider an application composed of three distinct frameworked subsystems.

- The graphical user interface (GUI)
- The data transport framework (DTF)
- The data storage framework (DSF)

The layering of this architecture is important. The order in which each domain is presented represents its sequence in the architecture. The GUI communicates to the DTF, and the DTF communicates to the DSF. From these relationships, you can assume that the GUI is buffered from the DSF; that is, no instances of the GUI communicate directly to the DSF. Changes in protocol or implementation in the DSF should not affect the protocol mechanism coded in the GUI, which interacts solely with the DTF.

NOTE For this discussion, I have imposed some constraints on the described architecture. In reality, there are variations on how layers interact, and not all scenarios will be as strict or oversimplified as this one.

By constraining the architecture in this manner and utilizing frameworks to address each category of problem domain, you can alter the implementation, including the underlying technologies between buffered layers, without affecting protocol. For example, suppose the DSF is coded to JDBC against a relational database. Information gathered within the GUI is passed to the DTF. The DTF is responsible for propagating the events and data to the DSF. Interaction between the GUI and the DTF remain constant, as possible implementations or protocol changes occur between the DTF and the DSF. This alleviates the burden of redesigning systems because of technical changes and minimizes the impact a change in implementation or protocol will have on the overall system architecture.

This type of architecture reduces the complexity of designing objects and structures at the application level by alleviating the details and operations of abstracted or buffered frameworks and class collections (which are not directly visible to the application programmer).

Meta-Frameworks

A *meta-framework* presents one or more frameworks by acting as a façade to those frameworks of subsets of them. The meta-framework maps classes or components from one or more frameworks, possibly distilling them in the process. This process masks complexity and provides a façade in the form of a unified set of classes and abstractions that map onto one or more actual frameworks that could, at some point, be replaced with other technologies or frameworks altogether. It can be argued that this extreme form of abstraction is not necessary; and in most cases, I would tend to agree. It is, however, an interesting concept to create cross-sections or consolidations of one or possibly multiple frameworks and reduce the complexity to provide faster, easier-to-wield objects and structures to application designers. The concept behind a façade is quite similar in that the specific objects (including their possible implementations) mapped to the meta-framework may undergo change while the meta-framework presents a consistent representation of them [Gamma et al., 1995].

Figure 6.11 shows a simple visualization model of a meta-framework in relation to the frameworks it aggregates. You can see two distinctly different kinds of framework classes: workflow and object persistence. The goal of the new derived meta-framework is to combine the utility of the two other frameworks and provide specialized abstractions, interfaces, and default implementations that meet only the functional needs for which the meta-framework is

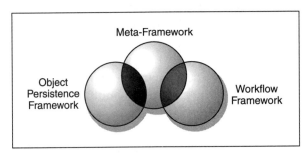

Figure 6.11 Meta-framework concept visualization.

designed. That is, each base framework may contain a wide spectrum of classes and utilities, but because not all are needed, the meta-framework effectively distills only the objective it is intended to serve and exposes the interfaces and object classes for doing that. From the developer's perspective, dealing with one reduced framework is much easier than tackling two larger frameworks that contain more complexity than is required for a given project.

Plug and Play

As previously mentioned, implementations of key framework classes and components can be inserted into a system architecture that is based on layered frameworks without affecting interacting frameworks or application objects, assuming their protocols are well-defined and followed. One of the key capabilities of any reusable framework is that it can insert specialized instances or provide implementations against framework interfaces.

Because of this capability, all client objects interacting with framework components through their interfaces will continue to operate in the same fashion against different implementations of those objects as long as each implementation provides semantically similar behavior. In addition, the entire DSF could be replaced without affecting the operation of the GUI against the DTF. For the developer, this means less time spent redesigning portions of the system to interoperate. Any technology changes within the DSF can be encapsulated in the proper interface implementations within the DTF, allowing earlier operating technologies between the two frameworks to continue to operate in their respective applications or environments.

Modularity and Isolation

Another key architectural concept centers on *modularity,* the characteristic of being composed from modules or modular components. Major components of an application or system are identified and ensured to operate in a modular fashion. Modular components can be identified at many levels, from individual objects or beans to composite beans, aggregate objects, collections, and frameworks or subsystems. You increase your awareness of both the small and large facets of the system by looking at each level; you don't have to contemplate the entire system at once.

Larger, more abstracted logical components can be composed within the architecture by assuring that facets of the system are properly modularized. For example, you might identify that an application is going to be used by many individuals and that it will emulate a business process involving different roles, permissions, and tasks. Further analysis can reveal this application as a good candidate for a workflow framework. The problem is generic enough to make this a reasonable approach. You could, of course, simply hard-code the business process within your application and still deliver a working product, but should changes to that process be necessary, you would need to recode and redesign. If, however, you isolate the workflow classes into a framework and separate its definition and abstractions from the application goals, then this collection of objects becomes a discrete piece, or module, that can provide services to one or many applications, not just the one you're designing.

The idea of modularity arises when developers attempt to understand the workflow characteristics of an application. If workflow characteristics are embedded in an application in a nonmodular way, tracking the workflow is difficult. If workflow activities are delegated to instances of a set of classes (framework or otherwise), it is much easier to go right to the source of the concern and examine it directly.

State Management

Properly isolating framework structures within a system architecture allows for better control of the state management of those systems. Chapter 1, "Framework Concepts," covered the concept of controlling the state of elements within a complex system. Recall that invalid states propagate negative effects that can escalate over time, which can lead to complete system failure.

Finding the source of problems is often an exploratory task.

This occurs when the number of elements or objects in a system become larger and more diverse. Because systems and applications are evolving toward complexity, it is important that they fit into an architecture design that accommodates a high degree of state management through modularity and isolation. This idea extends beyond the fundamental levels concerning simple objects (Java classes) or components (JavaBeans) and aggregates into algorithms, micro-architectures, frameworks, and collections of frameworks, or foundations upon which diverse applications can be built.

Separating constructs at a variety of simultaneous levels isolates effect propagation and leads to better state management. With solid exception handling and proper framework design, negative effects and invalid states can be tracked down and identified easily in the appropriate module or framework of origin. This is important to debugging systems. It can be frustrating to work with languages like C and C++ when you are tracking memory leaks and pointer violations. Fortunately, Java features solid exception handling, memory management, and runtime stack output, which can produce better-performing modules and allow the states of those modules to be better controlled and scrutinized. In addition, you can achieve higher levels of confidence in the efficacy of a system built on modules—if, of course, your confidence in those individual modules can be validated independently.

Optimal Reuse

As with any development effort, exploring the possibility of using existing code, classes, or libraries to solve a particular problem is of high importance. Developers are bored with reinventing solutions to recurring problems! Code reuse, either your own or someone else's, can save time and money on a project.

One of the benefits of the Composite Foundation Architecture (CFA) is a design approach for reusing code bases across similar and even dissimilar project efforts. Companies today are seeking to develop companywide strategies that can leverage development efforts from past projects. This problem is not easily solved, but strides are being taken to spawn newer and better ideas to accomplish this (e.g., component-based architectures, frameworks, and component vendors).

Framework Extension

The main goal of the CFA is to maximize the opportunity for code reuse by systematic structuring of architectural layers or frameworks. When constructing a universal architecture to support the existence of multiple frameworks, each hosting a variety of applications or other frameworks, diversity will certainly proliferate as the number of coexisting systems grows. Such complex architectures based around an object-oriented language like Java should allow for the optimum opportunity for reuse.

There are two kinds of extensions to base frameworks or class sets: *hybrids* and *variants*. Before we discuss those extensions, recall that *interacting frameworks* use object composition and *derived frameworks* to rely on class specialization. Consider a set of classes representing an application or another form of framework or class hierarchy. Logically, it would make use of existing classes in the form of class association or inheritance.

Because reuse is of the utmost concern in large evolving systems, it is likely that new subsystems will utilize a code base in the form of a collection of classes at some point in their life cycle. This does not necessarily mean a completely specialized form of an existing framework. It means that for specific applications, certain specializations based upon an existing framework or set of core classes, including classes from other variations or applications, are necessary. These specialized subclasses simply plug into their base *foundations* and continue to interoperate through object abstraction, which would execute their specialized code in place of the base code where it is overridden or implemented. It is appropriate, in this case, to term such a set of specializations as a *variant* of the base framework or class set that hosts the new specialized classes. The subclasses, including any interface implementations, represent a slight variation of the functionality provided for and defined by the base framework. This implies that a variation extends exactly one such framework or class hierarchy.

A set of specializations that extend multiple base classes as part of their core class family (not multiple inheritance) are called *hybrids*. Similar to meta-frameworks, a hybrid provides specializations across multiple class sets or frameworks.

> **NOTE** A meta-framework does not provide class specialization through subclassing. It provides a façade [Gamma et al., 1995] for only the required classes from various frameworks to create a refined aggregate framework with a combination of functionalities that more uniquely addresses a specific task domain, and hence can be easier to wield.

Composite Foundations

A *foundation* is a framework or set of classes that act as the basis upon which other class sets, frameworks, or applications can be implemented or derived. It goes without saying that the term is not technical in nature; a foundation is anything that acts as a supporting layer or mechanism for something else. A house is built upon a foundation, and without it, the house would not stand, but the foundation is not a noticeable feature of the house.

For the purposes of this discussion, however, the term foundation is used slightly differently from meaning a framework or class hierarchy. The foundation framework acts in conjunction with a variety of extensions, variants, and hybrids that, together, represent an architecture upon which a diversity of applications can be quickly built and efficiently managed. Here, then, "foundation" refers more to the mental architectural model and does not necessarily imply a framework.

The Composite Foundation Architecture is an architecture methodology that relies on the composition of foundations (or frameworks, if you prefer) into an application development strategy, using Java. The key concept is that, when designing a scalable architecture that will host present and future applications, you begin by composing the appropriate foundations to support them. This includes a variety of utility-, domain-, and application-level frameworks as well.

The term *composite foundation* is an extrapolation on the foundation theme, but encapsulates a wide-angle abstraction. To draw upon earlier discussions about how object concepts scale and aggregate, recall that the aggregation concept scaled from objects to collections to patterns and micro-architectures, then on to frameworks, macro-architectures, and applications. In a similar manner, a composite foundation is an abstract foundation that is composed of many other foundation frameworks. The composite foundation is not a tangible nor visible construct, as are base foundations. It is a virtual cross-section of frameworks that are constructed, buffered, or abstracted from one another. The composite foundation reduces cumbersome details and complexities contained within the composing layers, and typically is the topmost extension of a series of frameworks that is manifest as a composite foundation.

Figure 6.12 shows a layered model representing a series of frameworks that comprise a set of application foundation classes. Remember that the vertical orientation within a model suggests the level of utilization and order of propagation between layers. Specifically, the math extensions framework represents the most generic, most heavily utilized substrate in the system. Both the

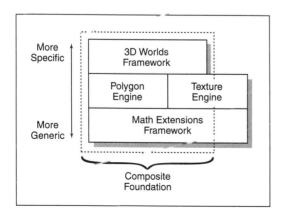

Figure 6.12 A composite foundation cross-section view.

polygon engine and texture engine utilize this framework, but not one another, as indicated by their adjacent relationship. Upon those frameworks resides the three-dimensional framework. It is this topmost composite foundation that developers will actually find useful because it encapsulates and reduces the difficulty of understanding and using the deeper strata in this model; it also exposes a set of refined and comprehensive classes and abstractions to solve a particular problem: generating three-dimensional worlds. As a developer and user of the 3D world framework, for future visualization purposes, you would only need to contemplate it as a single packaged layer and not be burdened with its internal complexity, unless, of course, it was required.

Foundation Implementations

Assuming that a particular foundation in your architecture represents a properly designed and sufficiently generic framework, multiple coexisting implementations of that framework can be provided to represent modules of an application or whole applications. The foundation framework remains a stable yet reusable component in a scalable environment. Figure 6.13 depicts some hypothetical applications residing on a composite foundation.

> **NOTE** Figure 6.13 presents nothing new. This type of structuring diagram is used throughout this book. Notice its simplicity. Even though it looks trivial, it is designed to be easy to understand at first glance. The complexities of the framework and application components are not described at this level, nor should they be.

Java Packages

Packages are important facilities provided by Java to help the developer create separate, modular components and frameworks. If you're already familiar with how packages work in Java or another language, you can breeze through the beginning of this section, but be on the lookout for topics beyond the basics that might be of interest to you.

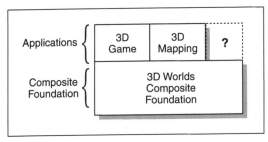

Figure 6.13 Applications residing on a composite foundation.

Package Basics

For any given Java class source file, you can specify a package in which that class resides and is scoped. Other classes outside of the specified package cannot "see" (that is, declare or use) objects of classes residing in the package without specifically allowing foreign package scopes to be visible via the *import* statement.

The following example has two classes: Letter and Number, shown in Listings 6.1 and 6.2, respectively. Notice that each class definition belongs to a package. Specifying the package to which a class belongs is done using the *package* keyword. It is the first line of each listing.

Because each class is defined in a separate package, neither class can declare objects of the other without the appropriate import statement, which tells the Java compiler which namespaces to search to resolve class declarations.

NOTE Contrary to common belief, the import statement does not "import" anything. It simply identifies which packages can be used to resolve name definitions within the given source file. Only the classes you declare in a particular source file are actually examined by the compiler. Java is not a statically linked language, and therefore, the concepts of importation/linking and/or object modules are not inherent, as they are in C for example.

Listing 6.1   Number class header.

```
// Number.java

package numeric;

public class Number {
   // Attributes/Code here
} . . .
```

Listing 6.2   Letter class header.

```
// Letter.java

package alpha;

public class Letter {
   // Attributes/Code here
}
```

Let's next consider a class called AlphaNumeric, shown in Listing 6.3. In this, two objects are declared: one each of type Letter and Number, respectively. However, the compiler will not be able to resolve the class Letter because the package to which Letter belongs is not indicated. Letter objects are not visible to the AlphaNumeric class. Listing 6.4 shows the corrected class definition.

The asterisk (*) wild card symbol is used to indicate that all class definitions in that package should be *scoped* within this class file. The visibility of packaged classes can be restricted easily by specifying classes by name in the import statement. For example:

```
import alpha.Letter;    // Only allows Letter to be visible
```

Some programmers prefer to explicitly state which classes are imported from any given package. But this does not reduce the workload of the compiler, nor does it reduce imported classes, because they are not imported anywhere. Using explicit importation can resolve naming conflicts between identically named objects in different packages; however, in general, it is up to you whether to use wild cards to indicate entire package visibility or explicitly list the objects in the package to be imported.

Listing 6.3 The AlphaNumeric Class header.

```
// AlphaNumeric.java

import numeric.*;

public class AlphaNumeric {
    Letter letter;
    Number number;
    // methods here
}
```

Listing 6.4 Revised AlphaNumeric class header.

```
// AlphaNumeric.java

import numeric.*;
import alpha.*;

public class AlphaNumeric {
    Letter letter;
    Number number;
    // methods here
}
```

Directory Mapping

Java enforces a direct *isomorphism* or mapping between the signature of packages and the directory structure in which packaged Java classes are defined. Because packages allow for *namespace shadowing*, classes of the same class name, but different packages, must be in different directories. Obviously, two classes of the same name cannot exist in the same directory because, in fact, they'd be one and the same file.

As you probably already know, Java resolves class names at compile *and* runtime by using a CLASSPATH environment variable containing root directories where class resolution can occur.[2] Each directory in the CLASSPATH can host Java classes, packaged or otherwise. If you were to complete the alphanumeric classes, you would have to place them in appropriately named directories on your computer, namely "alpha" and "numeric." Your directory structure might resemble the following:

C:\Java

C:\Java\alpha

C:\Java\alpha\Letter.java

C:\Java\numeric

C:\Java\numeric\Number.java

In this scenario, your CLASSPATH would be rooted at C:\Java, because it is the root of your package directories (alpha, numeric). All packaged class files offset from the CLASSPATH, and all package names extend from there as well.

You could easily provide deeper levels to your package structure by creating two additional and separate packages: "numeric.float" and "numeric.double." The directory structure would also reflect this:

C:\Java\numeric\float

C:\Java\numeric\double

Of course, classes created in either package would reside in the appropriate subdirectory. Notice that a hierarchical strategy is used for package name selection in this example. There is no restriction or typical naming convention used for packages other than common sense and personal preference. You could easily put float and double classes in separate packages like this:

C:\Java\float

C:\Java\double

C:\Java\numeric

---

[2] Java 2 provides other means of bootstrapping, so the use of CLASSPATH is optional.

TIP In this example, I've tried to use mnemonics with the package names to make it easier to identify where object families reside in the file system. This makes it easy to inspect the directory structure without having to interpret class names or review source code.

In the hierarchical approach to package name selection, the hierarchy developed is mimicked in the object model. A base class called Number is created with two subclasses: Float and Double, respectively, which depend upon the definition of Number, but not vice versa. For this reason, you need to stick with your first package structure. Note also that each package can contain any number of classes and therefore should closely resemble the family of classes that such a package would encapsulate. In this example, however, there is only one class in each package.

Figure 6.14 shows how a simple object model can contain structures similar to the directory and packaging structure that contain it, providing useful "external" information about how components of a system are grouped and relate.

Having organized your classes and file structure this way, you can understand the relationships between packages and objects external to the code. This is an important concept and a highlight of the CFA method.

Now let's examine what the source files for Float and Double would look like. It's fairly simple, and you've probably already figured this out. Listings 6.5 and 6.6 show the class headers for our Float and Double classes. Here, the package numeric.float exhibits a direct isomorphism between the directory structure (which is bound to the package name) and the class hierarchy of the classes

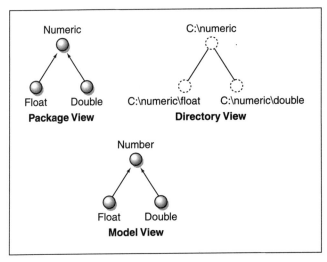

Figure 6.14 Object model directory mapping.

Listing 6.5 Float class header.

```
// Float.java

package numeric.float;

import numeric.Number;

public class Float extends Number {
   // methods
}
```

Listing 6.6 Double class header.

```
// Double.java

package numeric.double;

import numeric.Number;

public class Double extends Number {
   // methods
}
```

contained within the packages involved (namely, numeric, numeric.float). Likewise, Listing 6.6 shows the same relationship with a slightly different package structure.

These examples aren't intended to be a recommendation of how to package mathematical objects as such, but to serve as simple illustrations of the package concept. The key point to remember about these different packages is that they represent different namespaces and are therefore (by default) not visible to one another without explicit import statements. Doing it this way binds two packages together in a direction similar to framework dependencies, as discussed earlier. Specifically, a hierarchically linear dependency structure is created. In these examples, the dependency is more or less bottomup. That is, the deeper, more specific packages like numeric.double and numeric.float are dependent on the less specific, more generic package numeric.

RULE As a general rule, avoid *circular dependencies* between Java packages. A circular dependency occurs when classes residing in two different packages declare or reference objects in the other package. It's a chicken and egg kind of problem. Though Java can handle this situation, it often requires multiple compilations. It's best to avoid circular dependencies if at all possible.

Framework Packaging

There are no actual rules governing how to structure classes or frameworks in terms of packages. Still, there are some useful guidelines to follow, as well as advantages to organized package naming mechanisms. It's important that frameworks embody the same fundamental modularity, encapsulation, and information hiding as even the most basic of objects. These concepts continue to scale well and are useful at macro as well as micro levels. Java packages provide a way to segregate frameworks, class modules, and subsystems within a developmental configuration (recall the JFC and InfoBus frameworks presented in Chapter 5).

To summarize, here are some of the benefits of packages:

- Packages group similarly functioning objects or objects that require a common scope at all times (i.e., objects that are inseparable).

- Package naming can be done hierarchically, to mimic object relationships that can be useful in configuration management, thus contributing to easy viewing and understanding of a complexity of classes outside of those classes.

- Packages represent a macro-level structure that can be readily manipulated independent of users of the package; for example, it can be extended, upgraded, or replaced as a whole.

- Viewing a large, complex project in terms of a hierarchical package view of the system is easier to grasp than sifting through possibly hundreds or thousands of class files.

- Packaging your classes prevents name collisions and neatly organizes and identifies your objects. For example, all your company packages may be prefixed as com.mycompany.mypackage.

This list represents only some general thoughts on the utility of package structures. You will discover other reasons to use them as well.

A Real-World Scenario

A scalable architecture would have to allow for the evolution and insertion of classes, objects, and components over time in a manner that maximizes reusability. If you combined your architectural ideas with the appropriate package scheme to identify and isolate these evolving pieces, you would expect to find your system easier to manage and extend over time. To test this, let's take a look at a simple scenario.

Suppose you're developing a banking application that tracks a consumer loan application through its internal workflow process. When a customer strolls into a bank to request a loan, there are a number of sequences that must occur before he or she finally receives the loan funds. First, the customer must fill out a loan application, which is checked by a clerk for the proper information. From there, it is input into a computer system, where it is flagged for review. The review officer receives an electronic form of the application. He or she examines the application and verifies the information, then follows some general heuristics to determine if the customer qualifies for the requested amount. If the customer does, the review officer flags the application as "approved" and returns it, again in digital form, to the loan officer responsible for the customer's application.

As a software developer, you realize the broad base of banks and institutions that would find such an application useful in one form or another. You discover that the potential for this process, including the domain objects involved to be generalized across banks, is quite high. With only slight variations of data, each bank uses more or less, the same process, staff, and loan applications. It is the variations that you intend to identify and capture, because it would be wasteful time- and moneywise to re-create separate applications for every bank that requested this kind of software program. For this reason, you choose to begin to develop this application by defining and developing a core set of reusable frameworks so that variations can be quickly and easily implemented.

For the purposes of this discussion, we'll assume you want to focus on two primary facets of this system architecture: Specifically, you want to define frameworks that address the domain problem of banking or account-oriented applications, and one that deals with modeling a process in terms of a workflow as described in this scenario.

The Domain

A core set of classes is used to represent a subset of a possible, larger framework that addresses customers, accounts, and transactions, referred to as the CAT framework. It would seem reasonable to further define and apply that framework to solve this application problem. The goal of your hypothetical software company is to pay careful attention when designing this framework to ensure that it is sufficiently generic, so that it can address various banking customers applications by reusing code bases and frameworks.

Drawing on your knowledge about packages, visibility, and dependency, and some of the rules and guidelines provided by CFA, let's construct an initial package and object model for this *domain model framework*. Listings 6.7 through 6.10 show some class file headers for objects from the CAT framework used in earlier chapters.

The three listings represent different source files within a package labeled com.myco.cat. Presumably, there would be various other types of classes,

Listing 6.7   Customer class header.

```
// Customer.java

package com.myco.cat;

public class Customer {
    // implementation deferred
}
```

Listing 6.8   Account class header.

```
// Account.java

package com.myco.cat;

public class Account {
    // implementation omitted
}
```

Listing 6.9   Transaction class header.

```
// Transaction.java

package com.myco.cat;

public class Transaction {
    // implementation omitted
}
```

Listing 6.10   Statement class header.

```
// Statement.java

package com.myco.cat;

import java.util.Hashtable;

public class Statement extends Hashtable {
    // implementation omitted
}
```

organizational models, and collaboration model objects, but let's keep this example simple for illustration purposes.

The entire package will contain all the class and interface definitions provided by this framework. It could just as well contain a variety of packages with even finer-grained functionality, but this is a small and simple framework and therefore has only one package. The domain models as provided by this framework are included in the actual application by importing the package using either the wild card notation or on a class-by-class basis.

For the immediate purposes of your client's goal, the classes defined in this framework might be adequate and practical. Remember, one of the key capabilities a framework must provide is extensibility. Your company's vision of applying this framework across customers and applications can be reached only if the exact description of the object classes defined in the framework can evolve or be adapted in more detailed ways to address more specific needs should they arise. The point is, you must take extra care to make sure your classes are not too specific initially but allow for easy adaptation through subclassing.

Now let's assume that another client has requested a similar banking type of application, but with the specific requirement that its bank's domain models contain security authentication codes that are unique. Modifying the framework classes to include this new requirement would migrate the framework away from sufficiently generic to more specific and possibly break existing installed applications or otherwise present erroneous features or attributes. As suggested, the appropriate subclass can contain the delta requirements for the new client without affecting the operation of the framework proper or current clients and applications.

This is elementary to object-oriented programming, but you also need to provide a mechanism for these modifications to coexist peacefully within your architecture so that they don't disrupt the development of past, current, and future applications centering on these efforts. Package structures enforce a directory mapping that is isomorphic, which addresses how a system is laid out, viewed, and deployed, and affects the configuration management of the system.

To accommodate the newly refined domain models for the new client, you must create a new, more specific package that contains an inverse dependency to the base package of your framework. We'll call this new package com.myco.cat.secure, and it will contain subclasses of the important classes that require the security codes. Listings 6.11 through 6.13 show new class definitions for secure versions of your previous Customer, Account, and Transaction classes. All are contained within a single package.

The application constructed for your new client would import com.myco.cat.secure instead of com.myco.cat, and would instantiate objects like SecureCustomer, SecureAccount, SecureTransaction instead of Customer, Account,

Listing 6.11   SecureCustomer class header.

```
// SecureCustomer.java

package com.myco.cat.secure;

import com.myco.cat.*;

public class SecureCustomer extends Customer {
    int securityCode = 0;

    // implementation omitted
}
```

Listing 6.12   SecureAccount class header.

```
// SecureAccount.java

package com.myco.cat.secure;

import com.myco.cat.*;

public class SecureAccount extends Account {
    int securityCode = 0;

    // implementation omitted
}
```

Listing 6.13   SecureTransaction class header.

```
// SecureTransaction.java

package com.myco.cat.secure;

import com.myco.cat.*;

public class SecureTransaction extends Transaction {
    int securityCode = 0;

    // implementation omitted
}
```

or Transaction. Applications built with com.myco.cat would continue to operate normally and would not be affected by the presence of the new package.

Notice that a hierarchical relationship is maintained to address specificity and inheritance. This is a key concept of CFA with regard to organizing packages. The classes defined in com.myco.cat.secure represent a higher degree of specificity and directly descend from those defined in com.myco.cat. This can be explicitly inferred because the super-package name is nested within the variant package name. This type of organization provides valuable information outside of your application or source code. Clients who need the secure versions can easily locate where that code is defined. In addition, it is possible to conclude that the object relationship between objects defined in this package directly descends from definitions within the base foundation because com.myco.cat is one level higher. Furthermore, if additional requirements were identified that affected the secure framework variant, you could easily provide additional, deeper package structures that accurately reflected the object model relationship and properly isolated these variant extensions as easy-to-manipulate modules within their own nested directory structures.

Though this approach shows base classes with subclasses, often it is better to define the framework model as an interface and allow the framework variant implementations to exist in separate packages, while retaining the same class name. Remember, different implementations of the same interface must be separated into their own packages because no two files can have the same name in the same directory. Therefore, your package name contains the clue to which types of class or interface implementations it contains.

If you wrote the application this way, your Transaction object might resemble the interface called ITransaction shown in Listing 6.14. Application objects could provide implementations of this interface to suit their needs.

Listings 6.15 and 6.16 show two implementations of the same interface. Each class has the same name, and the package name contains a clue to what each Transaction class is designed to do. Generic code written to communicate to

Listing 6.14 ITransaction interface header.

```
// ITransaction.java

package com.myco.cat;

public interface ITransaction {
    // implementation omitted
}
```

Listing 6.15   Unsecure Transaction class header.

```java
// Transaction.java

package com.myco.cat.unsecure;

public class Transaction implements ITransaction {
    // implementation omitted
}
```

Listing 6.16   Secure Transaction class header.

```java
// Transaction.java

package com.myco.cat.secure;

public class Transaction implements ITransaction {
    // implementation omitted
}
```

Transaction objects or ITransaction interfaces would continue to operate regardless of which actual implementation was loaded.

The fact that these two Transaction classes are in packages residing at the same level inside the directory hierarchy is important. This might tell us that there are two extended variations of classes within the package com.myco.cat, and that because these variants are siblings, they specifically do not contain references to one another, and may in fact be mutually exclusive. This means simply that classes contained in either package offset or exclude the other. This is not necessarily directly implicit because of the sibling relationship of the directory level at which each package resides, but it at least indicates that some ancestral commonalties exist between the two packages.

The application built to reference ITransaction objects could be masked from the details about whether those ITransaction objects are secure or not. In other words, the implementation does not affect the application framework. In this case, you would dynamically load various implementations of ITransaction, possibly within a Factory method similar to the following code snippet. Figure 6.15 shows a model of what your architecture would look like to support these variations.

```java
ITransaction secureTransaction =
  Class.forName("com.myco.cat.secure.Transaction").newInstance();

ITransaction insecureTransaction =
  Class.forName("com.myco.cat.Transaction").newInstance();
```

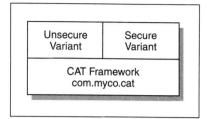

Figure 6.15   Framework architecture visualization.

For this banking application, the defined framework packages could provide a sufficient implementation, meaning that no subclassing or framework extensions were needed. If that is the case, you do not need to create a derived framework variant to host specifications unique to your application.

Workflow

In addition to accommodating evolving requirements and multiple existing frameworks at the domain level for your banking application, you must also address the workflow component of this system. This component will enable objects defined in the CAT framework to be managed inside a business process that contains rules specific to each application/customer. It makes sense for this to be a framework because it will attempt to capture the generic definition of office workflow, which can then be applied to your immediate application problem and be adapted to other slightly different customer requirements. Let's label the package for this framework as com.myco.workflow. In practice, you will find that one package is sufficient for most purposes. The goal is to keep things small and simple. You could just have easily used a range of packages to represent any given framework, but that extent of modularity is not relevant to this discussion.

The workflow framework will contain a number of generic classes and interfaces, such as WorkItem, WorkProcess, WorkStation, and Guard. The following list shows the qualified class names including packages.

```
com.myco.workflow.WorkItem;
com.myco.workflow.WorkProcess;
com.myco.workflow.WorkStation;
com.myco.workflow.Guard;
```

The workflow mechanism is a simple system. A WorkItem can be any object, and is typically supplied by the framework's client code or application. Because the framework is unaware of which kinds of objects might be WorkItems, this is an abstraction in the form of an interface. Therefore, any application class can become a workflow WorkItem simply by providing an implementation of this interface. A WorkStation is a juncture in a graph that represents the state transition of the workflow process being modeled. For example, as a loan application travels throughout the bank, each person who reviews the application performs some task on it, often, but not necessarily, different. As these tasks are performed, the state of the WorkItem—in this case, the application—changes or evolves. Before a WorkItem is passed to the next WorkStation in the workflow, the application system must ensure that the proper state change has occurred. Workflow applications provide a means to catch and control human process, and even errors!

Connecting each WorkStation is a Guard object that inspects the WorkItem traveling between two WorkStations (this is in the logical sense and does not necessarily imply physical relocation, although it could). If the logic contained within a specific Guard permits the WorkItem to pass, the WorkItem is transferred to the new WorkStation node because it has now assumed the state legitimate to the new WorkStation. In your system, this would mean labeling the WorkItem as belonging to the new WorkStation, whose owner might notice it in his or her application inbox. Therefore, each Guard connecting two distinct WorkStations would perform some distinct action as well. If a WorkItem does not pass the test at a given juncture, it does not transition state (i.e. move from one state to another) and therefore transfer to the desired WorkStation (in the logical sense). It remains at the current WorkStation.

A WorkProcess represents a graph of connected WorkStations and Guards. Stations themselves do not provide the necessary connections to model a given workflow process. Rather, the WorkProcess object decides how to construct the graph that represents the transitioning of WorkItems. Figure 6.16 shows a simple workflow state transition diagram.

WorkStation objects represent logical spaces where a particular WorkItem can reside. This can be someone's inbox, or the document can simply be flagged with a particular user's name. The meaning behind the state transition of a WorkItem is undefined by the framework and is, in fact, something only the application would be able to define.

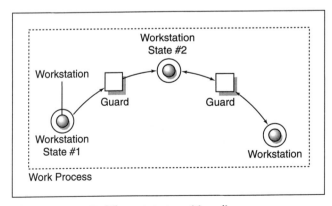

Figure 6.16 Workflow state transition diagram.

Let's look at some class definitions that would use these constructs. Listings 6.17 through 6.20 represent specialized classes and implementations relevant to your banking application project and accompanying framework.

Listing 6.17 Applicant class header.

```
// Applicant.java

package loanapp.cat;

import com.myco.cat.*;

public class Applicant extends Customer {
    // implementation omitted
}
```

Listing 6.18 LoanApplication class header.

```
// LoanApplication.java

package loanapp.workflow;

import com.myco.workflow.*;

public abstract class LoanApplication implements WorkItem {
    Applicant applicant;

    // implementation omitted
}
```

Listing 6.19 ReviewApplicationGuard class header.

```
// ReviewApplicationGuard.java

package loanapp.workflow;

import com.myco.workflow.*;

public abstract class ReviewApplicationGuard implements Guard {
    // implementation omitted
}
```

Listing 6.20   LoanOfficerDesktop class header.

```
// LoanOfficerDesktop.java

package loanapp.workflow;

import com.myco.workflow.*;

public abstract class LoanOfficerDesktop implements WorkStation {
    // implementation omitted
}
```

NOTE These listings are designed to give you an idea of what some class declarations would look like given our current package structure and rules, and hopefully are enough to help you begin to delve further into this topic. Figure 6.17 shows the class diagram for some of the classes discussed. The actual implementation of these frameworks and application is beyond the scope of this chapter.

Look closely at Listings 6.17 through 6.20 and you will notice that there are two packages that comprise the defined classes: loanapp.cat and loanapp.workflow. Each package holds classes that extend or implement base classes or interfaces from the com.myco counterpart package. That is, loanapp.workflow represents a *variant* of some entities in com.myco.workflow. Even though there is a specialization of classes contained in com.myco.workflow, loanapp packages are isolated from the hierarchy rooted by com.myco because you want the loanapp framework (which actually is two packages) to stand alone and separate from the com.myco hierarchy. However, the suffix *workflow* is retained. A specialization of the workflow portion of the com.myco package classes (namely those contained in com.myco.workflow) is also indicated. In this case, the package name is segmented to represent a prefix and a suffix. The prefix (e.g., com.myco or loanapp) represents the base foundation or variant identification; the suffix (i.e., workflow) represents the nature of the framework or extension. No matter how long a package suffix is, creating new variants to existing framework packages using this naming scheme simply involves replacing the prefix portion with the new (isolated) variant prefix while retaining the suffix descriptive part. This accomplishes two things:

- It allows variations on generic foundations to exist in their own rooted directory structures so they can evolve and be configuration managed as separate products or units—which they are.

- It identifies the origins of the new package name by retaining the suffix portion.

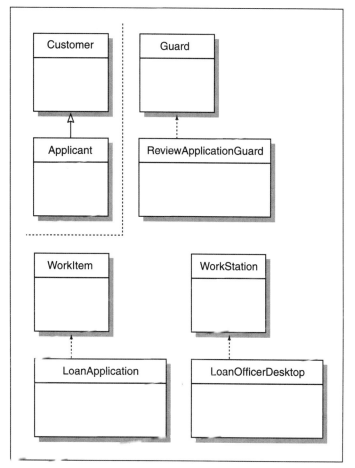

Figure 6.17 Class diagram.

NOTE The discussion of packages earlier in this chapter explained how to label them in a hierarchy that mimicked object relationships of the classes they contained (e.g., inheritance). That is, the greater the specificity, the deeper the package name and, hence, directory structure. The example in this section demonstrates why that method is not useful for configuration purposes. If your variant package name were com.myco.workflow.loanapp, then your loanapp package/framework would be contained within the subdirectory structure of your com.myco packages. This would not be a desirable place for a framework intended to be a distributable, self-contained product.

Also worth mentioning is that in your new composite foundation (loanapp), classes are defined as abstract classes that also implement interfaces. These interface methods can either be implemented directly by the abstract class or passed along as an abstract method where the subclass must provide the implementation. This subclass would be a client code object that resides at the application level. Again, the loanapp framework simply provides an aggregated set of objects (as a hybrid) that unify the CAT and workflow frameworks to provide a combined application framework that is more useful to designers of loan application systems.

In this example, a new composite foundation specific to loan applications is composed from two important frameworks that already provide most of the necessary pieces (see Figure 6.18). The loanapp framework will derive and implement objects and abstractions from two base foundations. This new loanapp framework is a more specific combination of two other less specific frameworks, a *domain model framework* and a *utility framework*.

You're probably wondering at this point: When do I begin coding the actual application? Bear in mind that with this new architecture process, you are looking for ways to create framework subsystems from your application engineering effort that would truly prove useful and reusable across domain applications, either horizontally or vertically, in *advance* of coding the actual application.

THOUGHTS The interesting development here is that a logical foundation is created upon which all future "loan application" type applications can be implemented. Even though this logical foundation is really the top-level manifest of other framework components or class libraries, the complexity of aggregating these subsystems into a finished product is reduced by refining their components into an almost out-of-the-box state. The final domain application can simply use the domain-specific components that were designed with this purpose in mind (as part of the newly created composite foundation).

Variations

Suppose you have two variations of your loan application system that are built upon the loanapp foundation. Because the details behind the underlying frameworks com.myco.cat and com.myco.workflow are abstracted or buffered by loanapp, the developer doesn't need to grapple with them directly. Rather,

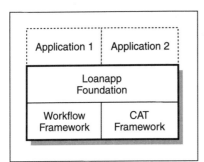

Figure 6.18 The loanapp composite foundation.

the developer is concerned only with how to code directly to the loanapp framework.

The issues of properly hosting the variations of a system within must be addressed in your development configuration. As mentioned previously in this chapter, as an architecture that supports multiple application variants over time, it must facilitate the peaceful coexistence of said applications. Within this discussion, you can use the proper package naming scheme to handle isolation of application differences within your system.

Consider another mini-scenario. Two customers, Customer A and Customer B, want loan applications. Their business processes are almost identical, including similar domain objects; however, certain of the rules governing the state transition of WorkItems are different. Obviously, you would not want to design two entirely new systems because of this difference; instead, you would prefer to make only those changes necessary to accommodate the differences, and reuse the bulk of the first application you write.

Assume also that you have developed a complete loan application system based on your loanapp framework and that you have deployed it. Your goal now is to analyze how much of that existing system is transferable to meet the new customers' needs. Because only a few Guard objects are affected, it would seem that many of the objects created for Customer A's system are indeed usable without cloning the complete baseline. However, you must ensure that the differences between the two deployed systems remain properly isolated from one another so that they are clearly manageable by humans.

In Figure 6.19, notice that the packages representing Customer A's application are defined as:

```
CustomerA.loanapp.workflow;
CustomerA.loanapp.cat;
```

The customerA.loanapp.workflow package within this application provides implementations to the abstractions provided by the loanapp.workflow pack-

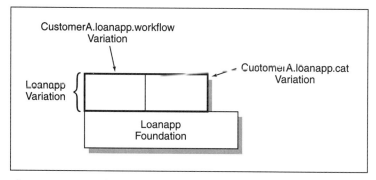

Figure 6.19 Application for Customer A.

age in the loanapp framework. Identifying exactly which portions of the loanapp framework are defined for Customer A is a simple matter of inspection. The configuration environment should contain directory structures that correspond to package names. Therefore, you can determine if Customer A's application implements workflow components, without exploring source code, by noticing that the customerA\loanapp\workflow directory exists and that the classes defined within that directory necessarily represent extensions and implementations of classes and interfaces in loanapp\workflow. The key here is the way the naming scheme works. As mentioned previously, the loanapp.workflow suffix is the descriptive antecedent of this particular variation, namely customerA. Any framework extensions defined by Customer A are placed in packages prefixed by customerA. Therefore, the directory of the same name will act as the root for all variants provided by Customer A. This makes its very easy and useful to explore how a multi-framework application architecture is laid out without resorting to source code or other documentation.

Customer B's application might only require class implementations for loanapp.workflow because only the differences between Customer A's and Customer B's application reside in the class logic in this package. For this reason, the directory structure might only contain one such package for Customer B's variation of your application: customerB.loanapp.workflow. Again, by inspecting the external configuration management layout of the system, you can determine exactly what Customer B's application variation involves. You would see that only the directory customerB\loanapp\workflow existed, and therefore represented the only portion that needed additional development for that system.

The question now for any external viewer of this system is: What are the other reusable foundations that comprise a deployable system for Customer B? Certainly guessing is not a good approach. It would be useful if such information were also available through inspection. This can be achieved by nesting the package for Customer B within the package hierarchy it requires, in order to represent a complete, deployable application (based on whatever foundations it intended to reuse). Specifically, the packages created for Customer A are, in fact, reusable except for the workflow segment. For this reason, Customer B's variant package can be renamed as customerA.customerB.loanapp.workflow. This embeds the Customer B-specific variations inside the directory tree rooted by Customer A because it is acting as the base- reusable foundation for Customer B's deployed system. As a result, acquiring Customer B's variations from this directory structure automatically acquires the foundation upon which it was built, since it resides within the directory hierarchy.

> **NOTE** The issue of separating or extracting only Customer A is a problem addressed by configuration management techniques. The key here is to understand how the system is built and how the foundations are reused without interpreting source code files.

This new package name indicates two important points:

■ Customer B has variant-specific code based in loanapp.workflow.

■ Customer B is also contained within the Customer A directory structure, which indicates that sibling directories (hence, packages) are part of the complete Customer B system as well. Put another way, the existence of the Customer B directory within Customer A's hierarchy says that Customer B's system is everything that Customer A's system is, but that any packages appearing within Customer B's subdirectory override any corresponding Customer A implementation.

Let's add another package to the mix to better illustrate this. Suppose that Customer A's application defines a package called customerA.domain. In this package are domain-specific extensions to the com.myco.cat framework. The directory/package structure now looks like Figure 6.20. Figure 6.21 shows a vertical layered visualization of Figure 6.20.

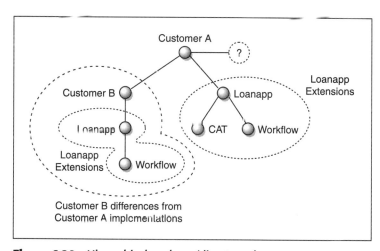

Figure 6.20 Hierarchical package/directory view.

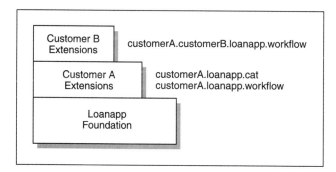

Figure 6.21 Layered hierarchical model.

> **NOTE** Remember, class names can remain the same as long as different packages are used and not included simultaneously. Therefore, customerA.loanapp.workflow and customerA.customerB.loanapp.workflow can define classes with the same name. This would not break any other classes that declare classes from within these packages; however, those modules would need to ensure the proper loading of the appropriate packaged classes.
>
> Also be aware that you are not restricted in the nomenclature for your packages. The example in this section uses customerA and customerB directly within the package name. This is not always the best option, but was used to keep the discussion succinct and easy to track. You will explore other useful names that fit the paradigm suggested here.

For the classes defined in customerA.customerB.loanapp.workflow to operate correctly with other classes defined in customerA.domain, let's say the application should be coded to dynamically load the appropriate instances from a particular package upon startup. The framework classes defined do not import classes from other frameworks (i.e., they are not composite foundations). Therefore, it is up to an overlying structure—possibly the application itself or even another framework—to properly import or dynamically load the appropriate class definitions from the desired packages at runtime. The following code snippet demonstrates the dynamic loading of a class implementation of the WorkItem interface.

```
WorkItem workItem =
Class.forName(
    "customerA.loanapp.workflow.LoanApplication").newInstance();
```

The important consideration here is that the directory structure and application architecture facilitates the reuse of packages and classes from prior efforts. In addition, useful information about how a system is defined, in terms of which foundations it extends, uses, and the like, can be gleaned directly from your system configuration—that is, external to the class definitions or source code. This alone makes managing and understanding a complex system through simple views and external inspection possible. Embedded extensions to existing packaged frameworks necessarily include those extended foundations within their directory hierarchy, so determining which pieces are needed to construct a given foundation extension is relatively automatic (specifically, if you acquire a package extensions directory, you automatically acquire its superstructure, which should contain the foundations it extends or builds upon; this dependency should exist only in this direction).

Summary

This chapter presented some architectural design considerations that can improve the organization of your framework-based systems. We addressed some of the concerns of large systems, including scalability through isolation, and segmentation of subsystems into modular frameworks or components using various Java package names and schemes. The important concept to remember is that modularity can extend beyond the object model representation and into the physical layout of the system. This contributes to a developer's understanding of complexity by allowing the visualizations of cross-sections or micro-views of a larger system. This can be accomplished if the components (including frameworks) are arranged in a hierarchical fashion that represents the foundations from which they are derived. It is important to distinguish between those components that are reused for a given application system and those that are not.

The methods discussed should allow for peaceful coexistence of multiapplication architectures that make it possible to share and reuse components while maintaining their separation as modules within the architecture. It would be difficult to manage the evolution of a system in terms of plugging in new modules and replacing packages, frameworks, and technologies if they were not properly segmented and visibly isolated within your system configuration management. A hierarchy is the best method for embedding framework packages and subsequent variations and extensions. Fortunately, directory structures are hierarchies, and package names map directly onto them.

This chapter also identified some simple visualization models that allow the developer to expand the details of the architecture and to represent the hierarchy of reuse within a system. Tracking the reusable components and how and where they are reused is important if an architecture strategy is to be used across similar or dissimilar applications and projects.

Chapter 7 on Java application architectures explores various domains of interest that arise when considering the architecture of an application or system. Frameworks present reusable constructs useful to such topics as common issues to consider when designing Java application systems, objects, user interfaces, data storage, and distributed systems. You will find it informative to delve into these topics in some detail.

References

Adair, Deborah. "Building Object-Oriented Frameworks" http://www.developer.ibm.com:8080/library/aixpert/feb95/aixpert_feb95_boof.htm, Taligent, Inc. Appearing in AIXpert February 1995.

Baumer, Dirk, Guido Gryczan, Rolf Knoll, Carola Lilienthal, Dirk Reihle, and Heinz Zullighoven. "Framework Development for Large Systems." *Communications of the ACM*, October 1997. Page 52-59.

D'Souza, Desmond, and Alan Cameron Wills. *Objects, Components and Frameworks with UML: The Catalysis Approach*. Reading, MA: Addison-Wesley, 1998.

Gamma, Erich, Richard Helm, Ralph Johnson, and John Vlissides. *Design Patterns: Elements of Reusable Object-Oriented Software*. Reading, MA: Addison-Wesley, 1995.

Govoni, Darren. "Java Frameworks." OOPSLA '98 midyear workshop, Denver, CO, July 1998.

Hofstadter, Douglas. *Godel, Escher, Bach: An Eternal Golden Braid*. New York: Basic Books, 1979.

Java Application Architectures

Previous chapters introduced a number of important topics pertaining to framework design and implementation. This chapter covers a number of architectural design techniques and patterns that can be used to develop Java applications. It focuses on the bigger picture of application architectures and explores architectural solutions at various levels, including systems architectures and object model architectures.

Frameworks, patterns, and components become even more compelling to use when considered as component parts of a greater system. Chapter 1, "Framework Concepts," introduced the concepts of scale and magnitude, and from there this book has offered fine-grained, detailed examples of those topics, while explaining how those details act as pieces of the whole. This chapter continues this trend by analyzing various architectural choices Java developers are faced with today. The emphasis is on architectural solutions and patterns and where framework components fit in, and less on how to construct or implement frameworks.

Specifically, this chapter covers:

- Data access models
- Front-end design models

- Business object paradigm
- Distributed architectures

Each section discusses pertinent Java technologies and techniques that address useful design considerations. The weight of this chapter, however, resides in the final section on distributed architectures. Today, the growing need for massively scalable and networked applications warrants a distributed approach. Fortunately, Java is an important technology on both the front end and, increasingly, on the back end as a server-side solution. Let's begin this discussion by exploring methods for accessing data from applications.

Data Access Models

There are two primary types of databases used by software developers today: *relational databases* (RDBMS) and *object databases* (ODBMS). Each has particular strengths and weaknesses and relies on a fundamentally different paradigm. After reading these sections, you should be well informed and be able to make sound judgments as to which approach is best for your project.

NOTE A number of readers may be already familiar with these subjects and should feel free to skim over this material.

The Relational Data Model

The *relational data model* has been around for more than 20 years. It stores raw information in what are called database *tables*. These tables are created within a database to hold specific kinds of data. Each table resembles a spreadsheet layout, that is, it is composed of rows and columns. A *cell* represents the value at an intersection of a column and row. Each *column* in a table has a label identifying the name of the values residing beneath it, often called a *field*. The column also has a data type associated with it, for example, strings, integers, dates, or objects. Data is input to a table by inserting a *row*. A row is a collection of values for each column in the table. The table as a whole is a collection of rows for a given set of columns.

When retrieving data from a relational database, a *query* is submitted that identifies the criteria for matching rows. If any rows exist in a given table that match the criteria in the query, that row is added to the *result set* for the query. The result set returned by the query will contain a simple enumeration of the matching rows found during the query search. The result set is always a subset of the table or tables involved in the search, possibly including the entire table.

Consider, for example, a simple relational table called People with the columns Name, Age, Occupation, and Birthdate. Each row in the People table will contain values, empty or otherwise, for each of the four defined columns. The column types might be String, Integer, String, and Date, respectively.

Java provides a convenient low-level *data access framework* (or API) that represents the abstracted concepts of relational information sources and data. Java DataBase Connectivity (JDBC) is designed to facilitate a standard mechanism for interacting with relational data sources. If the concept of relational data and relational databases can be masked by an appropriate set of classes and interfaces (like a framework), then subsequent implementation details governing access to vendor-specific products can be strictly separated. This will allow developers to focus on interacting with the paradigm interface and not a commercial proprietary API.

JDBC

JDBC is a uniform standard mechanism for accessing relational databases. Because it is rooted entirely in Java, JDBC is easy for Java developers to use. Although the actual data stored in a relational database is not represented as objects per se, JDBC performs simple type mapping that enables it to return qualified result sets containing native Java object types. Because JDBC maps to the data types provided by the database, which tend to be simple atomic structures, it is relatively a low-level API and can certainly be augmented and built upon. Table 7.1 highlights the conversion of basic types.

NOTE Higher-level data frameworks such as JavaBlend and TopLink build upon JDBC to provide a rich set of tools and services for managing relational data and objects.

JDBC interacts with a database through the Structured Query Language (SQL), an industry standard for accessing relational databases. Most important databases support SQL.

NOTE It is beyond the scope of this section to cover SQL comprehensively. There are a number of excellent books available on this subject at your local bookstore.

There are four primary components to JDBC:

DriverManager

Connection

Statement

ResultSet

Table 7.1   Relational /JDBC Type Conversions

SQL TYPE	CONVERTS TO JAVA OBJECT	CONVERTS TO SQL TYPE
CHAR	String	VARCHAR LONGVARCHAR
VARCHAR	String	
LONGVARCHAR	String	
TIME	java.sql.Time	TIME,CHAR,VARCHAR, LONGVARCHAR
TIMESTAMP	java.sql.Timestamp	TIMESTAMP VARCHAR,CHAR, LONGVARCAR,DATE,TIME
DATE	java.sql.Date	DATE CHAR,VARCHAR, LONGVARCHAR TIMESTAMP
NUMERIC	java.math.BigDecimal	NUMERIC
DECIMAL	java.math.BigDecimal	TINYINT, SMALLINT, BIGINT, INTEGER, REAL, DOUBLE, FLOAT, DECIMAL, BIT, CHAR, VARCHAR, LONGVARCHAR
BIT	Boolean	BIT
TINYINT	Integer	INTEGER
SMALLINT	Integer	
INTEGER	Integer	
BIGINT	Long	BIGINT
REAL	Float	REAL
FLOAT	Double	DOUBLE
DOUBLE	Double	DOUBLE
BINARY	byte[]	VARBINARY LONGVARBINARY
VARBINARY	byte[]	BINARY
LONGVARBINARY	byte[]	BINARY

each of which serves a fundamental purpose in connecting to, issuing queries to, and acquiring data from a relational data source.

DriverManager

The class java.sql.DriverManager is central to JDBC; it is responsible for managing a number of independent database drivers that can handle certain kinds of connection URLs. DriverManager will search for classes representing JDBC drivers in the Java property sql.drivers. In addition, new drivers can be loaded at runtime simply by loading the class into the current JVM as follows:

```
Class.forName("MyJDBCDriverClass");
```

When a driver class is loaded, it automatically registers with DriverManager, after which it becomes available to handle connections.

Requests for Connection objects are made through the DriverManager, which can then query the registered drivers and pass the connection URL to the driver capable of handling it. For example:

```
Connection conn = DriverManager.getConnection("jdbc:vendor_driver:
//host:port/source",userid,password);
```

The URL supplied to getConnection() can be somewhat complicated. Often, specialized middleware will receive connection requests that it then passes along to the actual database. None of these components must reside on the same machine, so depending on the driver vendor and system configuration, the URL can certainly involve many machines. Figure 7.1 shows the relationships between drivers, DriverManager, and the components involved in returning a valid connection. There are four primary types of JDBC drivers, and they are identified and defined in Table 7.2 [Berg, 1998].

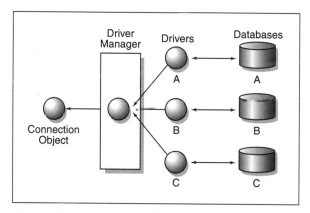

Figure 7.1 Drivers, DriverManager, and Connections.

Table 7.2 JDBC Driver Types

TYPE	NAME	DESCRIPTION
I	JDBC/ODBC	Cannot redirect to other database hosts. Furthermore, it requires an appropriately installed ODBC driver for the database it serves. Through a native interface, the JDBC driver passes through the ODBC driver, and vice versa.
II	Native API	Also does not provide host redirection. It interfaces directly to the database through the database's own native interfaces.
III	Open Protocol Network	Can redirect requests to remotely located data sources. It requires the presence of a network server component through which database connections are actually made.
IV	Proprietary Protocol Network	Identical to type III, except it communicates to a particular brand of database using that vendor's propriety communication protocol.

Determining which driver to use in your system depends on two important criteria.

- *The chosen database vendor.* Depending on the database vendor you choose to use, JDBC drivers may exist as one type but not the other.

- *Whether your system is a distributed architecture.* If you have more than one tier in your system, you will have to explore which JDBC driver types can connect to remote database sources; otherwise, you will have to provide a middleware component to your architecture.

These driver types will be revisited later in this chapter to explore some architectural schematics that apply to them.

Connection

Instances of the Connection class represent a single established connection to a data source. Because connecting to a database is vendor-specific at some level, it is the responsibility of the DriverManager using vendor-provided JDBC drivers to supply a fully linked Connection.

Multiple Connection objects can be obtained to either the same database or to other databases within your application or framework. Connection objects are retrieved by invoking DriverManager.getConnection(), as demonstrated in the code snippet in the previous subsection.

Once a Connection object is obtained, you can then create Statement objects, which are used to deliver SQL statements to the database for subsequent execution. Creating a Statement object is done by using the appropriately named createStatement() method:

```
Statement statement = connection.createStatement();
```

For a complete description of the Connection class, refer to the API documentation included in Java 2 under the java.sql package.

Statement

Statement objects deliver SQL-formatted strings, called *queries* or *statements*, to the database back end for execution. In JDBC, this is done through the executeQuery() method:

```
ResultSet result = statement.executeQuery("SELECT * FROM EMPLOYEE");
```

Statement objects can be reused any number of times. That is, a single instance can make additional calls to the database. The SQL query does not have to be a static string. The following code represents a method called executeSQL that takes a Statement and a String and executes the query represented by sqlString on the given Statement object, which is already bound to a Connection and subsequent database.

```
public ResultSet executeSQL(String sqlString, Statement statement)
{
    ResultSet result = statement.executeQuery(sqlString);
    return result;
}
```

This is a relatively trivial example, but serves to demonstrate the separation of query statements from JDBC Statement objects that can execute them and provide a ResultSet upon completion.

For a complete description of the Statement class, refer to the API documentation included in Java 2.

ResultSet

The ResultSet returned from a successfully executed SQL query contains the rows of data found by the query. JDBC offers three types of ResultSets that address different functional conditions:

- *forward-only.* The most typical type of ResultSet. Only allows forward scrolling of rows.

- *scroll-insensitive.* All rows retrieved are place in the ResultSet when the query is executed, regardless if further changes occur during the given transaction.

- *scroll-sensitive.* Allows dynamic forward and backward scrolling. The implementation of this will be vendor-specific.

Sometimes, the number of rows retrieved for a query is excessively large and therefore would be impractical to stuff in a ResultSet to return to a client-side applet or application. For this reason, ResultSets can be declared to scroll through the resulting rows returned by an executed query. In essence, this is like a moving window that sees only a smaller number of rows at any given time. Because you can only move the window forward or backward, you are shielded from the fact that rows not in the window are retrieved from the database caching mechanism automatically. This greatly reduces the amount of data needed by the database client, and so can greatly improve the perceived performance of your system.

Typically, a ResultSet is allowed forward-only scrolling; that is, you can iterate through the rows sequentially from beginning to end, but you cannot go backward. Only ResultSets of the scroll-sensitive type permit this action. Scrolling is an undefined behavior within the JDBC spec. Database vendors provide this capability, and JDBC invokes it through a common API. The functional behavior of the scrolling action depends on how the vendor provides it.

For a complete description of the ResultSet class, refer to the API documentation included in Java 2.

Object/Data Mapping

Traditional relational databases define a set of data types that can be stored within tables. The data stored in these tables usually are not objects as we understand them (i.e., including behavior), but only fundamental raw data. That is, the data in an RDBMS does not have any functionality. Any functionality applied to the data is provided strictly by the application and, to some degree, by the database server itself. When working with a primarily object-oriented language like Java, obtaining data from a relational database and associating it with well-defined domain-oriented objects that include behavior can be an intricate and unnatural process to undertake without assistance from other tools, frameworks, or APIs (e.g., JavaBlend or TopLink).

The process of taking fundamental data elements and inserting them into object instantiations is called *mapping*. Until recently, it was up to the developer to decide which data elements defined in the database model mapped to objects defined in the object model, and then to write the code to perform this *bidirectional mapping*—a rather cumbersome process. Rather than composing a single data- and behavior-driven model, there are two separate models, one for objects and one for data. Reconciling the two involves additional processing and steps.

Unfortunately, this *impedance mismatch* exists between data-only containers like relational databases and object-oriented languages like Java. But fortunately, new tools are now available that automatically supply the code needed to translate between one model and the other. One such tool is JavaBlend from

JavaSoft. JavaBlend provides a framework for automatically mapping between relational rows and Java objects. In addition, it has a set of tools that assist in defining a consistent and cohesive data and object model (for more information, go to www.javasoft.com).

Architectures with JDBC

Your choice of database drivers can influence your architecture. Figures 7.2 and 7.3 [Berg, 1998] show simple architectures based on type I and type II, respectively. They are almost identical, except that type I relies on ODBC as the ultimate connection protocol, whereas type II allows for the vendor to define the connection implementation to its own database.

Figure 7.4 shows the schematic for an architecture based on type III or IV drivers. Because these drivers require the presence of a middleware server (typically supplied by a database vendor or JDBC driver vendor), they establish a distributed architecture for your system. The network server will service requests for connections and execute queries against databases originating anywhere within reach by the network. This provides a common facility for client applications to make connections to data sources dynamically without having to provide direct support for connecting to those databases. The actual drivers specific to individual database connections reside along the middleware component, not the client.

Client applications forward requests to the network request server (the middleware component), and subsequent connections can be made to databases supported by the middleware. A commercial example of a product like this is Symantec's DBAnywhere (go to www.symantec.com for more details). DBAnywhere is a middleware component that contains many native drivers for connecting to a variety of commercial databases. Client applications need only connect to DBAnywhere and submit the appropriate URL for a particular database, and DBAnywhere will mitigate the connection between the database and the client and return an appropriate Connection object to the client on behalf of

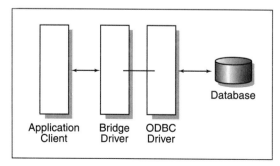

Figure 7.2 Type I driver schematic.

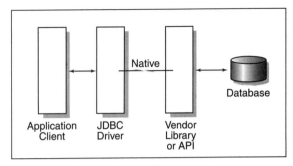

Figure 7.3 Type II driver schematic.

the database. The client only has to know how to contact and communicate with the middleware component, not where databases reside; also, the client does not have to obtain the necessary drivers for connecting to them.

Remarks

Though relational data models have proven to be highly successful over the past 10 years or so, with the growing popularity of object languages like Java, overcoming the basic impedance mismatch between data stored in relational format and an object-oriented world has proven to be a large hurdle for developers. Translating between the worlds of strictly data- and behavior-driven models involves tedious mapping.

Fortunately, commercial products are becoming available to make this task easier and more transparent to the developer. Still, the question remains: When is a relational data model desirable for a particular system? Making changes to relational structures like tables and fields can have a huge negative impact on an existing system; and, traditionally, relational databases have not offered provisions for evolution and dynamic versioning of data. These concerns have prompted a new movement toward object databases. Their imple-

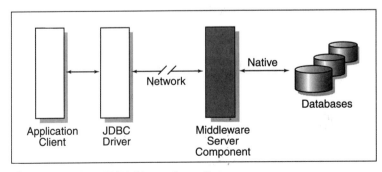

Figure 7.4 Type III/IV driver schematic.

mentation of data storage and retrieval is based entirely on the object data model.

The Object Data Model

The *object data model* serves as a method for persisting Java objects. The concept is not unique to a particular database vendor; many object database vendors implement what is called a Java language *binding*. The underlying object storage mechanisms are typically not language-specific, so one database engine can support various language bindings. For this reason, most object databases require extra steps to make your Java objects persistable in their database.

This can involve one of two current common approaches. The first approach involves extending all your persistent-capable objects from some common root class that provides the persistence mechanism for you. The second approach defines classes to be persistable in some externally resident file that is managed by the database. In addition, this often requires the postprocessing of Java class files. This processing inserts database-specific code into the class files to enable them to operate within the database.

There are pros and cons to both approaches. For example, using the inheritance mechanism, you are, at some level, bound to the specific database. This, however, can be avoided by implementing your business objects as primary interfaces. Though doing this does increase the workload for the developer, it adds the benefit of hiding database-specific hierarchies behind the interface. The second mechanism does not require any source-level binding, but does require classes to be processed. Then, those processed classes require database-specific libraries in order to run.

THOUGHTS Ideally, at runtime, you would want any Java class to be made persistable without requiring further work on the part of the developer. This includes not having to extend from a common class or run pre- or postcompile processors. This so-called holy grail of object persistence would likely be in the form of a custom ClassLoader that performs the necessary modifications on classes transparently. This would allow any class to be used at runtime within the database, a much needed capability.

How Object Databases Work

When using an object database, you often must decide which objects within your system to declare *persistent* and which to declare *transient*. Transient objects are not stored in the database, regardless of where they appear. Persistent objects can go to and from the database almost transparently to the developer. When an object is persisted into the database, all objects also declared persistent that can be reached by that object are also stored, thus maintaining the composition of the object tree. This method is called *persistence by reachability*. For example, if I have an object of type A that references an object of type B, both object A and B are stored in the database, providing that both objects are defined as persistent-capable. Retrieving object A also retrieves object B, and the reference within A is maintained. There is no translational difference between the objects represented in memory and in the database, which is the intent of object databases.

> **NOTE** Object databases are complex, and this discussion is not meant to be comprehensive; it only serves to introduce you to the concepts to help you make fundamental architectural decisions about which data model approach is suitable for your efforts.

Object Database Pros and Cons

Compared to the relational approach, there are two primary advantages to using an object database:

- An object database provides for the near-transparent access and storage of Java objects. This relieves the developer from learning SQL.

- Because Java objects are the persistable elements, there is no need to map data elements into object attributes, as between relational data sources (automatic or otherwise).

Object databases are just now starting to address concerns such as schema evolution and/or object versioning. Each of these issues centers on how data and objects change over time and how systems manage evolving data or objects. The following are fundamental issues regarding object databases that you will want to consider:

- *Retrieving an object automatically retrieves all persistent objects reachable by that object.* Although this is desirable, there are situations where you specifically do not want this to happen. For example, suppose you have an object called Transactions that contains possibly thousands of transaction objects for a given Account. When you retrieved the Transactions collection, all Transaction objects contained therein will be fetched as well. If the Transactions collection were subsequently streamed over a low-speed connection to a client application, thousands of transactions would also be streamed along. If the end user were expecting a listing of transactions on his or her screen, it could take several minutes for all the data to arrive. In this case, you would only want to send portions. Therefore, you would need to provide additional processing of the retrieved objects to prune uneeded portions to accomplish this. This dilemma is solved in the relational world by providing scrolling cursors for data.

■ *Sometimes, it makes sense for only chunks of data to be sent to a client application.* Complex behaviors may be associated with Transaction objects, but if the initial goal is to populate a scrolling list with transaction names and dates, then retrieving numerous objects and their behaviors in the form of Java objects may require more overhead in time and bandwith than merits the result. In this case, it would be nice to separate the data and only send the pertinent pieces for visualization on a remote client. If further actions by the user require the actual presence of real Java objects with their behavior, then the resources needed to allocate and retrieve these can be invoked.

■ *Java classes are typically not stored within the database.* In my experience, object databases do not provide the capability to store the entire object, which includes not only its data but its behavior (or class file) as well. This means that the object's class must be (and typically is) stored outside of the database. Because most ODBMS vendors implement a language-neutral engine, the engine typically does not recognize language-specific classes, and therefore only stores the data or attributes of the object, leaving the class file to be managed externally. This is a problem because it does not facilitate the proper versioning and schema evolution that object databases intend to deliver. If you were to change the external class file of a Java object whose attributes had already been stored in an object database, this mismatch would probably throw an exception.

Remarks

Object databases are just now starting to gain appeal, but they are not yet fully mature in the way they handle language-specific features. The Object Management Group (OMG) and Object Data Management Group (ODMG) are working to develop standards for transactional models and querying languages (e.g., OQL) that provide the same levels of maturity and functionality as the older and more mature relational model, but with the benefits of the object world. (For more information on these efforts, visit www.omg.org and www.odmg.org.)

The Object/Relational Data Model

In an effort to address the inherent problems of both the relational and object data models, a hybrid object/relational model was developed. This model permits the presence of qualified Java objects within a relational database table.

Beginning with all the capabilities of a relational database, this model adds the capability to store and retrieve persisted Java objects as fields. In order for a Java object to be persisted as a data field in an object/relational database, it is required to be *serializable*, that is, able to implement the java.io.Serializable interface.

Objects stored in a relational table can have their behavior invoked during queries to the database. This is an important feature and one that even most object databases lack (due to their language-independent engines). Consider the following SQL query that contains a method invocation to objects residing in a particular column:

```
SELECT City from CityTable where
City.getName().toLowerCase() = "paris"
```

This SQL query will scan the column City in the table CityTable. The fields residing beneath the column City are Java objects of type City. The method get-Name() returns the name attribute for that object, and toLowerCase() acts on the String type of that name, converting it to lowercase before testing for equality against "paris".

This capability gives you the flexibility to store raw (nonobject) data elements alongside real Java objects and to create associations between the two. In addition, Java objects stored in this model (as implemented by the vendor) will continue to behave as objects even in a nonreferenced state such as within a query. A good example of an object/relational Java database is Cloudscape's JBMS. JBMS is an embedded database implemented entirely in Java. An embedded database does not require a server component, which means you can create and use databases local to the application that utilizes the database classes and API. (Visit www.cloudscape.com for more information.)

Framework Considerations

Designing a *data access framework* involves integrating with a particular access model or, possibly, commercial vendor products. These integrations should be subordinate to the primary goal of the framework. Implementations of data access models and commercial databases should be well hidden behind the abstractions and interfaces of the framework proper.

The data access framework that hides this implementation will have the following characteristics:

- *Support for multiple access models and/or database vendors.* The interfaces defined by your framework will support the generic concepts for common entities such as Connections, Transactions, and ResultSets. JDBC does this entirely for the relational world. However, there could be domain-specific value-add that layers onto an API like JDBC that provides process and behavior specific to the goals of your framework.

■ *Facilities for including business logic extensions that drive interactions with the data model.* By wrapping a particular data access model (e.g., JDBC/relational) in a higher-order construct like a framework, you have the opportunity to provide slots for embedding application-specific business logic objects that manipulate and/or interact with the underlying data storage and retrieval mechanisms. By building such a capability into a data access framework, you relieve the application designer from instituting these mechanisms directly. In addition, these business logic objects can "massage" the data in response to certain events and data change notifications that may originate within the framework proper. These events and triggers can propagate back to the application, thereby creating a tight bond between the framework, the application, and stored data objects.

Front-End Design Models

Whether you're designing a standalone or a distributed application, there is always a *front end*, a colloquial term for the user interface or GUI. Aspects of an application that are foreground to the user and play a role in interaction are considered more frontal than aspects that are not visible or known to the user (e.g., a database server). With any large application, it is important that the front end be designed in such a way that promotes reusability, extensibility, scalability, and flexibility. Another goal is to minimize the impact of changes within your system to the front end.

There are approaches to front-end GUI design that facilitate higher levels of reuse and better control for complexity, readability, and abstraction. By now, you should be familiar with Java and its various packages and frameworks, the design and layout of the JFC, and how GUI components utilize common patterns. But before beginning the discussion of one approach to GUI design, it's important to understand where the potential problems in GUI design lie.

Let's begin by supposing you are writing a mini-application for a local factory. Take a moment and consider a thought process that you might adopt before coding some screens or views. Let's further assume that you decide that these screens are actually frames, and choose to use the Swing JFrame as the basis for each screen in your application. Let's also say that there are three screens you must design and code. The first screen, called the Dispatch-Screen, dispatches parts over an assembly line. The second screen, called the

A factory.

ProductionScreen, details the production metrics of the factory. The last screen is a DeliveryScreen; it shows you the status of deliveries made from your factory.

Through object analysis, you might decide that each screen is really a specific KIND-OF JFrame. In making this decision, you believe that some specialized behavior is present in each screen that is fundamentally unique to that screen, and conclude no further generalization is required. (It is not unreasonable to think that each screen might carry some distinctly different sets of actions and behavior, which would reinforce your decision to subclass each screen from JFrame, which is essentially a window on the user's desktop.) Listing 7.1 shows the skeleton for the DispatchScreen.

NOTE The method displayDispatch() is inserted in this Listing 7.1, but show() could have been called on the DispatchScreen to display it on-screen, because show() is inherited from JFrame and causes the frame to be displayed. However, it is important to ensure that data is retrieved from the dispatch database first, before showing the screen. This step is encapsulated inside displayDispatch(). Users of DispatchScreen are required to use this method.

Listing 7.1 DispatchScreen class definition.

```
// DispatchScreen.java
import javax.swing.*;

public class DispatchScreen extends JFrame {

    public void displayDispatch()
    {
        // Get dispatch data from the database

        // Show this JFrame on the desktop
        show();
    }

}
```

Now suppose that one of the many buttons and views present in this screen is a button labeled Dispatch. It triggers the dispatching of parts coming into the factory. The same line of reasoning can be used for this button as for the frame. If the Dispatch button is considered to be a special kind of button—namely, one that dispatches parts—the subclass DispatchButton, which extends JButton, can be created to contain the necessary behavioral traits associated with dispatching parts, as the following snippet depicts.

```
public class DispatchButton extends JButton {

    // some behavior goes here

}
```

If you continued to think along these lines, the result would be many, many classes and possibly a lot of redundant code, because functionality is encapsulated within the specialized subclass. If you wanted to alter various aspects of the DispatchScreen, such as when and where triggers occurred, you might have to examine a multitude of classes. This is the first problem.

Let's continue by supposing that the mini-application and all screens are complete and successfully deployed to the factory foreperson. (The application could also be deployed to many factories.) But there is a new requirement for future iterations of the software: Because the dispatch screen is too cluttered, it has to be divided into two separate windows or frames.

You know that all dispatching functionality is contained at some level within the class DispatchScreen, which is a one-to-one mapping with visible windows (because it is a single frame window). In addition, all object users of Dispatch-

Screen are invoking displayDispatch() exclusively, so adding another JFrame class would require modification of all object users wishing to display the dispatching screen information, which is now on two screens. Going through every class and determining where calls to the dispatch screen occur is painstaking and subject to error. The following code segment shows the modification to a possible object user of DipatchScreen:

```
DispatchScreen dispatchScreen = new DispatchScreen();
DispatchScreen2 dispatchScreen2 = new DispatchScreen2();

// probably some code here

dispatchScreen.displayDispatch();
dispatchScreen2.dispalyDispatch();
```

In this code, the presence of DispatchScreen2, which was created to accommodate the second frame requirement, is assumed. DispatchScreen2 could have been included within DispatchScreen as a member variable, but it doesn't make sense that a single specialization of a single JFrame should be a composite object containing other JFrames. In any event, the result of creating DispatchScreen2 is that object users must now accommodate both screens. This increases not only the amount of work involved, but also the complexity of your system. If this application were to continue evolving like this, it would become unmanageable and unstable at some point in time. In addition, you can see that similarities between DispatchScreen and DispatchScreen2 will force some factoring of behavior, thus increasing the generalization hierarchy as well. This is the second problem.

Let's stop and summarize these two primary problems with this style of design:

- Specializing GUI components through subclassing to include behavior of your application will proliferate and cause an increase in the number of classes involved in your application. It is generally considered good concise programming practice to create an application in the most efficient way possible, which means including a reasonable number of classes. Remember, the more classes you have, the more complex your application seems. Usually, this has undesirable consequences.

- Because there is a one-to-one mapping between most GUI component classes and their visual counterparts, it does not make sense to composite other objects of the same or higher level. In other words, it seems natural that a JFrame would contain JButtons, but not that a JButton would contain a JFrame. This places the burden on users of GUI components; and in doing that, you must make yet more changes to your system.

Now let's address how the system should be developed to solve these problems:

1. The developer should be able to make changes to the behavioral side of applications, without having to touch the visual, or view, side. That is, you would not want to change classes that represent visual aspects if you need to change only the nonvisual side effects. For example, if you wanted to change the button that triggers a process, you would not want to extract existing behavior from another class, altering two classes when altering only one would suffice.

2. In the event that multiple entities represent a collective discrete unit, like dispatching, the developer should be able to create a focal point of organization for those entities without having to manage the entities individually. In addition, objects that want to call out to or display the discrete unit need not be aware of the number of entities managed by the unit's focal point.

Solution 1 represents the traditional notion of separating view and behavior. The hierarchies representing view and behavior are separated so that they can change independent of one another. This is how most object-oriented programmers code.

Solution 2 suggests the notion of a non-GUI class that acts as a firm mediator between the GUI constituents of a collective unit and the object users of that unit. Again, this allows the representation of the constituents to change and evolve without any protocol changes between the mediator and its object users. (For the purposes of this discussion, I call this mediator the ViewMediator, but you can call it whatever you like.)

The ViewMediator Abstraction

The goal of the ViewMediator class is to provide a reliable and stable protocol for non-GUI object users to interact with discrete, possibly composite, view units. In the previous example, two view frames representing different but related portions of the dispatch portion of the application would composite quite nicely as a single atomic unit. The presence of a ViewMediator allows the number of GUI components and their representations and behavior to change without affecting the users that invoke the unit through the mediator. Figure 7.5 shows this simple relationship.

When thinking about redesigning that example, consider that individual GUI components perform specialized behavior simply because their triggers are visually associated with that behavior. As an example, think about a microwave oven. When you touch the buttons on the keypad, the oven responds. Hitting the Start button causes your food to cook, even though the Start button knows nothing about cooking food. The trigger associated with the Start button invokes the behavior embedded in the oven, and the oven performs the cooking process.

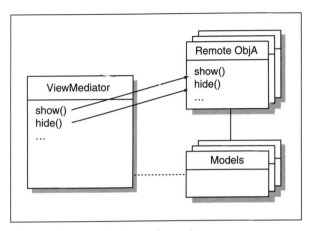

Figure 7.5 ViewMediator abstraction.

Switchboard Controller

One of the roles of the ViewMediator is to trap and route triggers from any GUI components encapsulated within it. This is very similar to how switchboard operators used to route incoming calls and connect them with destinations. Often, the caller was unaware that this routing was taking place; today it continues to takes place but with vastly complex digital electronics in place of human operators. You still hear a simple dial tone; the way phones are used hasn't been changed in decades.

In terms of GUI screens, components making up a screen will cause events to be generated and delivered. Those events can be delivered to many different kinds of objects, but the ViewMediator should capture these events and route them appropriately. Take a look at an example, shown in Listing 7.2.

This listing shows a simple example of how the mediator works. The mediator creates a simple window with a button and a label. The behavior of the button is linked to and executed by the mediator. That is, the button is unaware of the behavior it triggers, much like the Start button on a microwave. The mediator could have easily delegated to another object through proper composition.

To change the behavior associated with the button trigger, always start with the mediator. Changing the effect of the button click does not change the button class; in fact, a separate specialization of button wasn't necessary to contain this behavior.

The example mediator contains two methods: show() and hide(). These translate appropriately to show() and hide() in the actual frame view. Depending on how the mediators are implemented, these methods can involve additional steps—which will be examined later in this chapter.

Switchboard controllers connect incoming events with their end points (or behaviors).

It is also the responsibility of the mediator to construct the view appropriately. This could mean using a separate view class to represent the frame or other components in the view. This does not mean that other views used by the mediator must have their behavior wired to it. This architectural pattern provides much flexibility in design and implementation. The key concept is that object users of MyViewMediator are aware of the method protocol, including show() and hide(), and do not really know about the details they encapsulate. For this reason, MyViewMediator can be modified to address the same type of problem encountered with DispatchScreen. Listing 7.3 shows an altered MyViewMediator that accounts for multiple visual interfaces (GUIs).

Listing 7.3 shows that there are now two JFrame components contained in the collective unit called MyViewMediator. However, no changes were required of object users that still invoke show() and hide(), which now show and hide both frames respectively.

Creation Methods

Using an abstraction like the mediator affords some additional flexibility in how you can create, store, and retrieve the view components. In an object lan-

Listing 7.2 A ViewMediator acting as a "switchboard controller."

```java
//MyViewMediator.java
import javax.swing.*;
import java.awt.event.*;
import java.awt.*;

public class MyViewMediator implements ActionListener {

    private JFrame frame = new JFrame("Frame");
    private JButton button = new JButton("Hello");
    private JLabel label = new JLabel("Waiting for click. ");

    public MyViewMediator()
    {
        frame.getContentPane().setLayout(new BorderLayout());
        frame.getContentPane().add("Center",button);
        frame.getContentPane().add("North",label);

        // Now add the mediator as an actionlistener of
        // the button so it can trap events on it.
        button.addActionListener(this);
    }

    public void show()
    {
        frame.setVisible(true);
    }

    public void hide()
    {
        frame.setVisible(false);
    }

    public void actionPerformed(ActionEvent event)
    {
        if(event.getSource()==button) {
            label.setText("Hello World! ");
        }
    }

}
```

Listing 7.3   A ViewMediator comprising multiple view components.

```java
//MyViewMediator.java
import javax.swing.*;
import java.awt.event.*;
import java.awt.*;

public class MyViewMediator implements ActionListener {

    private JFrame frame = new JFrame("Frame");
    private JButton button = new JButton("Hello");
    private JLabel label = new JLabel("Waiting for click. ");

    private JFrame frame2 = new JFrame("Frame2");
    private JLabel label2 = new JLabel("Also waiting for click. ");

    public MyViewMediator()
    {
        frame.getContentPane().setLayout(new BorderLayout());
        frame.getContentPane().add("Center",button);
        frame.getContentPane().add("North",label);
        frame2.getContentPane().add(label2);

        // Now add the mediator as an actionlistener of
        // the button so it can trap events on it.
        button.addActionListener(this);
    }

    public void show()
    {
        frame.setVisible(true);
        frame2.setVisible(true);
    }

    public void hide()
    {
        frame.setVisible(false);
        frame2.setVisible(false);
    }

    public void actionPerformed(ActionEvent event)
    {
        if(event.getSource()==button) {
            label.setText("Hello World! ");
            label2.setText("Hello World 2! ");
        }
    }

}
```

guage like Java, objects of almost any class type can be persisted in a variety of ways, which means that displaying a view can involve retrieving the appropriate view components first. In the example, they were created dynamically. Aside from instantiating GUI components within the mediator, you can likewise select a different method for obtaining instantiated GUI objects, without disrupting users of the view mediator (i.e., it will not require any changes to object users). Some of these methods include the following:

- *Dynamic Instantiation.* Creating view components by providing instantiations for GUI classes directly within your mediator is called *dynamic instantiation.* This is the most common and practical approach. For more advanced applications, certain GUI components may need their state saved, which requires some form of permanent persistence.

- *Serialized Objects.* How the components within your mediator are created and connected is more or less hidden from the rest of the system. You could easily provide a different mechanism for instantiating GUI objects to which you want to link behavior. The basic bundled mechanism for streaming objects in Java is the serialization facility (in the java.io package). If you had an object such as a JFrame whose state was serialized to a file, your mediator could reinstate that frame through deserialization and proceed to use it normally, as in this code fragment:

```
FileInputStream serialObj = new FileInputStream("frame.ser");
ObjectInputStream ois = new
        ObjectInputStream(serialObj);

JFrame frame = (JFrame)ois.readObject();
```

Database Storage. In addition to default serialization, objects can be stored in databases that support persistable objects. If you chose to store your GUI objects inside a database, your view mediator could easily extract those object instances for display.

The goal of the previous subsections was to illuminate possibilities for acquiring object instances that can be easily adapted into an existing mediator class. At any point, you could change the underlying creation mechanism for the objects within your mediator without propagating unnecessary changes to other classes.

More on Abstract Classes and Interfaces

An approach to establishing mediators within your system that I recommend is to root them in a common abstract class that can provide reliable protocol support through interface implementation and abstract methods. Consider the class definition in Listing 7.4.

Listing 7.4 A generic ViewMediator base class definition.

```
//ViewMediator.java
import java.awt.event.*;

public abstract class ViewMediator implements ActionListener {
    String name = "";

    public void setName(String nm)
    {
        name = nm;
    }

    public String getName()
    {
        return name;
    }

    public abstract void show();
    public abstract void hide();

    public abstract void actionPerformed(ActionEvent event);

}
```

This listing shows a generic abstract base class called ViewMediator. All mediators within your application would subclass ViewMediator. Because ViewMediator is abstract, it can never be instantiated directly. Also, all subclasses are required to implement the abstract methods defined in ViewMediator. This includes actionPerformed(), which is part of the ActionListener interface; its implementation is passed along to subclasses that are uninformed about the ActionListener interface (i.e., they do not explicitly declare implementing it). This reduces the burden of knowledge for subclass implementors. Mediator subclasses will not compile unless a method block exists for all abstract methods. Placing this in ViewMediator and making it abstract ensures that all subclasses will contain the correct protocols; nothing is left to chance. Future interfaces can be added to this base class, forcing a recompile of all affected classes and instance notification of breakage points. This is quite useful for developers, as it reduces the time needed to track down where changes need to occur, and eliminates the possibility that some changes are accidentally omitted.

The other valuable aspect of the abstract base class is that it can provide implementations to common behaviors across all subclasses. Therefore, the mediator subclass can inherit useful functionality without duplicating it, much like setName() and getName() in Listing 7.4. This makes writing subclasses much easier and less time-consuming. (For more on abstract classes, refer to the discussion in Chapter 2, "Java Framework Design.")

Listing 7.5 shows the redesigned dispatch screen, using a mediator and two JFrames, per the requirement.

The new dispatch mediator is a bit cleaner. It no longer must include the "implements ActionListener" clause. This is enforced from the parent abstract class. As a developer, it would be hard to leave out a crucial implementation, because the compiler will notify you if something were missing.

Object users would contain code fragments as the following:

```
DispatchView dispatchView = new DispatchView();
dispatchView.displayDispatch();
```

or

```
ViewMediator dispatchView = new DispatchView();
dispatchView.show();
```

NOTE Depending on your preference, you can choose a common name for all your view mediators. I've chosen to simply call them "-Views" (e.g., DispatchView, ProductionView, DeliveryView) because the mediator is really a view abstraction; it appears to be a view, but hides the real view components.

By using the abstract base class, you dictate a strict policy for how view mediators should behave in your system. You can even institute a hierarchy of mediators that enforces different protocol policies on subclasses, or include default behavior. This is a highly recommended approach as it increases reusability and reduces necessary change and impact to a system because actual GUI representations and implementations can be altered freely.

Moreover, certain patterns, such as Factory Method or Builder, fit nicely with this model. Using these patterns, you could further separate discrete portions of a large complex application from each another in order to reduce the possibility of negative side effects or alteration, while providing support for dynamic subclass instantiation.

The View Observer

Another common dilemma arising on the presentation side of applications is that, often, multiple views show the same data. The views are either viewing representations of the same object or displaying identical data from a database. Consistent with the model-view pattern, any changes occurring within a particular model should propagate change notifications to any and all views so they may update accordingly. Using the JavaBean event model, you could

Listing 7.5 DispatchView mediator class definition.

```java
//DispatchView.java
import javax.swing.*;
import java.awt.event.*;

public class DispatchView extends ViewMediator {

    JFrame dispatchFrame1 = new JFrame("View 1");
    JFrame dispatchFrame2 = new JFrame("View 2");


    public DispatchView()
    {
    }

    // Convenience method
    public void displayDispatch()
    {
        show();
    }

    public void hideDispatch()
    {
        hide();
    }

    public void show()
    {
        dispatchFrame1.setVisible(true);
        dispatchFrame2.setVisible(true);
    }

    public void hide()
    {
        dispatchFrame1.setVisible(false);
        dispatchFrame2.setVisible(false);
    }

    public void actionPerformed(ActionEvent event)
    {
        // various events are captured here and either
        // handled directly or delegated to behavior
        // objects
    }

}
```

easily implement domain models that can be properly visualized within a view, and maintain proper notification through property change events. However, when adopting the ViewMediator approach, you want more control over the granularity of change notifications and when they get sent. This policy is something that might change from view to view and would be dictated by a particular ViewMediator. In addition, if you chose not to implement your domain models as JavaBeans, you would need another method to maintain data integrity within your views.

For example, suppose you have an object representing a list of individuals' names and phone numbers. Also suppose that there are two views that display this information, a list in window A and a table in window B. Both windows are part of your application. You are allowed to make edits to the phone number entries in either window, and if you change an entry in one window, you would want to see the other window update accordingly, otherwise you could get confused or, worse, commit data that you forgot you had changed, thereby compromising the accuracy of your data.

To prevent this problem, it's necessary to ensure that views or view mediators react to changes in shared data. If views or mediators could listen to other views and receive messages when changes to important objects occur, they could react appropriately and update their visual data without the need for a refresh or update action by the user. Take a look at the interface in Listing 7.6.

ViewObserver has a single method declaration: changedObjects(). This method requires a Vector of objects as a parameter. Theoretically, all views would implement this method, so it would make sense for the ViewMediator to implement this interface. In order for a view to receive changedObjects() messages, it must first register itself as a ViewObserver of another view. Therefore, each view would potentially have a list of observers that it would notify of important changes to its data objects. The methods for maintaining this list of observers can also be integrated into the evolving ViewMediator class. Listing 7.7 is a refined definition of the ViewMediator class.

The ViewMediator class can provide useful implementations that relieve the burden of the subclass developer. In this case, any ViewMediator subclass will automatically be a ViewObserver as well. In addition, the subclass will have

Listing 7.6 ViewObserver interface definition.

```
// ViewObserver.java
import java.util.*;

public interface ViewObserver {
    public void changedObjects(Vector objects);
}
```

Listing 7.7 Enhanced ViewMediator with ViewObserver.

```java
//ViewMediator.java
import java.util.*;
import java.awt.event.*;

public abstract class ViewMediator implements
ActionListener, ViewObserver {
    protected String name = "";
    protected Vector observers = new Vector();

    public void setName(String nm)
    {
        name = nm;
    }

    public String getName()
    {
        return name;
    }

    public void addViewObserver(ViewObserver observer)
    {
        observers.addElement(observer);
    }

    public void removeViewObserver(ViewObserver observer)
    {
        observers.removeElement(observer);
    }

    public abstract void show();
    public abstract void hide();

    public abstract void actionPerformed(ActionEvent event);

    public abstract void changedObjects(Vector objects);

}
```

protected access to the list of observers through which it can make the proper notification of data changes. Bear in mind that the implementation of changed-Objects() is left entirely to the developer. He or she can decide what sorts of actions need to be taken, if any. Let's revisit the example used previously in this section and try to solve for it. If you remember, there were two windows, A and B. Listing 7.8 shows how an implementation of each view component wrapped in a view mediator would look.

Listing 7.8 ViewA and ViewB class definitions.

```java
//ViewA.java
import javax.swing.*;
import java.util.*;
import java.awt.event.*;

public class ViewA extends ViewMediator {

    public JFrame windowA = new JFrame("Window A");
    PhoneList phoneList;

    public ViewA(PhoneList phoneList)
    {
        // populate windowA with phoneList data
        this.phoneList = phoneList;
    }

    public void show()
    {
        windowA.setVisible(true);
    }

    public void hide()
    {
        windowA.setVisible(false);
    }

    public void actionPerformed(ActionEvent event)
    {
      // Assuming a data change triggers an action event here

        Vector objects = new Vector();

        // Add any and all objects that we know we've
        // changed during this action cycle.
        objects.addElement(phoneList);

        for(int x=0;x<observers.size();x++) {
            ViewObserver vo = (ViewObserver)observers.elementAt(x);
            // Send the list of changed objects to observers
            // who might also be viewing them
            vo.changedObjects(objects);
        }

    }

    public void changedObjects(Vector objects)
    {
        for(int x=0;x<objects.size();x++) {
```

Listing 7.8 *(Continued)*

```
            if(objects.elementAt(x) instanceof PhoneList) {
                // update my view of the phone data
            }
        }
    }

}

//ViewB.java
import javax.swing.*;
import java.util.*;
import java.awt.event.*;

public class ViewB extends ViewMediator {

    public JFrame windowB = new JFrame("Window B");
    PhoneList phoneList;

    public ViewB(PhoneList phoneList)
    {
        // populate windowB with phoneList data
        this.phoneList = phoneList;
    }

    public void show()
    {
        windowB.setVisible(true);
    }

    public void hide()
    {
        windowB.setVisible(false);
    }

    public void actionPerformed(ActionEvent event)
    {
        // Assuming a data change triggers an action event here

        Vector objects = new Vector();

        // Add any and all objects that we know we've
        // changed during this action cycle.
        objects.addElement(phoneList);

        for(int x=0;x<observers.size();x++) {
            ViewObserver vo = (ViewObserver)observers.elementAt(x);
            // Send the list of changed objects to observers
            // who might also be viewing them
```

continues

Listing 7.8   ViewA and ViewB class definitions. *(Continued)*

```
            vo.changedObjects(objects);
        }
    }

    public void changedObjects(Vector objects)
    {
        for(int x=0;x<objects.size();x++) {
            if(objects.elementAt(x) instanceof PhoneList) {
                // update my view of the phone data
            }
        }
    }
}
```

Somewhere in this system you might have the following lines of code that links these two views:

```
viewA.addViewObserver(viewB);
viewB.addViewObserver(viewA);
```

It is now up to each view mediator to decide when notification should occur. This affords you a bit more freedom than at the JavaBean level, when a notification occurs as each property change occurs. In this approach, you can decide when to trigger changedObjects()notifications and include a variety of possible objects that your view mediator can manage for its view components. Therefore, you can make more decisions about the granularity of notifications. When a changedObjects() message is received, each ViewObserver will need to determine which objects are of interest to it. It is assumed that such objects exist because the ViewObserver would not receive a changedObjects() message from a view in which it was not interested (it would not be registered on the view anyway). By doing a simple comparison, the ViewObserver receiving the changeObjects() message can determine which objects it receives are also objects it manages, such as PhoneList. Because all views will be running within the same JVM, object references passing the equality test (= =) will be referring to the same object. At that point, the ViewObserver can reread the objects' data and update any view components accordingly.

Connecting Views and Models

One of the goals of designing an efficient and reusable front-end model is the proper separation of views that visualize domain data and models from the data containing the models themselves. For example, if you create a form component, called EmployeeForm, that displays employee information, you should be able to supply any object of type Employee and the view will display the associated data for that object. Therefore, any object whose type satisfies the prerequisites of the view can at least be partially displayed. This, of course, is the old Model-View pattern mentioned throughout this book. This paradigm can scale as well. You would not always expect a simple one-to-one relationship to exist between models and views (as might be seen on-screen). In some cases, you might have a visual form window that has various sections and each section stands as an independent view with an associated model. In this sense, the form view acts as a sort of *meta-view*, or composite view. That is, it does not necessarily have a model to which it maps, but it aggregates other subordinate views to create a collective unit. Figure 7.6 represents how a meta-view composites actual views.

Because of the model-view relationship, meta-views make it possible to reuse various subordinate views in a variety of contexts, without overwhelming the application user, by maintaining a medley of windows or separate interfaces. The idea of a meta-view is similar to that of view mediator in that neither is a GUI component itself, but both act as aggregators of GUI components and control the logical connection of event sequences that stem from a given discrete unit or context. Mediators can be used as meta-views as well. This permits the optimum reuse of actual views by isolating an aggregate logic for a composite meta-view in the meta-view itself. As an example, consider the meta-view MV that combines three view mediators A, B, and C in a certain manner. Another meta-view, MV1 might assemble them as C, A, and B and provide variation on logic to link them.

In general, it is considered good practice to optimize the separation of GUI views and the underlying data that drives them. Taking the model-view approach is but one way to do that, but it is, by and large, the most widely

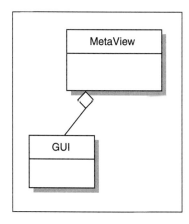

Figure 7.6 Meta-view diagram.

accepted. Using view mediators is a variation on that theme and affords some additional choices when deciding how your views will exchange, share, and propagate information.

Detached versus Attached

When considering ways to separate views and models, you should also consider how they are to be connected. Now that you've created a facility to isolate the code of views and models from one another, how exactly should they come together? Although this is not a compelling design issue, you can opt to design your views as either *attached* or *detached*. Attached views are bound to the models they visualize when they are instantiated and cannot obtain new references to different models after instantiation. Detached views can accept new models of the same type after instantiation. The following code snippets demonstrate these simple concepts.

```
// Attached view
public class AttachedView {

    public AttachedView(DataModel model)
    {
        // extract model data and visualize
    }

}


// Detached view
public class DetachedView {

    public DetachedView()
    {
    }

    public void setModel(DataModel model)
    {
        // extract model data and visualize
    }

}
```

When deciding which method to apply, consider whether or not you would expect to have instances of views before instances of particular models. Also, consider whether a given view instance should be allowed to have its model changed after instantiation. You can combine the two approaches to make it easy to create view instances initialized to a default model, which can subsequently have their models changed.

Design for Change

Regardless of which aspect of your system you are designing, it is vital to the longevity of your system that it be designed for change. By making use of abstraction and separation, you can minimize the complexity (amount of code and classes) and burden of change over time. It goes without saying that any representation that exists today will evolve and change tomorrow. Applications and systems engineers must design for that change at many levels, down to the object level. Keeping these design considerations in mind will help improve the quality and durability of your product.

Business Object Models

A *business object* is an object from the domain that is modeled within your application. Business objects are associated with *business logic* that imposes constraints on the range of values and behavior the object can be in or perform. The following items are examples of business objects:

- Employee
- Profile
- Document
- Folder
- Application (the paper kind)

In a typical object-oriented application, such objects will be properly modeled through *object decomposition*. Their relationships to one another, attributes, and behavior are all captured and implemented in the final application.

Defining the Domain

Earlier chapters explained the *domain,* or the real-world context, in which applications must assimilate. From this domain, abstracted representations of real-life processes and objects, with which humans are already familiar, are created. This familiarity makes the modeling of objects in an object-oriented language more intuitive. If you consider each object as a business object with associated business logic, human knowledge can be translated into predictable software behavior. For example, you can define an Application business object that represents a paper form, maybe for a credit card or loan. This Application object can be in one of three states: *pending, approved,* or *rejected.* The business logic for Application says that it must start out in a pending state and can then go to either approved or rejected. After moving from a pending state, the state of the Application object can no longer be changed. There are two ways to implement the business object: with or without behavior.

Data-Driven Models

A business object is identical to a domain model; they are one and the same. When implementing a business object, you consider what types of behavior are intrinsic to the object. Often, however, you will deem that certain models will contain no behavior at all, only properties or attributes. For example, the Application business object might contain only the information from the paper representation of the application, including its state. Typically, no real-world behavior is associated with a piece of paper. For example, you would not issue a "file" command to a folder sitting on your desk. The file just contains data. It is a data-driven model; no behavior is contained within it. This is one approach to implementing business objects. It requires that other objects contain the necessary behavior to complete the functionality of your system. For example, you might have a Filer object that takes Applications and puts them in their proper places. (In real life, this is a person.) Listing 7.9 shows a simple data representation for this Application example.

Listing 7.9   Data-centric application business object.

```java
// Application.java

// We assume the presence of a generalized base class
// called BusinessObject.
public class Application extends BusinessObject {
    public String applicantName;
    public String address;
    public String city;
    public String state;
    public String zipcode;

    public int age;
    public Date dob;

    final static int STATE_PENDING = 0;
    final static int STATE_APPROVED = 1;
    final static int STATE_REJECTED = 2;

    public int currentState = STATE_PENDING;
}
```

Behavior-Driven Models

Some developers code their business objects with methods representing the behavior associated with those objects. In some cases, this behavior is taken directly from the real-world counterpart, and in other cases, it is provided as a convenient facility to cause state changes to occur within the object model. For example, it's not unreasonable to code an Application class that contains a save() method that will cause the class instance to be saved to some persistent store. In real life, however, this behavior is strictly external to most real-world objects, which generally follow Newton's law of inertia: "Objects at rest tend to stay at rest. . . ." Determining the kind of behavior you want to link to your objects is part of developing the object model for your system.

Business Logic

Business logic is linked to one or more business objects and governs the state and behavior of these objects in a given domain context. Traditionally, once business logic was set forth for a particular application, changing it required a great deal of effort. It is generally considered good practice to provide for some degree of separation between the implementations of business objects and their business logic. This degree of separation should allow for changes to occur with less difficulty in either the object or the logic.

There are two approaches for implementing business logic for our example Application object. The first method includes the business logic as part of the object's intrinsic behavior, making it a behavior-driven business object. The second approach separates the logic from the business object and requires only a data-centric model.

Embedding the Business Logic

At this point, you need to modify the Application class to include functionality for setting or changing its state. As part of this functionality, you insert the appropriate business logic to ensure that state changes in Application objects follow those of their real-world counterparts. Listing 7.10 shows the necessary enhancements.

As you can see from this listing, you can now set the state of an Application object through the setState() method. This means that some outside process or object must perform this activity and know in advance to what state it wishes to set the Application object.

Within the setState() method, some business logic has been added that causes an exception to be thrown if the Application object is requested to be in an invalid state. It begins in a pending state and can be changed only to either

Listing 7.10   Enhanced Application class with embedded business logic.

```java
// Application.java
import java.util.*;

// We assume the presence of a generalized base class
// called BusinessObject.
public class Application extends BusinessObject {
    public String applicantName;
    public String address;
    public String city;
    public String state;
    public String zipcode;

    public int age;
    public Date dob;

    final static int STATE_PENDING = 0;
    final static int STATE_APPROVED = 1;
    final static int STATE_REJECTED = 2;

    public int currentState = STATE_PENDING;

    public void setState(int state)
    throws InvalidApplicationStateException
    {
        switch(currentState) {
            case STATE_PENDING:
            case STATE_REJECTED:
            case STATE_APPROVED:
                if(currentState!=STATE_PENDING)
                    throw new InvalidApplicationStateException();
                break;
        }
        currentState = state;
    }
}

class InvalidApplicationStateException extends Exception
{
}
```

approved or rejected. Once the state has been changed, no further changes can be made without generating an error.

There are now two constituents involved in setting the state of a particular Application: the invoker of setState() and the Application object itself. If the necessary logic or code is missing or changed between one of these two components, it could cause negative and/or unforeseen side effects. For example, if an Application object were discovered to be in an improper state, it would be because there was an error in the business logic within Application. It is also possible that the invoker did not invoke the proper setState() method when needed, and therefore did not cause a state change when there should have been one. Determining the source of such a problem in this scenario would not be possible through direct inspection, consequently, tracking down the source of such problems is time-consuming and difficult. In addition, should any changes in the type or value of states change for the Application class, subsequent users of the class would have to be changed to match. Often, it is not always known how many users there are for a given class, so tracking them down and making necessary changes requires more time as well.

Separating the Business Logic

Let's attempt to remedy some of the problems just described. There are a couple of interesting solutions, as well as a variety of other ways. Listing 7.11 shows the new ApplicationLogic class.

The revised class ApplicationLogic handles the business logic for Application within two methods: approveApplication() and rejectApplication(). Each method is specific in name and functionality. The notion of Application states is concealed from users of the ApplicationLogic class, and therefore is not important to objects wanting to cause these state changes in Application. This allows a good degree of flexibility when implementing Application and ApplicationLogic classes because they are well encapsulated, and states can be added or changed without negatively affecting users of ApplicationLogic. Note that the presence of ApplicationLogic does not alleviate the need for invokers, and is not designed to; it establishes a solid, reliable protocol with which invokers can communicate independent of the business logic. This prevents the invoker either from having to implement the business logic itself or knowing about specific details surrounding the state of a given object. There are probably going to be more invoker classes in a large system, and ensuring they all access the same business logic rules verifies that their behaviors will be properly accounted for. Fixing any problems in the business logic in one place effectively fixes all users (or invokers) of the business logic class.

Listing 7.12 shows another variation on the Application class. Here, the business logic is removed and a getter method is added to access the current state.

The getter and setter methods (collectively, the accessor methods), namely setState() and getState(), follow the standard JavaBeans naming convention for properties. Whenever possible, it is good practice to follow this standard for the sake of interoperability, consistency, and state management. Also, it permits the specifics behind the representation of the property (currentState) to change without affecting how it is accessed.

Listing 7.11   ApplicationLogic class definition.

```java
// ApplicationLogic.java

// We assume that we've created a universal generalization
// base class called BusinessLogic.
public class ApplicationLogic extends BusinessLogic {

    // This method will return true if the approval was allowed.
    public boolean approveApplication(Application application)
    {
        int state = application.getState();

        switch(state) {
            case Application.STATE_PENDING:
            case Application.STATE_APPROVED:
                try {
                    application.setState(Application.STATE_APPROVED);
                } catch (InvalidApplicationStateException e) {
                    // State changed invalid
                }
                break;
            case Application.STATE_REJECTED:
                return false;
        }
        return true;
    }

    // This method will return true if the rejection was allowed.
    public boolean rejectApplication(Application application)
    {
        int state = application.getState();

        switch(state) {
            case Application.STATE_PENDING:
            case Application.STATE_REJECTED:
                try {
                    application.setState(Application.STATE_REJECTED);
                } catch (InvalidApplicationStateException e) {
                    // State changed invalid
                }
                break;
            case Application.STATE_APPROVED:
                return false;
        }
        return true;

    }

}
```

Listing 7.12   Enhanced Application class with business logic removed.

```
// Application.java

// We assume the presence of a generalized base class
// called BusinessObject.
public class Application extends BusinessObject {
    public String applicantName;
    public String address;
    public String city;
    public String state;
    public String zipcode;

    public int age;
    public Date dob;

    final static int STATE_PENDING = 0;
    final static int STATE_APPROVED = 1;
    final static int STATE_REJECTED = 2;

    public int currentState = STATE_PENDING;

    public void setState(int state)
    throws InvalidApplicationStateException
    {
        // We simply set the state since the laws
        // governing this are now external
        currentState = state;
    }

    public int getState()
    {
        return currentState;
    }

}
```

Using JavaBeans

As the example Application business object evolves, it looks more and more like a JavaBean, through its proper use of getter and setter methods. (Recall the discussion on properties in Chapter 4, "JavaBean Components," which stated that implementing Application and ApplicationLogic as JavaBeans is another possibility for separating the business logic from Application. Using the Java-Bean event model, it would be possible to implement the currentState property of Application as a constrained property. As a constrained property, any attempt to set currentState would cause notification events to be sent to any registered VetoableChangeListeners. One such listener would be the ApplicationLogic class, which would receive a message indicating that a state change was about to occur for a given Application object. The ApplicationLogic object then could veto that change and prevent it from occurring. If this happened, the original invoker would be notified through a thrown exception.

In order to complete the transition to this approach, the Application and ApplicationLogic classes must be changed yet again. In Listing 7.13, further modifications have been made to the Application class. First, the capability to add and remove generic VetoableChangeListeners has been added; second, the convenience methods approve() and reject(), have also been added. Although the business logic is still separate from Application, you can now simply invoke approve() or reject() to cause a state change to occur, without wrapping business logic around such invocations or knowing about specific states.

The ApplicationLogic class also underwent some changes in the conversion to the JavaBean event model. It now implements the VetoableChangeListener interface. This interface allows it to be added as a property listener to any object that can receive it (namely the Application object). Listing 7.14 shows the ApplicationLogic class as a VetoableChangeListener.

The vetoableChange() method is called by any Application object to which this VetoableChangeListener has been added. The nice thing about this is that only one instance of ApplicationLogic has to apply to any and all instances of Application, because the same logic applies to all. This single reference point for business logic facilitates easy modification and enhancement over time. Should there ever be a functionality problem with the software system, the appropriate business logic object could be quickly identified.

Distributed Architectures

Much of the interest in Java as it applies to intranet or Internet class software centers on applying it as a distributed technology. A recent paper on IT architectures from Sun Microsystems states:

> Expected business growth, operational efficiencies, new business opportunities, and overall service reliability are driving many companies towards a more distributed business model. A company's Core Systems, and Services are moving from a centralized "hub and spoke" model to a more distributed network of operations. This distributed model is the evolution of years of success and will allow more effective service to customers. This will also provide a higher level of reliability and scalability by eliminating the potential catastrophic failure of a single point of operation and by balancing workloads among operational nodes.

The JavaSoft focus is to make Java the tool of choice for the distributed business model in demand today. Java offers a number of APIs and frame-

Listing 7.13 JavaBean version of Application class.

```
// Application.java
import java.util.*;
import java.beans.*;

// We assume the presence of a generalized base class
// called BusinessObject.
public class Application extends BusinessObject {
    Vector listeners = new Vector();

    public String applicantName;
    public String address;
    public String city;
    public String state;
    public String zipcode;

    public int age;
    public Date dob;

    final static int STATE_PENDING = 0;
    final static int STATE_APPROVED = 1;
    final static int STATE_REJECTED = 2;

    public int currentState = STATE_PENDING;

    public void addVetoableChangeListener(VetoableChangeListener
                                          listener)
    {
        listeners.addElement(listener);
    }

    public void removeVetoableChangeListener(VetoableChangeListener
                                          listener)
    {
        listeners.removeElement(listener);
    }

    public void setState(int state)
    throws InvalidApplicationStateException
    {
        try {
          for(int x=0;x<listeners.size();x++) {
            VetoableChangeListener listener =
                (VetoableChangeListener)listeners.elementAt(x);
            listener.vetoableChange(new
PropertyChangeEvent(this,"state",new Integer(currentState),
                        new Integer(state)));
          }
        } catch (PropertyVetoException e) {
```
continues

Listing 7.13   JavaBean version of Application class. *(Continued)*

```
            throw new InvalidApplicationStateException();
        }
        currentState = state;
    }

    public void approve()
    throws InvalidApplicationStateException
    {
        setState(Application.STATE_APPROVED);
    }

    public void reject()
    throws InvalidApplicationStateException
    {
        setState(Application.STATE_REJECTED);
    }

    public int getState()
    {
        return currentState;
    }
}
```

works for the enterprise to facilitate the development of complex distributed applications.

This section addresses the *distributed nature* of Java. It explores some of the methods and technologies involved in distributed architectures and how Java contributes to them.

The Common Web Applet

You probably have encountered a Java applet on a Web page in the form of some simple animation or input form. You also probably are aware that the Java code for that applet is retrieved from the Web host computer and loaded and executed automatically on your computer by the browser. In some cases, those applets communicate directly with the Web host to retrieve information from a database. When this occurs, the applet is running as a distributed application. That is, the processes needed to perform the task of the applet are spread across more than one machine, namely, yours and the Web host (running a database, for example). If either machine in the system fails to execute properly, the applet will not operate.

Listing 7.14 ApplicationLogic as a VetoableChangeListener.

```
// ApplicationLogic.java
import java.util.*;
import java.beans.*;
// We assume that we've created a universal generalization
// base class called BusinessLogic.
public class ApplicationLogic extends BusinessLogic
    implements VetoableChangeListener
{

    public void vetoableChange(PropertyChangeEvent vce)
    throws PropertyVetoException
    {
        Application application = (Application)vce.getSource();

        int oldstate = ((Integer)vce.getOldValue()).intValue();
        int newstate = ((Integer)vce.getNewValue()).intValue();

        switch(oldstate) {
            case Application.STATE_PENDING:
                // Since the old state was pending,
                // any change is allowed
                break;
            case Application.STATE_REJECTED:
            case Application.STATE_APPROVED:
                // Allow the change, if it never really changed
                if(newstate!=oldstate)
                 throw new PropertyVetoException("Invalid state.",vce);
                break;
        }

    }

}
```

Although much of Java's early success and recognition was a result of applets, the following subsections focus on Java applications, which run outside the context of a Web browser and are typically loaded on the end user's computer much like any other piece of software (although they can be loaded dynamically across a network as well use special deployment software). Applets do not require a browser or even the Web to run (depending on the application, of course). Java applications offer more flexibility and can be much larger and more complex than applets. For this reason, they tend to be more useful and interesting. Figure 7.7 shows a typical architecture for the distributed applet just described.

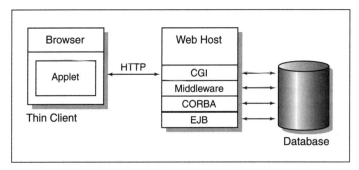

Figure 7.7 Typical distributed Web applet architecture.

Tiered Approach

The applet architecture can also be referred to as a *tiered architecture*. A tier is a logical representation of some processing juncture running as an individual process or processes. A tier can also map onto physical units, like a computer running a database server. Figure 7.7 showed that most applets contain two tiers, the computer the applet is running on and the computer host with which the applet communicates. There are also processes running on these systems. The tier does not necessarily mean a separate computer, but it could.

> **NOTE** Because of the Java security model, applets can only communicate directly to the host from which they were loaded. In other words, only the Web server that served the applet can be involved in any distributed processing performed by the applet directly. Further communication to other hosts would have to stem from the Web host itself and not the applet.

Client/Server Approach

Client/server is a two-tiered architecture developed during the '80s as the traditional mainframe/dumb terminal architecture was fading from mainstream popularity. Applications running on the user's PC are called *clients*. The client application is responsible for gathering data from the user, performing some processing on it and sending it to the *server*. The server is typically a database server. Centralizing the data on a single known computer allows everyone running a client to access the same set of data. This is useful for workgroups that share information.

Client/server became an attractive architecture because newer, more powerful PCs could replace dumb terminals. This gave software designers the freedom to write applications that could be run directly on the user's PC. In this sense, client/server was much like the Web/applet architecture; however, applications deployed under a client/server architecture were typically installed on the PC by an administrator or the user.

One of the advantages of client/server over traditional mainframe-type applications was the capability to separate or distribute some of the processing power. Older mainframe applications ran entirely on the mainframe computer and exported screens to a dumb terminal that would display them and return information typed in by the user. All logic was executed on the mainframe. Client/server meant you could perform logic processing on the client and let the server take care of more difficult things like synchronization, locking, and data persistence. This, of course, relieved much of the processing burden on the server and displaced it to the client.

Problems with Client/Server

Client/server met with mixed reviews over the years. For some types of applications, it was a success, but a number of problems led to its general demise. To illustrate some fundamental problems with the nature of client/server, let's consider an example application deployed using this approach. Suppose you wrote an electronic payroll application for your company, that you've deployed this application to 100 desktops within your company, and that your company is located in two buildings several miles from one another. One of the features of this application is to calculate the pay for a given user based on this simple formula:

pay = pay rate * hours worked

The pay field is a calculated field, and the calculation occurs within the client application on the user's PC.

After a while, you realize that due to federal labor laws, your calculation for pay should include the overtime rate of 1.5 times the normal rate. Therefore, the new calculation should be modified as follows:

overtime_pay = (pay_rate*1.5) * hours worked

You also realize that some employees are exempt from overtime pay and so you need to decide whether to use pay or overtime_pay. The problem with this scenario is that each time you need to make minor changes like this to your application (and I assure you, you will), you must upgrade *every* user's desktop application. The user interface portion of your application is not likely to change and, therefore, the experience is identical to the user of the user interface. Though only the business logic has changed, the side effects of that simple change are quite drastic. In practice, then, some client/server systems have proven costly to maintain and develop, and thus fail to deliver on the promise of cost-effective and streamlined systems. Regardless of the architecture, if it does not facilitate cost-effective solutions, it will not be used.

Three-Tiered Approach

Enter the three-tiered architecture. Distributed Java applications written today fall into this category. The question of where best to place the business logic of an application is answered effectively by the insertion of the middle tier. In a three-tiered approach, the second or middle tier is represented by a new class of software called, logically, middleware. The third tier in the sequence is the database server; the first tier is still the client application.

Middleware

Middleware is software that runs between (in the middle of) a client application and a database. A variety of middleware products are available to IT managers to perform a medley of tasks. Middleware can be very generic, where IT managers plug in their own objects, or it can be more specific. For example IBM's San Francisco project is a middleware component for deploying distributed financial applications.

In a three-tiered architecture, the client application will communicate directly to and only with the middle tier. It is the duty of the middleware process to mediate requests to and from the database server, which could be located on another machine.

In addition, middleware affords the developer the ability to locate some business logic processing on the server through which all applications communicate. Why is this important? Looking back at the pay example, suppose the calculation of a given user's pay rate could be encapsulated into a remote method call to the middleware, as in the following line of code:

```
pay = middleware.calculatePay(rate,hours);
```

This would allow the formula to change on the server without propagating changes to all installed client applications. The user's application would continue to make the correct call to the middleware server, which contains the formula for determining pay. In addition, this reduces the complexity of developing applications against a middleware component that contains much of the business logic processing. You can see how important this would be if you had hundreds or thousands of users.

You're probably wondering what the exact nature of the middleware object in the preceding line of code is. In Java, there are two major mechanisms that can provide middleware services: distributed objects and application servers. Figure 7.8 shows the structure of a typical three-tiered distributed architecture.

Isolating Business Logic

In a distributed architecture, the business logic hosting a number of client applications can be embedded within the middle tier. Whether you choose to

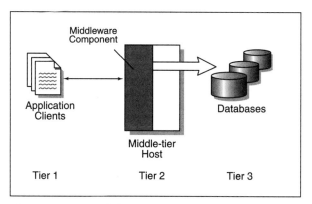

Figure 7.8 Typical three-tiered distributed architecture.

implement your business logic within your business object model or not is something you should consider on a case-by-case basis. Architecting your system such that the business logic is isolated solely on the middle tier and is well enough abstracted from direct client access will give you the future flexibility to change, enhance, or augment that logic, with minimal impact on other tiers in your system.

Distributed Objects

Couple the power of computer networks with the simplicity of an object-oriented language like Java, and you will soon discover how useful having objects in your application reside on different machines can be. Distributing objects across a network is an intuitive and natural way to code distributed applications. Simply, if you are already familiar with coding Java objects, coding distributed Java objects is almost the same process! The goal of distributed object programming is to make the "distributedness" of the objects as transparent as possible. Specifically, the developer coding or using a distributed object does not have to be aware of exactly where that object is located and how to code and decode messages to it.

The question is, precisely how do objects become distributed? The answer is: a process capable of locating and establishing connections to remote objects. In terms of a tiered architecture, the mechanics of locating and connecting to a remote object is transparently handled by an *object request broker*, or ORB for short.

ORBS

An object request broker is a separate process located on the middle tier that receives requests from client applications for specific object instances. The ORB can locate and instantiate (if necessary) the objects residing on the middle tier that the client application is requesting. Note: For the object to be truly distributed, it must reside on the middle tier exclusively. The client application does not receive the object directly, but receives what is called a *proxy* to the object. Technologies like CORBA and Remote Method Invocation (RMI; discussed shortly) use ORBs to provide access to remote objects written for them. Figure 7.9 depicts an ORB middleware component.

Stubs, Proxies, and Skeletons

A proxy to a remote object is an exact likeness of the object itself. The proxy contains all the method signatures of the remote object representation and is, in fact, an interface implementation of that object. The implementation of the proxy is, however, drastically different from that of the remote object. It is the duty of the proxy object to translate method calls made to it to the remote object, where the same method is executed; any values returned are also sent through the proxy back to the invoking context of the client.

How does this impact the client coding process? Depending on the ORB used, it might be necessary to take a few initial steps before being able to send messages to the remote object (in the case of CORBA) or nearly transparent to the client developer (in the case of RMI). The goal is for the remote object to "appear" as though it's just another object in your client application.

The process for making a Java class remote-enabled varies depending on the type of ORB you're using. Traditionally, this process involves creating the necessary interfaces and classes that play a role in identifying and connecting to your remote object. These include the following:

- *The proxy.* The Client implementation (of the remote objects interface) responsible for trafficking messages and objects to the actual remote object.

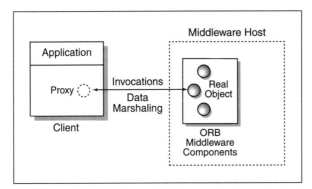

Figure 7.9 ORB middleware component.

- *The stub.* The local class responsible for connecting to a remote object. The proxy is an instance of the stub class.

- *The skeleton.* The server-side analog to the stub. This is the class that actually invokes methods on your remote object instance by receiving the appropriate message instructions and parameters from the client proxy.

The proxy is that portion of the remote object used by the client for sending messages. The skeleton is located on the server, where the ORB and remote object reside, and represents the server implementation of the object that the proxy communicates with through the ORB. With today's distributed object technologies, both the proxy and the skeleton can be generated automatically from a given Java class. The developer wishing to make his or her objects distributed is freed from the details about how their remote objects will accommodate network access.

Both the stub and skeleton objects play a role in *marshaling* objects to and from your remote object. Marshaling is the process of streaming an object hierarchy between two points. At some level within the RMI package, network communication code utilizes the socket layer of network (TCP/IP). This facility is a streamed input/output device; therefore, any data sent over a network socket must be streamed. Java uses *serialization* as the mechanism for streaming objects. Figure 7.10 shows the relationship between the common elements of a distributed object.

NOTE Serialization is built into Java. Any class implementing the java.io.Serializable interface can be streamed or marshalled. If you label a subclass as Serializable and its parent class is not, this will cause the attributes inherited from the superclass not to be serialized. Fortunately, most classes in Java implement Serializable where it makes sense. The java.io.Serializable interface contains no methods and therefore does not require any additional code other than that to specify that your class implement it.

Next let's take a look at some ways to create distributed objects using the mechanisms bundled with Java 2.

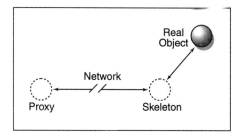

Figure 7.10 Components of a distributed object.

RMI

The Remote Method Invocation technology allows developers to instantiate remote versions of Java classes and to invoke methods that execute on the remote object. RMI is a package bundled with Java (in the java.rmi package). Executing methods (or passing messages) on remote objects is a somewhat involved process, but RMI makes it an easy-to-use API (compared to CORBA).

Using RMI, an object that requires remote enabling will implement an interface that it wishes to expose to clients over a network. It is this interface that binds the protocol (or method signatures) of the remote object with its reference obtained by client applications. Remember, the actual implementation of your remote object doesn't leave the host it is running on, and therefore, clients accessing it do not have direct access to it, but must use a proxy to it.

The actual remote object, sometimes called a *server object*, will extend the RMI-provided class java.rmi.server.UnicastRemoteObject. This enables the class to be accessed by the RMI ORB registry process. For example, if you wanted to create a remote object for a bell, you would first want to declare the interface it will implement. This interface is mandatory and used by the stub and skeleton classes that RMI will create for you. The following interface represents a simple remote interface extending java.rmi.Remote:

```
import java.rmi.*;

public interface Bell extends java.rmi.Remote
{
    public String ringBell() throws java.rmi.RemoteException;
}
```

Any method you define for your remote interface must throw RemoteException or a subclass thereof. These exceptions will be generated within the conversation processes set forth between the stub and skeleton classes; and should any error occur during that discussion, your client application would be notified through catching this exception. Your remote object can throw exceptions rooted by the RemoteException class, propagating to the client as well.

The next step is to create the server-side implementation of this interface. This will be the actual remote object in which methods will ultimately be called and executed. Listing 7.15 shows an implementation of Bell.

Notice in this listing that a main() method is included. It allows you to execute this class directly. By including this method, a runtime context is provided by which to instantiate and bind a BellImpl object to the RMI registry. Also, RMI requires the presence of an appropriate SecurityManager for applications, because one does not exist as default. Therefore, the default security manager is set to a new instance of RMISecurityManager.

Listing 7.15 BellImpl class definition.

```
//BellImpl.java
import java.rmi.*;
import java.rmi.server.*;

public class BellImpl extends java.rmi.server.UnicastRemoteObject
    implements Bell {

    public BellImpl()
    throws java.rmi.RemoteException
    {
        super();
    }

    public static void main(String args[])
    throws Exception
    {
        System.setSecurityManager(new java.rmi.RMISecurityManager());
        Bell myBell = new BellImpl();

        java.rmi.Naming.rebind("Bell",myBell);
    }

    public String ringBell()
    throws java.rmi.RemoteException
    {
        return "The Bell is ringing! ";
    }

}
```

NOTE The RMI registry is a process that runs on the remote host where your objects will be stored. It is included in the JDK. The registry listens on an RMI port where requests for objects arrive. The registry can then retrieve the appropriately named object and return a proxy to the requesting client. This is, in effect, what an ORB does, and the RMI registry serves this purpose.

Once the remote interface and implementation object is created, you must generate the stub and skeleton classes (BellImpl_Stub.class and BellImpl_Skel.class respectively for our BellImpl class) that will be used to access the remote instance of BellImpl. To do this, run the RMI rmic command. For this example, you would type the following:

```
rmic -d . BellImpl
```

TIP When specifying the –d option, you would supply the fully qualified directory where you would like the generated classes written. In addition, you would use the qualified package name for the input class name as well. For example,

```
rmic -d demo/bell demo.bell.BellImpl
```

would apply if the BellImpl class were placed in a package called demo.bell.

This invokes the RMI compiler and generates the stub and skeleton class files BellImpl_Stub and BellImpl_Skel. BellImpl_Stub will be used by the client application while BellImpl_Skel will be used by the server.

Now that you've set up an appropriate server object, your clients must be able to look up the remote object instance (once it has been registered within the RMI registry) and invoke methods on it. An example of this can be seen in Listing 7.16.

The Hunchback client does an RMI lookup, which contacts the RMI registry running on the host specified within the RMI URL in the lookup call. If

Listing 7.16   Hunchback class definition.

```
//Hunchback.java
import java.rmi.*;
import java.net.*;

public class Hunchback {

    public static void main(String argv[])
    {
        try {
            Bell bell = (Bell)java.rmi.Naming.lookup("//hostname/Bell");
            String message = bell.ringBell();

            System.out.println(message);
        } catch (RemoteException e) {
            System.out.println("Got a RemoteException!");
        } catch (NotBoundException e) {
            System.out.println("Got a NotBoundException!");
        } catch (MalformedURLException e) {
            System.out.println("Got a MalformedURLException!");
        }
    }
}
```

the registry finds a registered object with the name Bell, it returns a proxy implementation. The call to look up is a blocking method; it returns only if there is an error or when the object is found. Once the proxy is acquired in Bell, all subsequent method calls will travel across the network and run on the remote object in the JVM supplied by the server context (in this example, Bell-Impl provides its own runtime context because you execute it as an application directly).

The output (on the screen where the program was run) from the Hunchback class is, "The Bell is ringing!" This is a simplified example, but you can see how easy it is to construct remote objects using RMI. As mentioned, RMI will automatically marshal object parameters to and from methods on the remote object. In order for an object to be successfully marshaled, it must implement the java.io.Serializable interface. When an object is marshaled, it is actually copied. That is, the object instance running in a given context is not removed when it is serialized between two points; rather, a copy of it is passed through the serializing stream (a.k.a. pass-by-value). Therefore, when you write RMI remote objects that accept and return object parameters, realize that those objects are being copied. Depending on the architecture of your application, it may be desirable to use copies of objects as parameters. However, in some conditions, you can return proxies to other remote objects. From the client's perspective, it's still just an object, and there is no real discrepancy in that regard. Figure 7.11 shows a visual comparison of object references and marshaling.

RMI Architectures

Let's take a look at a hypothetical architecture based on RMI to see how the big components fit together to make a distributed application. Figure 7.12 shows a high-level view of this.

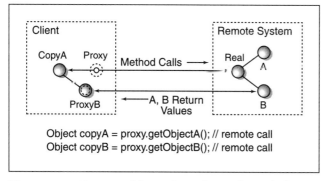

Client   Remote System

CopyA   Proxy   Method Calls ⟶   Real

ProxyB   ⟵ A, B Return Values   B

Object copyA = proxy.getObjectA(); // remote call
Object copyB = proxy.getObjectB(); // remote call

Figure 7.11 Remote object referencing and marshaling.

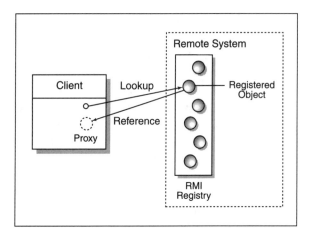

Figure 7.12   A generic RMI-based architecture.

Theoretically, you would have a number of remote objects running on the middle tier of your system. One design consideration is: How many of these objects need to be globally accessed through the registry? Or put another way: Which objects will the client application need to perform lookups on? One solution is to provide a primary remote object (or server object) that contains methods that return subsequent remote references to other remote objects running on the same system. Consider such a primary remote object interface called LoginObject. A client application would contact the LoginObject and invoke login(username,password). If an exception is not thrown, the login() method will return another remote object representing an application controller class called AppController (it's an invented term and doesn't necessarily imply any specific functionality). The classes involved in this scenario are defined in Listings 7.17 through 7.21.

Listing 7.17   LoginObject interface definition.

```
// LoginObject.java
import java.rmi.*;

public interface LoginObject extends Remote
{
    public Remote login(String username, String password)
    throws RemoteException;
}
```

Listing 7.18 LoginObjectImpl class definition.

```java
// LoginObjectImpl.java
import java.rmi.server.*;
import java.rmi.*;
import java.util.*;

public class LoginObjectImpl extends UnicastRemoteObject
    implements LoginObject
{
    Hashtable passwordRegistry = new Hashtable();
    AppController appController;

    public LoginObjectImpl()
    throws RemoteException
    {
        // This step performs some crucial initialization we would
        // otherwise have to do ourselves.
        super();

        // If the appController instantiates successfully, then
        // so will this LoginServer; if either fails, the system
        // will not be available and a RemoteException will be
        // thrown.
        appController = new AppControllerImpl();
    }

    public Remote login(String username, String password)
    throws RemoteException
    {
        // This assumes that passwordRegistry already contains
        // mappings between usernames and passwords. You can
        // decide how you wish this to happen though.
        try {
            String pwd = (String)passwordRegistry.get(username);
            if(!pwd.equals(password))
                throw new InvalidLoginException();
        } catch (Exception e) {
            throw new RemoteException(e.getMessage());
        }
        // Return a remote reference to our
        // ApplicationController object
        return appController;
    }

}
```

Listing 7.19   InvalidLoginException class definition.

```
// InvalidLoginException.java
public class InvalidLoginException extends java.rmi.RemoteException
{}
```

Just to give this method of design a name, let's called it the *focal point* method (it's very similar to the Façade pattern). It gives your clients access to all the distributed objects needed by your system through a single focal point. This relieves the client from having to perform multiple lookups for various distributed objects. Also, should you adopt a pattern approach to implementing retrieval of your focal point, you would be able to change the location and nature of the focal point without forcing modification on the client. In other words, once the focal point is acquired, all subsequent objects are obtained through it. Figure 7.13 diagrams the focal point architecture.

TIP By limiting access to remote objects in your system to a single focal point, you increase the level of security by reducing the number of entry points. This also allows you to establish a strong security policy for your "front door," which you don't have to duplicate for other "doors" in your architecture.

RMI Considerations

One of the primary questions to ask when implementing a distributed architecture with RMI is when to make objects in your system remote and when they can simply be serialized to and from the client as needed. This can be a

Listing 7.20   AppController interface definition.

```
// AppController.java
import java.rmi.*;

public interface AppController extends Remote
{
    public void lock() throws RemoteException;
    public void addUser(String name) throws RemoteException;
    public boolean hasUser(String name) throws RemoteException;
}
```

Listing 7.21 ApplicationControllerImpl class definition.

```
// AppControllerImpl.java
import java.rmi.server.*;
import java.rmi.*;

public class AppControllerImpl extends UnicastRemoteObject
    implements AppController
{
    public AppControllerImpl()
    throws RemoteException
    {
        super();
    }

    public void lock()
    throws RemoteException
    {
        // put your implementation here
    }

    public void addUser(String userName)
    throws RemoteException
    {
        // put your implementation here
    }

    public boolean hasUser(String userName)
    throws RemoteException
    {
        // put your implementation here
        return true;
    }

}
```

complex problem to address. Some of the trade-off considerations are listed in Tables 7.3 and 7.4.

Determining when to implement a particular object as a remote object or not is a matter of analyzing the trade-offs with respect to your chosen architecture and application needs. Unfortunately, there are no real guidelines; you must simply know the effects each has on your system. For distributed objects, consider the granularity with which you intend to send messages. In other words, how frequently will a particular remote object have methods called on it? If

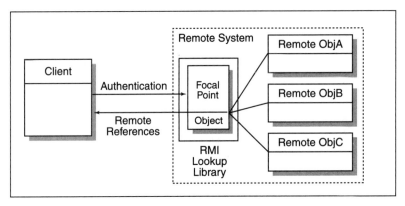

Figure 7.13   Focal point RMI architecture.

performance is a concern, you might consider serializing the object to the client, where it can run locally. But this is not always desirable; it depends on what the object does within your architecture. If you want a remote object to be visible to many clients or to reside strictly on the middle tier *and* it will receive many frequent method calls, system performance is guaranteed to suffer. Fortunately, there are a few alternatives in this case, none of which is addressed by the RMI mechanism, but some of which we'll talk about in Chapter 8, "Enterprise Frameworks".

Object Servers

An *object server* is really just another term for a remote object. Because there is an established client-side and server-side component to each remote object, object servers are sometimes viewed as mini-client/server architectures. The

Table 7.3   Serializing and Remote Objects: The Pros

Serializing objects	Because the object is re-created locally on the client (or server), all subsequent method calls take place in the local context quickly and without concern for network connectivity. In this sense, operations can be performed on objects locally, and the object state can be maintained as it is sent across a network and reinstated on the other side.
Remote objects	Because the object is remote-enabled, many clients can obtain proxies to it simultaneously. This means that state changes occurring within the object are noticeable to clients currently "looking" at it. For distributed systems, this is important because it means that state changes do not necessarily have to be broadcast to clients because they would already have a reference to the same object.

Table 7.4   Serializing and Remote Objects: The Cons

Serializing objects	Because serializing an object is, in effect, copying it, client applications cannot share state changes of these objects as they occur on local systems. Therefore, if an object's state is to be subsequently propagated to the remote system, you will have to provide for object cloning and synchronization, which require the tedious task of mapping object values and using locking. This requires a great deal of effort and so is very undesirable unless a framework system exists to make these tasks more transparent.
Remote objects	All method invocations on a remote object cause an RMI protocol mechanism to activate and contact the server-side components to make the method call happen. This requires time and resource overhead. If your object has methods that are called frequently, this could seriously impact the perceived latency and operation of your client application.

term object server can be interpreted in two ways. First, it can imply that the object being referred to is also the server—in other words, they are one and the same. The remote object is also acting as a server of itself.

The second interpretation of this term is that a different object acts as a server of other objects. In this sense, it's similar to our focal point architecture pattern. The nice thing about object servers in this sense is that they can provide objects much like Factory or Builder patterns do. This allows a decent level of abstraction or buffering to occur between objects residing on the middle tier and the client application. Subsequent changes in the way objects are served, or exactly which objects are returned by the object server, can be encapsulated and hidden from client application developers. This degree of separation should allow developers of the front end and middle tiers of a distributed application to work more or less independently, a highly desirable goal. This is, as we'll see, how Enterprise JavaBeans functions.

Choosing an Approach

Deciding how to architect your distributed Java applications is no trivial matter and certainly is worthy of a more in-depth discussion, which unfortunately is beyond the scope of this book. As a starting point, however, ask yourself the following questions when thinking about distributed solutions for your Java applications.

How many users will my system have? When it is a requirement that the user base be defined ahead of time (and therefore be authenticated in your system), you can answer this question. But a related question is: Will this system be used by an unknown number of users? Typically, systems that run on the Web operate this way because anyone who has access to the system is a potential user.

How secure must this system be? Although security hasn't been covered in detail in this book, it is an important issue for developers of distributed systems. There are many levels of security you might want to employ. If your user base is predefined, you will want to implement user authentication. And if the data moving between the nodes in your distributed system is highly sensitive, you will want some encryption mechanism like Secure Socket Layer (SSL).

How should my system scale? In general, building scalable applications is the goal of modern systems architecture today if they are to meet dynamic user demands. Available resources are plentiful, so addressing this really depends on how your system is to be deployed. Knowing the size and extent of your user base will help you determine how important scaling is for your system.

Will my system need to (or should it) integrate new technologies over time? This is a matter of conjecture, for obvious reasons, but in my experience, nothing built today will suffice long into the future. Therefore, it is important to get the "shell" of your distributed architecture right so that you can "plug in" components as technology changes or improves. This topic, too, deserves many more pages of discussion. Chapter 8, "Enterprise Frameworks," talks about Enterprise JavaBeans (EJB), which addresses this issue in various ways.

There is little doubt that priorities in systems design are moving toward distributed architectures. Java has much to offer in this area. You've seen how RMI can be simple yet powerful. The next chapter looks further into frameworks and mechanisms that address distributed systems for the enterprise.

Future Trends

Even as this discussion on distributed objects and tiered architectures concludes, new trends are emerging for creating highly scalable and distributed network systems in Java.

Spontaneous Networking

Spontaneous networking refers to the ability of networked applications or components to dynamically "arrive" on the network and discover and interact with other elements on the network. Rather than having a centralized server hosting a number of clients, there are instead independent nodes communicating to one another through a common lookup service like the Java Naming and Directory Interface (JNDI). Allowing each node, or peer, to remain independent allows it to handle local policies for itself on a node-by-node basis, while maintaining a presence in the overall system through solid contract and protocol mechanisms. In addition, an environment like this is subject to high degrees of separation and scalability, which have been identified as necessary traits in distributed systems. Spontaneous networking embodies the essence of a distributed computing model. Indeed, even your cellular phone is a node in a large intercontinental distributed network!

Voyager

Voyager is a framework class library that provides the facilities for creating complex and powerful distributed applications in Java. It does this by dynamically creating necessary pieces of your distributed object on the fly. That is, the components discussed previously, such as the proxy, the skeleton, and stub, are generated at runtime by the Voyager system. This enables you to create remote-enabled Java objects without taking the detailed steps before and after compilation. In addition, Voyager provides services to your application such as remote resource loading and resource and class serving as well. Voyager is a state-of-the-art ORB that provides many more interesting facilities to developers, such as mobile agents, object spaces, and others. (For more information on Voyager, visit www.objectspace.com.)

Jini

Jini is a new research technology from Sun Microsystems (see java.sun.com/products/jini/). It is the epitome of spontaneous disitributed computing because it is a true dynamic networking paradigm for applications and devices. In this form of distributed environment, nodes (or Jini services as they're called) are bound by solid contract and protocol, and that is what allows them to discover and collaborate with other services. The Jini core platform *is* that contract and protocol. For the first time, a standard for developing distributed applications and applications that collaborate over a network is underway. The philosophy of Jini is that application objects can make themselves available for "lease." Once available for lease, other application or device objects can discover the newly available object, inspect its services, and lease its use for a certain period of time.

This is the ultimate degree of separation; it means applications can be reused by other applications. It also promotes the highest levels of networking among objects of various levels (within applications, between applications, etc.). Using Jini, you will be able to design objects that provide services to other, yet unknown, objects, possibly developed by other individuals as part of entirely disparate efforts. Figure 7.14 shows the Jini architecture; for more information, go to java.sun.com/products/jini/index.htm.

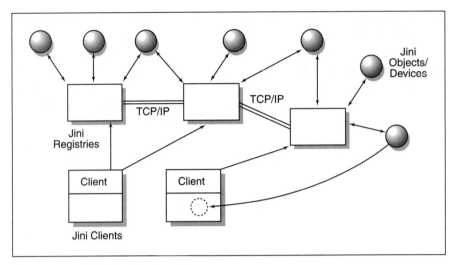

Figure 7.14 A Jini architecture view.

Framework Considerations

As with any discrete facet of a system, a system can be considered a framework in the sense that the duties of the component can be refined, encapsulated, and provided as services of a framework. The topics of distributed objects or middleware are certainly no exception; in fact, a number of fledgling frameworks in these areas are becoming available to the Java community. These include: Voyager from ObjectSpace (www.objectspace.com), Enterprise JavaBeans, and the CORBAfacilities provided with Java 2. Distributed frameworks and distributed components will become increasingly important in distributed systems architecture with Java as the need for network applications and architectures continues to rise.

Summary

This chapter covered various architectural issues such as data retrieval mechanisms, front-end view techniques, business object modeling, and distributed object architectures. Although the information presented represents the tip of the proverbial iceberg, it introduced the practical architectural issues that are likely to arise in Java application development today. Consider this chapter, then, as the foundation for making decisions regarding distributed application development, strengthened by the framework design and development discussions of previous chapters. Together, these approaches can facilitate easier and faster development of Java applications and systems through proven techniques.

Keep in mind that frameworks are becoming important in tiered or distributed architectures because different tiers within a system can be driven by the reusable architectures contained in a specific framework. Tiers in a distributed system can vary independently of each other, similar to the way frameworks can adapt different implementations of key interfaces and abstractions. This allows for front- and back-end modifications, each independent of the other and connected through either a framework abstraction or a patterned approach (as part of a framework). As stated, constructing applications (or groups of applications) with this fundamental principle across a distributed environment is the coming trend in Java systems development and will allow for higher degrees of evolution and interconnectedness among large complex systems and their components. These middleware frameworks will become the backbone for the large distributed Java systems of the future.

The final chapter in this book addresses enterprise frameworks. Using Enterprise JavaBeans and CORBA (via JavaIDL) as examples, you'll learn how such enterprise frameworks operate and why and when they're necessary. In addition, you will learn more about the coming trend in large-scale distributed frameworks This insight will help you in your own efforts to construct large systems by building and/or using such frameworks.

References

Berg, Clifford J *Advanced Java: Development for Enterprise Applications.* Upper Saddle River, NJ: Prentice-Hall, 1998.

Guttman, Michael, and David Frankel. "When Objects Mean Business." *Object Magazine*, May 1998, pp. 39–46.

CHAPTER

8

Enterprise Frameworks

Enterprise computing was one of the primary motivations behind the Java language/platform development. Recently, there has been an upsurge in the importance of enterprise class tools, languages, and components. The demands of enterprise systems are constantly being expanded, and technologies such as Java, with its frameworks and APIs, attempt to meet those demands.

An enterprise framework is designed to address specific kinds of application problems encountered in distributed enterprise systems. Most of these problems concern accessing, retrieving, and storing information across a network. Java has responded to this demand in a number of different ways. This chapter looks at two such enterprise-class frameworks: Enterprise JavaBeans (EJB) and the CORBAfacilities provided by JavaIDL. These Java frameworks and APIs allow business objects to be distributed across a network, facilitating a corporatewide strategy for gathering, accessing, and disseminating information. This chapter shows you how to use these framework components, discusses strategies for implementing architectures with them, and addresses the notion of distributed frameworks.

Enterprise JavaBeans

Java as a server-side technology is becoming more prevalent in businesses today for a variety of reasons. This list highlights some of the more important ones.

- *Java is Write Once, Run Everywhere (WORE).* Often, large distributed systems are not composed of entirely homogenous systems, and the platform portability of Java gives IT designers more choices.

- *Java frameworks and APIs meet the demands of today's systems.* This is true in terms of adaptability, flexibility, and plug-and-play architectures, thereby reducing development time and allowing for new technologies to be added over time.

- *Java is secure.* Java offers a number of advanced security features that make it attractive for developing network systems.

Enterprise JavaBeans (EJB) is a specification[1] that defines a set of interfaces, components, roles, and procedures for developing, deploying, and reusing server-side Java objects under the umbrella of a common transactional, concurrency, and deployment model. JavaSoft created this standard so that enterprises could reliably develop distributed component-based solutions.

> **NOTE** The preceding chapters have looked at using components as reactive models, possibly representing plug-in implementations of framework interfaces. Later, in the section on distributed frameworks, this chapter explores the use of component objects with the goal of using such distributed objects as implementations within frameworks that may reside on different systems.

EJB is a framework for deploying reusable components and objects on the middle tier of a multitiered distributed architecture. It provides near-transparent access to business objects and business logic deployed on a central server platform. Client applets, applications, and forms can interact with EJB from anywhere on a network. Chapter 7, "Java Application Architectures," introduced a multitiered distributed architecture that allows for corporations to isolate business logic away from their client. This is what makes such distributed systems attractive. EJB presents an implementation for deploying business object components within a distributed architecture.

EJB is a *middle-tier component*. Middle-tier components handle incoming requests from client applications distributed across a network. In addition, they offer a repository for business logic and/or business objects in a system.

---

[1] As a specification, EJB exists in its default form as a white paper, defining the roles and interfaces necessary to create an actual EJB server implementation. (For more information on the EJB spec, visit java.sun.com/products.ejb/white_paper.htm.)

But they can serve a variety of purposes in addition to hosting business objects or business logic. EJB defines a persistence model for persisting server-side objects and maintaining state between events such as network failures, server crashes, and power outages. In addition, it defines a transaction model provided transparently to beans, which means these capabilities do not have to be directly coded by the EJB developer.

EJB offers a number of other services at no "cost" to the developer (i.e., no special coding required) including *object persistence,* whereby objects have their internal state managed for them. Because the EJB framework provides these important and valuable services automatically, the developer is free to focus on the important business objects and business logic required by the application.

EJB is able to provide these transparent services to objects through special objects called *containers*. Enterprise beans are deployed into containers from which they can then be accessed through the EJB server across a network. Containers are provided by a specific vendor's implementation of the EJB server. Because EJB has a written specification, as well as core classes and interfaces, vendors have the opportunity to provide their own implementations of that specification. The EJB specification (or spec) clearly defines the behavior and services that each container implementation must provide its beans; therefore, numerous varying implementations (from different vendors) may exist.

Human Roles in EJB

One characteristic that separates EJB from other similar paradigms (such as CORBA, DCOM, etc.) is defined by the roles humans play in the process of developing and deploying EJB objects and components. This important in today's software development market, because it clearly explains where responsibilities in the ultimate creation of a system lie. In a component architecture paradigm, it is useful to know who provides components, who installs components, and who provides component services. Understanding these roles will help you to identify how and where you fit into the process.

There are at least four basic roles that emerge from the EJB specification:

- *Enterprise bean provider.* The individual or company that creates and packages an enterprise bean or set of beans. In the near future, the market for sophisticated business objects that can be used to quickly construct enterprise class applications will grow significantly as system developers generate a great demand for reusable, redeployable object components. Many types of enterprise business objects will find their way into the market, and developers will be able to choose appropriate business frameworks upon which they will construct their applications. Enterprise bean providers will build these business objects.

- *Bean deployer.* The person who installs enterprise beans into a third-party container. This role involves interacting with the EJB server through graphical deployment tools to make decisions about how the bean is to be deployed and managed. Configuration of an EJB when it is deployed is handled through its *deployment descriptor,* which contains information (e.g., access-control lists, bean names, etc.) about how the bean is to be managed by the container.

- *Application developer.* The individual or team of individuals who focus on solving application domain problems. These developers are more concerned with the domain use cases and user requirements of an application than with technical barriers such as persistence, concurrency, and transaction management.

- *EJB container provider.* A software vendor who is technically proficient in transaction management, data retrieval, and thread control, and implements these services to beans as required by the EJB specification. Container implementations provided the semantic behavior defined by EJB, but, currently, are strictly vendor-specific.

NOTE Currently, there is no standard interface between containers and servers. For this reason, it is not possible to take a container from one vendor and place it on another vendor's server. So, for the time being, server providers are also container providers.

These roles stem from the natural separation of interests in the process of application development. Previously, developers found themselves grappling with the same technological hurdles (such as transaction management, persistence, concurrency, etc.) and therefore could not focus on the application requirements. EJB has taken a big step forward to changing the way software is developed, by defining the semantics of these earlier hurdles and allowing skilled vendors to provide clean, transparent implementations.

EJB Features

As we just stated, EJB is essentially a specification and a small set of Java interfaces. The spec is a standard upon which vendors can provide implementations. Details about how facilities are implemented behind the EJB interfaces are undefined (e.g., persistence, transaction services, etc.).

NOTE Defining a system in terms of interfaces like those in the EJB spec is an example of black box reuse, as discussed in Chapter 1, "Framework Concepts."

Only the interfaces are exposed to the EJB developer. Vendors such as BEA WebLogic, IBM, and Oracle either have already implemented or are planning to implement EJB servers that provide the basic EJB services to beans using their own implementation. The EJB server's container is responsible for providing these critical services to enterprise beans it contains.

A Persistence Model

An EJB framework implementation must provide a mechanism for persisting beans. The specifics behind how persistence is performed is completely transparent to the bean developer, who needn't provide facilities for managing object persistence in this regard. Adhering to the EJB specification guarantees that persistence is available in any given EJB server implementation. Different container providers may provide this service in different ways. For example, an object database vendor might choose to implement object persistence in the object database. A relational database vendor might provide translation between relational row data and objects automatically.

Concurrency Control

Traditional server components in a client/server or multitiered architecture must address the issue of *concurrency*. Concurrency deals with the issue of multiple clients attempting to invoke the same routine or method (or data, for that matter) of a given object at the same time. For example, Internet Web servers listen for client socket connections on port 80. Each client that makes a request on this port is joined with a process thread spawned in the Web server to handle that request. This allows for other clients to acquire threads for handling their requests without queuing up to wait for previous threads to complete (otherwise, hundreds of clients could end up waiting in line!).

Writing servers that perform robust concurrency control is not easy. Furthermore, if it is necessary to manage database transactions, the problem grows exponentially. Because most application developers are not experts in concurrency control, a large commercial market exists for databases and server components that perform this difficult task.

Fortunately, EJB servers enable safe, concurrent access to your enterprise Java-Beans. The bean developer does not have to be concerned with how to make his or her beans handle concurrency. When beans are deployed into the EJB execution environment, they inherit these services from the deployment container.

A Transaction Model

Middleware software that interacts with a database must provide semantics for transaction management. A *transaction* is a temporal unit in which interactions to managed objects or data occurs. That is, in order to guarantee the integrity of such objects and data, access to them must be governed strictly. So, before an object can be accessed or altered, a transaction must be created to ensure proper access. *Transaction management* ensures that the integrity of the underlying data is not compromised in a multiuser, multithreaded environment. EJB defines a sophisticated set of transaction semantics that adhere to the OMG standard (visit www.omg.org for more information about this standard). Executing methods on a given EJB take place within the context of a transaction by default, and a number of settings can alter the transaction context required by a particular EJB. The result of the transaction model is that robust, reliable systems can be constructed without an overwhelming concern for data integrity and access governance.

Write Once, Drop in Anywhere

Another nice feature integrated by the EJB designers is that the developer can create an enterprise bean and deploy it (drop it in, if you will) into multiple servers without modification. This means that as a business object developer, you need not worry about which services are available in a particular EJB server or how to access them. The EJB specification is designed specifically to contain these semantics while deferring key implementations. The result is that your business objects and logic can migrate to different or better EJB environments without source-level modifications. In today's ever-shifting IT world, this is a huge plus.

Architecture

The EJB architecture contains a number of entities. We'll discuss these three in this subsection:

- Enterprise beans
- EJB servers
- Containers

Enterprise Beans

An *enterprise bean* is a Java object that represents a business object (for more information on business objects, refer to Chapter 7, "Java Application Architectures"), such as an Employee or Automobile (depending on the nature of the business). Each enterprise bean is registered and deployed into an EJB server, where it is placed in a corresponding container. Once deployed, the enterprise bean can be accessed remotely from distributed Java applications, components, and frameworks. In other words, a process in a remote Java Virtual Machine (JVM) can now discover and make invocations on the newly deployed enterprise bean.

There are two basic types of enterprise beans: *session beans* and *entity beans*. The key difference between them is that entity beans are required to have their state managed or persisted in permanent storage, whereas session beans are not. The current EJB specification does not require container implementations to provide support for entity beans at this time, and therefore, it is optional to vendors.

EJB Servers

An EJB server is a vendor-specific implementation of the EJB specification. Though different vendors will likely provide different server implementations, the semantics defined in the EJB specification will not vary. EJB containers operate within the context of a server. For this reason, a given EJB server implementation can provide its own semantics for allowing containers to reside within in.

Although the EJB spec does not define interactions between EJB servers and containers, at some point this will become important, because container vendors will want to deploy their containers into various server implementations such as BEA WebExpress. It is the role of the server to provide all the network-level connectivity and interaction between requests for enterprise beans and how those enterprise beans are stored in their respective containers. For this reason, EJB servers are typically located on the middle tier of a multitier system architecture. Client applications will interact directly with an EJB server to access to server-side enterprise objects.

Containers

As mentioned in the introduction to this chapter, EJB containers are special objects that contain enterprise beans. Containers provide crucial implementations of bean services, such as transaction management, concurrency, and object persistence. The interactions between an enterprise beans and its container are well defined and will vary only as the EJB spec varies. Before an enterprise bean can be used in a system, it must first be deployed into a container residing in an active EJB server. Containers are designed to run within the context of a server implementation, but details about how this occurs is currently vendor-specific.

Figure 8.1 highlights the containment relationships between the key components of Enterprise JavaBeans. A system built using EJB resembles a basic three-tiered architecture. Enterprise beans can access other enterprise beans that reside on the same server or on another server. This allows the developer to create an *n*-tier distributed system composed of many EJB servers.

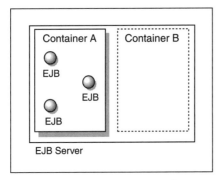

Figure 8.1   EJB containment diagram.

Connecting to an EJB

The EJB server serves enterprise beans over a network by answering to a standard lookup mechanism, such as Java Naming and Directory Interface (JNDI). Interaction occurs between the server and containers containing the enterprise beans. As just explained, beans residing in containers can be one of two types, session beans or entity beans. The current EJB spec requires that all EJB servers implement session beans; entity beans are optional. When a client requests a connection to an enterprise bean, the server returns an implementation of a special interface called the bean's *home interface*. Through a given home interface, a client can create new instances of the enterprise bean, acquire metadata about it, or possibly search for specific stored beans.

The client application or applet receives an interface either by retrieving an existing bean or creating a new one, which maps onto the enterprise bean. The client never actually obtains the enterprise bean directly, but communicates through a proxy implementation that forwards method invocations to the bean's container. The container then confers with the actual enterprise bean implementation to execute the appropriate method. This process is transparent to both the server and the client. Developers appear to be working with the bean itself, but in reality they are invoking on the EJB proxy. Figure 8.2 shows the relationship of the entities involved in connecting to and interacting with an EJB.

EJB Interfaces

Writing an enterprise bean is almost as simple as writing a basic Java class. Each enterprise bean defines an interface for accessing the bean's method implementations. The developer is responsible for providing the basic interfaces that his or her enterprise bean implements.

It is through these interfaces that enterprise beans are created, interacted with, and removed. Deploying an EJB causes a significant amount of process-

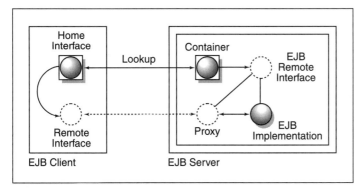

Figure 8.2 EJB architecture view.

ing to occur on these interfaces. There are two primary interfaces needed for each EJB: the *home interface* and the *remote interface*.

EJBHome Interface

Enterprise bean developers must provide a home interface to their bean by extending the interface EJBHome. This interface is the gateway (the home) to the enterprise bean's remote proxy. The home interface can provide valuable services to the client, such as creating new instances, performing find operations on existing beans of that type, or removing instances. Listing 8.1 shows the EJBHome interface provided in the javax.ejb package.

The default EJBHome interface provides method declarations for acquiring metadata about the bean and for removing specific enterprise beans whose

Listing 8.1 EJBHome interface definition.

```
package javax.ejb;
import java.rmi.RemoteException;

public interface javax.ejb.EJBHome extends java.rmi.Remote
{
    public abstract EJBMetaData getEJBMetaData()
        throws RemoteException;
    public abstract void remove(Handle handle)
        throws RemoteException, RemoveException;
    public abstract void remove(Object primaryKey)
        throws RemoteException, RemoveException;
}
```

class types are associated with that particular home interface. When an enterprise bean is deployed, the deployment process provides key implementations to these methods automatically.

In addition, an EJB's home interface represents the initial entry point for creating and connecting to the EJB. When a client performs a naming service lookup by name on a particular enterprise bean, it retrieves that bean's home interface. Enterprise beans are deployed by name in association with the class represented by the EJB. Therefore, when a lookup on a particular name is performed, a home interface is returned associated with the bean's class.

New instances of the bean's remote interface (its implementation proxy) can be acquired through the bean's home interface. Additional methods, such as find methods for retrieving specific instances of beans, can be placed in a bean's EJBHome subinterface, at the discretion of the developer. This allows you to tailor specific functionality to your type of enterprise bean and makes it possible for client applications that recognize your EJBHome subinterface to tap into that functionality as well as the defaults provided by the EJBHome base interface. Listing 8.2 is an example of the home interface that includes the find( ) method.

Notice in Listing 8.2 that a create( ) method has been added. It is the responsibility of the EJBHome subinterface to provide specific flavors of create( ) that allow instances of the specified enterprise bean to be created within the server. This allows client applications to create new enterprise beans that will subsequently have a lifetime of their own, possibly in permanent storage. For any given enteprise bean, you might provide a variety of create( ) methods. Each create( ) method maps onto a special method within your bean implementation that initializes the bean to a useful state much like an object constructor. This is, in fact, identical in purpose.

RULE For each create( ) signature appearing in your EJBHome subinterface, there must be an analagous ejbCreate( ) method appearing in your bean's implementation class. This is due to the fact that when your enterprise bean is

Listing 8.2 DomainObjectHome interface definition.

```
public interface DomainObjectHome extends javax.ejb.EJBHome
{
    public DomainObject create(int id)
    throws java.rmi.RemoteException, javax.ejb.CreateException;

    public DomainObject find(int id)
    throws java.rmi.RemoteException;
}
```

deployed, the support classes generated will map between the create( ) method in the home interface and your corresponding ejbCreate( ) method in your implementation class.

EJBObject Interface

The remote interface of your EJB is created by extending the base interface EJBObject. The remote interface to your enterprise bean represents the implementation proxy to your bean. That is, it represents all the key business methods provided by an enterprise bean, as well as a few EJB-specific methods. Enterprise JavaBeans will supply a proxy implementation of your remote interface to clients when they request access to your enterprise bean. Listing 8.3 shows a sample of the EJBObject interface.

Table 8.1 briefly describes the methods provided by the EJBObject base interface shown in Listing 8.3.

Listing 8.4 shows the remote interface represented in the DomainObject-Home interface. Similar to the DomainObject in Chapter 2, "Java Framework Design," accessor methods for the objectId property have been supplied, as well as a plug point for the save( ) method. By subclassing EJBObject, additional methods are provided that will ultimately be implemented in a bean implementation class for this interface. Specifically, the enterprise bean implementation class residing within the EJB server will implement getObjectId( ), setObjectId( ), and save( ) The EJB deployment process will create for you the necessary classes to translate onto your enterprise bean implementation from remote clients.

Listing 8.3   EJBObject interface definition.

```
package javax.ejb;
import java.rmi.*;

public interface javax.ejb.EJBObject
{
    public abstract EJBHome getEJBHome();
        throws java.rmi.RemoteException;
    public abstract Handle getHandle();
        throws java.rmi.RemoteException;
    public abstract Object getPrimaryKey();
        throws java.rmi.RemoteException;
    public abstract boolean isIdentical(EJBObject obj);
        throws java.rmi.RemoteException;
    public abstract void remove();
        throws RemoteException, RemoveException;
}
```

Table 8.1 EJBObject Interface Methods

METHOD	BRIEF DESCRIPTION
getEJBHome ( )	Returns the EJBHome interface representing this bean.
GetHandle ( )	Returns a Handle object that can be used for future reference to this bean.
GetPrimaryKey ( )	Returns the primary key used to uniquely identify and index this enterprise bean.
IsIdentical (EJBObject obj)	Tests two beans' remote interfaces to determine if they are identical
remove( )	Removes this specific enterprise bean.

The create( ) method present in the DomainObjectHome interface will return an object proxy implementing this DomainObject interface, which holds the key business methods you wish to access on your enterprise bean. You'll see shortly how this all fits together. For now, it's important that you understand what the remote interface represents.

EnterpriseBean Interface

Again, all enterprise beans fall into one of two categories provided by the EJB spec: session beans or entity beans. Each type is defined by an associated interface rooted by the common interface EnterpriseBean, shown in Listing 8.5. This interface is used for categorizing the entire family of enterprise beans and does not contain any generalized method declarations.

Listing 8.4 EJBDomainObject remote interface.

```
import javax.ejb.*;
import java.rmi.*;

public interface DomainObject extends EJBObject
{
    public int getObjectId()
        throws RemoteException;
    public void setObjectId(int id)
        throws RemoteException;
    public boolean save()
        throws RemoteException;
}
```

Listing 8.5   EnterpriseBean interface definition.

```
package javax.ejb;

public interface EnterpriseBean extends java.io.Serializable
{
}
```

Session Beans

Session beans implement the SessionBean interface. Beans of this type are only valid during a client's present session. A session is the connection a client has established with a particular EJB server. Each time a client connects to a server, a session is established when the two sides recognize one another. Session management is handled entirely within the server.

Listing 8.6 shows the SessionBean interface. Notice the three methods prefixed by "ejb": ejbActivate( ), ejbPassivate( ), and ejbRemove( ).

All of the methods in the SessionBean interface are *callback* methods that are invoked by the container to notify the bean about state changes and events. For example, after a SessionBean has been activated from a semi-persistent store, its ejbActivate( ) method is invoked. This allows the bean to perform any necessary operations, such as reestablish vital transient connections to information sources. Likewise, before a bean is passivated (a term meaning: persisted to a temporary storage space and unloaded from process memory), its ejbPassivate( ) method is called. Again, it is useful for the bean to know when these transitions occur so that proper resources can be allocated or freed. Table 8.2 summarizes the SessionBean interface methods.

Listing 8.6   SessionBean interface definition.

```
package javax.ejb;

public interface SessionBean extends EnterpriseBean
{
    public abstract void ejbActivate();
        throws RemoteException;
    public abstract void ejbPassivate();
        throws RemoteException;
    public abstract void ejbRemove();
        throws RemoteException;
    public abstract void setSessionContext(SessionContext ctx);
        throws RemoteException;
}
```

Table 8.2   SessionBean Interface Methods

METHOD	BRIEF DESCRIPTION
ejbActivate( )	Called immediately after the bean has been restored from a persistent state.
ejbPassivate( )	Called just before the bean is swapped out to persistent storage.
ejbRemove( )	Called when a client calls remove( ) on the bean's home or remote interface.
setSessionContext (SessionContext ctx)	Called by the container when the bean is first brought to life, and passes the context associated with the current session. The bean can interact with the container through its SessionContext object.

Session beans are useful for all-purpose client-server interactions. For example, suppose you have a Web-based order form that customers fill out and submit to your database. A session bean would process the incoming data from the form submitted by the client application and store it in the appropriate back-end database, where the order would be previewed and subsequently filled. A client interaction would be strictly with the session bean, and data would be marshaled and forwarded to the database on the middle tier.

NOTE Although session beans are swapped in and out (that is, they are activated and passivated dynamically) depending on the state of the connection, they are not guaranteed permanent persistent storage that would survive power outages or network failures. This type of functionality is reserved for entity beans. But because this discussion on EJB is necessarily limited, and entity beans are an optional portion of the spec, they are covered in less detail.

Entity Beans

In contrast to session beans, which are active only as long as the current client is connected, entity beans are indefinitely persistent. They maintain state across invocations or connections from a client, which means they can be shared by many clients simultaneously. Entity beans represent precise instances of business objects that are shared across a network. Because the enterprise bean model is based on beans or Java objects, any critical data used by an EJB system would represent that data as enterprise beans, or access to data would be through enterprise beans. Because entity beans are permanently persisted, it is not necessary to manually translate between data representation and object representation. In fact, an EJB container supporting entity beans would provide any mapping functionality automatically, thus freeing developers to focus on objects and only objects.

Table 8.3 shows the interface methods provided by the EntityBean interface. It is similar to the SessionBean interface, but with the addition of a few methods important only to EntityBeans, such as ejbLoad( ) and ejbStore( ).

Interface Implementations

In addition to the home and remote interfaces for an EJB, the implementation of the bean must also be provided by writing a simple Java class that implements either the SessionBean or EntityBean interface. The methods defined by those interfaces represent callback methods to the implementation class, notifying it of certain specific events. The business methods defined in the remote interface must also be implemented, but your class does not have to directly declare that it implements the remote interface. EJB will dynamically provide an implementation proxy that maps onto your EJB.

Table 8.3   EntityBean Interface Methods

METHOD	BRIEF DESCRIPTION
ejbActivate( )	Called immediately after the bean has been restored from a persistent state.
ejbPassivate( )	Called just before the bean is swapped out to persistent storage.
ejbRemove( )	Called when a client calls remove( ) on the bean's home or remote interface.
setEntityContext (EntityContext ctx)	Called by the container when the bean is first brought to life, and passes the EntityContext. The bean can interact with the container through its EntityContext object. New contexts are set as requests from clients are executed on the bean.
ejbLoad( )	In the case of bean-managed persistence, the bean should store itself to persistent storage when this is called. For container-managed persistence, this method will be called after the bean has been loaded from permanent storage.
ejbStore( )	A container invokes this method to instruct the instance to synchronize its state by storing it to the underlying database.
UnsetEntityContext( )	Removes the current EntityContext for the bean, possibly to allow a new request to be executed on the bean.

Accessing EJBs

Accessing an enterprise bean involves performing a lookup on the bean's name. A lookup involves locating an object somewhere on a network or within a system based on a key, name, or identifier. This process operates in a manner similar to RMI, discussed in Chapter 7, "Java Application Architectures." EJB uses the standard Java Naming and Directory Interface (JNDI) API as the basis for performing lookups on EJB. If the requested enterprise bean exists by name, its home interface is returned from the lookup call. The lookup call blocks until either the bean is found (on a particular server) or it is determined that no bean exists by the requested name.

> **NOTE** The Java Naming and Directory Interface (JNDI) provides a common set of interfaces for accessing objects across a network or on a file system. The exact mechanism by which objects are discovered and retrieved is part of a particular JNDI implementation. You can obtain a variety of JNDI implements such as RMI, CORBA COS, File System, and LDAP. This way, your client programs can be coded once and have access to objects residing in a variety of directories such as these, in addition to EJB.
>
> The following code snippet shows how a simple lookup occurs in JNDI.
>
> ```
> Context initCtx = new InitialContext();
> Object obj1 = (Object)initCtx.lookup('objecturl');
> ```

An EJB Example

Now that you understand the features and architecture of EJB, let's take a look at a simple example. Suppose you wanted to implement a simple EmployeePay enterprise bean that implements the calculatePay( ) method discussed in Chapter 7. If you remember, this method was used to calculate the amount of pay an employee would be eligible for given his or her number of hours and pay rate. Remember, too, that you also had to accommodate for certain business conditions, such as overtime pay.

With those parameters in mind, look at the following list, which identifies the four steps to creating the EmployeePay enterprise business-logic bean:

1. Define the home interface.
2. Define the remote interface.
3. Provide a single implementation class that satisfies the remote and SessionBean interfaces.
4. Discuss the deployment process and descriptors for your bean.

It makes more sense for this bean to be a SessionBean because it contains business logic and not persistent business data (it does not contain *state*, and is therefore stateless). It does establish a centrally accessible location containing logic used by various distributed applications. Because it is centrally located and can be accessed in a predefined manner (i.e., through a lookup mechanism such as JNDI), any application that can talk to the EJB server can utilize the bean's functionality.

The Home Interface

The home interface for the EmployeePay EJB in this example is called Employee-PayHome; it contains a single create method, shown in Listing 8.7. This create method will map onto an analogous ejbCreate( ) method in your bean implementation class.

Notice that the create( ) method throws RemoteException and CreateException. Because EJB uses RMI for its communications, all create methods in the home interface must throw RemoteException. A RemoteException will be thrown when some sort of network or connectivity error occurs, indicating that RMI cannot carry out its handshaking protocol between the server and the client. Because the create( ) method attempts to initialize a new instance of a server-side enterprise bean, it must also throw CreateException. In your analogous ejbCreate( ) method (in your implementation class), you can throw a CreateException if the new bean cannot be created or initialized. The client can trap for this exception and know the nature of the failure (i.e., whether it was an RMI network error or a bean thrown exception).

The Remote Interface

The remote interface represents the declaration of business methods on the enterprise bean. The EmployeePay interface has a single business method, called calculatePay( ), shown in Listing 8.8. This will be the remote interface. A proxy implementation of this interface will be provided to clients who acquire

Listing 8.7 EmployeePayHome interface definition.

```
// EmployeePayHome.java
import javax.ejb.*;
import java.rmi.*;

public interface EmployeePayHome extends DomainObjectHome
{
    public EmployeePay create()
        throws RemoteException, CreateException;
}
```

Listing 8.8 EmployeePay interface definition.

```
// EmployeePay.java
import javax.ejb.*;
import java.rmi.*;

public interface EmployeePay extends EJBObject
{
    public double calculatePay(int rate, int hours)
        throws RemoteException;
}
```

references to enterprise beans of this type through the appropriate home interface (in this case, EmployeePayHome).

The calculatePay( ) method, like all other method declarations seen thus far, also throws RemoteException. Again, this is because this interface will be seen remotely from a client. Any negative conditions preventing the execution of this method will throw a RemoteException. It's worth mentioning that your business methods can also throw user defined exceptions. You can provide an appropriate exception family for your business objects that are thrown from within your bean implementation class. These exceptions will be marshaled over the network where the client can trap for them as well.

The Bean Implementation

Now that you have provided the key interfaces, let's implement them in the bean implementation class, called EmployeePayBean. Because this is a simple session bean, it implements the SessionBean interface. Listing 8.9 shows the EmployeePayBean class.

In Listing 8.9 you can see that the implementation of calculatePay( ) is provided. It should already be familiar to you from the previous chapter. You will also notice the method blocks for the SessionBean interface methods summarized in Table 8.1. Although nothing useful is done in these methods, they must be there.

It's interesting to note that the EmployeePayBean enterprise bean is not all that complicated. In fact, it should seem quite simple; and not much is really required to take advantage of the services provided by EJB containers. Notice that nothing special is done to indicate how the object is to be accessed, synchronized, or otherwise used. This is done for you automatically.

Finally, notice that you were not required to provided special "throws" clauses in your method implementations. All the EJB interfaces defined required RemoteException to be thrown by all methods. When your enterprise bean is deployed, the appropriate classes necessary to proxy calls to and from

Listing 8.9 EmployeeBean interface definition.

```java
// EmployeeBean.java
import javax.ejb.*;
import java.io.*;
import java.util.*;

public class EmployeePayBean implements SessionBean
{
    protected final static int PAY_PERIOD_MAX = 80;
    private transient SessionContext ctx;
    private transient Properties     props;

    public void ejbCreate()
    {
    }

    // Here is our business method for calculated pay. We've opted
    // to include it in our session bean since all employees will
    // be using the same business object class. Changing the
    // business logic here changes it for all clients.
    public double calculatePay(int rate, int hours)
    {
        double pay = rate * hours;
        if(hours>PAY_PERIOD_MAX) {
            int diff=hours-PAY_PERIOD_MAX;
            double overtime = diff*(rate*1.5);
            return overtime;
        }
        return pay;
    }

    /*
     * SessionBean method blocks
     ****************************************************************/

        /**
         * This method is required by the EJB Specification,
         * but is not used by this example.
         *
         */
        public void ejbActivate() {
            System.out.println("ejbActivate called");
        }

        /**
         * This method is required by the EJB Specification,
         * but is not used by this example.
         *
         */
```

continues

Listing 8.9 EmployeeBean interface definition. *(Continued)*

```
        public void ejbRemove() {
            System.out.println("ejbRemove called");
        }


        /**
         * This method is required by the EJB Specification,
         * but is not used by this example.
         *
         */
        public void ejbPassivate() {
            System.out.println("ejbPassivate ");
        }


        /**
         * Sets the session context.
         */
        public void setSessionContext(SessionContext ctx) {
            System.out.println("setSessionContext called");
          this.ctx = ctx;
          props    = ctx.getEnvironment();
        }



    }
```

your enterprise bean will provide the required mechanics to generate and throw RemoteExceptions should they occur during a remote method invocation. But if you had defined your own exception classes in the business methods of your remote interface (EmployeePay), you would have been required to declare those in a "throws" clause appearing within the method header. Figure 8.3 shows a simple class diagram for this EJB example.

Bean Deployment

In order to deploy this bean and its interfaces into a container, you must provide some important information about the bean. This information will be contained in the SessionDescriptor class. EJB deployment environments expect to see a serialized instance of SessionDescriptor with the attributes set for the specific bean class being deployed (e.g., EmployeePayBean). Fortunately, the more advanced deployment environments for EJB servers provide a graphical interface to edit these properties, so you don't (if you choose) have to write a Java class and then serialize its state. For this reason, we won't dis-

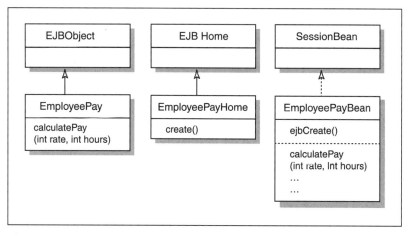

Figure 8.3   Class diagram for the EmployeePay example.

cuss the details of how the SessionDescriptor class behaves, but instead present the critical information typically provided by SessionDescriptors.

Table 8.4 identifies the properties needed to deploy the bean. The Value column is populated with the class or interface name from our example.

The deployment process is rather tricky to explain because how it works depends largely on the implementation. The property fields (shown in Table 8.4 in the Property column) needed to deploy the bean are fixed, which is why they were presented in Table 8.4; however, additional steps may be required, depending on the EJB server used. These steps might include putting the inter-

Table 8.4   Deployment Descriptor Properties for the EmployeePay Example

PROPERTY	VALUE	DESCRIPTION
BeanHomeName	EmployeePay	Represents the JNDI name used to look up and acquire the home interface for the SessionBean.
EnterpriseBeanClassName	EmployeePayBean	Represents the qualified class name of the bean implementation.
HomeInterfaceClassName	EmployeePayHome	The name of the home interface.
RemoteInterfaceClassName	EmployeePay	The name of the remote interface.
StateManagementType	STATELESS_SESSION	The type of persistence requested by the bean.

faces, classes, and descriptors into a jar file, and having the deployment environment inspect the jar file. Other environments might create the jar file for you, including the generated classes needed to complete the bean (such as the proxy implementations of the remote and home interfaces).

> **NOTE** A jar file is an acronym for a Java-archive file containing compressed files and directory structures. EJB deploys beans as jar files. A single jar file is much easier to manage and track than a fully expanded directory structure. There are many reasons why using jar files is a good idea.

The Client

Listing 8.10 shows a simple client that accesses the SessionBean and invokes the business logic based on two simple parameters. The two parameters represent the rate and hours, respectively. The calculation, or execution, of the calculatePay( ) method occurs within the EmployeePay enterprise bean back on the server.

This example, although simple, demonstrates the steps involved in creating session enterprise beans. Clearly, there are features of the EJB framework that interact with your application or business objects. The key concept is that this type of framework operates similar to application-level frameworks, but is distinct in nature in that it doesn't define an application architecture through which you supply critical objects and implementations as plug-ins. The EJB framework creates an environment through which you can supply application objects and subsequently interact with them across a network. Technologies like EJB (and other distributed object frameworks) can act as the functioning backbone to the concept of distributed frameworks (or components) in a network application architecture. This is discussed further later in this chapter.

Java IDL

The release of Java 2 included something quite exciting: a compiler that supports the Interface Definition Language (IDL), and a naming service that supports CORBA. CORBA, the now-familiar acronym Common Object Request Broker Architecture was developed by the Object Management Group (OMG) as a framework for connecting distributed objects. CORBA is an object-oriented approach to network programming and is fast becoming a tool for developing middleware. Because the OMG developed CORBA as an open standard, and because the consortium has a membership of more than 700 companies, the goal of CORBA is interoperability. CORBA is not programming

Listing 8.10 Client code for the EmployeePay example.

```java
// EmployeeClient.java
import javax.ejb.*;
import javax.naming.*;
import java.rmi.*;

public class EmployeeClient {

    InitialContext ic;
    EmployeePayHome home;

    public static void main(String argv[])
    {
        EmployeeClient ec = new EmployeeClient();
    }

    public EmployeeClient()
    {
        try {
            ic = new InitialContext();
            home = (EmployeePayHome)ic.lookup("EmployeePay");
                EmployeePay employeePay = home.create();
            System.out.println("Pay for this employee is"+
                    + employeePay.calculatePay(40,40));
        } catch (NamingException e) {
            // JNDI lookup of our home interface failed
        } catch (RemoteException f) {
            // A network error occurred when trying to create()
        } catch (CreateException g) {
            // For some reason our implementation bean could
            // not be created.
        }
    }
}
```

language-specific, platform-specific, or corporation-specific. The addition of the CORBA classes to and the IDL support in Java 2 offers the programmer a powerful tool for distributed object programming.

NOTE This section is intended only as a brief overview of CORBA and Java IDL. For more information on CORBA, visit OMG's Web site at www.omg.org and the Java home page at java.sun.com. And for a book that is a great introduction and reference, check out *Client/Server Programming with Java and CORBA,* Second Edition, by Robert Orfali and Dan Harkey [Wiley, 1999].

CORBA Overview

CORBA is the glue that can link objects that have been written in different programming languages, reside on different platforms, and reside in different server and client locations. The heart of CORBA is the object request broker (ORB). The ORB provides facilities for object management; it connects objects to other objects, and helps objects communicate with object services. Simply put, the ORB helps objects "talk" to other objects.

CORBA has often been described as an "object bus," where objects can register to talk to other objects. Though this metaphor is sometimes helpful in describing certain CORBA services, perhaps a better analogy is the *remote procedure call* (RPC). RPC is a facility that enables a program on a computer to make a "function call" on another remote computer in the network. CORBA extends this analogy to objects: Objects can call remote objects' methods, and these objects, no matter where they are on the network, can then communicate.

Figure 8.4 shows the basis for the Object Management Architecture (OMA), CORBA's base architecture. As you can see, the ORB is the key component. There are CORBA application objects, CORBA facilities, an ORB, and CORBA services. CORBA's common facilities provide generic functions that can be used in specific applications (database management, for example). CORBA's many services perform a number of object management functions, such as the aforementioned naming service. Objects register with this service to let the other objects know that they are out there. The naming service, provided by Java 2, is the focus of this subsection.

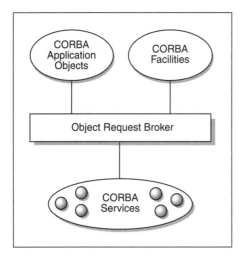

Figure 8.4 CORBA Object Management Architecture.

In CORBA, there are *client objects* and *server objects*. Server objects are those that perform a specific service, and will have their methods remotely invoked. Client objects simply invoke methods on the server objects.

In order to use CORBA, the developer must use the Interface Definition Language (IDL) to describe his or her server objects. IDL is a standard programming language-independent definition language that describes objects and is used to generate code that works with the CORBA environment. IDL describes the object's interface, the public methods, and member variables of an object. Because IDL is not programming language-specific, an interface definition for an object written in C++ would look the same as the same object written in Java.

A developer compiles the IDL with an IDL compiler to create code that his or her object uses in order to participate in the CORBA environment. Because the interfaces for CORBA objects are described in a standard, programming language-independent way (IDL), every one of these objects will have a common look and feel; that is, other objects won't know if the object is implemented in C++, Java, Smalltalk, or Ada! Objects calling CORBA objects only need to know the CORBA object's interfaces. Another benefit of CORBA is that it provides a method to *dynamically* discover an object's interfaces! If object A sees object B, and does not know how to access B, it simply asks the ORB, "What does this object's interface look like?" The ORB will respond, and Object A can then dynamically create a call to the object.

For objects to speak to each other using CORBA, a developer must create the IDL that describes the object's interface and must have an IDL compiler for his or her specific language. This compiler creates skeletons and stubs that are necessary for object-ORB communication. After the skeletons and stubs are created, an object adapter lets the objects speak to each other.

NOTE Server objects must be defined with IDL, whereas client objects only have to ask the ORB for the server objects.

Figure 8.5 shows an example of object invocation in CORBA. Client A registers with an ORB on a network, and asks the ORB to look up the Bank object. Because the Bank object is a CORBA server, which has IDL stubs, the ORB gives Client A an instance of the object. At the same time, the Bank object could call the StockWatcher object. Notice that the objects are written in three different languages. With CORBA, it does not matter, because the CORBA "glue" was generated with programming language-independent IDL!

Programming language independence is one of the main reasons that CORBA technology is becoming so instrumental for working with legacy systems. Instead of reinventing a good product that was written in an older language (COBOL, for instance), developers are using CORBA to bridge the gap between systems. At the same time, CORBA and related technologies (RMI,

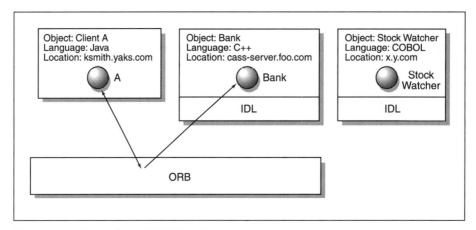

Figure 8.5 Invocation of CORBA objects.

DCOM) are being used in multitier architectures. Unlike DCOM, however, CORBA is platform-independent. Unlike Java RMI, it is language-independent.

Another reason that CORBA is becoming so popular is its flexibility. Different companies provide different ORBs. These ORBs (assuming they are CORBA-compliant) can communicate with each other via Internet Inter-Orb Protocol (IIOP). IIOP, a protocol above the TCP/IP layer, allows the flexibility of distribution of ORBs throughout the Internet.

The CORBA architecture is a framework that provides abstraction over the network layer. Instead of programming with sockets and having to worry about bits and bytes and streams, the programmer simply looks for an object and calls its methods. This is far easier. To the programmer, all objects look "local." In actuality, they don't have to be.

CORBA and Java

Java 2 includes an IDL compiler and a CORBA-compliant ORB that enables objects to speak to each other via IIOP. In this subsection, we will discuss how a developer can use these tools to build a CORBA application.

Creating IDL for Existing Objects

After an object is developed in Java, IDL has to be created. Though IDL looks like a skeleton class, it has a certain format:

NOTE Italicized text is used to indicate place holder names rather than literal names used in source code. For example, in the IDL listed below, the italicized type names are not real type names, but would be where the actual type names used would be placed.

```
module packageName
{
  interface className
  {
    attribute dataType variableName;
    ...
    dataType methodName();
    dataType methodName(in dataType variableName);
    ...
  }
}
```

Notice that IDL looks very similar to C++ interface classes. There are a fixed set of data types used with IDL:

boolean	long
char	unsigned long
octet	float
enum	double
short	object
unsigned short	void

Listing 8.11 shows a Bank Account object in package bank, along with the IDL that defines the bank's interfaces.

Listing 8.11 An example class with IDL.

```
//Here's an empty account object
package bank;
public class Account {
    private int cash_value;
    public Bank() {} // constructor
    public boolean withdraw(int money) {}; //Withdrawal
    public void deposit(int money) {}; //Deposits
    public int getCashValue(){} ; //Returns amount in account
}

//The IDL would look like this:

module bank {
   interface Account {
     boolean withdraw(in long money);
     void deposit(in long money);
     long getCashValue();
   }
}
```

Notice in this listing that the parameters for the methods withdraw( ) and deposit( ) are changed. Because CORBA has no support for "ints," the money parameter must be converted to the proper supported value. Here, a "long" was used, which is a long integer.

NOTE Using CORBA, it is not possible to create IDL for passing programming language-specific objects as parameters. Because CORBA's interfaces are language-independent, parameters must be specified using IDL's existing data types. For example, there is no comparable data type for an object of type, say, java.lang.Object. If a Java developer needs to pass an object as a parameter, he or she may choose to pass an array of bytes as a parameter instead. In Java, it is easy to convert a serialized object to bytes, and to convert bytes to objects. An array of bytes can be defined in IDL as an octet stream. For more information on the conversion of programming language-specific data types, see the documentation at java.sun.com/products/jdk/idl/index.html.

Compiling IDL

Using the idltojava compiler, the IDL can be compiled to create stubs and skeleton classes. If you have a C compiler on your system (and it's in your path), the idltojava compiler will try to use its preprocessor. Having a C compiler on your system is not required, however; you can use the -fno-cpp option to disable this functionality.

Running idltojava on the Account IDL in Listing 8.11, the command would be, simply:

```
idltojava Account.idl
```

This will automatically create a bank subdirectory, stub, and skeleton files: Account.java, AccountHelper.java, AccountHolder.java, and _AccountImpl-Base.java. These are the "glue" classes that help the ORB find the Account server object, and allow other client and server objects to invoke methods upon the Account object.

After the IDL generates code, the developer has to write the implementation of the server object, usually a "servant" that does the implementation, and a server that runs the servant and binds to the ORB.

A Java-CORBA Example

Remember the television-remote control example in Chapter 4, "JavaBean Components"? Here we extend that example using CORBA. Listing 8.12 shows the IDL for the television object, called CORBATV.

At the end of Chapter 4, the public methods of the television were discussed. These methods are defined in the interface in Listing 8.12. Although an "int" is passed, you must define this as a "long" in your IDL.

Listing 8.12 The television IDL.

```
module corbabeans {
  interface CORBATV {
     void incrementChannel();
     void decrementChannel();
     void onOff();
     void setChannel(in long c);
  };
};
```

Listing 8.13 shows the servant code that does all the real work. Notice that the servant needs to extend _CORBATVImplBase, one of the files generated in the idltojava compilation. The code looks pretty simple, doesn't it? That's because the code was designed by abstracting the implementation of the television from its transport. That is, instead of having all of the internals of the television in this code, a TelevisionBean object is instantiated, and its method is called. This is useful because it allows you to use different transport mechanisms, such as RMI, CORBA, or even another implementation, depending on the situation.

As you can see from this listing, a television bean is instantiated in the constructor, and the television bean's methods are called as the servant's methods are invoked.

Listing 8.14 shows the code for the Television server object. Notice that it has most of the CORBA-specific calls in it. In this code, a reference to the ORB must be initialized via the ORB.init( ) method; the CORBATVServant is instantiated; and the CORBATVServant is registered to the ORB via the ORB.connect( ) method. You must register your CORBATVServant with the naming service. This naming service registration allows other objects to find the television object.

Whew! Now you've created a bonafide CORBA server object. All that's left to do is to build the remote control. Listing 8.15 shows the code for the remote control (CORBARemote.java). The CORBARemote class extends the RemoteControlGUI, to abstract the GUI interface. The most important part of this code is the section where the client talks to the ORB. The ORB's naming service looks for the CORBATV and returns a reference.

Notice that the only reference to CORBA in this code involves contacting the naming service in the constructor. Because the remote control is a CORBA client object, all the remote control has to do is find the Television object with the naming service. From that point on, the remote control can invoke the Television's methods.

CORBA in Enterprise Frameworks

CORBA has become the tool of choice for developing middleware. When integrating with legacy systems, in which operating systems, database systems,

Listing 8.13   The television servant.

```
package corbabeans;

import org.omg.CORBA.*;
import org.omg.CosNaming.*;
import org.omg.CosNaming.NamingContextPackage.*;
import beandemo.*;

public class CORBATVServant extends _CORBATVImplBase
{

    TelevisionBean tv = null;

    public CORBATVServant()
    {
      super();
      tv = new TelevisionBean();
    }
    public void incrementChannel()
    {
      tv.incrementChannel();
    }

    public void decrementChannel()
    {
      tv.decrementChannel();
    }

    public void onOff() {
      tv.onOff();
    }

    public void setChannel(int c) {
      try {
          tv.setChannel(c);
      }
      catch (Exception e) {
          e.printStackTrace();
      }
    }
    }
}
```

and programming languages are different and use different interfaces, developers have found that CORBA is a convenient solution. CORBA-based collaboration solutions in which applications on networks can share audio, video, and application capability with numerous people are being developed in conferences on the Internet. Many innovative government systems, such as the

Listing 8.14   The television server.

```
package corbabeans;

import org.omg.CORBA.*;
import org.omg.CosNaming.*;
import org.omg.CosNaming.NamingContextPackage.*;
import beandemo.*;

public class CORBATVServer {

  public static void main(String[] argv)
  {
    try {
        //Initialize a reference to the ORB
          ORB orb = ORB.init(argv,null);
        //Instantiate a TV servant
          CORBATVServant tv = new CORBATVServant();

        //Connect the ORB to the servant
        orb.connect(tv);

        //Get a reference to the Naming Service
org.omg.CORBA.Object objref =
            orb.resolve_initial_references("NameService");
//Make a NamingContext Object
        NamingContext ncref = NamingContextHelper.narrow(objref);

        //Create a name component for the server
        NameComponent nc = new NameComponent("CORBATV","");
        NameComponent path[] = {nc};

        //Bind the path with the servant & wait for invocations
        ncref.rebind(path,tv);
        java.lang.Object sync = new java.lang.Object();
        synchronized(sync) {
            sync.wait();
        }
    }
    catch (Exception e) {
        e.printStackTrace();
    }

  }
}
```

Listing 8.15 The remote control client.

```
/****************************************************************/
/*  Filename:    CORBARemote.java                               */
/*                                                              */
/*  Description: This class is the main remote control that     */
/*               acts as a client talking to the television!    */
/****************************************************************/
package corbabeans;

import java.awt.event.*;
import java.beans.*;
import java.io.*;
import org.omg.CORBA.*;
import org.omg.CosNaming.*;
import beandemo.*;


/*=======================================================
  This will be the class that interacts with the TV!
  It inherits from the RemoteControlGUI, and it handles
  all of the events of the contained beans, and handles
  the connections with the tv!
  =======================================================*/

public class CORBARemote extends RemoteControlGUI
implements PropertyChangeListener, ActionListener
{
   CORBATV tv = null;

   //constructor
   public CORBARemote()
   {
     super();

     //Listen to the beans!
     keypad.addPropertyChangeListener(this);
     up.addActionListener(this);
     down.addActionListener(this);
     onoff.addActionListener(this);

     //Register with the server
     try
     {
     String[] foo = {"foo"};
     ORB orb = ORB.init(foo, null);
     org.omg.CORBA.Object objRef =
orb.resolve_initial_references("NameService");
     NamingContext ncRef = NamingContextHelper.narrow(objRef);
     NameComponent nc = new NameComponent("CORBATV","");
     NameComponent path[] = {nc};
```

Listing 8.15 *(Continued)*

```
        tv = CORBATVHelper.narrow(ncRef.resolve(path));
    }
    catch (Exception e)
    {
        System.out.println("Couldn't find the tv!");
        System.exit(-1);
    }
}

//This will change the channel on the TV..
public void propertyChange(PropertyChangeEvent pcEvent)
{
    String changedProperty = pcEvent.getPropertyName();
    java.lang.Object newval = pcEvent.getNewValue();
    Integer i = (Integer)newval;
    tv.setChannel(i.intValue());
}

// This handles all of the remote control's buttonpress
// events.
public void actionPerformed(ActionEvent ae)
{
    java.lang.Object source = ae.getSource();

    if (source.equals(up))
        tv.incrementChannel();
    if (source.equals(down))
            tv.decrementChannel();
    if (source.equals(onoff))
        tv.onOff();
}

//main
public static void main(String[] argv)
{
    new CORBARemote();
}
}
```

Joint Deployable Intelligence Support System (JDISS) are leveraging CORBA as a framework for collaboration, and are using CORBA to integrate with similar systems for real-time data sharing at a new level.

Enterprise JavaBeans is an exciting development that can use CORBA in the enterprise, extending the component model to distributed systems in a transactional processing model. Increasingly, electronic commerce solutions using CORBA are being developed. Companies are finding easier ways to develop distributed applications with CORBA as their base model. ObjectSpace's Voyager is a good example. Its architecture dynamically creates CORBA stubs and skeletons at runtime, leaving out the step of creating IDL. Other companies are also pursuing similar solutions. CORBA is a scalable and flexible architecture, and its potential in the next few years is enormous.

Distributed Frameworks

With enterprise frameworks such as EJB, CORBA, RMI and others, you can construct façades to network distributed frameworks and components. Applications across a network can interact with the remote frameworks either by passing local application objects directly to the framework or by providing callbacks into the application through remote proxies. This is possible because a proxy object referencing a remote object is indeed an object itself and can be passed around a network using object serialization. Regardless of where that proxy resides, it can translate method calls (either from the application or the framework) across the network to the remote object.

In a distributed framework architecture, the application and the framework used by the application (or vice versa) are located on different systems (meaning different computers separated by a network). In order for this to work properly, the application side of the system must have access to the framework classes or interfaces it implements. This requires that there be a clear distinction between the interfaces and classes the framework provides solely for client implementations and the classes representing the core functionality of the framework (i.e., the internal parts of the framework not intended for client visibility or direct interaction).

Framework designers must consider this when laying out the functionality and package structure of the framework. If the client portions of the framework are separated from the internals of the framework through reliable protocols (or interfaces), then clients wishing to supply objects to the framework need only see those interfaces. The interfaces can be cleanly separated from the functional component of the framework, thereby allowing any application client to utilize the framework without having to know details about the classes used internally to the framework. This is especially important in large distributed systems because client applications should not have to carry server-side classes (rather, only lightweight interfaces) along with them.

This type of approach will allow the remote framework implementation to undergo change without affecting the way client applications utilize and interact with such a framework. The usefulness of enterprise frameworks such as EJB and CORBA has been established in this chapter. They offer excellent solutions to distributing objects across a network. From there, you can construct large-grained framework components that rely on these other frameworks to

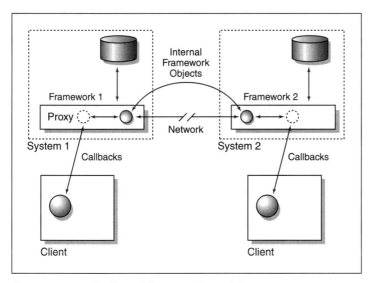

Figure 8.6   A distributed framework model.

create a composite framework foundation through which network Java applications can receive useful services using the framework paradigm.

The interactions among remote Java applications and a distributed framework would occur as a remote method invocation that executes within (possibly) the Java application, much like a resident (or local) framework would call back to application client code that has been plugged into it. The key difference is that the method invocation travels across the network and arrives at the application, where it executes. Likewise, any direct method calls into the framework from the application would carry over the network as well. This necessarily assumes a common method of remote interaction. Depending on how you design your framework, the bidirectionality of method calls may or may not exist.

Assuming this type of bidirectional (method calling) capability, complex distributed systems can be built that utilize frameworks at various tiers within the system (that is, the client, the middle, or the back end). Applications of slightly different natures can make use of the same remotely available set of business objects, which subsequently are tied into frameworks residing on the remote systems. Figure 8.6 shows a possible visualization of this concept.

Summary

This chapter covered two important types of enterprise frameworks: Enterprise JavaBeans and CORBA (via Java IDL). Because distributed systems, and therefore, distributed architectures, are of paramount value to Java developers, frameworks and APIs provided by Java for creating such systems and architectures should be practical and valuable. Enterprise JavaBeans represents a new type of framework that allows server-side business objects to be easily deployed in a variety of commercial containers. This type of standardized specification will make developing distributed objects and systems much less complex than it is today. Java is far ahead of the pack in terms of distributed capabilities, and it is important to know what those capabilities are.

In the area of Java frameworks, it is important understand how frameworks can coexist across a network, how a distributed architecture utilizes frameworks, and how interactions between distributed applications and frameworks occur. Much of this is open to more exploration, but the fundamentals and the tools provided by Java pave the path for creating such complex systems. The current trend toward component architectures and distributed systems warrants technologies that facilitate their design and development. Using distributed object frameworks to build distributed frameworks that can function as independent (possibly service-based) components will promote higher degrees of reusability and increase the separation between complex entities in a distributed system that need not be tightly bound. By doing this, you can quickly adapt large systems to new or different technologies simply by replacing or changing key components or framework implementations independent of the many client applications utilizing them.

Index